Acquisitions, Collection Development, and Collection Use

HANDBOOKS FOR LIBRARY MANAGEMENT

Administration, Personnel, Buildings and Equipment
Acquisitions, Collection Development, and Collection Use
Reference Services and Library Instruction
Cataloging and Catalogs
Circulation, Interlibrary Loan, Patron Use, and Collection Maintenance
Library Education and Professional Issues

Acquisitions, Collection Development, and Collection Use
A Handbook for Library Management

David F. Kohl

Foreword by Hugh Atkinson

ABC-CLIO
Santa Barbara, California
Oxford, England

©1985 by David F. Kohl

All rights reserved. No part of this publication may be reproduced, stored in a retrieval system, or transmitted, in any form or by any means, electronic, mechanical, photocopying, recording, or otherwise, except for the inclusion of brief quotations in a review, without prior permission in writing from the publishers.

This book is Smyth sewn and printed on acid-free paper to meet library standards.

Library of Congress Cataloging in Publication Data

Kohl, David F., 1942–
   Acquisitions, collection development, and collection use.

   (Handbooks for library management)
   Bibliography: p.
   Includes index.
     1. Acquisitions (Libraries)—Handbooks, manuals, etc.
2. Collection development (Libraries)—Handbooks, manuals, etc.
3. Library administration—Handbooks, manuals, etc.
I. Title. II. Series: Kohl, David F., 1942–
Handbooks for library management.
Z689.K6   1985   025.1   85-6023

ISBN 0-87436-431-0 (v. 1)
ISBN 0-87436-433-7 (v. 2)
ISBN 0-87436-399-3 (set) (alk. paper)

10 9 8 7 6 5 4

ABC-Clio, Inc.
2040 Alameda Padre Serra
P.O. Box 4397
Santa Barbara, CA 93140-4397

Clio Press Ltd.
55 St. Thomas Street
Oxford OX1 1JG, England

Manufactured in the United States of America

CONTENTS

FOREWORD, **xxi**

INTRODUCTION, **xxv**
  Arrangement, **xxv**
  Scope, **xxvi**
  Acknowledgements, **xxvii**

SAMPLE ENTRIES, **xxix**
  (from Contents, Text, Bibliography, and Index)

LIST OF JOURNALS SURVEYED, **xxxi**

1. Acquisitions

APPROVAL PLANS, **3**
  Academic, **3**

CLAIMS, **3**
  Academic, **3**

COLLECTION GROWTH RATE—GENERAL ISSUES, **4**
  Academic, **4**
  Special, **5**

COLLECTION GROWTH RATE—MAPS, **6**
  Academic, **6**

COSTS—GENERAL ISSUES, **6**
  Academic, **6**
  Public, **7**

School, **8**
Special, **9**

COSTS—GOVERNMENT DOCUMENTS, **9**
Academic, **9**

COSTS—MAPS, **10**
Academic, **10**

COSTS—MONOGRAPHS, **10**
Academic, **10**
Public, **11**
School, **11**
Special, **12**

COSTS—OUT-OF-PRINT MATERIALS, **12**
General, **12**
Academic, **12**

COSTS—PER CAPITA, **13**
School, **13**
Special, **13**

COSTS—PERIODICAL DUAL PRICING, **14**
General, **14**
Academic, **14**
Special, **15**

COSTS—SUBSCRIPTION INCREASES, **16**
General, **16**
Academic, **16**
Special, **19**

COSTS—VENDOR DISCOUNTS, **21**
Public, **21**

GIFT AND EXCHANGE PROGRAMS, **22**
General, **22**

GOVERNMENT DOCUMENTS, **23**
Academic, **23**

ISSN, **24**
General, **24**

MAPS, **25**
Academic, **25**

MICROFORMS, **25**
Academic, **25**

Contents

OUT-OF-PRINT MATERIALS—GENERAL ISSUES, **27**
General, **27**
Academic, **28**

OUT-OF-PRINT MATERIALS—PROCEDURES, **28**
Academic, **28**

PAPERBACKS, **29**
Academic, **29**
Public, **29**

PROCEDURES—GENERAL ISSUES, **30**
Academic, **30**
Public, **32**
School, **32**
Special, **34**

PROCEDURES—GOVERNMENT DOCUMENTS, **34**
Academic, **34**

PUBLISHING INDUSTRY ISSUES, **36**
General **36**
School, **36**

REPRINTS, **37**
General, **37**

SPEED, **37**
Academic, **37**
Public, **39**

VENDORS—BOOK, **39**
Academic, **39**
Public, **41**

VERIFICATION, **42**
General, **42**
Academic, **45**

WHOLE COLLECTIONS, **47**
General, **47**
Academic, **47**
Public, **47**

2. Collection Development

AGE OF MATERIAL—GENERAL ISSUES, **51**
  Academic, **51**
  School, **53**
  Special, **53**

AGE OF MATERIAL—BOOKS, **54**
  Academic, **54**
  Special, **55**

AGE OF MATERIAL—PERIODICALS, **56**
  Academic, **56**
  Special, **59**

AGE OF MATERIAL—PHYSICAL CONDITION, **61**
  Academic, **61**

AGE OF MATERIAL—SUBJECT, **62**
  Academic, **62**
  Special, **63**

APPROVAL PLANS, **64**
  Academic, **64**
  Special, **65**

BUDGET, **65**
  Academic, **65**
  Public, **66**
  School, **67**
  Special, **68**

CENSORSHIP, **69**
  General, **69**
  Public, **70**
  School, **71**

CHARACTERISTICS OF THE LITERATURE—LANGUAGE, **71**
  Academic, **71**
  Special, **74**

CHARACTERISTICS OF THE LITERATURE—OTHER, **75**
  General, **75**
  Academic, **76**
  Public, **79**

School, **80**
Special, **80**

CHARACTERISTICS OF THE LITERATURE—
PUBLICATION FORMAT, **83**
General, **83**
Academic, **84**
Special, **87**

COLLECTION EVALUATION, **88**
Academic, **88**

COLLECTION GROWTH, **89**
Academic, **89**
School, **92**
Special, **94**

COSTS—BOOKS, **95**
General, **95**
Academic, **95**
Public, **96**
School, **96**
Special, **97**

COSTS—GOVERNMENT DOCUMENTS, **97**
Academic, **97**

COSTS—MAPS, **98**
Academic, **98**

COSTS—OUT-OF-PRINT MATERIALS, **98**
General, **98**
Academic, **99**

COSTS—PER CAPITA, **99**
Academic, **99**
Public, **100**
School, **100**
Special, **101**

COSTS—PERIODICALS, DUAL PRICING, **101**
General, **101**
Academic, **102**
Special, **103**

COSTS—PERIODICALS, SUBSCRIPTION INCREASES, **103**
General, **103**
Academic, **104**
Special, **107**

COSTS—VENDOR DISCOUNTS, **109**
  Public, **109**

DUPLICATION OF COPIES, **110**
  Academic, **110**
  Special, **111**

ESTIMATING SIZE, **113**
  Academic, **113**

FOREIGN LANGUAGES—GENERAL ISSUES, **113**
  Public, **113**

FOREIGN LANGUAGES—
PATRON SKILLS AND ATTITUDES, **114**
  Academic, **114**

GIFT AND EXCHANGE PROGRAMS, **115**
  General, **115**
  Academic, **116**

GIFTS, **116**
  Academic, **116**

HOLDINGS—GENERAL ISSUES, **118**
  General, **118**
  Academic, **119**
  Public, **123**
  School, **124**
  Special, **127**

HOLDINGS—MEDIA, **130**
  Academic, **130**
  School, **131**
  Special, **133**

LEASE PLANS, **134**
  Academic, **134**

METHOD OF SELECTION, **134**
  Academic, **134**

OUT-OF-PRINT MATERIALS, **136**
  General, **136**
  Academic, **137**

OUTREACH AND EXTENSION, **138**
  Academic, **138**
  Special, **138**

Contents

OVERLAP, **139**
General, **139**
Academic, **140**
Public, **142**
School, **142**
Special, **142**

PRACTICES AND PROCEDURES, **143**
Academic, **143**
School, **146**
Special, **148**

RETRENCHMENT, **149**
Academic, **149**

SELECTION—GENERAL ISSUES, **150**
Academic, **150**
Public, **151**
School, **151**

SELECTION, MONOGRAPHS—GENERAL ISSUES, **152**
Academic, **152**

SELECTION, MONOGRAPHS—
HARDBACK VERSUS PAPERBACK, **153**
General, **153**
Academic, **154**
Public, **154**

SELECTION, MONOGRAPHS—
SUBJECT AREA (AFRICAN STUDIES), **156**
Academic, **156**

SELECTION, MONOGRAPHS—
SUBJECT AREA (ANTHROPOLOGY), **156**
Academic, **156**

SELECTION, MONOGRAPHS—
SUBJECT AREA (BUSINESS), **157**
Academic, **157**

SELECTION, MONOGRAPHS—
SUBJECT AREA (ENGINEERING), **158**
Academic, **158**

SELECTION, MONOGRAPHS—
SUBJECT AREA (HISTORY), **158**
Academic, **158**

SELECTION, MONOGRAPHS—
SUBJECT AREA (LIBRARY SCIENCE), **160**
  Academic, **160**

SELECTION, MONOGRAPHS—SUBJECT AREA (MUSIC), **161**
  Academic, **161**
  Special, **161**

SELECTION, MONOGRAPHS—
SUBJECT AREA (PHILOSOPHY), **161**
  Academic, **161**

SELECTION, MONOGRAPHS—
SUBJECT AREA (POLITICAL SCIENCE), **162**
  Academic, **162**

SELECTION, MONOGRAPHS—
SUBJECT AREA (SOCIOLOGY), **163**
  Academic, **163**

SELECTION, OTHER—GENERAL ISSUES, **163**
  Academic, **163**
  Public, **164**
  Special, **164**

SELECTION, OTHER—DISSERTATIONS, **165**
  Academic, **165**

SELECTION, OTHER—ENCYCLOPEDIAS, **165**
  Public, **165**

SELECTION, OTHER—GOVERNMENT DOCUMENTS, **167**
  Academic, **167**
  Public, **169**

SELECTION, OTHER—MEDIA, **169**
  Academic, **169**
  School, **170**
  Special, **170**

SELECTION, OTHER—MICROFORMS, **171**
  Academic, **171**
  Public, **173**
  School, **173**

SELECTION, OTHER—REPRINTS, **174**
  General, **174**

SELECTION, OTHER—WORKING PAPERS, **174**
  Academic, **174**

SELECTION, PERIODICALS—GENERAL ISSUES, **175**
General, **175**
Academic, **176**
Public, **180**
School, **181**
Special, **182**

SELECTION, PERIODICALS—
BRADFORD DISTRIBUTION, EXPLICIT, **186**
General, **186**
Academic, **186**

SELECTION, PERIODICALS—
BRADFORD DISTRIBUTION, IMPLICIT, **187**
General, **187**
Academic, **188**
School, **191**
Special, **192**

SELECTION, PERIODICALS—ISSN, **194**
General, **194**

SELECTION, PERIODICALS—
SUBJECT AREA (BIOLOGY), **194**
Academic, **194**

SELECTION, PERIODICALS—
SUBJECT AREA (BUSINESS), **195**
General, **195**
Academic, **196**

SELECTION, PERIODICALS—
SUBJECT AREA (ECONOMICS), **197**
Academic, **197**

SELECTION, PERIODICALS—
SUBJECT AREA (ENGLISH), **197**
Academic, **197**

SELECTION, PERIODICALS—
SUBJECT AREA (GEOLOGY), **197**
Academic, **197**

SELECTION, PERIODICALS—
SUBJECT AREA (HISTORY), **198**
Academic, **198**

SELECTION, PERIODICALS—
SUBJECT AREA (LIBRARY SCIENCE), **199**
Academic, **199**

SELECTION, PERIODICALS—
SUBJECT AREA (MEDICINE, GENERAL), 202
- Academic, 202
- Special, 205

SELECTION, PERIODICALS—
SUBJECT AREA (MEDICINE, CARDIOLOGY), 208
- Academic, 208
- Special, 209

SELECTION, PERIODICALS—
SUBJECT AREA (MEDICINE, PHYSIOLOGY), 210
- Academic, 210
- Special, 212

SELECTION, PERIODICALS—
SUBJECT AREA (MEDICINE, TROPICS), 213
- Academic, 213
- Special, 214

SELECTION, PERIODICALS—
SUBJECT AREA (MICROBIOLOGY), 215
- Academic, 215
- Special, 216

SELECTION, PERIODICALS—SUBJECT AREA (MUSIC), 217
- General, 217

SELECTION, PERIODICALS—
SUBJECT AREA (PHARMACEUTICALS), 217
- Special, 217

SELECTION, PERIODICALS—
SUBJECT AREA (PHARMACOLOGY), 218
- Academic, 218
- Special, 219

SELECTION, PERIODICALS—
SUBJECT AREA (PHYSICS), 220
- Academic, 220

SELECTION, PERIODICALS—
SUBJECT AREA (POLITICAL SCIENCE), 221
- Academic, 221

SELECTION, PERIODICALS—
SUBJECT AREA (SOCIAL WORK), 222
- Academic, 222

SELECTION, PERIODICALS—
SUBJECT AREA (SOCIOLOGY), 223
   Academic, 223

SELECTION TOOLS—GENERAL ISSUES, 225
   General, 225
   Academic, 225
   Public, 228
   School, 229
   Special, 230

SELECTION TOOLS—BOOK REVIEWS, 230
   General, 230
   Academic, 232
   Public, 233
   School, 237
   Special, 240

SELECTION TOOLS—MEDIA, 242
   Academic, 242
   Special, 243

SELECTION TOOLS—MONOGRAPHS, 243
   General, 243
   Academic, 243
   School, 243

SELECTION TOOLS—PERIODICALS, 245
   General, 245
   Academic, 249
   Special, 250

SOURCES OF MATERIALS, 250
   Academic, 250
   Special, 251

SPECIAL COLLECTIONS—FACULTY LIBRARIES (LAW), 252
   Academic, 252

SPECIAL COLLECTIONS—LABOR, 253
   Public, 253

SPECIAL COLLECTIONS—MAPS, 253
   Academic, 253

SPECIAL COLLECTIONS—NEWSPAPERS, 255
   Academic, 255

SPECIAL COLLECTIONS—RECREATIONAL READING, 256
   Academic, 256

SPECIAL COLLECTIONS—TEACHER COLLECTIONS, **256**
School, **256**

SPECIAL COLLECTIONS—UNIVERSITY COLLECTIONS, **257**
Academic, **257**

STANDARDS, **257**
Academic, **257**

TRANSLATIONS—PERIODICALS, **259**
General, **259**

WHOLE COLLECTIONS, **260**
General, **260**
Academic, **260**
Public, **260**

3.

Collection Use

AGE OF MATERIAL—GENERAL ISSUES, **263**
General, **263**
Academic, **264**
School, **265**
Special, **265**

AGE OF MATERIAL—BOOKS, **266**
Academic, **266**
Special, **268**

AGE OF MATERIAL—GIFTS, **269**
Academic, **269**

AGE OF MATERIAL—NEWSPAPERS, **269**
Academic, **269**

AGE OF MATERIAL—PERIODICALS, **270**
Academic, **270**
Special, **273**

BOOKS—GENERAL ISSUES, **275**
Academic, **275**
School, **278**
Special, **278**

Contents

BOOKS—BRADFORD DISTRIBUTION, IMPLICIT, 279
Academic, 279
School, 280

BOOKS—HARDBOUND VERSUS PAPERBACK, 280
Public, 280

BOOKS—TYPE OF PATRON, 281
Academic, 281
Public, 282
Special, 282

BOOKS VERSUS PERIODICALS, 283
General, 283
Academic, 283
School, 285
Special, 285

BROWSING, 286
General, 286
Academic, 286
Public, 287
Special, 288

COPYRIGHT—RESERVES, 288
Academic, 288

COSTS, 289
Academic, 289

DISSERTATIONS AND THESES, 290
Academic, 290
Special, 290

FOREIGN LANGUAGES, 291
General, 291
Academic, 291
Public, 292
Special, 293

GIFTS, 293
Academic, 293

GOVERNMENT DOCUMENTS, 295
Academic, 295
School, 297

IN-HOUSE, 298
Academic, 298

Public, **299**
Special, **300**

MAPS, **300**
Academic, **300**

MEDIA, **302**
Academic, **302**
School, **302**
Special, **303**

METHOD OF SELECTION, **303**
Academic, **303**

MICROFORMS, **305**
Academic, **305**
Special, **307**

NEWSPAPERS, **307**
Academic, **307**
School, **308**

OUTREACH AND EXTENSION, **309**
Academic, **309**
Special, **310**

PERIODICALS—GENERAL ISSUES, **311**
Academic, **311**
Public, **314**
School, **315**
Special, **316**

PERIODICALS—BRADFORD DISTRIBUTION, IMPLICIT, **316**
Academic, **316**
School, **318**
Special, **319**

PERIODICALS—CORE, **319**
General, **319**
Academic, **320**
School, **322**
Special, **323**

PERIODICALS—TYPE OF PATRON, **323**
Academic, **323**
Special, **326**

REFERENCE MATERIALS AND TOOLS, **326**
Academic, **326**

Public, **327**
School, **328**

RELATION TO PERSONAL COLLECTION, **329**
Academic, **329**

RESTRICTIONS, **329**
Academic, **329**
Special, **330**

STACK POLICY, **331**
General, **331**
Academic, **331**
Special, **332**

SUBJECT AREAS, **333**
Academic, **333**
Public, **335**
Special, **335**

SUCCESS RATE AND PROBLEMS—GENERAL ISSUES, **336**
Academic, **336**
Public, **340**
Special, **341**

SUCCESS RATE AND PROBLEMS—AGE OF MATERIAL, **342**
Academic, **342**

SUCCESS RATE AND PROBLEMS—LOAN PERIOD, **342**
Academic, **342**

BIBLIOGRAPHY OF ARTICLES, **343**

AUTHOR INDEX TO BIBLIOGRAPHY OF ARTICLES, **399**

FOREWORD

All professions must live with their own mythologies as well as their own realities. They have as part of the decision-making environment both the history and the future. Included in that history is the record of the past, the investigation of the phenomenon, and a description of observed activity. Also included is the belief present in the minds of the practitioners of what the history means, of what the research means. Much of that belief is not based on the facts of research but rather on a series of attitudes, commitments, and dogmas that have been handed down in the great oral tradition and as well have found their way into the textbooks for the training of the new members of the profession.

Librarianship, as I have noted, is not alone in this, but it is certainly one of those professions that have spent less time in the promulgation and understanding of research and more time in the promulgation of mythology. One should not assume that all mythology is wrong or untrue. However, one should be equally committed to the verification of that mythology by research and to the description of the previously unknown. The basic tenets of librarianship should be analyzed by controlled scientific investigations if possible and if not at least by verifiable observations.

It is upon the ascertainable facts of librarianship that management decisions should be based. In an era of more scientific management, or at least management that is attempting to divest itself of the styles and strictures of the past, a greater commitment to the use of research in the process of administering libraries is needed. The daily decisions that in sum are administration should be founded on reality as compared with an earlier time when they were based on intuition. It may well be a hallmark of our age and our society that the procedures, ethics, commitments, and attitudes of the past have so often proved themselves to be not only wrong but inhibiting progressive human action. Almost all of the previously held and commonly believed lore is to be distrusted until reproven.

In librarianship one can point to whole areas of our field where almost nothing is known scientifically and in fact large areas where there is no "received wisdom." We really don't know how people use our catalogues and our libraries. We really don't know why they use them, and we don't know yet what is the best way for us to provide library service. The debate over these issues is so often presented in terms of a moral imperative or a practicality based on a biased attitude that any administrator is hard pressed to make a rational decision. We are in an age of computers and rationality—a rationality different from that of the eighteenth-century "age of reason." The earlier period depended on human thought and logic rather than concentrating on the collection and testing of data as our present time does. It is to the research that we must turn if we are both to be held accountable and to provide an administrative role that is acceptable to our colleagues and those who evaluate us, be it taxpayers, citizens, university administrators, city managers, or an institutional hierarchy. We are just beginning to apply controlled experiment and rigorous observation to the phenomena that surround us.

In this volume Dr. Kohl has provided the library administrator, whether in technical services or in a general administrative role, the distillation of the past quarter-century of research in a form that is usable. While the demand for more rational decision making is being made, the time available to perform that rational action has decreased. Thus, more and more rational decisions are needed, and there is less and less time for each individual administrator to investigate and to make those decisions. The value of this book is that it presents the research in a useful and handy format, even though it is assumed we are keeping up with the literature. The indexing will be particularly helpful for the administrator. The language and topics chosen for the indexes are the language and topics about which decisions must be made rather than the language and topics the observers or researchers might choose. This book contains not the language and topics of the theorists of librarianship but rather those of its practitioners. It is true that much of the library research would not stand the kind of rigorous and formalistic criteria that a first-class library school would apply to the dissertations of its Ph.D. candidates. Nevertheless, the research published in the library literature provides a set of data that is so far superior to the instinct of the individual administrator or to received wisdom that it is essential that it be accessible so that it can in turn be applied to the individual decision. The editor and compiler of this volume, Dr. Kohl, has critically evaluated the research, eliminating the internally inconsistent and that which is not replicatable. Therefore he has provided some quality assurance on the research itself. He has further limited himself to only that research which has a relatively high degree of statistical significance in the application of the data to the researcher's hypotheses and findings. He has thus eliminated the "maybe yes, maybe no" investigations. This criterion is one of the devices that make this volume useful, since in fact those "maybe" investigations do not aid the decision-maker in bringing an issue to closure.

The area covered in this volume is basically the first of the four great functional tasks of librarianship—that of procuring library materials. The others are arranging the material for patron use (cataloging), lending material to people (circulation), and answering questions about the material and from it

Foreword

(reference). The previous volume in this series dealt with the administrative issues surrounding the management of libraries. The later ones will, in addition to the three other basic tasks, consider topics on library education and professional issues. This volume considers acquisition and collection development in a broad sense that includes not only the techniques of acquisition but also the use of the collection and the characteristics of library collections. In fact it does not particularly concentrate on techniques; rather it reports the research on the effectiveness of various techniques, such as approval plans and claims, and provides a basis for administrative decisions concerning the costs of acquisitions and of material. It also speaks to problems in acquisitions, such as those encountered in obtaining government documents, dealing with gifts and exchanges, procuring periodicals, maps, and microforms.

Some of the most valuable reporting occurs in the sections on the characteristics of the literature. What is it? Who uses it? In what form does it occur? The questions surrounding selection and the selection tools, including book reviews and the like, are examined. Some of the most interesting research studies the age of material in libraries. The reporting on the usefulness of library collections is also valuable. It is in just this area where so much technology occurs and where we so desperately need at least seriously compiled and observed data, if not a perfectly designed research experiment. In this area, after all, librarianship is as primitive as chemistry and physics were some two hundred years ago. It is the era of close observation and the building of hypotheses about the causes of the phenomena observed. This series of books should provide the basic data base for administrative decisions, and it is to be hoped and expected that both the author and the press continue to update the series even as the new volumes are in preparation.

—*Hugh C. Atkinson*
University of Illinois,
Urbana-Champaign

INTRODUCTION

The *Library Administrator's Handbook* series has been designed for library managers and decision makers who regularly need information, but who are chronically too short of time to do involved and time-consuming literature searches each time specific, quantitative information is desired. This unusual tool, rather than abstracting complete studies or providing only citations to research, instead presents summaries of individual research findings, grouped by subject. By looking under the appropriate subject heading in the *Handbook,* librarians can find summaries detailing the research findings on that topic. For example, what percentage of reference questions are answered correctly, and does it make a difference whether professional or nonprofessional staff are doing the answering? As a result, helpful information can be found in minutes and without an extensive literature review. Furthermore, if a more complete look at the study is desired, the user is referred to the bibliographic citation number so that the full study can be consulted.

Arrangement

The series consists of six volumes, with each volume covering two or more of the sixteen basic subject areas that divide the volumes into parts. While most of these basic subject divisions reflect such traditional administrative divisions of library work as administration, circulation, and reference, at least two subject areas go somewhat further. "Library Education" may be of interest, not just to library school administrators, but to faculty and students as well, and "Professional Issues" should be of interest to all career-oriented library professionals. Each basic subject division is further divided by specific subject headings, which are further subdivided by type of library: General (more than one library type), Academic, Public, School, and Special. For example, readers seeking information on book loss rates in academic libraries would consult the basic subject division "Collection Maintenance" and look under the specific subject heading "Loss Rates (Books)," in the "Academic" libraries subdivision. There they would find the summarized results of studies on book loss rates in academic libraries followed by the number referring to the full citation in the Bibliography of Articles.

Each volume in the series follows the same basic pattern: The introduction; a list of the journals surveyed; a detailed table of contents listing all subject headings used in that volume; the research findings arranged by subject; the complete bibliography of articles surveyed for the series with page numbers indicating locations of corresponding research summaries in the text; and an alphabetically arranged author index to the Bibliography of Articles.

The summaries of the research findings also tend to follow a standard format. First the study is briefly described by giving location, date, and, when appropriate, population or survey size and response rate. This information is provided to help users determine the nature, scope, and relevance of the study to their needs. The actual findings, signaled by an italicized *"showed that,"* follow and include, when appropriate, such supporting data as significance level and confidence interval. Information in brackets represents editorial comment, for example "[significance level not given]" or "[remaining cases not accounted for]," while information in parentheses merely represents additional data taken from the article.

The Sample Entries on page xxix identify the elements and illustrate the interrelationships between the subject organization of the volume, research summaries of the text, corresponding article citations in the bibliography, and the author index entries.

Scope

In order to keep the *Handbook* series manageable, a number of scope limitations were necessary. The time period, 1960 through 1983, was selected since it covers the time when quantitative research began to come of age in library research. Only journal literature has been surveyed, because the bulk of quantitative library research is reported in that medium, and because the editorial and refereeing process required by most journals helps ensure the quality of the research reported. This limitation does ignore a number of important studies reported in monographic form, however, and we hope to cover this area at a later date. Further, only North American journals and research were reviewed since they constitute the main body of quantitative library research reported. Again, this ignores several journals reporting significant library research, particularly journals from Great Britain. We plan to expand our focus and include these in later editions or updates of the *Handbook* series.

Although we generally followed the principle that research good enough to publish was research worth including in the *Handbook* series, several caveats must be stated. First, no research findings with statistical significance exceeding .05 were reported. This follows general Social Science practice and, in recent years, almost universal library research practice. Second, occasional findings, and sometimes whole studies, were not reported in the *Handbook* series when there were serious problems with internal consistency and/or ambiguous and confusing text. At issue here is not the occasional typographical error or arithmetical miscalculation, but those situations where charts and text purportedly presenting the same information differed in

Introduction

substantial and unaccountable ways. Fortunately, such problems were not excessive. And third, as a general rule, only original and supported findings were used in the *Handbook* series. Findings that were reported second-hand, or where the study documentation was reported elsewhere (often the case with doctoral research), were generally not used in the series. Only in those instances when the second-hand data were used to show a pattern or otherwise resulted in new data by their juxtaposition, were such findings reported.

Finally, under the category of unsought limitations, we, like many library users, were not always able to find all the journal articles we needed in the time available to us. However, the excellent holdings and services of the University of Illinois Library Science Library provided us with access to almost all of the journal issues actually published and received by March 1984—a fact that should probably be listed as a record rather than as a limitation.

Acknowledgements

As might be expected, a project of this size required assistance from many quarters. Both the University of Illinois Library Research and Publication Committee and the University of Illinois Research Board provided invaluable assistance in the form of financial support for graduate assistants. The assistants themselves, Becky Rutter, Nicki Varyu, and Bruce Olsen, constituted a dedicated, bright and hardworking team. The Undergraduate Library staff deserve special thanks for their support and cooperation, as do the Library Science Library staff, who were unfailingly courteous and helpful in making their truly outstanding collection available. The staff at ABC-Clio, particularly Gail Schlachter and Barbara Pope, provided much needed encouragement and good advice, even in the face of several delays and at least one nasty shock. And last, but by no means least, I would like to acknowledge the patience and support of my wife, Marilyn, and my son, Nathaniel, who have given up much in the way of a husband and father so that this *Handbook* series could be completed on schedule.

—David F. Kohl
Urbana, Illinois

SAMPLE ENTRIES

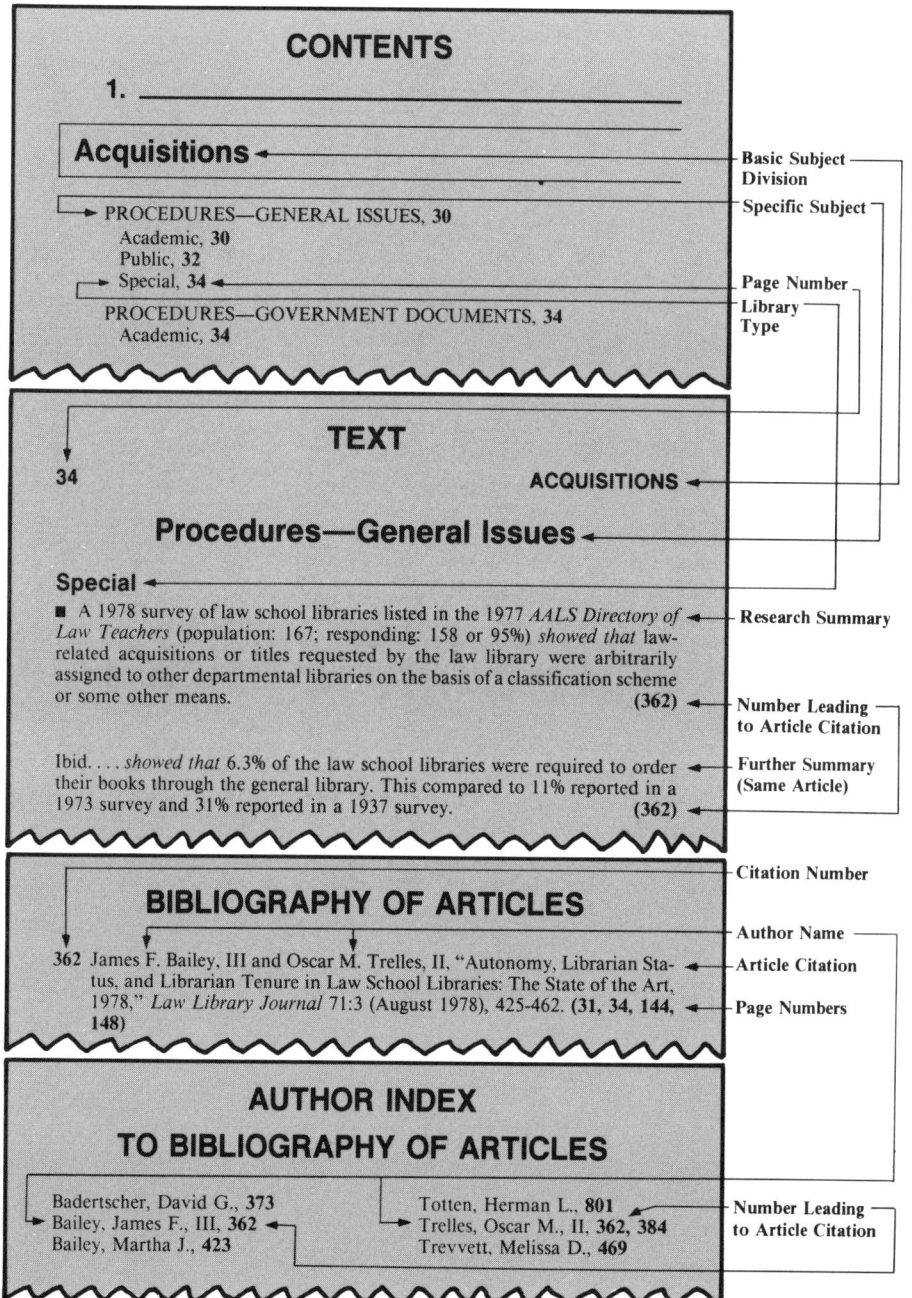

xxix

LIST OF JOURNALS SURVEYED

American Libraries. Chicago: American Library Association, 1970– . Monthly. LC 70-21767. ISSN 0002-9769. (Formerly *ALA Bulletin,* 1907–1969.)

American Society for Information Science. Journal. (JASIS) New York: John Wiley & Sons, 1970– . Bimonthly. LC 75-640174. ISSN 0002-8231. (Formerly *American Documentation,* 1950–1969.)

Canadian Library Journal. Ottawa: Canadian Library Association, 1969– . Bimonthly. LC 77-309891. ISSN 0008-4352. (Formerly *Bulletin,* 1944–March 1960; *Canadian Library,* 1960–1968.)

Catholic Library World. Haverford, PA: Catholic Library Association, 1929– . Monthly. LC 39-41. ISSN 0008-820X.

Collection Building. New York: Schuman, 1978– . Quarterly. LC 78-645190. ISSN 0160-4953.

Collection Management. New York: Haworth Press, 1975– . Quarterly. LC 78-640677. ISSN 0146-2679.

College and Research Libraries. Chicago: American Library Association, 1939– . Bimonthly. LC 42-16492. ISSN 0010-0870.

Drexel Library Quarterly. Philadelphia: Centrum Philadelphia, 1965– . Quarterly. LC 65-9911. ISSN 0012-6160.

Harvard Library Bulletin. Cambridge: Harvard University Library, 1947– . Quarterly. LC 49-1965//R802. ISSN 0017-8136.

International Journal of Legal Information. Camden, NJ: International Association of Law Libraries, 1982– . 6/yr. LC 82-643460. ISSN 0731-1265. (Formerly *Bulletin. International Association of Law Libraries,* 1960–1972; *International Journal of Law Libraries,* 1973–1979.)

International Library Review. London: Academic Press, 1969– . Quarterly. LC 76-10110. ISSN 0020-7837.

Journal of Academic Librarianship. Ann Arbor, MI: Mountainside Publishing, 1975– . Bimonthly. LC 75-647252. ISSN 0099-1333.

Journal of Education for Librarianship. State College, PA: Association of American Library Schools, 1960– . 5/yr. LC 63-24347. ISSN 0022-0604.

Journal of Library Administration. New York: Haworth Press, 1980– . Monthly. LC 80-644826. ISSN 0193-0826.

Journal of Library Automation. Chicago: American Library Association, 1968–. Quarterly. LC 68-6437//R82. ISSN 0022-2240.

Journal of Library History, Philosophy and Comparative Librarianship. Austin, TX: 1966–. Quarterly. LC 65-9989. ISSN 0275-3650. (Formerly *Journal of Library History,* 1966–1975.)

Law Library Journal. Chicago: American Association of Law Libraries, 1908–. Quarterly. LC 41-21688//R6. ISSN 0023-9283.

Library Acquisitions: Practice and Theory. Elmsford, NY: Pergamon Press, 1977–. Quarterly. LC 77-647728. ISSN 0364-6408.

Library Journal. New York: R.R. Bowker, 1876–. Semimonthly, except July–August. LC 76-645271. ISSN 0363-0277.

Library Quarterly. Chicago: University of Chicago, 1931–. Quarterly. LC 32-12448. ISSN 0024-2519.

Library Research. Norwood, NJ: Ablex Publishing, 1979–. Quarterly. LC 79-643718. ISSN 0164-0763.

Library Resources and Technical Services. Chicago: American Library Association, 1957–. Quarterly. LC 59-3198. ISSN 0024-2527. (Formed by the merger of *Serial Slants* and *Journal of Cataloging and Classification.*)

Library Trends. Champaign: University of Illinois at Urbana-Champaign, 1952–. Quarterly. LC 54-62638. ISSN 0024-2594.

Medical Library Association. Bulletin. Chicago: Medical Library Association, 1911–. Quarterly. LC 16-76616. ISSN 0025-7338.

Microform Review. Westport, CT: Meckler Publishing, 1972–. Quarterly. LC 72-620299. ISSN 0002-6530.

Notes. Philadelphia: Music Library Association, 1942–. Quarterly. LC 43-45299//R542. ISSN 0027-4380.

Online. Weston, CT: Online, 1977–. Quarterly. LC 78-640551. ISSN 0416-5422.

Public Libraries. Chicago: American Library Association, 1978–. 4/yr. ISSN 0163-5506. (Formerly *Just Between Ourselves,* 1962–1969; *PLA Newsletter,* 1962–1977.)

RQ. Chicago: American Library Association, 1960–. Quarterly. LC 77-23834. ISSN 0033-7072.

RSR Reference Services Review. Ann Arbor, MI: Perian Press, 1972–. LC 73-642283//R74. ISSN 0090-7324.

School Library Journal. New York: R.R. Bowker, 1954–. Monthly except June and July. LC 77-646483. ISSN 0362-8930.

School Library Media Quarterly. Chicago: American Library Association, 1981–. 4/yr. LC 82-640987. ISSN 0278-4823. (Formerly *School Libraries,* 1951–1972; *School Media Quarterly,* 1972–1980.)

List of Journals Surveyed

Special Libraries. New York: Special Libraries Association, 1910– . 4/yr. LC 11-25280rev2*. ISSN 0038-6723.

Wilson Library Bulletin. Bronx, NY: H.W. Wilson, 1914– . Monthly except July and August. LC 80-9008(rev.42). ISSN 0043-5651.

1. Acquisitions

Approval Plans

Academic

■ A study reported in 1975 at California State Polytechnic University, Pomona, comparing approval book selections with traditional faculty and librarian selections over a year's time, involving imprints for 1974 in economics and biological sciences, *showed that*, of 286 economics titles received through the approval program, 15 (5.2%) were also independently requested by faculty and librarians, while 63 of 78 faculty and librarian requests (80.8%) were not received on the approval plan. However, only 96 (33.6%) of the approval titles were returned to the vendor. **(669)**

Ibid. . . . *showed that*, for 255 titles in the biological sciences received on the approval program, 60 (23.5%) were also independently requested by faculty and librarians, while 152 of 212 faculty and librarian requests (71.7%) were not received on the approval plan. However, only 33 (12.9%) of the approval titles were returned to the vendor. **(669)**

■ A 1976 study at the Health Sciences Library of the University of Iowa involving 1,288 books received during a 6-month period *showed that*, of 730 (57%) books received on the approval plan, 330 (25%) were received due to orders placed on the basis of book reviews or publishers fliers; 131 (10%) were received due to orders generated as a result of patron request; and 97 (8%) were received due to standing order. **(467)**

Claims

Academic

■ A survey reported in 1977 of moderate-sized (120,000-500,000 volumes) U.S. academic libraries listed in the 1972-73 *American Library Directory* (survey size: 200; responding: 147 or 74%) *showed that*, when claiming issues of periodical titles ordered through a subscription agency, 34% of responding libraries did not rely solely on the subscription agency to initiate or follow up on claims, while 14% did not rely on the subscription agency for any help at all with claims. To wit:

    77 (52%) libraries reported that both first and subsequent claims were sent to the agency;

    20 (14%) libraries reported that both first and subsequent claims were sent directly to the publisher;

18 (12%) libraries reported that the first claim was sent to the publisher and all subsequent claims to the agency;

12 (8%) libraries reported that the first claim was sent to the agency with all subsequent claims sent to the agency;

16 (11%) libraries reported some other procedure was used. **(454)**

Collection Growth Rate—General Issues

Academic

■ A review in 1960 of library growth figures for the 25 university libraries listing holdings of over 1 million volumes in order to check Fremont Rider's finding that American college and university libraries tended to double their holdings every 15 years *showed that* only 4 had increased their holdings by 100% or more during the previous 15-year period. The overall average growth for the 25 was 78%. **(116)**

■ A comparison of 25 university libraries listing holdings of over 1 million volumes in 1960 with the 22 top-ranked graduate institutions *showed that* only 5 of the university libraries reporting holdings of 1 million or more were not ranked as one of the top 22 graduate institutions. These 5 were Texas, Brown, Iowa State, Duke, and Missouri. Only 2 of the top 22 institutions had libraries whose holdings were less than 1 million. These were MIT and Cal Tech. **(116)**

■ A 1963 update of the growth rates of the 20 libraries originally studied by Rider *showed that* collection growth rates have clearly decreased. His first group of "10 large university libraries of respectable age" had a collection doubling time of 16 years based on the average growth rate for the period 1831-1938. However, based on their average growth rate for the period 1938-60, their average doubling time was 25.1 years. **(129)**

■ A 1963 restudy using partially new data of the growth rates of those U.S. university libraries whose collections exceeded 1 million on June 30, 1960 (original study by Axford; citation 116) *showed that* the average time it took library collections to double in size, given their average growth rate of 3.5% during the period 1946-60, was 20.1 years. However, there was great variability among the libraries, with the doubling time required ranging from 9.8 years to 43.3 years. **(129)**

Collection Growth Rate 5

Ibid. . . . *showed that* in the 14 years previous to 1946-60 (1932-46) the average time it took library collections to double in size, given their average growth rate of 3.4% during this period, was 20.7 years. Here, too, there was great individual variability, with the doubling time ranging from 9.3 years to 33.3 years. **(129)**

Ibid. . . . *showed that* Rider's second group of 10 more recently founded university libraries had a collection doubling time of 9.5 years (according to the author of the article's recalculation, it was actually 10.9 years) based on their average growth rate for the period 1938-60. However, based on their average growth rate for the period 1938-60, their average doubling time was 22 years. **(129)**

Ibid. . . . *showed that* there was no statistically significant relationship between library growth rate and university excellence. Specifically, if library growth rate rank order was compared with the "correct" Keniston-Berelson rank order of university excellence in their graduate teaching and research programs, the correlation between the two during the 14-year period 1946-60 was r = −.24. This was not a statistically significant finding. **(129)**

Ibid. . . . *showed that*, if the Keniston-Berelson rank order of university excellence in graduate teaching and research programs was used to create a top group of 10 universities and a second-level group of 10 universities while the remaining members of the Association of Graduate Schools made up the third level of universities, the mean collection size of the first group had over twice as many volumes as the mean of the second group and over 3 times as many volumes as the mean of the third group in 1946 and 1960. The same ratio and relationship held for the means of absolute volumes added. **(129)**

Special

■ A 1976 survey of head law librarians in North American schools (sample size: 178; responding: 154 or 86.7%) *showed that* the modal numbers of volumes acquired per year by size of library were as follows:

small (50,000 volumes or less)	0-5,000 vol./year
medium (50,001-100,000)	0-5,000 vol./year
med-large (100,001-200,000)	5,001-10,000 vol./year
large (over 200,000)	10,000-15,000 vol./year **(357)**

Collection Growth Rate—Maps

Academic

■ A survey reported in 1981 of 85 North American academic map libraries that have medium or large research collections (usable responses: 49 or 58%) in conjunction with data from the 2nd and 3rd editions of *Map Collections in the United States and Canada* showed that the average size of map collections had grown from 83,650 sheets in 1968 to 113,816 in 1975 (an increase of 36.0%) to 157,696 in 1980 (a further increase of 38.6%). The average annual accession rate for 1968 was 4,654 sheets; for 1975 it was 5,565 (an increase of 19.6%); and for 1980 it was 5,734 (a further increase of 3.0%). **(216)**

Costs—General Issues

Academic

■ A study reported in 1981 of data on 1,146 2-year colleges, as reported in the 1977 Higher Education General Information Surveys and compared to the 1979 Association of College and Research Libraries standards, *showed that* overall the average library operating expenditures totaled $166,000 with median expenditures totaling $102,000, including average expenditures for privately supported schools (235 reporting) of $42,000 and average expenditures for publicly supported schools (911 reporting) of $198,000. **(500)**

Ibid. . . . *showed that* overall the average library materials budget was $39,000 with a median of $27,000, including average expenditures for privately supported schools (235 reporting) of $11,000 and average expenditures for publicly supported schools (911 reporting) of $46,000. **(500)**

Ibid. . . . *showed that* overall the average library salaries and wages budget was $99,000 with a median of $55,000, including average salaries and wages budgets in privately supported schools (235 reporting) of $23,000 and average salaries and wages budgets in publicly supported schools (911 reporting) of $118,000. **(500)**

■ A study reported in 1980 at the University of Rochester, comparing costs of 1-year versus 3-year journal subscriptions based on a sample of 20 business administration and management science periodicals, *showed that,*

Costs

when 4 variables were considered (cost of capital, reorder costs, average inflation rate for 1-year subscriptions, and ratio of 3-year to 1-year subscription costs), the 3-year subscription period was always the most advantageous in terms of cost. Specifically, the least projected savings for the 20 periodicals was 12%, while the most in projected savings that could be realized was 106%. The savings was due to locking in advantageous subscription rates for a 3-year period and to reduced staff costs caused by reduced renewal activity. **(627)**

■ A study reported in 1983 of surveys of medical school libraries for the period 1960-61 through 1980-81, made by the American Medical Association, the Medical Library Assoication, the Association of Academic Health Sciences Library Directors, and the National Library of Medicine, *showed that* during the 3-year period 1978-79 through 1980-81, on the basis of regular funds spent (excluding special contracts and grants), medical school libraries spent "more than three times as much on serials as they do on monographs." Even as expenditures increased during this period, the ratio remained constant. **(746)**

■ An Indiana University survey for the National Science Foundation reported in 1979 *showed that* major academic libraries increased their materials budget by an average of 9.4% in the period 1973-76; a 15-18% increase was reported necessary to maintain equivalent coverage. **(016)**

Ibid. . . . *showed that* library administrators responded to shortages in the library materials serials budget primarily by canceling duplicates and shifting funds from monographic to serials accounts. The third most common tactic was to halt new subscriptions in order to renew old ones. **(016)**

Ibid. . . . *showed that* during the period 1969-76 large academic libraries increased the percentage of their budget spent on serials at the expense of monographs. In 1969 $2 was spent on serials for every $1 on monographs; by 1976 a steady decrease had reduced the ratio to $1.23 for serials for each $1 spent on monographs. **(016)**

Public

■ An attempt reported in 1982 to establish 4 input measures and 4 output measures for public libraries, based on published statistical reports for 301 New Jersey public libraries over a 6-year period (1974-79) and survey data for 96 public libraries in New Jersey, *showed that* (per capita based on number of residents in the library's service area):

INPUT MEASURES

The proportion of budget spent on materials averaged 19.9%, with a standard deviation of .081 (based on 301 libraries).

The new volumes per capita averaged .181, with a standard deviation of .097 (based on 301 libraries).

The periodical titles per capita averaged .0094, with a standard deviation of .0054 (based on 301 libraries).

The circulation per volume averaged 1.79, with a standard deviation of .77 (based on 301 libraries).

OUTPUT MEASURES

The circulation per capita averaged 5.04, with a standard deviation of 3.07 (based on 301 libraries).

The patron visits per capita averaged 2.82, with a standard deviation of 1.82 (based on 96 libraries).

The reference questions per capita averaged 1.12, with a standard deviation of .79 (based on 96 libraries).

The in-library uses of materials per capita averaged 2.29, with a standard deviation of 2.02 (based on 96 libraries). **(576)**

■ A survey of 53 U.S. public libraries (all responding) reported in 1983 concerning circulation and expenditures *showed that*, using 1980 as a base year (index value = 100), expenditures rose 10% by 1981 (index value = 110), while expenditures had risen a further 11% by 1982 (index value = 121). However, when expenditures were adjusted for inflation using the Consumer Price Index, there was no increase in real expenditures in 1981 (index value = 100), although there was a 4% real increase in expenditures the following year, in 1982 (index value = 104). Further, between 1980-82 the amount of expenditures spent on salaries rose from 63% to 64%, while the amount of expenditures spent on materials dropped from 16% to 15%. The amount spent on "other" remained constant at 21%. **(791)**

School

■ A 1983 survey of a systematic sample of school library media centers concerning data for fiscal year 1982-83 (survey size: 2,000 centers; responding: 1,297; usable: 1,251 or 62%) *showed that* a comparison of privately supported (72) and publicly supported (1,179) school library media centers revealed that media specialists in private schools served fewer students, had more money to spend on resources, administered smaller collections, and earned more modest salaries. Specifically:

Costs

enrollment averaged 460 students for private schools and 669 for public schools;

total materials expenditure per student averaged $12.55 for private schools and $9.62 for public schools;

the number of books per student averaged 27.08 for private schools and 18.44 for public schools;

the number of AV items per student averaged 3.2 for private schools and 3.26 for public schools;

in private schools the media specialist averaged 8.92 years of experience with a salary of $13,880, while in public schools the media specialist averaged 11.08 years of experience with a salary of $20,389. **(798)**

Special

■ A study reported in 1983 of surveys of medical school libraries for the period 1960-61 through 1980-81, made by the American Medical Association, the Medical Library Assoication, the Association of Academic Health Sciences Library Directors, and the National Library of Medicine, *showed that* during the 3-year period 1978-79 through 1980-81, on the basis of regular funds spent (excluding special contracts and grants), medical school libraries spent "more than three times as much on serials as they do on monographs." Even as expenditures increased during this period, the ratio remained constant. **(746)**

Costs—Government Documents

Academic

■ A 1977 survey of academic depository libraries (sample size: 200; responding: 160 or 80%) concerning the impact of commercially produced microforms *showed that* the top 3 reasons given by the 73 respondents who reported purchasing commercially produced government documents for selecting a particular publisher were (multiple responses allowed): cost (64 or 88%); format, i.e., fiche, card, or film (57 or 78%); and reputation of company (43 or 59%). **(318)**

■ A 1977-78 study at Duke University involving acquisition of state government documents (population: "approximately 2,000 items" ordered during an 18-month period; sample size: 591 items) *showed that* overall

88.7% of the state government document requests did not require payment. However, between April 1977 and April 1978 the average number of responses to requests for state government documents that required payment rose from "about 5%" to "about 12%." **(310)**

Ibid. . . . *showed that* 96.8% of the material ordered from LC cards was gratis; 92.2% of the material from the LC's *MonthlyChecklist* was gratis; 89.4% of the material ordered from "other" sources was gratis; 88.7% of the material ordered from state checklists was gratis; and 73.3% of the material ordered from PAIS was gratis. **(310)**

Costs—Maps

Academic

■ A survey reported in 1981 of 85 North American academic map libraries that had medium or large research collections (usable responses: 49 or 58%) *showed that* the prices for selected foreign topographic series sold by GeoCenter during the period 1970-80 rose by 245.7% for Latin American maps and by 277.4% for European maps. **(216)**

Costs—Monographs

Academic

■ A 1969 study at San Fernando Valley State College involving out-of-print acquisitions over a year's time *showed that*, of 17,689 titles ordered, 4,720 titles (27%) were received. Further, the average unit cost of in-print books (all subjects) for that year was $9.19 compared to the average unit cost of $10.18 for the 4,720 out-of-print books. **(593)**

■ An Indiana University survey for the National Science Foundation reported in 1979 *showed that* library administrators responded to shortages in the library materials serials budget primarily by canceling duplicates and shifting funds from monographic to serials accounts. The third most common tactic was to halt new subscriptions in order to renew old ones.
(016)

Costs

Ibid. . . . *showed that* during the period 1969-76 large academic libraries increased the percentage of their budget spent on serials at the expense of monographs. In 1969 $2 was spent on serials for every $1 on monographs; by 1976 a steady decrease had reduced the ratio to $1.23 for serials for each $1 spent on monographs. **(016)**

Public

■ A study reported in 1979 at the Oklahoma City/County Metropolitan Library System *showed that*, for 18,996 adult hardback books and 19,126 adult paperback books purchased in FY 1976-77, the cost ratio, based on purchase price alone, of hardback to paperback was 4.1 to 1, while the cost per circulation (again based on purchase price only) of hardback to paperback was 4.2 to 1. For slightly more materials in FY 1977-78 the cost ratio of hardbound to paperback was 3.7 to 1, and the cost per circulation was 3.89 to 1. **(231)**

Ibid. . . . *showed that*, for 5,624 juvenile hardback books and 6,031 paperback books purchased in FY 1976-77, the cost ratio, based on purchase price alone, of hardback to paperback was 5.9 to 1, while the cost per circulation (again based on purchase price only) of hardback to paperback was 2.7 to 1. For approximately the same number of materials purchased in FY 1977-78 the cost ratio of hardbound to paperback was 4.8 to 1, and the cost per circulation was 2.6 to 1. **(231)**

■ A 1982 survey of American and Canadian public libraries (sample size: 279; responding: 68 or 24%) *showed that* approximately 10.5% (±3.2%, representing a 95% confidence interval for the population at large) of respondents' current book acquisitions budgets had been allocated for the purchase of mass market paperbacks, while about 9.2% (±3.1%, representing a 95% confidence interval for the population at large) of their last year's book budget was spent on mass market paperbacks. There was a small statistical correlation ("y's = .26 and .30 respectively") between the book budget percentages and size of populations served, with the libraries serving larger populations tending to allocate more money for the purchase of paperbacks (significance level not given). **(273)**

School

■ A review of textbook costs during the period 1958-63 undertaken at the University of Illinois Research Center for the U.S. Office of Education in 1964 *showed that* during the 1958-63 period inflation increased by 7% but textbook (elementary through college combined) prices increased by 15% from an average price of $2.60 each to $2.99 each. **(081)**

Special

■ A study reported in 1974 of 3,347 biomedical book reviews (2,067 titles), taken from the 1970 issues of 54 English-language biomedical journals (excluding *Science* and *Nature*) that contained "bona fide" book reviews, *showed that* the average price of a subsample (1,077 titles) of the books available in the U.S. was $16.20 per volume. Further, of 39 paperback books available in the U.S. (all the paperbacks in the sample available in the U.S.), the average price was $3.82 per volume. **(704)**

■ An annual study reported in 1982 of prices for legal publications *showed that* in 1980-81 prices for monographs increased 0.5% from the previous year, while prices for all categories of serials together increased 9.8% from the previous year. **(378)**

Ibid. . . . *showed that* between 1973-74 and 1980-81 the cost per average legal monograph title (based on over 2,400 titles published in each year) increased from $11.16 to $26.39 for an increase of 136.47%. **(378)**

Costs—Out-of-Print Materials

General

■ A survey reported in 1973 of out-of-print dealers concerning common dealer practices and preferences (survey size: 54 dealers; responding: 22 or 40.7%) *showed that* (multiple responses allowed) the most commonly reported basis of assigning prices was book trade experience (reported by 19 or 86.4% respondents); "next in order" [no numbers given] were *Bookman's Price Index* and *American Book Prices Current.* Only 1 major retrospective guide to book prices was mentioned, Wright Howes's *U.S. iana* (reported by 50% of the respondents). **(601)**

Academic

■ A 1969 study at San Fernando Valley State College involving out-of-print acquisitions over a year's time *showed that,* of 17,689 titles ordered, 4,720 titles (27%) were received. Further, the average unit cost of in-print books (all subjects) for that year was $9.19 compared to the average unit

Costs

cost of $10.18 for the 4,720 out-of-print books. **(593)**

■ A study at Indiana State University in 1971 comparing 2 methods of acquiring out-of-print books, using 168 titles divided into 2 equal groups, *showed that* a search of 98 out-of-print catalogs located 15 (18%) acceptable titles, compared to placing an ad in *Library Bookman*, which located 32 (38%) of the titles in that group. Further, if one was willing to pay 3 or more times the original publisher's price, then an additional 17 titles could be added to the success rate for the second method, making a total success rate for the second method of 59%. **(124)**

Ibid. . . . *showed that* the average price of books located through out-of-print catalogs was 1.56 times the original publisher's price, whereas the average price of books located through the *Library Bookman* ad was 1.78 times the original price. **(124)**

Costs—Per Capita

School

■ A 1983 survey of a systematic sample of school library media centers concerning data for fiscal year 1982-83 (survey size: 2,000 centers; responding: 1,297; usable: 1,251 or 62%) *showed that* the average total materials expenditure per pupil by type of library media center was as follows:

elementary school (587 schools)	$ 9.06 per student
junior high/middle school (308 schools)	$ 8.99 per student
senior high (304 schools)	$11.54 per student
other (49 schools)	$12.50 per student **(798)**

Special

■ The annual survey of law school libraries and librarians conducted in 1980 by the American Bar Association, American Association of Law Libraries, and Association of American Law Schools (population not given; response: 168 libraries) *showed that* the median amounts expended per FTE student for books was overall $317, while by size of library it was:

small (under 70,000 vols.)	$228
medium (70,000-99,999 vols.)	$344

continued

medium-large (100,000-199,999 vols.) $304
large (200,000+ vols.) $317 **(382)**

Costs—Periodical Dual Pricing

General

■ A study reported in 1977 of a 10-year run (1966-75) of 200 U.S. journal titles, selected at random from 10 well-known Wilson indexes, *showed that* the number of periodical titles with a dual price structure (individual subscription rate different from institutional subscription rate) rose from 4% of the titles in 1966 to 15% of the titles in 1975. (With a 95% confidence level, the 1975 number ranged between 9.8% and 20.2% of the titles.) Further, the percentage of titles with dual pricing increased most sharply in 1968-70, in 1971-72, and again in 1973-74. **(458)**

Ibid. . . . *showed that* dual pricing began at least as early as 1956, when the *Philosophical Review* instituted a differential subscription rate ($3.00 for individuals; $6.00 for institutions). **(458)**

Ibid. . . . *showed that*, while the difference between the average institutional subscription rate and the average individual subscription rate was not great for the sample as a whole, for the 27 journals with dual pricing the difference between individual and institutional subscription rates was considerable by 1975—"almost 7 dollars" per title. **(458)**

Academic

■ A study reported in 1980 of core health science journals ("500 Key Titles" prepared by Felter in 1973 and updated by Brown and Moore in 1978) and the journal holdings of 3 university medical center libraries (State University of New York at Buffalo Health Sciences Library, Cleveland Health Sciences Library-Health Center Library, and Northeastern Ohio Universities College of Medicine Basic Medical Sciences Library) *showed that* of the 500 core journals 61 (12.2%) had a dual pricing structure, i.e., individual and institutional subscribers were charged different rates. **(732)**

Costs

Ibid. . . . *showed that*, of a total of 281 health science journals identified as having a dual pricing structure, the average individual subscription rate (of the 264 titles for which the rates were known) was $30.61, while the average institutional subscription rate was $63.90 or 102.14% higher.
(732)

■ A study reported in 1983 of 76 academic journals related to economics and business *showed that* 59% charge libraries higher subscription rates than they charge individuals. In more detail, of 30 journals published by professional associations, 47% have a differential subscription price; of 26 journals published by universities, 58% have a differential; and of 20 journals published by private publishers, 80% have a differential subscription price. **(271)**

Ibid. . . . *showed that* the 14 journals with differential subscription rates published by a professional association averaged $19.18 for an individual subscription compared to an average library price of $36.96; for 15 such journals published by universities the average individual price was $13.27 compared to an average library price of $20.73; and for 16 such journals published by private publishers the individual price averaged $20.22 compared to an average library price of $45.30. The average subscription cost for 16 journals without differential rates published by a professional association averaged $23.50; for 11 such journals published by universities the price averaged $10.36; and for 4 such journals published by private publishers the price averaged $29.78. **(271)**

Special

■ A study reported in 1980 of core health science journals ("500 Key Titles" prepared by Felter in 1973 and updated by Brown and Moore in 1978) and the journal holdings of 3 university medical center libraries (State University of New York at Buffalo Health Sciences Library, Cleveland Health Sciences Library-Health Center Library, and Northeastern Ohio Universities College of Medicine Basic Medical Sciences Library) *showed that* of the 500 core journals 61 (12.2%) had a dual pricing structure, i.e., individual and institutional subscribers were charged different rates. **(732)**

Ibid. . . . *showed that*, of a total of 281 health science journals identified as having a dual pricing structure, the average individual subscription rate (of the 264 titles for which the rates were known) was $30.61, while the average institutional subscription rate was $63.90 or 102.14% higher. **(732)**

Costs—Subscription Increases

General

■ A study reported in 1983 of subscription costs for 100 serial titles (50 U.S./Canadian titles; 25 non-U.S./non-Canadian titles; and 25 reference services) over a 7-year period (1975-81) *showed that*:

> the average price increase of the U.S./Canadian titles was 84.7%, with 4 titles (8%) maintaining their prices and 18 titles (36%) showing an increase of 100% or more;

> the average price increase of the non-U.S./non-Canadian titles was 121.44%, with no titles maintaining their price and 14 titles (56%) showing increases of 100% or more;

> the average price increase of the reference services was 67.6%, with 2 of the titles (8%) maintaining their prices and 6 titles (24%) showing increases of 100% or more. **(441)**

Ibid. . . . *showed that* the overall average price increase was 76.2%, compared to the Consumer Price Index increase for the same period of 69% in the U.S. and 71% in Canada. **(441)**

Academic

■ A study reported in 1972 of price and page increases for 20 physics journals between 1959 and 1969 *showed that* the average overall price increase was 202% with an overall average increase in the number of pages in these journals of 147%. Subtracting out the percent of page increase, the price increase falls to 55% for this 10-year period. **(399)**

Ibid. . . . *showed that* during this period the number of issues increased from 264 to 481, an increase of 82%. **(399)**

Ibid. . . . *showed that* the average page and price increase during this period by publishing group was as follows:

> for the 8 American Institute of Physics journals the page increase was 161% with a price increase of 157% for a net price increase of −4%;

> for the 6 commercially published journals the page increase was 171% with a price increase of 283% for a net price increase of 112%;

Costs

and for 6 other society or nonprofit journals the page increase was 72% with a price increase of 189% for a net price increase of 117%. **(399)**

■ A study reported in 1975 comparing book price increases reported in the *Bowker Annual of Library and Book Trade Information* with actual price increases encountered on English-language material acquired through approval plans at 3 universities (University of Nebraska, years 1966-67 and 1967-68; Florida Atlantic University, 1969-70 and 1970-71; and Arizona State University, 1971-72) during the period 1967-72 *showed that* Bowker indicated a 48.1% increase, while the libraries showed an 18.5% increase for this period. **(630)**

■ An Indiana University survey for the National Science Foundation reported in 1979 *showed that* library administrators in major academic libraries responded to shortages in the library materials serials budget primarily by canceling duplicates and shifting funds from monographic to serials accounts. The third most common tactic was to halt new subscriptions in order to renew old ones. **(016)**

Ibid. . . . *showed that* during the period 1969-76 large academic libraries increased the percentage of their budget spent on serials at the expense of monographs. In 1969 $2 was spent on serials for every $1 on monographs; by 1976 a steady decrease had reduced the ratio to $1.23 for serials for each $1 spent on monographs. **(016)**

■ A study reported in 1980 at the University of Rochester comparing costs of 1-year versus 3-year journal subscriptions, based on a sample of 20 business administration and management science periodicals, *showed that*, when 4 variables were considered (cost of capital, reorder costs, average inflation rate for 1-year subscriptions, and ratio of 3-year to 1-year subscription costs), the 3-year subscription period was always the most advantageous in terms of cost. Specifically, the least projected savings for the 20 periodicals was 12%, while the most in projected savings that could be realized was 106%. The savings was due to locking in advantageous subscription rates for a 3-year period and to reduced staff costs caused by reduced renewal activity. **(627)**

■ A study reported in 1981 of the annual price indexes and average prices of academic periodicals reported in *Library Journal* for the 12-year period 1967-79 *showed that* the overall price increase of periodicals for this period was 250.7%. This compared to a price increase of 89.7% for the previous 12-year period, 1957-69. **(272)**

Ibid. . . . *showed that*, even if periodical budgets increased at the same rate as overall inflation as measured by the Consumer Price Index for the 1967-79 period, the overall periodical purchasing power of those budgets would have declined from 100% in 1967-69 (base years) to 62% in 1979. **(272)**

Ibid. . . . *showed that*, even if periodical budgets increased at the same rate as overall inflation as measured by the Consumer Price Index for the 1967-79 period, the periodical purchasing power declined differentially by subject area from 100% in 1967-69 (base years) to the following figures in 1979: law (90%), history (89%), general interest (86%), literature and language (84%), zoology (72%), agriculture (72%), medicine (66%), library science (65%), chemistry and physics (45%), and labor/industrial relations (41%). **(272)**

Ibid. . . . *showed that*, if a library had the same acquisitions budget in 1979 that it had in 1967, it would be able to purchase overall only 29% of the periodicals in 1979 it could have purchased in 1967. **(272)**

■ A study reported in 1983 at Harvard University updating an earlier study and comparing the average periodical prices of the Widener price index (based on humanities and social science periodicals published in the U.S., France, Germany, Great Britain, and Italy) with the average periodical prices in comparable sections of 2 published indexes (an international index compiled by John B. Merriam of Blackwell and published in the *Library Association Record*; and a domestic index compiled by Norman Brown and Jane Phillips and published in the *Library Journal*) *showed that*, while the average prices for all 3 indexes were quite different during the 12-year period 1970-82, the Widener index was nevertheless highly correlated with the 2 published indexes so that the published indexes were effective tools to predict average periodical prices for the Widener humanities and social science collection. Specifically, in 1970 the average Widener periodical cost $9.45, the average Blackwell periodical cost $12.96, and the average LJ periodical cost $10.41; by 1982 these costs were $38.11, $46.58, and $44.80 respectively. On the other hand, the Widener and the Blackwell average periodical prices for the same 12-year period had a correlation coefficient of $r = .9971$, while the Widener and the LJ average periodical prices had a correlation coefficient of $r = .9662$ (Widener index for U.S. periodicals only had a correlation coefficient with LJ periodicals of $r = .9938$). **(777)**

Ibid. . . . *showed that* using the Blackwell published data to predict changes in the Widener index (based on at least 9 years of Widener average periodical data to establish the regression line) enabled Harvard to predict humanities and social science average periodical prices within at least 1.4%

Costs

each year over a 4-year period. Over the 4-year period, the cumulative error in prediction was 1%. **(777)**

Special

■ A study reported in 1980 comparing the subscription rates as reported in *Ulrich's International Periodicals Directory* for 135 journals on the 1977 Brandon list (for the small hospital library) for the years 1958, 1963, 1968, 1973, and 1978 showed that the average cost per journal increased from $11.38 in 1958 to $36.16 in 1978. This represented a cost increase of 218%, compared to a cost increase of 126% for the Consumer Price Index for the same period. **(729)**

Ibid. . . . *showed that* for the 5 5-year periods, the lowest rate of increase was during the period 1958-63 (9% increase), while the highest rate of increase was during the 1973-78 period (56% increase). In all 5 periods the rate of journal increase exceeded the Consumer Price Index increase.
(729)

Ibid. . . . *showed that*, without adjusting the increase in journal costs for inflation, 1978 dollars would only have bought 31% of the journal subscriptions they would have bought in 1958. If adjustments for inflation were made (using the Consumer Price Index), the 1978 dollars would still only have bought 70% of the journal subscriptions they would have bought in 1958. **(729)**

Ibid. . . . *showed that* the rate of increase in journal costs for the 135 journals on the 1977 Brandon list, while large, was nevertheless substantially lower than the increases generally for U.S. periodicals or generally for medical periodicals. For example, based on the Brown annual price surveys in *Library Journal* for the period 1968-78, the cost increases for the various groups of journals during this period can be shown as follows:

for the 135 Brandon list journals, the 1968 dollars would have purchased only 46% of the 1978 journal subscriptions;

for medical periodicals on the Brown list, the 1968 dollars would have purchased only 34% of the 1978 journal subscriptions;

for U.S. periodicals on the Brown list, the 1968 dollars would have purchased only 31% of the 1978 journal subscriptions.

All of these drops in purchasing power were greater than the general rate of inflation for this period as measured by the Consumer Price Index. The CPI dollar dropped to 53% of its 1968 value by 1978. **(729)**

■ An annual study reported in 1982 of prices for legal publications *showed that* in 1980-81 prices for monographs increased 0.5% from the previous year, while prices for all categories of serials together increased 9.8% from the previous year. **(378)**

Ibid. . . . *showed that* between 1973-74 and 1980-81 the cost per average legal serial title (based on over 700 serial titles published in each year), including periodicals, commercially published court reporters, looseleaf services, and legal continuations, increased from $50.08 to $106.44 for an increase of 112.54%. **(378)**

Ibid. . . . *showed that* between 1973-74 and 1980-81 the cost per average legal periodical (based on over 340 periodical titles published in each of the years) rose from $11.95 to $21.07 for an increase of 76.32%. **(378)**

Ibid. . . . *showed that* between 1973-74 and 1980-81 the cost per average legal looseleaf service title (based on 92 looseleaf service titles in each of the years) rose from $181.80 to $374.65 for an increase of 106.08%. **(378)**

Ibid. . . . *showed that* between 1973-74 and 1980-81 the cost per average commercially published court reporter (based on at least 14 such reporters in each of the years) rose from $173.63 to $326.19 for an increase of 87.86%. **(378)**

Ibid. . . . *showed that* between 1973-74 and 1980-81 the cost per average legal continuation (based on 260 or more continuation titles for each of the years) rose from $44.07 to $130.32 for an increase of 195.71%. **(378)**

■ A study reported in 1983, concerning inflation of medical journal prices and based on prices of 111 journals listed on the 1983 Brandon list, *showed that* the average costs of these journals at 5-year intervals between 1963 and 1983 were as follows:

1963	$11.81	average journal cost
1968	$14.00	average journal cost
1973	$21.16	average journal cost
1978	$33.35	average journal cost
1983	$59.67	average journal cost

(749)

Costs 21

Ibid. . . . *showed that* for the 20-year period not only did the cost of the average journal subscription increase, but the rate of increase increased as well. Further, the increase in the average journal subscription was always greater than the increase in the Consumer Price Index. For example, the percentage increase in journal costs and in the Consumer Price Index by 5-year intervals for the period 1963-1983 was as follows:

                1963-68   19% journal/12% CPI increase
                1968-73   51% journal/28% CPI increase
                1973-78   58% journal/47% CPI increase
                1978-83   79% journal/50% CPI increase

Further, for the overall period 1963-83, the journals increased a total of 405%, while the Consumer Price Index increased a total of 219%. **(749)**

Ibid. . . . *showed that* during the period 1963-83 a journal budget that increased at the same rate as the Consumer Price Index would by 1983 only purchase 65% of the journal titles it could purchase in 1963. **(749)**

Ibid. . . . *showed that* a comparison of price increases for Brandon list journals, compared to price increases for medical journals and overall U.S. periodicals listed by Brown in *Library Journal*, revealed that during each of the 3 5-year periods between 1968-83, the increases for overall U.S. periodicals and for medical journals were almost always larger than for the Brandon journals. For example:

> in 1968-73 U.S. periodicals increased 87%, medical periodicals increased by 73%, and the Brandon list journals increased by 51%;

> in 1973-78 U.S. periodicals and medical periodicals both increased by 70%, while Brandon list journals increased by 58%;

> in 1978-83 (data for U.S. periodicals and medical periodicals based on 1982 data) U.S. periodicals increased 63%, medical periodicals increased by 80%, and Brandon list journals increased by 79%. **(749)**

Costs—Vendor Discounts

Public

■ A 1979 study of vendor performance (Baker & Taylor, Brodart) over a 5-month period in 8 small- to medium-sized public libraries and 1 regional

ACQUISITIONS

resource center on Maryland's eastern shore *showed that* the average discounts received from each vendor were as follows:

TYPE OF BOOK	BAKER & TAYLOR	BRODART
adult fiction	38.91%	37.6%
adult nonfiction	36.1%	33.2%
juvenile	28.15%	20.4%
paperbacks	37.5%	32.7%

(385)

Gift and Exchange Programs

General

■ A 1973 survey of all Duplicates Exchange Union (formerly Periodicals Exchange Union) members (survey size: 399 libraries; responding: 229 or 58%) *showed that*, of 228 respondents, 205 (89.5%) were college libraries; 15 (6.6%) were special libraries including hospital, art museum, and company libraries; and 8 (3.5%) were public libraries. **(635)**

Ibid. . . . *showed that* most of the Duplicates Exchange Union libraries were small. For example, the "approximate number of [periodical] subscriptions" per library broke down as follows:

1-300 subscriptions	42 (18.3%) libraries
301-600 subscriptions	78 (34.1%) libraries
601-1,000 subscriptions	52 (22.7%) libraries
over 1,000 subscriptions	45 (19.6%) libraries
no response	12 (5.3%) libraries

(635)

Ibid. . . . *showed that* respondents' estimates of the percentage of exchange lists received that proved useful were as follows (only 10 categories of usefulness were reported, e.g., 10%, 20%, etc., nothing in between):

30% or less of the lists received were useful to 65 (28.4%) of the respondents;

40-50% of the lists received were useful to 42 (18.3%) of the respondents;

60-80% of the lists received were useful to 66 (28.8%) of the respondents;

and 90% or more of the lists received were useful to 51 (22.2%) of the respondents

(5 or 2.3% of the respondents did not reply to this particular question). **(635)**

Ibid. . . . *showed that* the average number of items requested from a list was as follows: 22.7% of the libraries requested 4 or fewer items; 48.5% requested 8 or fewer items; and 70.8% requested 12 or fewer items. Further, 61.6% of the libraries estimated they received less than 30% of the items requested, while 87.4% estimated they received less than 50% of the items requested. **(635)**

Ibid. . . . *showed that*, although 24 (10.5%) libraries reported that use of the Duplicates Exchange Union resulted in a financial loss, most libraries considered it useful. Specifically, the libraries reported as follows:

very useful	98 (42.8%)	libraries
useful	93 (40.6%)	libraries
of some use	35 (15.3%)	libraries
useless	3 (1.3%)	libraries

(635)

Ibid. . . . *showed that* generally libraries supported the idea of continuing to include books and documents in the exchange program. Of 221 respondents, 160 (69.9%) favored the idea, while 61 (26.6%) did not.
(635)

Government Documents

Academic

■ A 1977-78 study at Duke University involving acquisition of state government documents (population: "approximately 2,000 items" ordered during an 18-month period; sample size: 591 items) *showed that* 85% of all requests for state government documents evoked a response within the first 5 weeks, after which "the response rate declined dramatically." **(310)**

Ibid. . . . *showed that* "about 75%" of the documents requested were serial publications and "about 25%" were monographs. The average response time was 4.3 weeks and ranged from a response rate of 15.2% for serials and 19.0% for monographs within 1 week through a response rate of 85.3% for serials and 83.9% for monographs within 5 weeks to a response rate of 92.7% for serials and 93.3% for monographs within 9 weeks.
(310)

ACQUISITIONS

■ A 1981 survey of U.S. depository libraries, both academic and public (sample size: 221; responding: 171 or 77%) concerning their use of online data bases (DIALOG, ORBIT, and BRS), particularly with regard to government documents, *showed that* the top 3 reasons given by respondents for not ordering government documents microfiche as the result of an online search were: library does not have computer terminals (academic depositories, 33%; public depositories, 59%), didn't know that microfiche government documents could be ordered online (academic depositories, 24%; public depositories, 25%), and prefer hard copy to microfiche copy (academic depositories, 27%; public depositories, 20%). **(317)**

Ibid. . . . *showed that* none of the public depositories had ever ordered microfiche online as the result of a government document search, while only 3% of the academic libraries had ever done so. **(317)**

ISSN

General

■ A study reported in 1977 at Brock University Library (Canada) of 532 titles from the university serials list that had International Standard Serial Numbers (ISSNs) reported both in *Irregular Serials and Annuals: an International Directory* (2nd issue) and in *New Serial Titles* showed that 32 (6.01%) titles did not have the same ISSN listed both places but instead had 2 different numbers listed. Of these 32, 30 (93.8%) had the "05" factor, i.e., the ISSN began with "05." **(546)**

Ibid. . . . *showed that*, of 497 serial titles taken from 10 "representative" publishers' lists and searched in all the Bowker publications providing ISSNs (including *Irregular Serials and Annuals: an International Directory*, 2nd edition) and in *New Serial Titles*, 428 (86.1%) had ISSNs of which 398 titles had ISSNs reported in more than 1 publication. Of these 398 titles, 31 (7.79%) titles did not have the same ISSN listed in all publications but instead had different ISSN numbers listed. Of these 31, the "05" factor, i.e., the ISSN began with "05," figured in 58.06% of the cases. **(546)**

■ A study reported in 1977 of "Corrections to Previous ISSN Assignments" listed in *Ulrich's International Periodicals Directory*, 15th edition, and in *Irregular Serials and Annuals: an International Directory*, 3rd edition, *showed that* using the "lower/lowest" ISSN did not lead to substantially greater agreement among sources. Specifically, of 67 ISSNs listed in *Ulrich's*, 57 (85.1%) were the lower of the 2 assigned numbers; while of 44 ISSNs listed in *Irregular*, 25 (56.82%) were the lower of the 2 assigned numbers. **(546)**

Maps

Academic

■ A survey reported in 1981 of 85 North American academic map libraries that had medium or large research collections (usable responses: 49 or 58%) in conjunction with data from the 2nd and 3rd editions of *Map Collections in the United States and Canada* showed that the average size of map collections had grown from 83,650 sheets in 1968 to 113,816 in 1975 (an increase of 36.0%) to 157,696 in 1980 (a further increase of 38.6%). The average annual accession rate for 1968 was 4,654 sheets; for 1975 it was 5,565 (an increase of 19.6%); and for 1980 it was 5,734 (a further increase of 3.0%). **(216)**

Ibid. . . . *showed that* 77% of the respondents reported depository membership in the United States Geological Survey in 1968, 94% in 1975, and 96% in 1980. 84% reported depository membership in the Defense Mapping Agency in 1968, 86% in 1975, and 88% in 1980. 13% reported depository membership in the National Ocean Survey in 1968, 27% in 1975, and 49% in 1980. **(216)**

Microforms

Academic

■ A survey reported in 1976 of 120 randomly selected patrons of the Bobst Library Microform Center of New York University *showed that*, given the statement "When I find what I want it makes no difference whether it is in regular form or microform," 64 (53%) respondents reported "strongly agree" or "agree"; 19 (16%) gave no opinion; and 37 (31%) reported "disagree" or "strongly disagree." However, when given the statement "The advantages of microforms outweigh the disadvantages," 102 (85%) reported "strongly agree" or "agree"; 12 (10%) gave no opinion; and 6 (5%) reported "disagree" or "strongly disagree." **(224)**

■ A 1977 survey of academic depository libraries (sample size: 200; responding: 160 or 80%) concerning the impact of commercially produced microforms *showed that* 73 (46%) respondents reported purchasing microforms of governmental publications from commercial publishers. Of these 73, 52 (71%) reported that they systematically consult reviewing sources related to microforms. **(318)**

Ibid. . . . *showed that* the top 6 sources consulted by the 73 respondents for information concerning commercially produced microforms were (multiple responses allowed):

publishers' brochures	50 (68.5%) respondents
Documents to the People	42 (57.5%) respondents
Government Publications Review	39 (53.4%) respondents
advice from colleagues	36 (49.3%) respondents
faculty recommendations	34 (46.6%) respondents
Microform Review	33 (45.2%) respondents **(318)**

Ibid. . . . *showed that* the top 3 reasons given by the 73 respondents who reported purchasing commercially produced documents for selecting a particular publisher were (multiple responses allowed): cost (64 or 88%); format, i.e., fiche, card, or film (57 or 78%); and reputation of company (43 or 59%). **(318)**

Ibid. . . . *showed that* the commercial firms most relied on by responding librarians (N = 73) to supply government publications in microform were (multiple responses allowed):

Readex	49 (67%) respondents
CIS	43 (59%) respondents
University Microfilms	33 (45%) respondents
Greenwood Press	31 (43%) respondents
Research Publications	14 (19%) respondents **(318)**

■ A 1981 survey of U.S. depository libraries, both academic and public (sample size: 221; responding: 171 or 77%) concerning their use of online data bases (DIALOG, ORBIT, and BRS), particularly with regard to government documents, *showed that* the top 3 reasons given by respon-

Out-of-Print Materials

dents for not ordering government documents microfiche as the result of an online search were: library does not have computer terminals (academic depositories, 33%; public depositories, 59%), didn't know that microfiche government documents could be ordered online (academic depositories, 24%; public depositories, 25%), and prefer hard copy to microfiche copy (academic depositories, 27%; public depositories, 20%). **(317)**

Ibid. . . . *showed that* none of the public depositories had ever ordered microfiche online as the result of a government document search, while only 3% of the academic libraries had ever done so. **(317)**

Out-of-Print Materials—General Issues

General

■ A survey reported in 1973 of out-of-print dealers concerning common dealer practices and preferences (survey size: 54 dealers; responding: 22 or 40.7%) *showed that* 13 (59.1%) reported a book stock of less than 25,000 volumes, while "nearly 30%" reported a book stock of 50,000 volumes or more. **(601)**

Ibid. . . . *showed that* (multiple responses allowed) the most commonly reported basis of assigning prices was book trade experience (reported by 19 or 86.4% respondents); "next in order" [no numbers given] were *Bookman's Price Index* and *American Book Prices Current*. Only 1 major retrospective guide to book prices was mentioned, Wright Howes's *U.S. iana* (reported by 50% of the respondents). **(601)**

Ibid. . . . *showed that* 4 categories of sales were ranked as follows by respondents from most important to least important:
 1. catalog sales
 2. want list sales
 3. specific title requests
 4. on-premises sales **(601)**

Ibid. . . . *showed that*, based on responses from 15 respondents, 53% of the want list quotes were filled; based on responses from 12 respondents, on the average 58% of the items listed in a catalog were sold. Further, 5 respondents advised ordering from catalogs within 2 weeks of receipt, while 4 reported that ordering within a month was acceptable if a library wanted to have a good chance of getting a desired item. **(601)**

Ibid. . . . *showed that*, based on responses from 5 respondents, 11.8% of the items in a catalog were sold within 1 week of issue, 26% of the items were sold within 2 weeks of issue, and 45% of the items were sold within 1 month of issue. **(601)**

Academic

■ A survey reported in 1973 of U.S. and foreign out-of-print dealers concerning their practices (survey size: 286; responding: 157 or 54.9%, including 108 U.S. and 49 foreign dealers) by California State University, Northridge, *showed that* dealer methods for locating out-of-print books were as follows (multiple responses allowed):

supply from own stock	99 (92%) U.S.; 45 (92%) foreign
advertise	89 (82%) U.S.; 28 (57%) foreign
check other dealers' catalogs	82 (76%) U.S.; 38 (78%) foreign
visit other dealers	82 (76%) U.S.; 32 (65%) foreign
contact other dealers by letter	68 (63%) U.S.; 31 (63%) foreign

Further, the most effective method reported by both U.S. (34 or 35%) and foreign (22 or 52%) dealers was supplying from own stock. **(603)**

Ibid. . . . *showed that* 84 (82%) of the U.S. and 38 (83%) of the foreign dealers reported that they made more than 1 attempt to locate the titles on the university's list. Of these 84 dealers, the length of time they continued to search was as follows:

indefinitely	42 (54%) U.S.; 22 (59%) foreign
2-5 years	4 (5%) U.S.; 5 (14%) foreign
1 year	18 (23%) U.S.; 3 (8%) foreign
6 months	10 (13%) U.S.; 3 (8%) foreign
1-3 months	4 (5%) U.S.; 4 (11%) foreign	**(603)**

Out-of-Print Materials—Procedures

Academic

■ A study at Indiana State University in 1971 comparing 2 methods of acquiring out-of-print books, using 168 titles divided into 2 equal groups, *showed that* a search of 98 out-of-print catalogs located 15 (18%) acceptable titles compared to placing an ad in *Library Bookman*, which located 32

Paperbacks 29

(38%) of the titles in that group. Further, if one were willing to pay 3 or more times the original publisher's price, then an additional 17 titles could be added to the success rate of the second method, making a total success rate for the second method of 59%. **(124)**

Ibid. . . . *showed that* the average staff time required to locate a book in out-of-print catalogs was 1 hour and 40 minutes per title, whereas only 12 minutes of staff time on the average were required to locate a title by placing an ad in *Library Bookman.* **(124)**

Ibid. . . . *showed that* the success rate in actually acquiring from dealers titles located in out-of-print catalogs was 9 out of 15 compared to the success rate in actually acquiring from dealers titles located through ads in *Library Bookman* which was 30 out of 32. **(124)**

Paperbacks

Academic

■ A 1967 survey by the Institute of Higher Education at Teachers College, Columbia University, of innovative programs in libraries in academic institutions with liberal arts programs (sample size: 1193; responding 781 or 65%) *showed that* 71 responding libraries (9%) reported that they did not use paperbound books in their collections. **(190)**

■ A study reported in 1968 of monographic acquisitions during the last 7 months of 1966 at the University of North Carolina *showed that* 29.6% of all books acquired were paperbound, while for the same period in 1967 the figure had risen to 46.7%. **(189)**

Public

■ A study reported in 1979 at the Oklahoma City/County Metropolitan Library System *showed that*, for 18,996 adult hardback books and 19,126 adult paperback books purchased in FY 1976-77, the cost ratio, based on purchase price alone, of hardback to paperback was 4.1 to 1, while the cost per circulation (again based on purchase price only) of hardback to paperback was 4.2 to 1. For slightly more materials in FY 1977-78 the cost ratio of hardbound to paperback was 3.7 to 1, and the cost per circulation was 3.89 to 1. **(231)**

Ibid. . . . *showed that*, for 5,624 juvenile hardback books and 6,031 paperback books purchased in FY 1976-77, the cost ratio, based on purchase price alone, of hardback to paperback was 5.9 to 1, while the cost per circulation (again based on purchase price only) of hardback to paperback was 2.7 to 1. For approximately the same number of materials purchased in FY 1977-78 the cost ratio of hardbound to paperback was 4.8 to 1, and the cost per circulation was 2.6 to 1. **(231)**

■ A 1982 survey of American and Canadian public libraries (sample size: 279; responding: 68 or 24%) *showed that* approximately 10.5% (±3.2%, representing a 95% confidence interval for the population at large) of respondents' current book acquisitions budgets had been allocated for the purchase of mass market paperbacks, while about 9.2% (±3.1%, representing a 95% confidence interval for the population at large) of their last year's book budget was spent on mass market paperbacks. There was a small statistical correlation ("y's = .26 and .30 respectively" [no further information or type of statistical test given]) between the book budget percentages and size of populations served, with the libraries serving larger populations tending to allocate more money for the purchase of paperbacks (significance level not given). **(273)**

Ibid. . . . *showed that* the top 3 types of 86 problems indentified by responding libraries were lack of adequate reviewing media for paperbacks (24%), backlist ordering (13%), and partial order fulfillment (12%). **(273)**

Ibid. . . . *showed that* the top 4 vendors (of 120 given) of paperback books used by respondents were Baker & Taylor (42%), Ingram (9%), Bookman (7%), and Brodart (6%). **(273)**

Procedures—General Issues

Academic

■ A 1959 survey of libraries in public midwestern institutions of higher education with a student population of 300+ (sample size: 116; respond-

Procedures 31

ing: 107) *showed that* 102 libraries may order books anytime during the period for which the fund was appropriated. **(113)**

Ibid. . . . *showed that* book orders were placed by means of a variety of channels. 37 libraries ordered through their own order departments; 36 were required to use the services of a central agency (e.g., Board of Education); and 33 used the facilities of their college or university business office. **(113)**

Ibid. . . . *showed that* 98 libraries reported they were the sole agencies for the ordering of library books. The only notable exceptions were 6 of the libraries in junior/community colleges. **(113)**

Ibid. . . . *showed that* 92 of the libraries were not allowed to carry over unencumbered balances from the appropriated fund into subsequent years. **(113)**

■ A survey reported in 1977 of moderate-sized (120,000-500,000 volumes) U.S. academic libraries listed in the 1972-73 *American Library Directory* (survey size: 200; responding: 147 or 74%) *showed that*, in order to fill a gap, 45% of responding libraries reported they would purchase microform, 26% reported they would purchase paper, and 29% reported they might do either. **(454)**

■ A 1978 survey of law school libraries listed in the 1977 *AALS Directory of Law Teachers* (population: 167; responding: 158 or 95%) *showed that* law-related acquisitions or titles requested by the law library were arbitrarily assigned to other departmental libraries on the basis of a classification scheme or some other means. **(362)**

Ibid. . . . *showed that* 6.3% of the law school libraries were required to order their books through the general library. This compared to 11% reported in a 1973 survey and 31% reported in a 1937 survey. **(362)**

■ A 1978-79 study underwritten by the NSF Division of Information Science and Technology of academic and research journal subscription and cancellation for both individuals and libraries (individual questionnaires: 2,817; usable responses: 1,190; library questionnaires: 4,997; usable responses: 1,905) of journals at least 5 years old *showed that* publisher information about library subscriptions was suspect. In 514 or 42.4% of the cases libraries disputed publisher claims that they had entered new subscriptions for a journal, while in 853 or 50.9% of the cases they disputed publisher claims that they had canceled a journal subscription. **(264)**

■ A 1980 study at the University of Northern Colorado (Michener Library) over a 3-month period (February through May), involving 477 separate invoices from 115 individual vendors, *showed that* the average time lapse between vendor's invoice date and date of the check generated by the acquisitions department was 35 days (on average 16 days lapsed between vendor's invoice date and receipt of invoice in the library); the average time lapse between receipt of vendor's invoice in the library to generation of check by the acquisitions department was 19 days; and average time lapse between payment authorization for vendor's invoice to generation of check by acquisitions department was 4 days. **(313)**

■ A study reported in 1980 at the University of Rochester comparing costs of 1-year versus 3-year journal subscriptions, based on a sample of 20 business administration and management science periodicals, *showed that*, when 4 variables were considered (cost of capital, reorder costs, average inflation rate for 1-year subscriptions, and ratio of 3-year to 1-year subscription costs), the 3-year subscription period was always the most advantageous in terms of cost. Specifically, the least projected savings for the 20 periodicals was 12%, while the most in projected savings that could be realized was 106%. The savings was due to locking in advantageous subscription rates for a 3-year period and to reduced staff costs caused by reduced renewal activity. **(627)**

Public

■ A 1982 survey of American and Canadian public libraries (sample size: 279; responding: 68 or 24%) *showed that* the top 4 vendors (of 120 given) of paperback books used by respondents were Baker & Taylor (42%), Ingram (9%), Bookman (7%), and Brodart (6%). **(273)**

School

■ A survey reported in 1978 of factors influencing selection of school media materials and involving 107 wholesaler/distributors (25 responses or 27%), 106 publishers/producers (46 responses or 49%), and 516 media program personnel (222 responses or 44%) *showed that* media program personnel reported final responsibility for selecting books resided as follows:

Procedures 33

media specialists	63%
acquisitions or order librarians	17%
district media coordinator	10%
other	6%
principal	2%
teachers and reviewing group	1% each
students	0%

(217)

Ibid. . . . *showed that* media program personnel reported final responsibility for selecting nonprint materials resided as follows:

media specialists	64%
district media coordinators	13%
acquisitions or order librarians	12%
other	6%
principals and teachers	2% each
reviewing group	1%
students	0%

(217)

Ibid. . . . *showed that* publishers and producers rated the following individuals or groups as "very important" in selecting books for school media centers (multiple responses allowed):

reviewing group	58%
media specialists	57%
acquisitions or order librarians	48%
district media coordinators	36%
teachers	29%
curriculum coordinators	21%
principals	13%
students	0%

(217)

Ibid. . . . *showed that* publishers and producers rated the following individuals or groups as "very important" in selecting nonprint materials for school media centers (multiple responses allowed):

media specialists	62%
reviewing group	54%
teachers	52%
district media coordinators	50%
curriculum coordinators	42%

continued

acquisitions or order librarians	35%	
principals	28%	
students	4%	**(217)**

Special

■ A 1978 survey of law school libraries listed in the 1977 *AALS Directory of Law Teachers* (population: 167; responding: 158 or 95%) *showed that* law-related acquisitions or titles requested by the law library were arbitrarily assigned to other departmental libraries on the basis of a classification scheme or some other means. **(362)**

Ibid. . . . *showed that* 6.3% of the law school libraries were required to order their books through the general library. This compared to 11% reported in a 1973 survey and 31% reported in a 1937 survey. **(362)**

■ A 1980 survey of the private law library and corporate law library membership of the American Association of Law Libraries, excluding part-time librarians (population: 585; responding: 382; usable: 360 or 61%) *showed that* overall, while 75% of the respondents were responsible for planning library acquisitions expenses, only 23% were allowed to authorize expenditures over $200. **(377)**

Procedures—Government Documents

Academic

■ A 1977 survey of academic depository libraries (sample size: 200; responding: 160 or 80%) concerning the impact of commercially produced microforms *showed that* the top 3 reasons given by the 73 respondents who reported purchasing commercially produced government documents for selecting a particular publisher were (multiple responses allowed): cost (64 or 88%); format, i.e., fiche, card, or film (57 or 78%); and reputation of company (43 or 59%). **(318)**

Ibid. . . . *showed that* the commercial firms most relied on by responding librarians (N = 73) to supply government publications in microform were (multiple responses allowed):

Procedures

Readex	49 (67%) respondents	
CIS	43 (59%) respondents	
University Microfilms	33 (45%) respondents	
Greenwood Press	31 (43%) respondents	
Research Publications	14 (19%) respondents	**(318)**

■ A 1977-78 study at Duke University involving acquisition of state government documents (population: "approximately 2,000 items" ordered during an 18-month period; sample size: 591 items) *showed that* 85% of all requests for state government documents evoked a response within the first 5 weeks, after which "the response rate declined dramatically." **(310)**

Ibid. . . . *showed that* "about 75%" of the documents requested were serial publications and "about 25%" were monographs. The average response time was 4.3 weeks and ranged from a response rate of 15.2% for serials and 19.0% for monographs within 1 week to a response rate of 85.3% for serials and 83.9% for monographs within 5 weeks to a response rate of 92.7% for serials and 93.3% for monographs within 9 weeks.
(310)

Ibid. . . . *showed that* the 2 most common sources of ordering information for state government documents were LC's *Monthly Checklist* (41.5% of all order requests) and state checklists (25.5% of all order requests).
(310)

Ibid. . . . *showed that* the average number of weeks a response was outstanding, broken down by source of request, was as follows:

LC Card	2.42 weeks	
LC's *Monthly Checklist*	3.45 weeks	
state checklists	3.73 weeks	
PAIS	4.0 weeks	
other	5.44 weeks	**(310)**

■ A survey reported in 1981 of 85 North American academic map libraries that have medium or large research collections (usable responses: 49 or 58%) in conjunction with data from the 2nd and 3rd editions of *Map Collections of the United States and Canada* showed that 77% of the respondents reported depository membership in the United States Geological Survey in 1968, 94% in 1975, and 96% in 1980. 84% reported depository membership in the Defense Mapping Agency in 1968, 86% in 1975, and 88% in 1980. 13% reported depository membership in the National Ocean Survey in 1968, 27% in 1975, and 49% in 1980. **(216)**

Publishing Industry Issues

General

■ A study reported in 1968 of Book Trade Statistics sections of the *Bowker Annual* 1967-69 *showed that* the increase of sales of hardbound books rose from 32,298,000 in 1958 to 40,213,000 in 1963 (increase of 24.2%), while sales of paperbound books rose in the same period from 5,661,000 to 48,874,000 (for an increase of 763.3%). **(189)**

■ A study of book trade mergers during the period 1958-70 *showed that* during this 12-year period 307 book trade mergers were reported. Mergers involving 2 or more publishers accounted for 224 (72.9%) of the mergers; mergers between a publisher and a company in the field of communications accounted for 33 (10.7%) of the mergers; mergers between a publisher and some other kind of company accounted for 22 (7.2%) of the mergers; and partial purchases and joint ventures accounted for 28 (9.2%), the remainder. **(396)**

Ibid. . . . *showed that* there were 2 peak periods of merging activity during this period. The first was 1960 and 1961, with 28 and 24 mergers, respectively; and the second was 1968 and 1969, with 49 and 46 mergers, respectively. **(396)**

Ibid. . . . *showed that* the 15 largest publishing companies accounted for 108 (35.2%) of the mergers during this period. **(396)**

School

■ A survey reported in 1978 of factors influencing selection of school media materials and involving 107 wholesaler/distributors (25 responses or 27%), 106 publishers/producers (46 responses or 49%), and 516 media program personnel (222 responses or 44%) *showed that* publishers/producers reported the following dollar sales volume for various media: books (54%); sound filmstrips (16%); 16mm film (6%); kits (4%); audio cassettes (2%); super 8 loops, filmstrips, records, reel-to-reel tapes, videotapes, and study prints (approximately 1% each). **(217)**

Reprints

General

■ A 1969 survey of U.S. reprint publishers (population: 274; survey size: 250; responding: 157 or 62.8%) *showed that*, of 216 firms for which data was available (some firms were interviewed directly rather than being sent a questionnaire), reprints were reported available in the following formats from the following numbers of firms:

hardcover books	183 (85.1%) firms
paperbound books	103 (47.7%) firms
microfilm	31 (14.4%) firms
microfiche	15 (6.9%) firms
xerographic	12 (5.6%) firms
microcards	8 (3.7%) firms
micro-opaques	3 (1.4%) firms
ultramicrofiche	3 (1.4%) firms

(592)

Speed

Academic

■ A study reported in 1960 at San Franscisco State College Library concerning length of time for book ordering and processing over a 7-year period (academic 1950-51 through academic 1956-57) and involving 500 randomly selected order cards per year (excluding materials with special problems such as "out of print," etc.) *showed that* (using calendar days rather than working days):

> the median time between order received in acquisitions to time order was placed ranged from 6.3 days in 1955-56 to 18.94 days in 1951-52;

> the median time between order being placed and books received ranged from 24.47 days in 1951-52 to 32.75 days in 1954-55;

> the median time between book being received and book being released [cataloged and marked] ranged from 16.24 days in 1955-56 to 46.80 days in 1950-51. **(578)**

ACQUISITIONS

■ A study during the 1975-76 fiscal year at Louisiana State University comparing 5 different [not identified] U.S. book dealers based on ordering 400 titles from each dealer *showed that* there were substantial differences between the dealers in a number of areas, including:

number of titles received—ranged from 342 (85.5%) to 371 (92.8%);

length of time between purchase order and receipt of invoice—ranged from 29 days to 55 days;

length of time between purchase order and receipt of book—ranged from 45 days to 70 days;

and average discount—ranged from 5.29% to 16%. **(640)**

■ A 1977-78 study at Duke University involving acquisition of state government documents (population: "approximately 2,000 items" ordered during an 18-month period; sample size: 591 items) *showed that* 85% of all requests for state government documents evoked a response within the first 5 weeks, after which "the response rate declined dramatically." **(310)**

Ibid. . . . *showed that* "about 75%" of the documents requested were serial publications and "about 25%" were monographs. The average response time was 4.3 weeks and ranged from a response rate of 15.2% for serials and 19.0% for monographs within 1 week to a response rate of 85.3% for serials and 83.9% for monographs within 5 weeks to a response rate of 92.7% for serials and 93.3% for monographs within 9 weeks.
(310)

Ibid. . . . *showed that* the average number of weeks a response was outstanding, broken down by source of request, was as follows:

LC Card	2.42 weeks
LC's *Monthly Checklist*	3.45 weeks
state checklists	3.73 weeks
PAIS	4.0 weeks
other	5.44 weeks **(310)**

■ A 1978-79 study of domestic book vendors undertaken at the University of Utah Libraries and involving "approximately 800 orders" divided among 3 vendors (Baker & Taylor, Academic Book Center, and Taylor-Carlisle) *showed that* books whose publishers were listed in BIP were more likely to be delivered than books whose publishers were not listed in BIP. Within 180 days of placing the orders for books with publishers listed in

Vendors

BIP, both Baker & Taylor and Academic Book Center had delivered 92.6% of the ordered titles, while Taylor-Carlisle had delivered 85.6% of the ordered items. Within the same 180-day period for books whose publishers were not listed in BIP, Baker & Taylor had delivered 60% of the requested titles; Taylor-Carlisle had delivered 58.3% of the requested titles; and Academic Book Center had delivered 52.7% of the titles.

(308)

Ibid. . . . *showed that*, for books with publishers listed in BIP, Baker & Taylor delivered a substantial number of items more quickly than the smaller vendors, although within 3 months of order placement the difference had reversed. Specifically, Baker & Taylor delivered 31.0% of the total number of requested items within 30 days and 60.1% within 90 days; Academic Book Center delivered 0% within 30 days and 78.8% within 90 days; and Taylor-Carlisle delivered 4.1% within 30 days and 73.6% within 90 days.

(308)

Public

■ A 1979 study of vendor performance (Baker & Taylor, Brodart) over a 5-month period in 8 small- to medium-sized public libraries and 1 regional resource center on Maryland's eastern shore *showed that* the time lag between placing the order and receiving the book for each of the vendors was as follows:

TYPE OF BOOK	BAKER & TAYLOR	BRODART
adult hardback	33.7 days	42.9 days
juvenile	24.9 days	44.25 days
paperbacks	22.7 days	17.3 days

(385)

Vendors—Book

Academic

■ A study reported in 1970 of 3 types of book selection procedures in 4 midwestern 4-year institutions of higher education with graduate programs that had used at least 2 methods of book selection for current imprint, English-language titles (sample size: 6,891 books including 2,559 selected on approval plan, 2,196 selected by faculty, and 2,136 selected by librarians) *showed that*, on the basis of subsequent book circulation (at least once in the 12 months following public availability), the librarians were the best selectors, faculty the next best, and approval plans the worst. 80.4% of librarians' books circulated; 69.7% of the faculty books circulated; and 61.8% of the approval plan books circulated. These differences were statistically significant at the .05 level. **(246)**

■ A study reported in 1975 comparing book price increases reported in the *Bowker Annual of Library and Book Trade Information* with actual price increases encountered on English-language material acquired through approval plans at 3 universities (University of Nebraska, years 1966-67 and 1967-68; Florida Atlantic University, 1969-70 and 1970-71; and Arizona State University, 1971-72) during the period 1967-1972 *showed that Bowker* indicated a 48.1% increase, while the libraries showed an 18.5% increase for this period. **(630)**

■ A study during the 1975-76 fiscal year at Louisiana State University comparing 5 different [not identified] U.S. book dealers based on ordering 400 titles from each dealer *showed that* there were substantial differences between the dealers in a number of areas, including:

number of titles received—ranged from 342 (85.5%) to 371 (92.8%);

length of time between purchase order and receipt of invoice—ranged from 29 days to 55 days;

length of time between purchase order and receipt of book—ranged from 45 days to 70 days;

and average discount—ranged from 5.29% to 16%. **(640)**

■ A performance survey in 1977 of 3 book vendors undertaken by the University of Louisville Library over a 4-month period *showed that* Ballen supplied books in the shortest amount of time; BNA and Baker & Taylor were tied in supplying the most accurate bibliographic information; and Baker & Taylor had the best discounts. **(011)**

■ A 1978-79 study of domestic book vendors undertaken at the University of Utah Libraries and involving "approximately 800 orders" divided among 3 vendors (Baker & Taylor, Academic Book Center, and Taylor-Carlisle) *showed that* books whose publishers were listed in BIP were more likely to be delivered than books whose publishers were not listed in BIP. Within 180 days of placing the orders for books with publishers listed in BIP, both Baker & Taylor and Academic Book Center had delivered 92.6% of the ordered titles, while Taylor-Carlisle had delivered 85.6% of the ordered items. Within the same 180-day period for books whose

Vendors   **41**

publishers were not listed in BIP, Baker & Taylor had delivered 60% of the requested titles; Taylor-Carlisle had delivered 58.3% of the requested titles; and Academic Book Center had delivered 52.7% of the titles.
                                                                          (308)

Ibid. . . . *showed that*, for books with publishers listed in BIP, Baker & Taylor delivered a substantial number of items more quickly than the smaller vendors, although within 3 months of order placement the difference had reversed. Specifically, Baker & Taylor delivered 31.0% of the total number of requested items within 30 days and 60.1% within 90 days; Academic Book Center delivered 0% within 30 days and 78.8% within 90 days; and Taylor-Carlisle delivered 4.1% within 30 days and 73.6% within 90 days.   **(308)**

Ibid. . . . *showed that*, for books with publishers listed in BIP, Baker & Taylor provided neither books nor information on 6% of the orders placed and canceled .9% of the orders; Academic Book Center provided neither books nor information on 3.7% of the orders placed and canceled 1.4% of the orders; and Taylor-Carlisle provided neither information nor books for 10.4% of the orders placed and canceled 3.1% of the orders. For non-BIP books Baker & Taylor, Academic, and Taylor-Carlisle, respectively, provided neither books nor information for 14.5%, 27.3%, and 41.7% of the orders placed, while they canceled 14.5%, 20.0%, and 0% of the orders respectively.   **(308)**

■ A 1980 study at the University of Northern Colorado (Michener Library) over a 3-month period (February through May) involving 477 separate invoices from 115 individual vendors *showed that* the average time lapse between vendor's invoice date and date of the check generated by the acquisitions department was 35 days (on average 16 days lapsed between vendor's invoice date and receipt of invoice in the library); the average time lapse between receipt of vendor's invoice in the library to generation of check by the acquisitions department was 19 days; and average time lapse between payment authorization for vendor's invoice to generation of check by acquisitions department was 4 days.   **(313)**

Public

■ A 1979 study of vendor performance (Baker & Taylor, Brodart) over a 5-month period in 8 small- to medium-sized public libraries and 1 regional resource center on Maryland's eastern shore *showed that* the average discounts received from each vendor were as follows:

TYPE OF BOOK	BAKER & TAYLOR	BRODART	
adult fiction	38.91%	37.6%	
adult nonfiction	36.1%	33.2%	
juvenile	28.15%	20.4%	
paperbacks	37.5%	32.7%	**(385)**

Ibid. . . . *showed that* the time lag between placing the order and receiving the book for each of the vendors was as follows:

TYPE OF BOOK	BAKER & TAYLOR	BRODART
adult hardback	33.7 days	42.9 days
juvenile	24.9 days	44.25 days
paperbacks	22.7 days	17.3 days

(385)

■ A 1982 survey of American and Canadian public libraries (sample size: 279; responding: 68 or 24%) *showed that* the top 4 vendors (of 120 given) of paperback books used by respondents were: Baker & Taylor (42%), Ingram (9%), Bookman (7%), and Brodart (6%). **(273)**

Verification

General

■ A 1967 study comparing *Cumulative Book Index* (CBI) with *Canadiana* in terms of its coverage of English-language books published in Canada (209 titles from the first 3 months of 1966 *Canadiana* searched in CBI for 1965-66-67) *showed that* 154 titles (74%) were located in CBI, while 55 (26%) were not found. Of the 55 titles not found in CBI, 26 (12.4% of the total) were the products of publishers not on CBI's list of publishers, while 29 (13.9% of the total) were on CBI's list of publishers. **(595)**

Ibid. . . . *showed that*, of the 154 titles located in CBI, 17 (11%) of the titles appeared in CBI before they appeared in *Canadiana*; 22 (14%) titles appeared in CBI within a month or 2 of their appearance in *Canadiana*; and 115 (75%) appeared in CBI at least 2 months after appearing in *Canadiana*. Further, 93 (60.4%) of the titles found in CBI appeared 4-5 months after appearing in *Canadiana*. **(595)**

Verification

■ A 1974 survey of the 47 charter members of the OCLC network, including site visits and interviews (148) with all levels of library personnel in member libraries, *showed that* 35 libraries (76%) made some use of OCLC for pre-order searching. However, of these only 24 (54% of total sample) searched for all monographs or all monographs published since 1968, and their pre-order find rate averaged 71% with a range of 50-90%.
(112)

Ibid. . . . *showed that* 24 (83%) of the libraries making full use of the OCLC data base in pre-order searching reported that use of the data base had decreased the average delay time caused by searching. The estimated reductions in 14 of these libraries ranged from 4 weeks to 1 week. **(112)**

■ A study reported in 1977 of a sample of titles with 1974, 1975, and 1976 imprint dates *showed that* OCLC was substantially more effective as a verification tool (with a 92.7% verification rate) than Library of Congress depository cards (73.2%), *American Book Publishing Record* (69.9%), *National Union Catalog* (44.6%), and *Cumulative Book Index* (32.8%).
(048)

■ A study reported in 1981 comparing 6 "commonly used library tools" (*American Book Publishing Record, Books in Print, Cumulative Book Index, Micrographic Catalog Retrieval Systems, National Union Catalog* and the OCLC online service) as to their effectiveness for verification of monographs before acquisition, using a sample of 360 books from 9 subject areas (including some foreign imprints), *showed that* the success in locating the 360 titles was as follows:

OCLC online service	97.5% of the books	
MCRS	94.4% of the books	
NUC	93.0% of the books	
BIP	83.6% of the books	
CBI	81.7% of the books	
BPR	73.9% of the books	**(767)**

Ibid. . . . *showed that*, of the combinations of 2 tools, the highest find rate was 98.9% using CBI and OCLC, while of the combinations of 3 tools, the highest find rate was 99.4% using BIP, OCLC, and MCRS. Further addition of tools did not increase the find rate; even using all 6 tools the last 0.6% could not be found.
(767)

Ibid. . . . *showed that*, when searching for books only in the imprint year of the book, BIP was as effective a tool as OCLC. 70% of the books were located in both. Further, using both tools together increased the find rate to 83.3% of the sample. Other effective combinations that used only print tools were NUC + BIP (find rate = 79.2%) and BPR + BIP (find rate = 77.5%). Finally, even when using all 6 tools to search for books during the imprint year, 13.1% of the books could not be found. **(767)**

Ibid. . . . *showed that*, when searching for books in the imprint year plus the following year, OCLC was the most effective tool (find rate = 92.5%), followed by MCRS (find rate = 90.6%) and NUC (find rate = 88.9%). However, combinations of printed tools were also effective for this period. NUC + BIP had a find rate of 94.7%; NUC + CBI had a find rate of 93.6%; and NUC + BPR had a find rate of 92.5%. Further, searching more than 1 year after the imprint year resulted in only a very small increase in the effectiveness of any of the tools, ranging from 0.3% for BPR to 5.0% for OCLC. **(767)**

Ibid. . . . *showed that* the speed of searching for each of the tools was as follows:

OCLC online service	1.15 minutes per item
MCRS	1.31 minutes per item
BPR	2.10 minutes per item
CBI	2.17 minutes per item
BIP	2.25 minutes per item
NUC	2.94 minutes per item **(767)**

Ibid. . . . *showed that* the cost per item searched and cost per item found based only on labor cost ($12.00 per hour) was as follows:

OCLC online service	$.230 searched; $.236 found
MCRS	$.262 searched; $.277 found
BPR	$.420 searched; $.568 found
CBI	$.434 searched; $.531 found
BIP	$.450 searched; $.538 found
NUC	$.588 searched; $.632 found **(767)**

■ A study reported in 1983 comparing the OCLC data base and *New Serial Titles* as information resources for serials, based on searching 200 titles randomly selected from OCLC in *New Serial Titles* and 200 titles randomly selected from *New Serial Titles* in OCLC, *showed that* there was only a moderate amount of overlap between the 2 tools. Specifically, a

Verification

total of 217 (54.3%) titles were found in both. Further, 96 (48%) of the OCLC titles were found in *New Serial Titles*, while 121 (60.5%) of the *New Serial Titles* were found in OCLC. **(776)**

Ibid. . . . *showed that* different information appeared to be contributed by OCLC and NST for the 217 serial titles they reported in common. For example, bibliographic information present in the NST record but absent in the OCLC record was as follows:

ISSN	21 (9.7%) records
Dewey number	127 (58.5%) records
beginning date/number	21 (9.7%) records
place of publication	4 (1.8%) records
publisher's address	24 (11.1%) records
price	10 (4.6%) records
frequency	9 (4.1%) records **(776)**

Ibid. . . . *showed that* information absent from both the OCLC and NST for the 217 records held in common was as follows:

ISSN	absent from 108 (49.8%) records
beginning date/number	absent from 76 (35.0%) records
publisher's address	absent from 119 (54.8%) records
price	absent from 161 (74.2%) records
frequency	absent from 89 (41.0%) records **(776)**

Ibid. . . . *showed that*, of the 217 titles held in common, OCLC records contained 273 notes, while NST records held 220 notes. 102 (37.4%) of the OCLC notes supplied information not contained in the NST notes, while 15.9% [no raw number given] of the NST notes provided information not contained in the OCLC notes. **(776)**

Academic

■ A study reported in 1966 [at the University of North Carolina Library], involving a random selection of 100 [monographic] titles from among American imprints for 1965 that were searched in 6 bibliographic tools to confirm or establish the correct bibliographic information preparatory to ordering, *showed that* the most efficient searching technique was to search 3 bibliographic tools in the following order: Library of Congress proof-slip file, 40 (of 100) titles found; *Publishers' Weekly Announcements*, 26 (of the remaining 60) titles found; and *Cumulative Book Index*, 5 (of the remaining 34) titles found. Altogether 71 (71%) of the titles were found. Further, with 1 exception every title found in the *National Union Catalog, American Book Publishing Record*, and *Publisher's Weekly* was also found in the LC proof-slip file. **(585)**

■ A 1977 survey of academic depository libraries (sample size: 200; responding: 160 or 80%) concerning the impact of commercially produced microforms *showed that* the top 6 sources consulted by 73 (46%) respondents for information concerning commercially produced microforms were (multiple responses allowed):

publishers' brochures	50 (68.5%) respondents
Documents to the People	42 (57.5%) respondents
Government Publications Review	39 (53.4%) respondents
advice from colleagues	36 (49.3%) respondents
faculty recommendations	34 (46.6%) respondents
Microform Review	33 (45.2%) respondents **(318)**

■ A 1977 study at the University of North Carolina, Chapel Hill, based on the time logs of 6 searchers in the Bibliographic Searching Section over a 4-month period and involving just under 14,000 items, *showed that* rush searching of current or previous-year materials averaged 14.5 minutes per order, while retrospective rush searching averaged 19.4 minutes per order; regular searching ranged from an average of 3.8 minutes per order for "copy, no series" to 22.0 minutes for "problems, sets, serials"; and book searching ranged from an average of 5.9 minutes per item for "University Press titles received on approval" to 25.8 minutes for "Pre-order problem follow up." **(305)**

Ibid. . . . *showed that* during the 4-month period the 6 searchers actually worked only 77.4% of the salaried hours (due to sick leave, vacations, etc.), and of the time actually worked only 71% of the time was actually spent searching (due to breaks, meetings, etc.). Consequently, only 55% of the salaried hours were spent actually searching. **(305)**

■ A study reported in 1977 of a sample of titles with 1974, 1975, and 1976 imprint dates *showed that* OCLC was substantially more effective as a verification tool (with a 92.7% verification rate) than Library of Congress depository cards (73.2%), *American Book Publishing Record* (69.9%), *National Union Catalog* (44.6%), and *Cumulative Book Index* (32.8%). **(048)**

Whole Collections

■ A 1977-78 study at Duke University involving acquisition of state government documents (population: "approximately 2,000 items" ordered during an 18-month period; sample size: 591 items) *showed that* the 2 most common sources of ordering information for state government documents were LC's *Monthly Checklist* (41.5% of all order requests) and state checklists (25.5% of all order requests). **(310)**

Whole Collections

General

■ A review of the acquisition of whole collections to libraries during the period 1940-70 as reported in *College and Research Libraries* and *College and Research Libraries News*, involving 1,454 collections and 301 libraries, *showed that* the acquisition of the collections was not equally distributed among libraries. In the total sample, 148 (49%) of the libraries reported adding only one collection, while 45 (15%) reported adding 10 or more. **(104)**

Academic

■ A review reported in 1975 of the acquisition of whole collections to libraries during the period 1940-70 as reported in *College and Research Libraries* and *College and Research Libraries News*, involving 1,454 collections and 301 libraries, *showed that*, among academic libraries reporting acquisition of collections, the receipt of collections was distributed unevenly. 15% of the academic libraries accounted for 66% of the collections acquired by academic libraries. In more detail, 21.5% of the public academic libraries accounted for 66% of the collections acquired by that type of library, while 10.5% of the private academic libraries accounted for 62% of the collections acquired by that type of library. **(104)**

Public

■ A review reported in 1975 of the acquisition of whole collections to libraries during the period 1940-70 as reported in *College and Research Libraries* and *College and Research Libraries News*, involving 1,454 collections and 301 libraries, *showed that* the Library of Congress accounted for 77 (75%) of the collections acquired by public libraries. A similar situation holds for state libraries, with one state library (Virginia) receiving 10 (71.5%) of the collections received by this type of library.

(104)

2. Collection Development

Age of Material—General Issues

Academic

■ A 1968-69 study over a period of 9 months of the use of materials at the Midwest Regional Medical Library (John Crerar Library), involving a random sample of 1,071 requests for material, *showed that*, of 1,061 requests, the age of the materials requested was as follows: under 1 year old (18.0%), 5 years old or less (53.8%), 10 years old or less (66.2%), and more than 10 years old (33.7%). **(688)**

■ A study of the citations in 186 doctoral dissertations of the 190 completed between the years 1969-72 in ALA-accredited library science programs (population: 43,500 citations; sample size: 2,139 citations, providing a sampling error of ±2% at 95% confidence level) *showed that* for all categories of dissertations combined, the age of cited work from dissertation date was as follows: 0-5 years (24.2%), 6-10 years (12%), 11-20 years (12.5%), 20+ years (51.3%). The most striking exceptions to this general pattern were dissertations on automation (9% of the dissertations overall), which had 68.2% of their citations in the 0-5 year category, and historical dissertations (28% of the dissertations overall), which had 76.9% of their citations in the 20+ category. **(633)**

■ A 1972 study comparing the rates of intergenerational information transfer in different scientific fields by reviewing citations in approximately 100 articles taken from a single representative journal in each of 15 biomedical scientific speciality fields (articles cited that were at least 25 years old were considered to be evidence of intergenerational information transfer) *showed that* the rates of intergenerational information transfer varied considerably among the various fields. Physiology had the highest rate of intergenerational information transfer with 87 papers cited that were 25 years old or older in 128 articles reviewed (68% rate), while molecular biology had the lowest rate of intergenerational information transfer with 14 papers cited that were 25 years old or older in 97 articles reviewed (14.4% rate). **(707)**

Ibid. . . . *showed that* the amount of intergenerational information transfer may change over time in a field. A comparison of physiology and microbiology showed changes in different directions, with physiology citing an increasing amount of older literature in the past 50 years and microbiology citing a decreasing amount of older literature in the past 50 years. Specifically, the transfer rate in physiology (number of cited papers 25 years old or older/number of articles reviewed) was 68.0% in 1972, 50% in

1947, and 40.2% in 1922. The transfer rate in microbiology was 19.4% in 1972, 30.1% in 1947, and 34.3% in 1922. **(707)**

■ A study reported in 1974 investigating the materials used by master's and doctoral candidates completing theses after 1966 in public health at 5 universities (Yale; Harvard; University of California, Los Angeles; University of California, Berkeley; and California State University, Northridge), involving 3,456 citations taken from 44 theses *showed that*, of 3,360 citations to materials for which the date of publication was known, 2,020 (61%) citations were to materials published after 1960, while 1,340 (39%) citations were to materials published before 1960. **(698)**

■ Ibid. . . . *showed that*, of 3,360 citations to materials for which the date of publication was known, 2,020 (61%) citations were to materials published after 1960, while 1,340 (39%) citations were to materials published before 1960. **(698)**

■ A 1982 study at the University of Wisconsin, Milwaukee, concerning the use of gift books in 2 separate parts of the collection, both the PS 3537-PS 3545 section (American literature, 1,039 nongift books and 104 gift books) and the QC 6-QC 75 section (physics, 1,023 nongifts and 16 gift books) *showed that* gift books tended to be older than nongift books. For example, in the PS section 375 (36.1%) of the nongift books had been published after 1970 compared to 11 (10.6%) of the gift books; in the QC section 380 (37.1%) of the nongift books had been published after 1970 compared to 2 (12.5%) of the gift books. **(807)**

Ibid. . . . *showed that* gift books tended to be old when given to the library. For example, in the PS section 68 (65.4%) of the gift books were over 20 years old when given to the library, while of the PS and QC sections combined, 105 (87.5%) of the gifts were over 10 years old when given to the library. **(807)**

■ A study reported in 1983 comparing 2 related variations of collection evaluation in political science based on citation checking (1st method: 1 citation selected at random from each article in *American Political Science Review* during a 3-year period for a total of 150 citations; 2nd method: 1 citation selected at random from each article in a single bibliographical volume of 5 political science journals, including *Comparative Politics, World Politics, American Journal of Political Science, Journal of Politics*, and *Political Theory* for a total of 142 citations) and applied to 5 university libraries in the greater Washington, D.C., area *showed that* of 576 citations for which the date of publication was known, 341 (59.2%) were published in 1970 or after [within approximately 8 years of the citing articles], while

Age of Material

518 (89.9%) citations were published in 1960 or after [within approximately 18 years of the citing articles]. **(774)**

School

■ A study reported in 1979 of term paper bibliographies of high school students (270 students/papers from 6 high schools, involving 3,165 identifiable references) *showed that* the students did not use particularly recent sources for their papers. Only 14% of the papers had more than half of their citations referring to sources published within 5 years of the study, while only 30% of the papers had more than half of the citations referring to sources published within 10 years of the study. **(564)**

Special

■ A study reported in 1966 at the library of the Electronics Systems Center of the International Business Machines Corporation (Owego, New York) concerning periodical usage during a 2-year period(1963-64) and involving 4,221 separate uses during this time *showed that*:

current-year requests totaled 1,470 (34.8% of the total);

requests for materials between 1 and 2 years old totaled 812 (19% of the total);

requests for materials between 2 and 3 years old totaled 480 (11% of the total);

requests for materials 5 years old or less totaled 3,379 (80.1% of the total);

requests for materials 10 years old or less totaled 3,874 (91.8% of the total). **(587)**

■ A 1968-69 study over a period of 9 months of the use of materials at the Midwest Regional Medical Library (John Crerar Library), involving a random sample of 1,071 requests for material, *showed that*, of 1,061 requests, the age of the materials requested was as follows: under 1 year old (18.0%), 5 years old or less (53.8%), 10 years old or less (66.2%), and more than 10 years old (33.7%). **(688)**

■ A 1972 study comparing the rates of intergenerational information transfer in different scientific fields by reviewing citations in approximately 100 articles taken from a single representative journal in each of 15 biomedical scientific speciality fields (articles cited that were at least 25 years old were considered to be evidence of intergenerational information transfer) *showed that* the rates of intergenerational information transfer varied considerably among the various fields. Physiology had the highest rate of intergenerational information transfer with 87 papers cited that were 25 years old or older in 128 articles reviewed (68% rate), while molecular biology had the lowest rate of intergenerational information transfer with 14 papers cited that were 25 years old or older in 97 articles reviewed (14.4% rate). **(707)**

Ibid. . . . *showed that* the amount of intergenerational information transfer may change over time in a field. A comparison of physiology and microbiology showed changes in different directions, with physiology citing an increasing amount of older literature in the past 50 years and microbiology citing a decreasing amount of older literature in the past 50 years. Specifically, the transfer rate in physiology (number of cited papers 25 years old or older/number of articles reviewed) was 68.0% in 1972, 50% in 1947, and 40.2% in 1922. The transfer rate in microbiology was 19.4% in 1972, 30.1% in 1947, and 34.3% in 1922. **(707)**

Age of Material—Books

Academic

■ A 1964 study at the Yale Medical Library involving patron use of books (survey size: 831 borrowers; responding: 430) during a 5-month period *showed that* the frequency of books used by year of publication was as follows:

1 year old	15 (3.5%) books
2 years old or less	92 (21.4%) books
5 years old or less	243 (56.6%) books
9 years old or less	324 (75.5%) books **(672)**

■ A 1-year study during 1964-65 at the Yale Medical Library concerning book and journal circulation (34,825 circulations) *showed that* currency was more important for journals than books. For example, 71% of the journals circulated had been published within the last 9 years, while only 66% of the books that circulated had been published within 9 years.

Age of Material 55

Further, 90% of the journal circulations involved materials no more than 22 years old, while 90% of the book circulations required materials up to 28 years old. **(674)**

Ibid. . . . *showed that* the importance of book currency varied considerably by subject area. For example, in the areas of biochemistry, neurology, and neoplasms, 90% of the circulations were accounted for by imprints going back 12 years, 17 years, and 17 years, respectively, while in the areas of surgery, biology, and infectious diseases, 90% of the circulations were accounted for by imprints going back 42 years, 39 years, and 37 years, respectively. **(674)**

■ A study reported in 1975 of the research literature of physiology over the 3-year period 1970-72 involving citation counting (first 3 months of each year) in 8 internationally known journals (31,669 citations) *showed that*, of the 2,955 citations to monographs, 1,586 (54.672%) of the citations referred to titles published within 8 years of the citation and 2,335 citations (79.018%) referred to titles published within 13 years of citation. **(355)**

■ A survey reported in 1978 of 31 Ph.D. dissertations in the field of business/management (13 from the State University of New York at Buffalo and 18 from SUNYAB incoming faculty but completed at other schools) *showed that*:

42.7% of the periodical citations and 36.0% of the monographic citations were to materials 5 years old or less;

72.8% of the periodical citations and 66.2% of the monographic citations were to materials 10 years old or less;

87.0% of the periodical citations and 80.7% of the monographic citations were to materials 15 years old or less;

and 93.0% of the periodical citations and 89.5% of the monographic citations were to materials 20 years old or less. **(461)**

Special

■ A 1964 study at the Yale Medical Library involving patron use of books (survey size: 831 borrowers; responding: 430) during a 5-month period *showed that* the frequency of books used by year of publication was as follows:

1 year old	15 (3.5%) books
2 years old or less	92 (21.4%) books

continued

5 years old or less 243 (56.6%) books
9 years old or less 324 (75.5%) books **(672)**

■ A 1-year study during 1964-65 at the Yale Medical Library concerning book and journal circulation (34,825 circulations) *showed that* currency was more important for journals than books. For example, 71% of the journals circulated had been published within the last 9 years, while only 66% of the books that circulated had been published within 9 years. Further, 90% of the journal circulations involved materials no more than 22 years old, while 90% of the book circulations required materials up to 28 years old. **(674)**

■ A study reported in 1975 of the research literature of physiology over the 3-year period 1970-72 involving citation counting (first 3 months of each year) in 8 internationally known journals (31,669 citations) *showed that*, of the 2,955 citations to monographs, 1,586 (54.672%) of the citations referred to titles published within 8 years of the citation and 2,335 citations (79.018%) referred to titles published within 13 years of citation. **(355)**

Age of Material—Periodicals

Academic

■ A 1-year study during 1964-65 at the Yale Medical Library concerning book and journal circulation (34,825 circulations) *showed that* currency was more important for journals than books. For example, 71% of the journals circulated had been published within the last 9 years, while only 66% of the books that circulated had been published within 9 years. Further, 90% of the journal circulations involved materials no more than 22 years old,while 90% of the book circulations required materials up to 28 years old. **(674)**

Ibid. . . . *showed that* the importance of journal currency varied considerably by subject area. For example, in the areas of nursing, science, and the cardiovascular system, 90% of the circulations were accounted for by 12 years, 13 years, and 15 years of backfiles of journal materials, respectively, while in the areas of anatomy, pathology, and psychology, 90% of the circulations required 30 years of backfiles of journal materials each.
(674)

Age of Material   57

■ A 6-month study during 1967-68 in the Medical Library of the Children's Hospital of Michigan concerning periodical use through circulation, room use, and interlibrary loan (1,898 uses) *showed that* current-year journal issues accounted for 753 (39.67%) uses, journal issues 5 years old or less accounted for 1,408 (74.18%) uses, and journal issues 15 years old or less accounted for 1,813 (95.51%) uses. **(686)**

■ A citation study reported in 1969 of a sample of article citations from 10 major journals in geology published in 1960 and 1965 (400 citations chosen for each year) *showed that* on the average researchers in geology would have to go back 15 years to find approximately 70% of the useful literature and about 25 years to find approximately 80% of the useful literature. **(193)**

■ A study reported in 1970 of 3,610 citations in the area of political science taken from a book of readings (Harry Eckstein and David E. Apter, *Comparative Politics*, 1963), *American Political Science Review* (1963-66) and 2 British journals, *Political Studies* and *Political Quarterly* (1958-66) *showed that*, of the 103 periodicals (1,493 citations) that were cited more than 4 times, 89% of the citations were after 1950, while 1955-67 provided 63% of the citations. **(352)**

■ A 1971 study at the MIT Science Library of in-room use (journals do not circulate) of 220 physics journals over a 3.5-month period *showed that* journal use by age of journal was as follows:

1 year old or less	288 (6.7%)	of total uses
3 years old or less	1,250 (29.1%)	of total uses
6 years old or less	2,239 (52.2%)	of total uses
10 years old or less	3,174 (74.0%)	of total uses
17 years old or less	4,039 (94.1%)	of total uses

Only 253 (5.9%) uses were made of journals more than 17 years old, i.e., 18 years old or older. **(608)**

Ibid. . . . *showed that* journals receiving heavy use have a later "point of obsolescence" than journals receiving light use. For example, for *Physical Review* (a heavy use item), volumes more than 10 years old accounted for 33.2% of its total use, compared to the overall group of 220 journals, whose volumes more than 10 years old accounted for only 26% of their use. **(608)**

■ A 1971-72 study of the articles supplied by the University of Oklahoma Health Sciences Center Library to state health professionals and institutions during a 4-month period, involving 1,756 articles (from 373 journals) sent to individual health professionals and 1,620 articles (from 527 journals) sent to health institutions, *showed that*, in terms of publication dates of the articles, 69.3% of the information requests could have been filled with a journal backfile of 5 years, while 85.5% of the information requests could have been filled with a journal backlog of 10 years. **(409)**

■ A 1972 study at the University of Minnesota Bio-Medical Library concerning in-house use of periodicals during 2 1-week periods (1st period: 727 uses involving 269 different titles; 2nd period: 533 uses involving 209 different titles) *showed that* combined data from both periods indicated that 58% of total use came from periodicals 5 years old or less. Further, for every 3.4 years of material age (for materials in the 1st period) and every 3.2 years of material age (for materials in the 2nd period) the materials use decreased by half. **(697)**

■ A study reported in 1974 investigating the materials used by master's and doctoral candidates completing theses after 1966 in public health at 5 universities (Yale; Harvard; University of California, Los Angeles; University of California, Berkeley; and California State University, Northridge), involving 3,456 citations taken from 44 theses, *showed that* the median age of materials cited was 7 years. The median age of materials in various other scientific disciplines as reported in 8 other studies and summarized in this study was 5 years. **(698)**

■ A study reported in 1975 of the research literature of physiology over the 3-year period 1970-72, involving citation counting (first 3 months of each year) in 8 internationally known journals (31,669 citations), *showed that*, of the 28,714 serial citations, 7,992 (27.833%) of the citations were to articles published within 5 years of citation, 15,077 citations (52.507%) of the citations were to articles published within 8 years of citation, and 21,248 (73.767%) citations were to articles published within 13 years of citation. **(355)**

■ A study reported in 1977 of English-language articles in 6 "major musicological journals" for the years 1973-75 (*Musical Quarterly, Journal of the American Musicological Society, Music and Letters, Music Review, Acta Musicologica*, and *Musica Disciplina*), involving 1,374 citations in 304 articles, *showed that* the literature in musicology did not "obsolesce" in the same manner as literature in science and technology. For example, of the 1,374 citations, the decades in which the cited materials were published were as follows:

        1966-75 412 (30% [40% reported]) citations
        1956-65 294 (21%) citations
        1946-55 195 (14%) citations

continued

Age of Material

        1931-45 119 (9%) citations
        1900-30 200 (15%) citations
        pre-1900 154 (11%) citations   (755)

■ A 1978 study in the Biology Library of Temple University involving a citation analysis of publications by full-time Temple biology faculty, doctoral dissertations of Temple biology Ph.D.'s, and preliminary doctoral qualifying briefs written by second-year graduate biology students at Temple during the 3-year period 1975-77 (153 source items with 4,155 citations) *showed that* in 51 of the 60 most frequently cited periodical titles "over 80%" of the citations were to articles published within 18 years.
(**650**)

■ A survey reported in 1978 of 31 Ph.D. dissertations in the field of business/management (13 from the State University of New York at Buffalo and 18 from SUNYAB incoming faculty but completed at other schools) *showed that*:

    42.7% of the periodical citations and 36.0% of the
    monographic citations were to materials 5 years old or less;

    72.8% of the periodical citations and 66.2% of the
    monographic citations were to materials 10 years old or less;

    87.0% of the periodical citations and 80.7% of the
    monographic citations were to materials 15 years old or less;

    and 93.0% of the periodical citations and 89.5% of the
    monographic citations were to materials 20 years old or less.   (**461**)

Special

■ A 1-year study during 1964-65 at the Yale Medical Library concerning book and journal circulation (34,825 circulations) *showed that* currency was more important for journals than books. For example, 71% of the journals circulated had been published within the last 9 years, while only 66% of the books that circulated had been published within 9 years. Further, 90% of the journal circulations involved materials no more than 22 years old, while 90% of the book circulations required materials up to 28 years old. (**674**)

Ibid. . . . *showed that* the importance of journal currency varied considerably by subject area. For example, in the areas of nursing, science, and the cardiovascular system, 90% of the circulations were accounted for by 12

years, 13 years, and 15 years of backfiles of journal materials, respectively, while in the areas of anatomy, pathology, and psychology, 90% of the circulations required 30 years of backfiles of journal materials each.
(674)

■ A 6-month study during 1967-68 in the Medical Library of the Children's Hospital of Michigan concerning periodical use through circulation, room use, and interlibrary loan (1,898 uses) *showed that* current-year journal issues accounted for 753 (39.67%) uses, journal issues 5 years old or less accounted for 1,408 (74.18%) uses, and journal issues 15 years old or less accounted for 1,813 (95.51%) uses. **(686)**

■ A 1971-72 study of the articles supplied by the University of Oklahoma Health Sciences Center Library to state health professionals and institutions during a 4-month period, involving 1,756 articles (from 373 journals) sent to individual health professionals and 1,620 articles (from 527 journals) sent to health institutions, *showed that* in terms of publication dates of the articles, 69.3% of the information requests could have been filled with a journal backfile of 5 years, while 85.5% of the information requests could have been filled with a journal backlog of 10 years. **(409)**

■ A 1972 study at the University of Minnesota Bio-Medical Library concerning in-house use of periodicals during 2 1-week periods (1st period: 727 uses involving 269 different titles; 2nd period: 533 uses involving 209 different titles) *showed that* combined data from both periods indicated that 58% of total use came from periodicals 5 years old or less. Further, for every 3.4 years of material age (for materials in the 1st period) and every 3.2 years of material age (for materials in the 2nd period) the materials use decreased by half. **(697)**

■ A study reported in 1974 investigating the materials used by master's and doctoral candidates completing theses after 1966 in public health at 5 universities (Yale; Harvard; University of California, Los Angeles; University of California, Berkeley; and California State University, Northridge), involving 3,456 citations taken from 44 theses, *showed that* the median age of materials cited was 7 years. The median age of materials in various other scientific disciplines as reported in 8 other studies and summarized in this study was 5 years. **(698)**

■ A study reported in 1975 of the research literature of physiology over the 3-year period 1970-72 involving citation counting (first 3 months of each year) in 8 internationally known journals (31,669 citations) *showed that*, of the 28,714 serial citations, 7,992 (27.833%) of the citations were to articles published within 5 years of citation, 15,077 citations (52.507%) of the citations were to articles published within 8 years of citation, and 21,248 (73.767%) citations were to articles published within 13 years of citation. **(355)**

■ A 1975 study of interlibrary loan requests initiated by 21 hospitals in central and western Massachusetts for their patrons during 1975 (4,368 requests for copies of periodical articles from 1,071 different journals) *showed that* the age of requested items was as follows:

5 years old or less	2,729 (62.48%) items
10 years old or less	3,501 (80.15%) items
20 years old or less	4,086 (93.54%) items
30 years old or less	4,262 (97.57%) items

This compared to the number of items 5 years old or less in 4 other studies reported in the literature, which ranged from 50-65%, and the number of items in 3 other studies reported in the literature which were 10 years old or less, which ranged from 69-85%. **(718)**

■ A study reported in 1977 of English-language articles in 6 "major musicological journals" for the years 1973-75 (*Musical Quarterly, Journal of the American Musicological Society, Music and Letters, Music Review, Acta Musicologica*, and *Musica Disciplina*), involving 1,374 citations in 304 articles, *showed that* the literature in musicology did not "obsolesce" in the same manner as literature in science and technology. For example, of the 1,374 citations, the decades in which the cited materials were published were as follows:

1966-75	412 (30% [40% reported]) citations
1956-65	294 (21%) citations
1946-55	195 (14%) citations
1931-45	119 (9%) citations
1900-30	200 (15%) citations
pre-1900	154 (11%) citations

(755)

Age of Material—Physical Condition

Academic

■ A study reported in 1983 at the University of North Carolina investigating the quality of paper in French books dealing with French literature and criticism and history published during the period 1860-1914 (1,349 imprints held in the Wilson Library of the University of North Carolina examined) *showed that*, for 5-year periods on the basis of the paper in the book, the number of books in "good" condition declined from 94% in 1860 to 56% in 1894, while the books in "bad" condition increased from 4% in 1860 to 17% in 1894. Thereafter, the number of books in "good" condition generally ran about 40% up to 1914, while the books in "bad" condition generally ran between 22-28% up to 1914. **(775)**

Ibid. . . . *showed that* for the period 1895-1914 the numbers of books in "good" or "bad" condition (based on their paper) by major publishers of the period were as follows:

Calmann-Levy	51% good; 12% bad
Champion	36% good; 23% bad
Charpentier	19% good; 72% bad
Hachette	16% good; 39% bad
Mercure de France	24% good; 5% bad
Perrin	31% good; 26% bad
Plon	61% good; 13% bad

For all publishers sampled (77) the overall average of "good" books for this time period was 39%, while the overall average of "bad" books was 24%. **(775)**

Ibid. . . . *showed that* between 1860 and 1914 the paper in the history books had generally held up better than the paper in the literature books. Specifically, 66% of the history books were in "good" condition compared to 55% of the literature books, while 12% of the history books were in "bad" condition compared to 20% of the literature books. **(775)**

Age of Material—Subject

Academic

■ A 1-year study during 1964-65 at the Yale Medical Library concerning book and journal circulation (34,825 circulations) *showed that* not all subject areas covered in the library are equally used. Specifically, of 67 subject fields covered in the library, "over half" of the book and journal circulations fell into 7 subject fields, while 82% of the circulations fell into 21 of the subject fields. **(674)**

Ibid. . . . *showed that* the importance of book currency varied considerably by subject area. For example, in the areas of biochemistry, neurology, and neoplasms, 90% of the circulations were accounted for by imprints

Age of Material 63

going back 12 years, 17 years, and 17 years, respectively, while in the areas of surgery, biology, and infectious diseases, 90% of the circulations were accounted for by imprints going back 42 years, 39 years, and 37 years, respectively. **(674)**

■ A study reported in 1981 of citations in English-language research papers dealing with library science research appearing in 39 North American, British, or international journals for selected years during the period 1950-75 (716 papers; 5,334 citations) *showed that* 25% of the citations were 7 years old or older at the time the citing article was published. **(571)**

■ A study reported in 1983 of the scholarly materials supporting research on 3 creative authors (John Milton, Henry James, and W. H. Auden), taken from the 1976-80 volumes of the *Arts and Humanities Citation Index* and involving 327 source articles and 2,876 citations found in the source articles, *showed that*:

> 37.4% of the citations involving Milton were 20 years old or less, while 23% of the citations involving Milton were 10 years old or less at the time the source documents were written;
>
> 45.2% of the citations involving James were 20 years old or less, while 21.5% of the citations involving James were 10 years old or less at the time the source documents were written;
>
> 51.5% of the citations involving Auden were 20 years old or less, while 20.4% of the citations involving Auden were 10 years old or less at the time the source documents were written. **(520)**

■ The same study also reported in 1983 of the scholarly materials supporting research on 3 literary topics (symbolism, existentialism, and structuralism) involving 352 source articles and 4,144 citations taken from those source articles *showed that*, of the 4,144 citations, 58.5% were to materials 20 years old or less when the source material was written, while 30.3% were to materials 10 years old or less when the source material was written. **(520)**

Special

■ A 1-year study during 1964-65 at the Yale Medical Library concerning book and journal circulation (34,825 circulations) *showed that* the importance of book currency varied considerably by subject area. For example, in the areas of biochemistry, neurology, and neoplasms, 90% of the circulations were accounted for by imprints going back 12 years, 17 years, and 17 years, respectively, while in the areas of surgery, biology, and infectious diseases, 90% of the circulations were accounted for by imprints going back 42 years, 39 years, and 37 years, respectively. **(674)**

Ibid. . . . *showed that* not all subject areas covered in the library are equally used. Specifically, of 67 subject fields covered in the library, "over half" of the book and journal circulations fell into 7 subject fields, while 82% of the circulations fell into 21 of the subject fields. **(674)**

Approval Plans

Academic

■ A study reported in 1975 comparing book price increases reported in the *Bowker Annual of Library and Book Trade Information* with actual price increases encountered on English-language material acquired through approval plans at 3 universities (University of Nebraska, years 1966-67 and 1967-68; Florida Atlantic University, 1969-70 and 1970-71; and Arizona State University, 1971-72) during the period 1967-1972 *showed that Bowker* indicated a 48.1% increase, while the libraries showed an 18.5% increase for this period. **(630)**

■ A study reported in 1975 at California State Polytechnic University, Pomona, comparing approval book selections with traditional faculty and librarian selections over a year's time, involving imprints for 1974 in economics and biological sciences, *showed that*, of 286 economics titles received through the approval program, 15 (5.2%) were also independently requested by faculty and librarians, while 63 of 78 faculty and librarian requests (80.8%) were not received on the approval plan. However, only 96 (33.6%) of the approval titles were returned to the vendor. **(669)**

Ibid. . . . *showed that*, for 255 titles in the biological sciences received on the approval program, 60 (23.5%) were also independently requested by faculty and librarians, while 152 of 212 faculty and librarian requests (71.7%) were not received on the approval plan. However, only 33 (12.9%) of the approval titles were returned to the vendor. **(669)**

■ A 1976 study at the Health Sciences Library of the University of Iowa involving 1,288 books received during a 6-month period *showed that*, of 730 (57%) books received on the approval plan, 330 (25%) were received due to orders placed on the basis of book reviews or publishers fliers; 131 (10%) were received due to orders generated as a result of patron request; and 97 (8%) were received due to standing order. **(467)**

Special

■ A 1976 study at the Health Sciences Library of the University of Iowa involving 1,288 books received during a 6-month period *showed that*, of 730 (57%) books received on the approval plan, 330 (25%) were received due to orders placed on the basis of book reviews or publishers fliers; 131 (10%) were received due to orders generated as a result of patron request; and 97 (8%) were received due to standing order. **(467)**

Budget

Academic

■ An Indiana University survey reported in 1979 for the National Science Foundation *showed that* major academic libraries increased their materials budget by an average of 9.4% in the period 1973-76; a 15-18% increase was reported necessary to maintain equivalent coverage. **(016)**

Ibid. . . . *showed that* library administrators responded to shortages in the library materials serials budget primarily by canceling duplicates and shifting funds from monographic to serials accounts. The third most common tactic was to halt new subscriptions in order to renew old ones. **(016)**

Ibid. . . . *showed that* during the period 1969-76 large academic libraries increased the percentage of their budget spent on serials at the expense of monographs. In 1969 $2 was spent on serials for every $1 on monographs; by 1976 a steady decrease had reduced the ratio to $1.23 for serials for each $1 spent on monographs. **(016)**

■ A study reported in 1981 of data on 1,146 2-year colleges, as reported in the 1977 Higher Education General Information Surveys and compared to the 1979 Association of College and Research Libraries standards, *showed that* overall the average library operating expenditures totaled

$166,000 with median expenditures totaling $102,000, including average expenditures for privately supported schools (235 reporting) of $42,000 and average expenditures for publicly supported schools (911 reporting) of $198,000. **(500)**

Ibid. . . . *showed that* overall the average library materials budget was $39,000 with a median of $27,000, including average expenditures for privately supported schools (235 reporting) of $11,000 and average expenditures for publicly supported schools (911 reporting) of $46,000.
(500)

■ A study reported in 1983 of surveys of medical school libraries for the period 1960-61 through 1980-81, made by the American Medical Association, the Medical Library Association, the Association of Academic Health Sciences Library Directors, and the National Library of Medicine, *showed that* during this 20-year period medical school library expenditures increased "some 100%" or "approximately doubled" every 5 years during the 15-year period between 1960 and 1975. In the most recent 5-year period the growth in expenditures had decreased to 53%, and if the expenditures for 1980-81 were projected for a 5-year period, the growth rate would decrease to 39%. **(746)**

Ibid. . . . *showed that*, even if adjustments were made for inflation, library support had increased. For example, while the purchasing power of the dollar decreased 60% in the 13-year period 1967-1980, average medical school library expenditures increased 599% for the 15-year period 1965-1980. For the 20-year period from 1960-61 through 1980-81 average medical school library expenditures increased 1,341%. **(746)**

Ibid. . . . *showed that* during the 3-year period 1978-79 through 1980-81, on the basis of regular funds spent (excluding special contracts and grants), medical school libraries spent "more than three times as much on serials as they do on monographs." Even as expenditures increased during this period, the ratio remained constant. **(746)**

Public

■ An attempt reported in 1982 to establish 4 input measures and 4 output measures for public libraries, based on published statistical reports for 301 New Jersey public libraries over a 6-year period (1974-79) and survey data for 96 public libraries in New Jersey, *showed that* (per capita based on number of residents in the library's service area):

Budget

INPUT MEASURES

The proportion of budget spent on materials averaged 19.9%, with a standard deviation of .081 (based on 301 libraries).

The new volumes per capita averaged .181, with a standard deviation of .097 (based on 301 libraries).

The periodical titles per capita averaged .0094, with a standard deviation of .0054 (based on 301 libraries).

The circulation per volume averaged 1.79, with a standard deviation of .77 (based on 301 libraries).

OUTPUT MEASURES

The circulation per capita averaged 5.04, with a standard deviation of 3.07 (based on 301 libraries).

The patron visits per capita averaged 2.82, with a standard deviation of 1.82 (based on 96 libraries).

The reference questions per capita averaged 1.12, with a standard deviation of .79 (based on 96 libraries).

The in-library uses of materials per capita averaged 2.29, with a standard deviation of 2.02 (based on 96 libraries). **(576)**

■ A survey of 53 U.S. public libraries (all responding) reported in 1983 concerning circulation and expenditures *showed that*, using 1980 as a base year (index value = 100), expenditures rose 10% by 1981 (index value = 110), while expenditures had risen a further 11% by 1982 (index value = 121). However, when expenditures were adjusted for inflation using the Consumer Price Index, there was no increase in real expenditures in 1981 (index value = 100), although there was a 4% real increase in expenditures the following year, in 1982 (index value = 104). Further, between 1980-82 the amount of expenditures spent on salaries rose from 63% to 64%, while the amount of expenditures spent on materials dropped from 16% to 15%. The amount spent on "other" remained constant at 21%. **(791)**

School

■ A 1983 survey of a systematic sample of school library media centers concerning data for fiscal year 1982-83 (survey size: 2,000 centers; responding: 1,297; usable: 1,251 or 62%) *showed that* a comparison of schools with (666 schools) and without (597 schools) district-level library media coordinators revealed that schools without district coordinators spent more money per student on resources and had more books per student than schools with district coordinators. However, schools with district coordinators paid media specialists higher salaries, had more AV items per student, had more clerical assistance, and used more adult volunteers than schools without district coordinators. Specifically:

> total materials expenditure per student in schools with coordinators averaged $8.80, and in schools without coordinators averaged $10.92;

> average books per student in schools with coordinators averaged 18, and in schools without coordinators averaged 20;

> number of AV items per student in schools with coordinators averaged 3.45, and in schools without coordinators averaged 3.03;

> media specialist salary in schools with coordinators averaged $20,699, and in schools without coordinators averaged $19,354;

> the number of clerical assistants and adult volunteers in schools with coordinators averaged .83 and 2.46, respectively, and in schools without coordinators averaged .77 and 1.85, respectively. **(056)**

Ibid. . . . *showed that* [in 1982-83] the average expenditure for microcomputer software reported by 81 elementary centers was $595; for 37 junior high/middle school centers was $322; for 46 senior high centers was $381; and for 5 combinations of the above schools was $523. **(056)**

Special

■ A study reported in 1983 of surveys of medical school libraries for the period 1960-61 through 1980-81, made by the American Medical Association, the Medical Library Association, the Association of Academic Health Sciences Library Directors, and the National Library of Medicine, *showed that* during this 20-year period medical school library expenditures increased "some 100%" or "approximately doubled" every 5 years during the 15-year period between 1960 and 1975. In the most recent 5-year period the growth in expenditures had decreased to 53%, and if the expenditures for 1980-81 were projected for a 5-year period, the growth rate would decrease to 39%. **(746)**

Ibid. . . . *showed that*, even if adjustments were made for inflation, library support had increased. For example, while the purchasing power of the dollar decreased 60% in the 13-year period 1967-1980, average medical school library expenditures increased 599% for the 15-year period 1965-1980. For the 20-year period from 1960-61 through 1980-81 average medical school library expenditures increased 1,341%. **(746)**

Ibid. . . . *showed that* during the 3-year period 1978-79 through 1980-81, on the basis of regular funds spent (excluding special contracts and grants), medical school libraries spent "more than three times as much on serials as they do on monographs." Even as expenditures increased during this period, the ratio remained constant. **(746)**

Censorship

General

■ A reanalysis of a 1970 survey of 2,486 American adults undertaken by the Commission on Obscenity and Pornography, based on dividing the sample into those favoring library censorship, i.e., librarians keeping sexually explicit materials off the shelves (1,877 respondents) and those opposing such censorship (473 respondents) (data were missing on the remaining 136 individuals), *showed that* there was a statistically significant difference between the 2 groups in the following areas, with people who opposed censorship by librarians:

> expressing more liberal sexual attitudes and claiming more exposure to erotica in the 2 years preceding the survey;
>
> reporting an average educational attainment of "some college" (12.8 years) as opposed to 11.3 years of education;
>
> reporting an average age of 38.5 versus an average age of 45.4 years;
>
> scoring higher on reported consumption of mass media (books, magazines, and movies) and on the willingness to take citizen's actions on important social or political problems;
>
> reporting church attendance an average of 1.8 times a month versus 3.1 times a month.

(All differences were significant at .001 significance level.) **(781)**

Ibid. . . . *showed that* older age groups were more likely to favor sexual censorship by librarians (women: gamma −.32; men: gamma −.44), while increasing levels of education (women: gamma .37; men: gamma .48), increasing levels of mass media consumption, i.e., books, magazines, and movies (women: gamma .24; men: gamma .40), and increasing levels of recent exposure to erotica (women: gamma .38; men: gamma .40) were associated with a tendency to oppose sexual censorship by librarians. (All findings were significant at the .001 level.) **(781)**

Ibid. . . . *showed that* there was no statistically significant relationship between either of the 2 groups (for or against library censorship) and sexual activity or degree of satisfaction with one's sex life. "Opposition to [or advocacy of] censorship is apparently not explained by people's sex lives." **(781)**

Public

■ A study reported in 1981 of 197 undergraduate and graduate students enrolled in children's literature classes at the University of Iowa and Michigan State University *showed that* a warning indicator signaling possible objectionable content arbitrarily assigned an otherwise favorable book review statistically significantly (significant at the .05 level) reduced the chances for that book to be chosen for a school library collection.
(220)

Ibid. . . . *showed that* a warning indicator signaling possible objectionable content arbitrarily assigned an otherwise favorable book review did not affect books chosen for grades none through second, third through fifth, and sixth through eighth in a statistically significant differential manner. The warning indicator reduced selection probability equally across the 3 groups. **(220)**

■ A study reported in 1981 of 339 undergraduate and graduate students primarily enrolled as education and library science majors at the University of Iowa and Michigan State University (142 in treatment group; 197 in control group) *showed that* the group exposed to an educational censorship unit were statistically significantly less likely to reject books for a school library collection whose positive book reviews had been arbitrarily assigned a warning indicator signaling that the book might contain objectionable material than the control group. **(221)**

Ibid. . . . *showed that* the treatment effects were across the board and made no statistically significant differential increase in the number of books with warning indicators selected for older children as compared to younger children. **(221)**

Characteristics of the Literature

School

■ A study reported in 1981 of 197 undergraduate and graduate students enrolled in children's literature classes at the University of Iowa and Michigan State University *showed that* a warning indicator signaling possible objectionable content arbitrarily assigned an otherwise favorable book review statistically significantly (significant at the .05 level) reduced the chances for that book to be chosen for a school library collection.
(220)

Ibid. . . . *showed that* a warning indicator signaling possible objectionable content arbitrarily assigned an otherwise favorable book review did not affect books chosen for grades none through second, third through fifth, and sixth through eighth in a statistically significant differential manner. The warning indicator reduced selection probability equally across the 3 groups.
(220)

■ A study reported in 1981 of 339 undergraduate and graduate students primarily enrolled as education and library science majors at the University of Iowa and Michigan State University (142 in treatment group; 197 in control group) *showed that* the group exposed to an educational censorship unit were statistically significantly less likely to reject books for a school library collection whose positive book reviews had been arbitrarily assigned a warning indicator signaling that the book might contain objectionable material than the control group.
(221)

Ibid. . . . *showed that* the treatment effects were across the board and made no statistically significant differential increase in the number of books with warning indicators selected for older children as compared to younger children.
(221)

Characteristics of the Literature—Language

Academic

■ A citation study reported in 1969 of a sample of article citations from 10 major journals in geology published in 1960 and 1965 (400 citations chosen for each year) *showed that* 87.5% of the 1965 citations were to materials published in English, while 87.3% of the 1960 citations were to English-language materials.
(193)

COLLECTION DEVELOPMENT

■ A study of the citations in 186 doctoral dissertations of the 190 completed between the years 1969-72 in ALA-accredited library science programs (population: 43,500 citations; sample size: 2,139 citations, providing a sampling error of ±2% at 95% confidence level) *showed that* 88.6% of the citations were to English-language publications, 5.6% were to German-language publications, 0.2% to French-language publications, and the remainder to "other" language publications. **(633)**

Ibid. . . . *showed that* 1,610 (75.3%) citations were to publications published in the U.S.; 240 (11.2%) citations were to foreign, English-language publications; and 289 (13.5%) were to foreign, non-English language publications. **(633)**

■ A study reported in 1972 of the citations listed in articles presented in the *Annual Review of Medicine* (international coverage) for the years 1965-69 (975 periodical titles; 14,201 periodical citations) *showed that*, of the 275 most cited journals (13,023 citations), 217 (78.91%) journals were published in English; 35 (12.73%) were published in multilingual text using a combination of English, French, or German; 11 (4%) were published in French; 6 (2.18%) were published in German; and 6 (2.18%) were published in some other language or combination of languages. **(351)**

■ A study reported in 1974 of citations in articles listed in the *Annual Review of Microbiology* (vols. 22-24, 1968-70), involving 624 titles and 10,408 citations, *showed that*, of the 141 most cited journals, the top 3 language formats were English (83 or 58.87% of total journals); multilingual, involving English, French, or German (27 or 19.15% of total); and multilingual, involving 4 languages of which English, French, and German were 3 of the languages (9 or 6.38% of total). **(353)**

■ A study reported in 1974 of the citations listed in the 1968-70 volumes of the *Annual Review of Pharmacology*, involving 11,424 citations, *showed that*, of the 229 most cited journals, the 3 main language formats used were English (167 or 72.93% journals); multilingual involving various combinations of English, French, or German (36 or 15.72%); and French (7 or 3.06%). **(354)**

■ A study reported in 1974 using 52 sociological subject headings in *Social Science and Humanities Index* (1970-71) to identify 446 different journal articles, which in turn produced 8,926 citations to different publications (3,651 serial publications; 5,275 nonserial publications),

Characteristics of the Literature 73

showed that only 4.78% of the total citations (2.99% of the serial citations and 6.03% of the nonserial citations) referred to non-English language publications. **(252)**

■ A study reported in 1975 of the research literature of physiology over the 3-year period 1970-72 involving citation counting (first 3 months of each year) in 8 internationally known journals (31,669 citations) *showed that* 23,118 (80.52%) of the serial citations referred to articles in English, while 4,696 (16.36%) of the citations referred to polylingual articles. Of the 909 serial titles identified as containing at least 1 of the 28,714 serial citations, 535 (58.85%) were English-language titles, while 237 (26.08%) were polylingual in format. **(355)**

■ A study reported in 1977 of English-language articles in 6 "major musicological journals" for the years 1973-75 (*Musical Quarterly, Journal of the American Musicological Society, Music and Letters, Music Review, Acta Musicologica,* and *Musica Disciplina*), involving 1,374 citations in 304 articles, *showed that* the languages of the citations were as follows:

English	64.4% articles
German	21.5% articles
French	9.9% articles
Italian	2.5% articles
all other languages	1.7% articles

Further, for each of the journals separately, the number of citations to English-language items ranged from 51% to 71% of the citations. **(755)**

■ A survey reported in 1978 of 31 Ph.D. dissertations in the field of business/management (13 from the State University of New York at Buffalo and 18 from SUNYAB incoming faculty but completed at other schools) *showed that*, of the 2,805 citations, only 4 (0.1%) were to non-English titles. These included 2 citations to French-language materials and 1 citation each to Spanish- and German-language materials. **(461)**

■ A study reported in 1978 of all articles indexed in 48 issues (1972-75) of the *Tropical Diseases Bulletin* (11,174 articles taken from 611 different journals) *showed that* the distribution of journal titles (and articles) by language was as follows for the 4 most frequently used languages:

English (439 titles)	8,963 (80.21%) articles
French (48 titles)	724 (6.48%) articles
Spanish (61 titles)	395 (3.53%) articles
Portuguese (27 titles)	361 (3.23%) articles

(719)

■ A study reported in 1983 comparing 2 related variations of collection evaluation in political science, based on citation checking (1st method: 1 citation selected at random from each article in *American Political Science Review* during a 3-year period for a total of 150 citations; 2nd method: 1 citation selected at random from each article in a single bibliographical volume of 5 political science journals, including *Comparative Politics, World Politics, American Journal of Political Science, Journal of Politics,* and *Political Theory* for a total of 142 citations) and applied to 5 university libraries in the greater Washington, D.C., area, *showed that* the 2 most frequently occurring languages of the 584 citations (2 samples of 150 and 2 samples of 142) were English (546 or 93.5% citations) and French (18 or 3.1% citations). **(774)**

Special

■ A study reported in 1972 of the citations listed in articles presented in the *Annual Review of Medicine* (international coverage) for the years 1965-69 (975 periodical titles; 14,201 periodical citations) *showed that,* of the 275 most cited journals (13,023 citations), 217 (78.91%) journals were published in English; 35 (12.73%) were published in multilingual text using a combination of English, French, or German; 11 (4%) were published in French; 6 (2.18%) were published in German; and 6 (2.18%) were published in some other language or combination of languages. **(351)**

■ A study reported in 1974 of the citations listed in the 1968-70 volumes of the *Annual Review of Pharmacology,* involving 11,424 citations, *showed that,* of the 229 most cited journals, the 3 main language formats used were English (167 or 72.93% journals); multilingual involving various combinations of English, French, or German (36 or 15.72%); and French (7 or 3.06%). **(354)**

■ A study reported in 1974 of citations in articles listed in the *Annual Review of Microbiology* (vols. 22-24, 1968-70) involving 624 titles and 10,408 citations *showed that,* of the 141 most cited journals, the top 3 language formats were English (83 or 58.87% of total journals); multilingual, involving English, French, or German (27 or 19.15% of total); and multilingual, involving 4 languages of which English, French, and German were 3 of the languages (9 or 6.38% of total). **(353)**

■ A study reported in 1975 of the research literature of physiology over the 3-year period 1970-72 involving citation counting (first 3 months of

Characteristics of the Literature

each year) in 8 internationally known journals (31,669 citations) *showed that* 23,118 (80.52%) of the serial citations referred to articles in English, while 4,696 (16.36%) of the citations referred to polylingual articles. Of the 909 serial titles identified as containing at least 1 of the 28,714 serial citations, 535 (58.85%) were English-language titles, while 237 (26.08%) were polylingual in format. **(355)**

■ A study reported in 1977 of English-language articles in 6 "major musicological journals" for the years 1973-75 (*Musical Quarterly, Journal of the American Musicological Society, Music and Letters, Music Review, Acta Musicologica,* and *Musica Disciplina*), involving 1,374 citations in 304 articles, *showed that* the languages of the citations were as follows:

English	64.4%	articles
German	21.5%	articles
French	9.9%	articles
Italian	2.5%	articles
all other languages	1.7%	articles

Further, for each of the journals separately, the number of citations to English-language items ranged from 51% to 71% of the citations. **(755)**

■ A study reported in 1978 of all articles indexed in 48 issues (1972-75) of the *Tropical Diseases Bulletin* (11,174 articles taken from 611 different journals) *showed that* the distribution of journal titles (and articles) by language was as follows for the 4 most frequently used languages:

English (439 titles)	8,963 (80.21%)	articles
French (48 titles)	724 (6.48%)	articles
Spanish (61 titles)	395 (3.53%)	articles
Portuguese (27 titles)	361 (3.23%)	articles

(719)

Characteristics of the Literature—Other

General

■ A 1972 study comparing the rates of intergenerational information transfer in different scientific fields by reviewing citations in approximately 100 articles taken from a single representative journal in each of 15 biomedical scientific speciality fields (articles cited that were at least 25 years old were considered to be evidence of intergenerational information transfer) *showed that* the rates of intergenerational information transfer varied considerably among the various fields. Physiology had the highest rate of intergenerational information transfer with 87 papers cited that were 25 years old or older in 128 articles reviewed (68% rate), while molecular biology had the lowest rate of intergenerational information transfer with 14 papers cited that were 25 years old or older in 97 articles reviewed (14.4% rate). **(707)**

Ibid. . . . *showed that* the amount of intergenerational information transfer may change over time in a field. A comparison of physiology and microbiology showed changes in different directions, with physiology citing an increasing amount of older literature in the past 50 years and microbiology citing a decreasing amount of older literature in the past 50 years. Specifically, the transfer rate in physiology (number of cited papers 25 years old or older/number of articles reviewed) was 68.0% in 1972, 50% in 1947, and 40.2% in 1922. The transfer rate in microbiology was 19.4% in 1972, 30.1% in 1947, and 34.3% in 1922. **(707)**

■ A study reported in 1982 of the number of cases received by West Publishing Company annually during the period 1900 to 1980 *showed that* the number of cases had increased from 18,937 in 1900 to 52,214 in 1980, with the greatest increase coming in the last 20 years. 26,241 cases were received in 1960; 36,892 were received in 1970; and 52,214 in 1980. **(373)**

Academic

■ A study reported in 1964 of the number of citations to medical dissertations in the period 1821-1960, based on the citations found in a sample of 10 American and European medical journals for that period, *showed that* there was a steady growth in the percentage of citations of dissertations from 0.8% of all citations in 1821-30 to a high of 4% in the 1881-1910 period followed by a marked and generally steady decline in dissertation citations up to 1951-60 with a new low of 0.7% for that period.
(168)

■ A study reported in 1971 investigating the number of papers published concerning a drug before the first human test was reported (involving 30 drugs) *showed that* often the report on the human test of a drug was among the earliest papers published. Specifically, in 6 (20%) cases a human test was the first paper published on a drug, while in 8 (27%) cases the human test was the second paper published on the drug. Overall, the median number of papers published before the first human

Characteristics of the Literature

test was reported was 2. In only 2 cases was a large number of papers published on a drug before a paper reported a human test. These were neomycin with 18 previous papers and griseofulvin with 81 previous papers. **(689)**

Ibid. . . . *showed that* in terms of the number of papers published prior to the report of the first human test, there was no statistically significant difference between the number of papers published on antimicrobial and the number of papers published on pharmacologic drugs. **(689)**

■ A summary reported in 1976 of a study of 46 political science books published in 1948 and 1949 *showed that* 30.9% of the books' citations were from other political science works and 69.1% of the citations came from other disciplines. **(053)**

■ A study reported in 1979 of footnotes in 9 law reviews and 2 journals *showed that* the footnote metric (the number of lines of footnotes per page divided by the number of lines of text plus the number of lines of footnotes on that page) had increased in the last 50 years:

1928	.25	footnote metric
1938	.26	footnote metric
1948	.23	footnote metric
1958	.20	footnote metric
1968	.26	footnote metric
1978	.31	footnote metric

(253)

Ibid. . . . *showed that* the *Columbia Law Review* was the most densely footnoted journal with an average footnote metric of .37, compared to the *Tulane Law Review*, which had the smallest footnote metric, .22. **(253)**

Ibid. . . . *showed that*, in terms of the sole or senior author of the articles considered, the footnote metric was as follows:

full professors	.25
associate/assistant professors	.27
other academics/professionals	.20
attorneys	.25
judiciary	.15
law students	.32

(253)

■ A study reported in 1982 comparing co-authorship in musicology during the period 1949-75 (970 articles, [source of articles not given]) with a previously published study of co-authorship in the sciences [not further defined] (533 articles) *showed that* 823 (21%) of the musicology articles were single-author items, while 147 (15%) were co-authored by 2 or more authors. This was compared to the study on scientists, in which 114 (21%) articles were single-author items and 419 (79%) articles were co-authored by 2 or more authors. **(655)**

Ibid. . . . *showed that* the 27 most prolific authors in musicology (5% of the total authors) were responsible for 334 (29%) of the total articles.
(655)

■ A study reported in 1983 investigating the relationship between the scholarliness of academic papers and their impact by comparing the number of references in each of 110 papers (taken from the *American Sociological Review* and the *American Journal of Sociology* during the years 1972-73) to the number of citations listed for each of the papers in *Social Science Citation Index*, 1972-81, *showed that* there was a very modest but statistically significant relationship between scholarliness and impact. Specifically, the correlation coefficient (partial gamma coefficient) was .26 and significant at the .03 level. **(659)**

■ A study reported in 1983 comparing peer rating of medical articles with citation counts (taken from *Science Citation Index* for the 5 years following the articles' date of publication), involving 279 "first order papers" (all 1974 research papers abstracted in the 1975 or 1976 volumes of the *Year Book of Cancer*, highest peer rating), 276 "second order papers" (random sample of the 1974 research papers that were only listed in the 1975 or 1976 volumes of the *Year Book of Cancer*, next highest peer rating), and 315 "average" papers (no special peer rating) published in 1974 on the subject of cancer research randomly selected from *Biological Abstracts*, *showed that* the more highly regarded articles tended to be cited more than other articles to a statistically significant degree (significant at the .005 level). Specifically, the average percentage of papers cited per year was as follows:

first-order group	73.7% of papers
second-order group	72.7% of papers
average group	55.7% of papers

while the average number of citations per paper for the 5-year period was as follows:

Characteristics of the Literature

         first-order group   30.59 citations
         second-order group 24.60 citations
         average group   11.17 citations   **(657)**

Ibid. . . . *showed that* comparison of citation ratings for the 3 groups using only 1974 and 1975 citations (citations made during these 2 years took place before the *Yearbook of Cancer* could have been a factor in calling attention to the articles) indicated as well that the more highly regarded articles were cited more than other articles to a statistically significant degree (significant at the .001 level). This suggested that the quality of the article itself was the factor leading to the generally higher number of citations. **(657)**

Public

■ An analysis reported in 1974 of how 56 fathers were portrayed in 50 junior high novels with twentieth-century U.S. settings (excluding fantasy and science fiction), randomly selected from 227 items in the 2nd edition of *Junior High School Library Catalog* and its 1971 and 1972 supplements, *showed that* 80% of the 56 fathers were portrayed as members of the broad middle class, 16% from the lower class, and 3% from the upper class. Further, 84% were white, 13% black, and 3% from other ethnic groups. **(280)**

Ibid. . . . *showed that* 45% of the fathers were involved in professional or business careers; 31% in sales, farm/ranch, skilled, or unskilled occupations; and 21% could not be clearly determined. Additionally, 74% of the fathers were portrayed in rural, suburban, or small town environments, while only 25% were portrayed in urban environments. **(280)**

Ibid. . . . *showed that* 18% of the fathers were portrayed as absent from the home due to death, divorce/separation, or work. Divorce/separation accounted for 50% of the father absences. **(280)**

Ibid. . . . *showed that* 71% of the fathers were portrayed as the major breadwinner. Additionally, of 35 home-centered tasks performed by these fathers, 10 involved driving children to school or social functions and 9 involved disciplining children. **(280)**

Ibid. . . . *showed that* 38% of the fathers were portrayed as democratic, 34% as authoritative, 5% combination democratic/authoritative, and 23% undeterminable. **(280)**

School

■ An analysis reported in 1974 of how 56 fathers were portrayed in 50 junior high novels with twentieth-century U.S. settings (excluding fantasy and science fiction), randomly selected from 227 items in the 2nd edition of *Junior High School Library Catalog* and its 1971 and 1972 supplements, *showed that* 80% of the 56 fathers were portrayed as members of the broad middle class, 16% from the lower class, and 3% from the upper class. Further, 84% were white, 13% black, and 3% from other ethnic groups. **(280)**

Ibid. . . . *showed that* 45% of the fathers were involved in professional or business careers; 31% in sales, farm/ranch, skilled, or unskilled occupations; and 21% could not be clearly determined. Additionally, 74% of the fathers were portrayed in rural, suburban, or small town environments, while only 25% were portrayed in urban environments. **(280)**

Ibid. . . . *showed that* 18% of the fathers were portrayed as absent from the home due to death, divorce/separation, or work. Divorce/separation accounted for 50% of the father absences. **(280)**

Ibid. . . . *showed that* 71% of the fathers were portrayed as the major breadwinner. Additionally, of 35 home-centered tasks performed by these fathers, 10 involved driving children to school or social functions and 9 involved disciplining children. **(280)**

Ibid. . . . *showed that* 38% of the fathers were portrayed as democratic, 34% as authoritative, 5% combination democratic/authoritative, and 23% undeterminable. **(280)**

Special

■ A study reported in 1964 of the number of citations to medical dissertations in the period 1821-1960, based on the citations found in a sample of 10 American and European medical journals for that period, *showed that* there was a steady growth in the percentage of citations of

Characteristics of the Literature 81

dissertations from 0.8% of all citations in 1821-30 to a high of 4% in the 1881-1910 period followed by a marked and generally steady decline in dissertation citations up to 1951-60 with a new low of 0.7% for that period.
(168)

■ A study reported in 1971 investigating the number of papers published concerning a drug before the first human test was reported (involving 30 drugs) *showed that* often the report on the human test of a drug was among the earliest papers published. Specifically, in 6 (20%) cases a human test was the first paper published on a drug, while in 8 (27%) cases the human test was the second paper published on the drug. Overall, the median number of papers published before the first human test was reported was 2. In only 2 cases was a large number of papers published on a drug before a paper reported a human test. These were neomycin with 18 previous papers and griseofulvin with 81 previous papers. **(689)**

Ibid. . . . *showed that* in terms of the number of papers published prior to the report of the first human test, there was no statistically significant difference between the number of papers published on antimicrobial and the number of papers published on pharmacologic drugs. **(689)**

■ A 1972 study comparing the rates of intergenerational information transfer in different scientific fields by reviewing citations in approximately 100 articles taken from a single representative journal in each of 15 biomedical scientific speciality fields (articles cited that were at least 25 years old were considered to be evidence of intergenerational information transfer) *showed that* the rates of intergenerational information transfer varied considerably among the various fields. Physiology had the highest rate of intergenerational information transfer with 87 papers cited that were 25 years old or older in 128 articles reviewed (68% rate), while molecular biology had the lowest rate of intergenerational information transfer with 14 papers cited that were 25 years old or older in 97 articles reviewed (14.4% rate). **(707)**

Ibid. . . . *showed that* the amount of intergenerational information transfer may change over time in a field. A comparison of physiology and microbiology showed changes in different directions, with physiology citing an increasing amount of older literature in the past 50 years and microbiology citing a decreasing amount of older literature in the past 50 years. Specifically, the transfer rate in physiology (number of cited papers 25 years old or older/number of articles reviewed) was 68.0% in 1972, 50% in 1947, and 40.2% in 1922. The transfer rate in microbiology was 19.4% in 1972, 30.1% in 1947, and 34.3% in 1922. **(707)**

■ A study reported in 1974 of 3,347 biomedical book reviews (2,067 titles) taken from the 1970 issues of 54 English-language biomedical journals (excluding *Science* and *Nature*) that contained "bona fide" book reviews *showed that*, of the 1,674 titles available in the U.S., 1,479 (88.35%) were published by trade publishers, while 147 (8.78%) were published by university presses. **(704)**

Ibid. . . . *showed that* the 3 presses that had published the most books in the present sample (together accounting for 26.46% of the 1,674 titles available in the U.S.) were Williams and Wilkins of Baltimore (177 books or 10.57% of the U.S. books), Charles C. Thomas of Springfield, Illinois (159 or 9.50% of the U.S. books), and Academic Press of New York (107 or 6.39% of the U.S. books). Further, the 18 most active presses published 75.70% of the 1,674 titles available in the U.S. The full 1,674 titles were published by 161 publishers. **(704)**

Ibid. . . . *showed that*, of the 2,067 books, 1,370 (66.3%) titles were originally published in the U.S.; 354 (17.1%) titles were published in Great Britain (of which 274 titles were reprinted or distributed by American publishers and/or distributors); and 343 (16.6%) titles were published elsewhere. **(704)**

■ A study reported in 1979 of footnotes in 9 law reviews and 2 journals *showed that* the footnote metric (the number of lines of footnotes per page divided by the number of lines of text plus the number of lines of footnotes on that page) had increased in the last 50 years:

1928	.25 footnote metric
1938	.26 footnote metric
1948	.23 footnote metric
1958	.20 footnote metric
1968	.26 footnote metric
1978	.31 footnote metric

(253)

Ibid. . . . *showed that* the *Columbia Law Review* was the most densely footnoted journal, with an average footnote metric of .37, compared to the *Tulane Law Review*, which had the smallest footnote metric, .22. **(253)**

Ibid. . . . *showed that*, in terms of the sole or senior author of the articles considered, the footnote metric was as follows:

full professors	.25
associate/assistant professors	.27

continued

Characteristics of the Literature

other academics/professionals	.20	
attorneys	.25	
judiciary	.15	
law students	.32	**(253)**

■ A study reported in 1982 comparing co-authorship in musicology during the period 1949-75 (970 articles, [source of articles not given]) with a previously published study of co-authorship in the sciences [not further defined] (533 articles) *showed that* 823 (21%) of the musicology articles were single-author items, while 147 (15%) were co-authored by 2 or more authors. This was compared to the study on scientists, in which 114 (21%) articles were single-author items and 419 (79%) articles were co-authored by 2 or more authors. **(655)**

Ibid. . . . *showed that* the 27 most prolific authors in musicology (5% of the total authors) were responsible for 334 (29%) of the total articles.
(655)

Characteristics of the Literature—Publication Format

General

■ A study of the citations in 186 doctoral dissertations of the 190 completed between the years 1969-72 in ALA-accredited library science programs (population: 43,500 citations; sample size: 2,139 citations, providing a sampling error of ±2% at 95% confidence level) *showed that* 917 (42.9%) of the citations were to books, 498 (23.2%) to journals, 457 (21.4%) to unpublished materials (due primarily to the 15% of the dissertations on historical topics), 70 (3.3%) to proceedings, 64 (3%) to annual reports, 59 (2.8%) to dissertations, 43 (2%) to newspapers and magazines, and 31 (1.4%) to reports. **(633)**

■ A study reported in 1982 of publication and citation patterns in *College and Research Libraries* during the 40 years between 1939-79 and involving 1,775 articles *showed that*, of 11,658 citations to materials in *College and Research Libraries* articles, periodicals accounted for 5,205 (44.65%)

citations; monographs accounted for 4,245 (36.41%) citations; and U.S. government publications accounted for 464 (3.98%) citations. **(511)**

Academic

■ A citation study reported in 1969 of a sample of article citations from 10 major journals in geology published in 1960 and 1965 (400 citations chosen for each year) *showed that* of the 1965 citations 75.5% were to periodicals, 21.5% to books, and the remainder (3%) divided among maps, theses, and other unpublished papers. The data for 1960 was similar.
(193)

■ A study reported in 1970 of 3,610 citations in the area of political science taken from a book of readings (Harry Eckstein and David E. Apter, *Comparative Politics*, 1963), *American Political Science Review* (1963-66), and 2 British journals, *Political Studies* and *Political Quarterly* (1958-66), *showed that* of the citations in the book alone (1,700 citations) 66% (1,124 citations) were to monographs, 23% (398 citations) were to periodicals, 3% (56 citations) were to newspapers, and 8% were to other sources. **(352)**

Ibid. . . . *showed that*, of the citations in the book alone (1,700 citations), 967 (86.0%) of the monographic citations, 65 (16.3%) of the periodical citations, and 12 (21.4%) of the newspaper citations were to English-language materials. **(352)**

■ A study reported in 1972 of the 1967 *RILM Abstracts (Repertoire International de la Litterature Musicale)* involving every 10th entry from the subject index (158 items), *showed that* an examination of every 12th entry in the 1967 cumulative index (1125 entries) indicated that the 4 most common publication forms were articles from periodicals (612 or 54.4%), monographs (145 or 13.7%), articles from Festschriften (75 or 6.7%), and book reviews (72 or 6.4%). **(401)**

■ A study of the citations in 186 doctoral dissertations of the 190 completed between the years 1969-72 in ALA-accredited library science programs (population: 43,500 citations; sample size: 2,139 citations, providing a sampling error of ±2% at 95% confidence level) *showed that* 917 (42.9%) of the citations were to books, 498 (23.2%) to journals, 457 (21.4%) to unpublished materials (due primarily to the 15% of the dissertations on historical topics), 70 (3.3%) to proceedings, 64 (3%) to

Characteristics of the Literature

annual reports, 59 (2.8%) to dissertations, 43 (2%) to newspapers and magazines, and 31 (1.4%) to reports. **(633)**

Ibid. . . . *showed that*, for all categories of dissertations combined, the age of cited work from dissertation date was as follows: 0-5 years (24.2%), 6-10 years (12%), 11-20 years (12.5%), 20+ years (51.3%). The most striking exceptions to this general pattern were dissertations on automation (9% of the dissertations overall), which had 68.2% of their citations in the 0-5 year category, and historical dissertations (28% of the dissertations overall), which had 76.9% of their citations in the 20+ category. **(633)**

Ibid. . . . *showed that* 88.6% of the citations were to English-language publications, 5.6% were to German-language publications, 0.2% to French-language publications, and the remainder to "other" language publications. **(633)**

Ibid. . . . *showed that* 1,610 (75.3%) citations were to publications published in the U.S.; 240 (11.2%) citations were to foreign, English-language publications; and 289 (13.5%) were to foreign, non-English language publications. **(633)**

■ A study reported in 1974 of the citations listed in the 1968-70 volumes of the *Annual Review of Pharmacology*, involving 11,424 citations, *showed that* journals accounted for 9,596 citations (84.00% of the total); nonprimary serial publications (e.g., annual review articles, recent advances, etc.) accounted for 714 citations (6.25% of total); and nonserial publications accounted for 1,114 citations (9.75% of total). **(354)**

■ A study reported in 1975 of the research literature of physiology over the 3-year period 1970-72 involving citation counting (first 3 months of each year) in 8 internationally known journals (31,669 citations) *showed that* serial titles accounted for 28,714 (90.67%) citations, while monographs accounted for 2,955 (9.3%) citations. **(355)**

■ A study reported in 1978 at the West Virginia University College of Engineering of the citations found in the master's theses accepted over a 4-year period (126 theses between 1971-74) *showed that* nonjournal (i.e., book) literature was more important in the engineering sciences than previously thought by showing that, of 3,002 references overall, only 1,000 (33.3%) were journal citations, with the proportion of journal citations by department ranging from 11.4% of the references in aerospace theses to 49.4% of the references in chemical theses. **(460)**

■ A survey reported in 1978 of 31 Ph.D. dissertations in the field of business/management (13 from the State University of New York at Buffalo and 18 from SUNYAB incoming faculty but completed at other schools) *showed that* the overall distribution of 2,805 citations by form was:

        periodicals   1,377 (49.1%) citations
        monographs   895 (31.9%) citations
        serials   266 (9.5%) citations
        miscellaneous 267 (9.5%) citations   **(461)**

■ A study reported in 1981 of citations in English-language research papers dealing with library science research appearing in 39 North American, British, or international journals for selected years during the period 1950-75 (716 papers; 5,334 citations) *showed that*, of 4,946 citations (excluding official documents), the distribution by form of publication was as follows:

        journals   2,323 (47%) citations
        books   1,387 (28%) citations
        reports   713 (14%) citations
        proceedings   185 (4%) citations
        collective works 238 (5%) citations
        theses   100 (2%) citations   **(571)**

■ A study reported in 1982 of publication and citation patterns in *College and Research Libraries* during the 40 years between 1939-79 and involving 1,775 articles *showed that*, of 11,658 citations to materials in *College and Research Libraries* articles, periodicals accounted for 5,205 (44.65%) citations; monographs accounted for 4,245 (36.41%) citations; and U.S. government publications accounted for 464 (3.98%) citations.   **(511)**

■ A study reported in 1983 of the scholarly materials supporting research on 3 creative authors (John Milton, Henry James, and W. H. Auden) taken from the 1976-80 volumes of the *Arts and Humanities Citation Index* and involving 327 source articles and 2,876 citations found in the source articles, *showed that*:

of 174 source items on John Milton, 56.3% were book reviews and 43.7% were articles;

of 106 source items on Henry James, 58.5% were book reviews and 41.5% were articles;

Characteristics of the Literature

and of 47 source items on W. H. Auden, 34% were book reviews and 66% were articles. **(520)**

Ibid. . . . *showed that*, of the 2,876 citations, 82.7% were references to books; 15.1% were references to articles; and 2.2% were references to other sources, such as dissertations, manuscripts, etc. **(520)**

■ A study reported in 1983 of the scholarly materials supporting research on 3 literary topics (symbolism, existentialism, and structuralism), involving 352 source articles and 4,144 citations taken from those source articles, *showed that* 45.5% of the source materials were book reviews and 54.5% were articles. Of the 4,144 citations, 78.8% were to books, 16.5% were to articles, and 4.6% were to other types of material. **(520)**

■ A study reported in 1983 comparing 2 related variations of collection evaluation in political science, based on citation checking (1st method: 1 citation selected at random from each article in *American Political Science Review* during a 3-year period for a total of 150 citations; 2nd method: 1 citation selected at random from each article in a single bibliographical volume of 5 political science journals, including *Comparative Politics, World Politics, American Journal of Political Science, Journal of Politics,* and *Political Theory*, for a total of 142 citations) and applied to 5 university libraries in the greater Washington, D.C., area, *showed that*, of the 584 citations (2 samples of 150 and 2 samples of 142), 362 (62.0%) referred to monographs, while 222 (38.0%) referred to serials. **(774)**

Special

■ A study reported in 1972 of the 1967 *RILM Abstracts (Repertoire International de la Litterature Musicale)* involving every tenth entry from the subject index (158 items) *showed that* an examination of every twelfth entry in the 1967 cumulative index (1125 entries) indicated that the 4 most common publication forms were articles from periodicals (612 or 54.4%), monographs (145 or 13.7%), articles from Festschriften (75 or 6.7%), and book reviews (72 or 6.4%). **(401)**

■ A study reported in 1974 of the citations listed in the 1968-70 volumes of the *Annual Review of Pharmacology*, involving 11,424 citations, *showed that* journals accounted for 9,596 citations (84.00% of the total); nonprimary serial publications (e.g., annual review articles, recent advances, etc.) accounted for 714 citations (6.25% of total); and nonserial publications accounted for 1,114 citations (9.75% of total). **(354)**

COLLECTION DEVELOPMENT

■ A study reported in 1975 of the research literature of physiology over the 3-year period 1970-72 involving citation counting (first 3 months of each year) in 8 internationally known journals (31,669 citations) *showed that* serial titles accounted for 28,714 (90.67%) citations, while monographs accounted for 2,955 (9.3%) citations. **(355)**

Collection Evaluation

Academic

■ A comparison in 1960 of 25 university libraries listing holdings of over 1 million volumes with the 22 top-ranked graduate institutions *showed that* only 5 of the university libraries reported holdings of 1 million or more were not ranked as one of the top 22 graduate institutions. These 5 were Texas, Brown, Iowa State, Duke, and Missouri. Only 2 of the top 22 institutions had libraries whose holdings were less than 1 million. These were MIT and Cal Tech. **(116)**

■ A 1963 restudy using partially new data of the growth rates of those U.S. university libraries whose collections exceeded 1 million on June 30, 1960 (original study by Axford; reported 1962) *showed that*, if library growth rate rank order were compared with the correct Keniston-Berelson rank order of university excellence in their graduate teaching and research programs, the correlation between the 2 during the 14-year period 1946-60 was r = −.24. This was not a statistically significant finding. **(129)**

Ibid. . . . *showed that* the correlation between the Keniston-Berelson rank order of university excellence in their graduate teaching and research programs and the rank order of absolute size of library holdings proved statistically significant for the 1946 holdings with an r = .76, as well as for the 1960 holdings with an r = .87. [Significance level not given.] **(129)**

Ibid. . . . *showed that* when the Keniston-Berelson rank order of university excellence in graduate teaching and research programs was used to create a top group of 10 universities and a second-level group of 10 universities while the remaining members of the Association of Graduate Schools were used to make up the third level of universities, the mean collection size of the first group had over twice as many volumes as the mean of the second group and over 3 times as many volumes as the mean of the third group in 1946 and 1960. The same ratio and relationship held for the means of absolute volumes added. **(129)**

■ A study reported in 1983 comparing 2 related variations of collection evaluation in political science, based on citation checking (1st method: 1 citation selected at random from each article in *American Political Science Review* during a 3-year period for a total of 150 citations; 2nd method: 1 citation selected at random from each article in a single bibliographical volume of 5 political science journals, including *Comparative Politics, World Politics, American Journal of Political Science, Journal of Politics*, and *Political Theory* for a total of 142 citations) and applied to 5 university libraries in the greater Washington, D.C., area, *showed that*, when each method was applied twice (using different citations) to the group of 5 libraries, both methods gave fairly consistent results. Specifically, for method 1 the difference between the number of citations found on the first check and the number found on the second check ranged from 1.3% (78.7% found first time; 77.7% found second time at Howard) to 6.4% (83.3% found first time; 89.0% found second time at Georgetown), while for method 2 the difference between the number of citations found on the first check and the second check ranged from 1.3% (54.9% found first time; 55.6% found second time at George Mason) to 3.9% (82.0% found first time; 78.9% found second time at Georgetown). **(774)**

Collection Growth

Academic

■ A study reported in 1972 of price and page increases for 20 physics journals between 1959 and 1969 *showed that* the average overall price increase was 202%, with an overall average increase in the number of pages in these journals of 147%. Subtracting out the percent of page increase, the price increase fell to 55% for this 10-year period. **(399)**

Ibid. . . . *showed that* during this period the number of issues increased from 264 to 481, an increase of 82%. **(399)**

Ibid. . . . *showed that* the average page and price increase during this period by publishing group was as follows:

> for the 8 American Institute of Physics journals the page increase was 161% with a price increase of 157%, for a net price increase of −4%;

> for the 6 commercially published journals the page increase was 171% with a price increase of 283%, for a net price increase of 112%;

and for 6 other society or nonprofit journals the page increase was 72% with a price increase of 189%, for a net price increase of 117%. **(399)**

■ A 1976 survey of head law librarians in North American schools (sample size: 178; responding: 154 or 86.7%) *showed that* the modal number of volumes acquired per year by size of library were as follows:

    small (50,000 volumes or less)   0-5,000 vol./year
    medium (50,001-100,000)   0-5,000 vol./year
    med-large (100,001-200,000)   5,001-10,000 vol./year
    large (over 200,000)   10,000-15,000 vol./year   **(357)**

■ A study reported in 1976 of the 25 largest Association for Research Libraries libraries (based on 1973-74 ARL statistics) and their growth during the 12-year period 1962-63 through 1973-74 *showed that* as collection size increases the rate of growth decreases. Such deceleration in growth rate showed up most clearly once library collections began to exceed 3 million volumes. For example:

for collections up to 1.49 million volumes, there were no growth rates less than 4% and 7 that were 4% or greater;

for collections of 1.5-1.99 million volumes, 3 had growth rates less than 4%, while 5 had growth rates 4% or greater;

for collections of 2-2.49 million volumes, 1 had a growth rate of less than 4%, while 3 had growth rates 4% or greater;

for collections of 2.5-2.99 volumes, none had growth rates less than 4%, while 1 had a growth rate of 4% or greater;

for collections of 3+ million volumes, 5 had growth rates less than 4%, while none had growth rates of 4% or greater.   **(446)**

Ibid. . . . *showed that* Fremont Rider's thesis of collection doubling every 16 years (which requires an annual growth rate of 4.5%) was not universally true of the largest research libraries. During the period under study, 11 libraries maintained an average growth rate of 4.5% or better, but 14 did not.   **(446)**

Ibid. . . . *showed that* reviewing the growth rate for the 11 libraries that appeared in both Fremont Rider's study and the present study by 16-year intervals over the period 1938 through 1970 *showed that* only 2 libraries

Collection Growth

(University of North Carolina and University of Illinois) met or exceeded Rider's predictions of collection size for 1954 and 1970. **(446)**

■ A study of 1977 survey information gathered by the National Center for Educational Statistics (U.S. Office of Education), concerning the degree to which 1,146 college and university libraries (Liberal Arts Colleges I and II; Comprehensive Universitites and Colleges I and II) met the 1975 Standards for College Libraries (ACRL), *showed that* 53% of the libraries added fewer than 1,000 books per year per librarian, 39% added 1,000-1,999 books per year per librarian, and 8% added 2,000 books or more per year per librarian. **(486)**

Ibid. . . . *showed that* 63% of the libraries did not meet the minimum standards for annual new monographic acquisitions in that the number of new books added annually to the collection was less than 5% of the collection. However, the average number of new annual acquisitions based on collection size was 5.3%, while the median number of new annual acquisitions based on collection size was 4.3%. Further, the average number of actual volumes added was 7,490, while the median was 4,770 volumes. **(486)**

■ A survey reported in 1981 of 85 North American academic map libraries that have medium or large research collections (usable responses: 49 or 58%), in conjunction with data from the 2nd and 3rd editions of *Map Collections in the United States and Canada*, *showed that* the average size of map collections had grown from 83,650 sheets in 1968 to 113,816 in 1975 (an increase of 36.0%) to 157,696 in 1980 (a further increase of 38.6%). The average annual accession rate for 1968 was 4,654 sheets; for 1975 it was 5,565 (an increase of 19.6%); and for 1980 it was 5,734 (a further increase of 3.0%). **(216)**

■ A study reported in 1981 of data on 1,146 2-year colleges, as reported in the 1977 Higher Education General Information Surveys and compared to the 1979 Association of College and Research Libraries standards, *showed that*, overall, 37% of the respondents, including 60% of the privately supported schools and 31% of the publicly supported schools did not increase their book stock by 5% per year as specified in the standards. However, the overall average increase was 8.8%, with the overall median increase 6.1%. **(500)**

■ A study reported in 1983 of surveys of medical school libraries for the period 1960-61 through 1980-81, made by the American Medical Association, the Medical Library Association, the Association of Academic Health Sciences Library Directors, and the National Library of Medicine, *showed that* the average number of net volumes added to collections in the years 1974-75, 1979-80, and 1980-81 was "approximately 5,000" volumes (monographs and serial volumes bound) per library per year. Further, between 1965-66 and 1980-81 the average number of bound volumes increased by 90%. **(746)**

Ibid. . . . *showed that* the average number of serial titles increased by 10.8% in the 5-year period ending in 1969-70, by 14.8% in the 5-year period ending in 1974-75, and by 9.4% in the 5-year period ending in 1979-80. Overall, between 1965-66 and 1980-81 the average number of current serial titles increased from 1,698 titles to 1,415 titles (42%).
(746)

■ A study reported in 1983 of 3 surveys made by the American Medical Association's Division of Library and Archival Services in 1969, 1973, and 1979 concerning the status of health sciences libraries in the U.S. (survey size for each survey ran between 12,000-14,000 health-related organizations, with a response rate for each survey around 95%) *showed that* between 1973 and 1979 the total number of bound volumes (monographs and serials combined) reported rose from 30,519,759 volumes in 1973 to 34,706,434 volumes in 1979, a 14% increase. Total current serial titles, however, decreased from 736,588 in 1973 to 732,408 in 1979, a 1% decrease. **(745)**

School

■ A 1983 survey of a systematic sample of school library media centers concerning data for fiscal year 1982-83 (survey size: 2,000 centers; responding: 1,297; usable: 1,251 or 62%) *showed that* the average number of books per pupil and average total volumes added in 1982-83 by type of library media center was as follows:

elementary school (587 schools): 20.42 books per student with an average of 295.8 volumes added;

junior high/middle school (308 schools): 16.29 books per student with an average of 393.01 volumes added;

senior high school (304 schools): 17.06 books per student with an average of 465.96 volumes added;

other (49 schools): 28.62 books per student with an average of 364.97 volumes added. **(056)**

Collection Growth

Ibid. . . . *showed that* the average number of AV items per pupil and the average total AV items added in 1982-83 by type of library media center was as follows:

    elementary school (587 schools): 3.71 items per student with an average of 61.13 items added;

    junior high/middle school (308 schools): 2.97 items per student with an average of 68.56 items added;

    senior high school (304 schools): 2.70 items per student with an average of 112.97 items added;

    other (49 schools): 3.06 items per student with an average of 87.53 items added. **(056)**

Ibid. . . . *showed that* a comparison of schools with (666 schools) and without (597 schools) district-level library media coordinators revealed that schools without district coordinators spent more money per student on resources and had more books per student than schools with district coordinators. However, schools with district coordinators paid media specialists higher salaries, had more AV items per student, had more clerical assistance, and used more adult volunteers than schools without district coordinators. Specifically:

    total materials expenditure per student in schools with coordinators averaged $8.80, and in schools without coordinators averaged $10.92;

    average books per student in schools with coordinators averaged 18, and in schools without coordinators averaged 20;

    number of AV items per student in schools with coordinators averaged 3.45, and in schools without coordinators averaged 3.03;

    media specialist salary in schools with coordinators averaged $20,699, and in schools without coordinators averaged $19,354;

    the number of clerical assistants and adult volunteers in schools with coordinators averaged .83 and 2.46, respectively, and in schools without coordinators averaged .77 and 1.85, respectively. **(056)**

Ibid. . . . *showed that* [in 1982-83] the average expenditure for microcomputer software reported by 81 elementary centers was $595; for 37 junior high/middle school centers was $322; for 46 senior high centers was $381; and for 5 combinations of the above schools was $523. **(056)**

Special

■ A 1976 survey of head law librarians in North American schools (sample size: 178; responding: 154 or 86.7%) *showed that* the modal numbers of volumes acquired per year by size of library were as follows:

    small (50,000 volumes or less) 0-5,000 vol./year
    medium (50,001-100,000)   0-5,000 vol./year
    med-large (100,001-200,000)   5,001-10,000 vol./year
    large (over 200,000)   10,000-15,000 vol./year **(357)**

■ A study reported in 1983 of 3 surveys made by the American Medical Association's Division of Library and Archival Services in 1969, 1973, and 1979 concerning the status of health sciences libraries in the U.S. (survey size for each survey ran between 12,000-14,000 health-related organizations, with a response rate for each survey around 95%) *showed that* between 1973 and 1979 the total number of bound volumes (monographs and serials combined) reported rose from 30,519,759 volumes in 1973 to 34,706,434 volumes in 1979, a 14% increase. Total current serial titles, however, decreased from 736,588 in 1973 to 732,408 in 1979, a 1% decrease. **(745)**

■ A study reported in 1983 of surveys of medical school libraries for the period 1960-61 through 1980-81, made by the American Medical Association, the Medical Library Association, the Association of Academic Health Sciences Library Directors, and the National Library of Medicine, *showed that* the average number of net volumes added to collections in the years 1974-75, 1979-80, and 1980-81 was "approximately 5,000" volumes (monographs and serial volumes bound) per library per year. Further, between 1965-66 and 1980-81 the average number of bound volumes increased by 90%. **(746)**

Ibid. . . . *showed that* the average number of serial titles increased by 10.8% in the 5-year period ending in 1969-70, by 14.8% in the 5-year period ending in 1974-75, and by 9.4% in the 5-year period ending in

1979-80. Overall, between 1965-66 and 1980-81 the average number of current serial titles increased from 1,698 titles to 1,415 titles (42%). **(746)**

Costs—Books

General

■ A study reported in 1974 of 3,347 biomedical book reviews (2,067 titles) taken from the 1970 issues of 54 English-language biomedical journals (excluding *Science* and *Nature*) that contained "bona fide" book reviews *showed that* the average price of a subsample (1,077 titles) of the books available in the U.S. was $16.20 per volume. Further, of 39 paperback books available in the U.S. (all the paperbacks in the sample available in the U.S.), the average price was $3.82 per volume. **(704)**

■ An annual study reported in 1982 of prices for legal publications *showed that* in 1980-81 prices for monographs increased 0.5% from the previous year, while prices for all categories of serials together increased 9.8% from the previous year. **(378)**

Ibid. . . . *showed that* between 1973-74 and 1980-81 the cost per average legal monograph title (based on over 2,400 titles published in each year) increased from $11.16 to $26.39, for an increase of 136.47%. **(378)**

Academic

■ An Indiana University survey for the National Science Foundation reported in 1979 *showed that* during the period 1969-76 large academic libraries increased the percentage of their budget spent on serials at the expense of monographs. In 1969 $2 was spent on serials for every $1 on monographs; by 1976 a steady decrease had reduced the ratio to $1.23 for serials for each $1 spent on monographs. **(016)**

■ A study reported in 1983 of surveys of medical school libraries for the period 1960-61 through 1980-81, made by the American Medical Association, the Medical Library Association, the Association of Academic Health Sciences Library Directors, and the National Library of Medicine, *showed that* during the 3-year period 1978-79 through 1980-81, on the basis of regular funds spent (excluding special contracts and grants), medical school libraries spent "more than three times as much on serials as they do on monographs." Even as expenditures increased during this period, the ratio remained constant. **(746)**

Public

■ A study reported in 1979 at the Oklahoma City/County Metropolitan Library System *showed that* for 18,996 adult hardback books and 19,126 adult paperback books purchased in FY 1976-77 the cost ratio, based on purchase price alone, of hardback to paperback was 4.1 to 1, while the cost per circulation (again based on purchase price only) of hardback to paperback was 4.2 to 1. For slightly more materials in FY 1977-78, the cost ratio of hardbound to paperback was 3.7 to 1, and the cost per circulation was 3.89 to 1. **(231)**

Ibid. . . . *showed that* for 5,624 juvenile hardback books and 6,031 paperback books purchased in FY 1976-77 the cost ratio, based on purchase price alone, of hardback to paperback was 5.9 to 1, while hardback to paperback was 2.7 to 1. For approximately the same number of materials purchased in FY 1977-78, the cost ratio of hardbound to paperback was 4.8 to 1, and the cost per circulation was 2.6 to 1. **(231)**

■ A 1982 survey of American and Canadian public libraries (sample size: 279; responding: 68 or 24%) *showed that* approximately 10.5% (±3.2%, representing a 95% confidence interval for the population at large) of respondents' current book acquisitions budgets had been allocated for the purchase of mass market paperbacks, while about 9.2% (±3.1%, representing a 95% confidence interval for the population at large) of their last year's book budget was spent on mass market paperbacks. There was a small statistical correlation ("y's = .26 and .30 respectively") between the book budget percentages and size of populations served, with the libraries serving larger populations tending to allocate more money for the purchase of paperbacks (significance level not given). **(273)**

School

■ A review of textbook costs during the period 1958-63 undertaken at the University of Illinois Research Center for the U.S. Office of Education in 1964 *showed that* during the 1958-63 period inflation increased by 7% but

Costs 97

textbook (elementary through college combined) prices increased by 15% from an average price of $2.60 each to $2.99 each. **(081)**

Special

■ A study reported in 1983 of surveys of medical school libraries for the period 1960-61 through 1980-81, made by the American Medical Association, the Medical Library Association, the Association of Academic Health Sciences Library Directors, and the National Library of Medicine, *showed that* during the 3-year period 1978-79 through 1980-81, on the basis of regular funds spent (excluding special contracts and grants), medical school libraries spent "more than three times as much on serials as they do on monographs." Even as expenditures increased during this period, the ratio remained constant. **(746)**

Costs—Government Documents

Academic

■ A 1977 survey of academic depository libraries (sample size: 200; responding: 160 or 80%) concerning the impact of commercially produced microforms *showed that* the top 3 reasons given by the 73 respondents who reported purchasing commercially produced government documents for selecting a particular publisher were (multiple responses allowed): cost (64 or 88%); format, i.e., fiche, card, or film (57 or 78%); and reputation of company (43 or 59%). **(318)**

■ A 1977-78 study at Duke University involving acquisition of state government documents (population: "approximately 2,000 items" ordered during an 18-month period; sample size: 591 items) *showed that* overall 88.7% of the state government document requests did not require payment. However, between April 1977 and April 1978 the average number of responses to requests for state government documents that required payment rose from "about 5%" to "about 12%." **(310)**

Ibid. . . . *showed that* 96.8% of the material ordered from LC cards was gratis; 92.2% of the material from the LC's *Monthly Checklist* was gratis; 89.4% of the material ordered from "other" sources was gratis; 88.7% of the material ordered from state checklists was gratis; and 73.3% of the material ordered from PAIS was gratis. (310)

Ibid. . . . *showed that* 85% of all requests for state government documents evoked a response within the first 5 weeks, after which "the response rate declined dramatically." (310)

Ibid. . . . *showed that* "about 75%" of the documents requested were serial publications and "about 25%" were monographs. The average response time was 4.3 weeks and ranged from a response rate of 15.2% for serials and 19.0% for monographs within 1 week through a response rate of 85.3% for serials and 83.9% for monographs within 5 weeks to a response rate of 92.7% for serials and 93.3% for monographs within 9 weeks. (310)

Costs—Maps

Academic

■ A survey reported in 1981 of 85 North American academic map libraries that have medium or large research collections (usable responses: 49 or 58%) *showed that* the prices for selected foreign topographic series sold by GeoCenter during the period 1970-80 rose by 245.7% for Latin American maps and by 277.4% for European maps. (216)

Costs—Out-of-Print Materials

General

■ A survey reported in 1973 of out-of-print dealers concerning common dealer practices and preferences (survey size: 54 dealers; responding: 22 or 40.7%) *showed that* (multiple responses allowed) the most commonly reported basis of assigning prices was book trade experience (reported by 19 or 86.4% respondents); "next in order" [no numbers given] were *Bookman's Price Index* and *American Book Prices Current.* Only 1 major retrospective guide to book prices was mentioned, Wright Howes's *U.S. iana* (reported by 50% of the respondents). **(601)**

Academic

■ A 1969 study at San Fernando Valley State College involving out-of-print acquisitions over a year's time *showed that*, of 17,689 titles ordered, 4,720 titles (27%) were received. Further, the average unit cost of in-print books (all subjects) for that year was $9.19, compared to the average unit cost of $10.18 for the 4,720 out-of-print books. **(593)**

■ A study at Indiana State University in 1971 comparing 2 methods of acquiring out-of-print books, using 168 titles divided into two equal groups, *showed that* a search of 98 out-of-print catalogs located 15 (18%) acceptable titles, compared to placing an ad in *Library Bookman*, which located 32 (38%) of the titles in that group. Further, if one was willing to pay 3 or more times the original publisher's price, then an additional 17 titles could be added to the success rate for the second method, making a total success rate for the second method of 59%. **(124)**

Ibid. . . . *showed that* the average price of books located through out-of-print catalogs was 1.56 times the original publisher's price, whereas the average price of books located through the *Library Bookman* ad was 1.78 times the original price. **(124)**

Costs—Per Capita

Academic

■ The annual survey of law school libraries and librarians conducted in 1980 by the American Bar Association, American Association of Law Libraries, and Association of American Law Schools (population not given; response: 168 libraries) *showed that* the median amount expended per FTE student for books was overall $317, while by size of library it was:

small (under 70,000 vols.)	$228
medium (70,000-99,999 vols.)	$344
medium-large (100,000-199,999 vols.)	$304
large (200,000+ vols.)	$317 **(382)**

Public

■ An attempt reported in 1982 to establish 4 input measures and 4 output measures for public libraries, based on published statistical reports for 301 New Jersey public libraries over a 6-year period (1974-79) and survey data for 96 public libraries in New Jersey, *showed that* (per capita based on number of residents in the library's service area):

INPUT MEASURES

The proportion of budget spent on materials averaged 19.9%, with a standard deviation of .081 (based on 301 libraries).

The new volumes per capita averaged .181, with a standard deviation of .097 (based on 301 libraries).

The periodical titles per capita averaged .0094, with a standard deviation of .0054 (based on 301 libraries).

The circulation per volume averaged 1.79, with a standard deviation of .77 (based on 301 libraries).

OUTPUT MEASURES

The circulation per capita averaged 5.04, with a standard deviation of 3.07 (based on 301 libraries).

The patron visits per capita averaged 2.82, with a standard deviation of 1.82 (based on 96 libraries).

The reference questions per capita averaged 1.12, with a standard deviation of .79 (based on 96 libraries).

The in-library uses of materials per capita averaged 2.29, with a standard deviation of 2.02 (based on 96 libraries). **(576)**

School

■ A 1983 survey of a systematic sample of school library media centers concerning data for fiscal year 1982-83 (survey size: 2,000 centers; responding: 1,297; usable: 1,251 or 62%) *showed that* a comparison of schools with (666 schools) and without (597 schools) district-level library media coordinators revealed that schools without district coordinators spent more money per student on resources and had more books per student than schools with district coordinators. However, schools with district coordinators paid media specialists higher salaries, had more AV items per student, had more clerical assistance, and used more adult volunteers than schools without district coordinators. Specifically:

total materials expenditure per student in schools with

Costs

coordinators averaged $8.80, and in schools without coordinators averaged $10.92;

average books per student in schools with coordinators averaged 18, and in schools without coordinators averaged 20;

number of AV items per student in schools with coordinators averaged 3.45, and in schools without coordinators averaged 3.03;

media specialist salary in schools with coordinators averaged $20,699, and in schools without coordinators averaged $19,354;

the number of clerical assistants and adult volunteers in schools with coordinators averaged .83 and 2.46, respectively, and in schools without coordinators averaged .77 and 1.85, respectively. **(056)**

Ibid. . . . *showed that* [in 1982-83] the average expenditure for microcomputer software reported by 81 elementary centers was $595; for 37 junior high/middle school centers was $322; for 46 senior high centers was $381; and for 5 combinations of the above schools was $523. **(056)**

Special

■ The annual survey of law school libraries and librarians conducted in 1980 by the American Bar Association, American Association of Law Libraries, and Association of American Law Schools (population not given; response: 168 libraries) *showed that* the median amount expended per FTE student for books was overall $317, while by size of library it was:

small (under 70,000 vols.)	$228
medium (70,000-99,999 vols.)	$344
medium-large (100,000-199,999 vols.)	$304
large (200,000+ vols.)	$317

(382)

Costs—Periodicals, Dual Pricing

General

■ A study reported in 1977 of a 10-year run (1966-75) of 200 U.S. journal titles, selected at random from 10 well-known Wilson indexes, *showed that* the number of periodical titles with a dual price structure (individual subscription rate different from institutional subscription rate) rose from 4% of the titles in 1966 to 15% of the titles in 1975. (With a 95% confidence level, the 1975 number ranged between 9.8% and 20.2% of the titles.) Further, the percentage of titles with dual pricing increased most sharply in 1968-70, in 1971-72, and again in 1973-74. **(458)**

Ibid. . . . *showed that* dual pricing began at least as early as 1956, when the *Philosophical Review* instituted a differential subscription rate ($3.00 for individuals; $6.00 for institutions). **(458)**

Ibid. . . . *showed that*, while the difference between the average institutional subscription rate and the average individual subscription rate was not great for the sample as a whole, for the 27 journals with dual pricing the difference between individual and institutional subscription rates was considerable by 1975—"almost 7 dollars" per title. **(458)**

Academic

■ A study reported in 1980 of core health science journals ("500 Key Titles" prepared by Felter in 1973 and updated by Brown and Moore in 1978) and the journal holdings of 3 university medical center libraries (State University of New York at Buffalo Health Sciences Library, Cleveland Health Sciences Library-Health Center Library, and Northeastern Ohio Universities College of Medicine Basic Medical Sciences Library) *showed that* of the 500 core journals 61 (12.2%) had a dual pricing structure, i.e., individual and institutional subscribers were charged different rates. **(732)**

Ibid. . . . *showed that*, of a total of 281 health science journals identified as having a dual pricing structure, the average individual subscription rate (of the 264 titles for which the rates were known) was $30.61, while the average institutional subscription rate was $63.90 or 102.14% higher.
(732)

■ A study reported in 1983 of 76 academic journals related to economics and business *showed that* 59% charge libraries higher subscription rates than they charge individuals. In more detail, of 30 journals published by professional associations, 47% have a differential subscription price; of 26 journals published by universities, 58% have a differential subscription price; and of 20 journals published by private publishers, 80% have a differential subscription price. **(271)**

Costs

Ibid. . . . *showed that* the 14 journals with differential subscription rates published by a professional association averaged $19.18 for an individual subscription compared to an average library price of $36.96; for 15 such journals published by universities the average individual price was $13.27 compared to an average library price of $20.73; and for 16 such journals published by private publishers the individual price averaged $20.22 compared to an average library price of $45.30. The average subscription cost for 16 journals without differential rates published by a professional association averaged $23.50; for 11 such journals published by universities the price averaged $10.36; and for 4 such journals published by private publishers the price averaged $29.78. **(271)**

Special

■ A study reported in 1980 of core health science journals ("500 Key Titles" prepared by Felter in 1973 and updated by Brown and Moore in 1978) and the journal holdings of 3 university medical center libraries (State University of New York at Buffalo Health Sciences Library, Cleveland Health Sciences Library-Health Center Library, and Northeastern Ohio Universities College of Medicine Basic Medical Sciences Library) *showed that* of the 500 core journals 61 (12.2%) had a dual pricing structure, i.e., individual and institutional subscribers were charged different rates. **(732)**

Ibid. . . . *showed that*, of a total of 281 health science journals identified as having a dual pricing structure, the average individual subscription rate (of the 264 titles for which the rates were known) was $30.61, while the average institutional subscription rate was $63.90 or 102.14% higher. **(732)**

Costs—Periodicals, Subscription Increases

General

■ An annual study reported in 1982 of prices for legal publications *showed that* in 1980-81 prices for monographs increased 0.5% from the previous year, while prices for all categories of serials together increased 9.8% from the previous year. **(378)**

Ibid. . . . *showed that* between 1973-74 and 1980-81 the cost per average legal serial title (based on over 700 serial titles published in each year), including periodicals, commercially published court reporters, looseleaf services, and legal continuations, increased from $50.08 to $106.44 for an increase of 112.54%. **(378)**

Ibid. . . . *showed that* between 1973-74 and 1980-81 the cost per average legal periodical (based on over 340 periodical titles published in each of the years) rose from $11.95 to $21.07 for an increase of 76.32%. **(378)**

Ibid. . . . *showed that* between 1973-74 and 1980-81 the cost per average legal looseleaf service title (based on 92 looseleaf service titles in each of the years) rose from $181.80 to $374.65 for an increase of 106.08%.
(378)

Ibid. . . . *showed that* between 1973-74 and 1980-81 the cost per average commercially published court reporter (based on at least 14 such reporters in each of the years) rose from $173.63 to $326.19 for an increase of 87.86%. **(378)**

Ibid. . . . *showed that* between 1973-74 and 1980-81 the cost per average legal continuation (based on 260 or more continuation titles for each of the years) rose from $44.07 to $130.32 for an increase of 195.71%. **(378)**

■ A study reported in 1983 of subscription costs for 100 serial titles (50 U.S./Canadian titles; 25 non-U.S./non-Canadian titles; and 25 reference services) over a 7-year period (1975-81) *showed that*:

> the average price increase of the U.S./Canadian titles was 84.7%, with 4 titles (8%) maintaining their prices and 18 titles (36%) showing an increase of 100% or more;
>
> the average price increase of the non-U.S./non-Canadian titles was 121.44%, with no titles maintaining their price and 14 titles (56%) showing increases of 100% or more;
>
> the average price increase of the reference services was 67.6%, with 2 of the titles (8%) maintaining their prices and 6 titles (24%) showing increases of 100% or more. **(441)**

Ibid. . . . *showed that* the overall average price increase was 76.2%, which compared to the Consumer Price Index increase for the same period of 69% in the U.S. and 71% in Canada. **(441)**

Academic

■ A study reported in 1972 of price and page increases for 20 physics journals between 1959 and 1969 *showed that* the average overall price increase was 202%, with an overall average increase in the number of

Costs

pages in these journals of 147%. Subtracting out the percent of page increase, the price increase falls to 55% for this 10-year period. **(399)**

Ibid. . . . *showed that* during this period the number of issues increased from 264 to 481, an increase of 82%. **(399)**

Ibid. . . . *showed that* the average page and price increase during this period by publishing group was as follows:

> for the 8 American Institute of Physics journals the page increase was 161% with a price increase of 157%, for a net price increase of −4%;

> for the 6 commercially published journals the page increase was 171% with a price increase of 283%, for a net price increase of 112%;

> and for 6 other society or nonprofit journals the page increase was 72% with a price increase of 189%, for a net price increase of 117%. **(399)**

■ A study reported in 1975 comparing book price increases reported in the *Bowker Annual of Library and Book Trade Information* with actual price increases encountered on English-language material acquired through approval plans at 3 universities (University of Nebraska, years 1966-67 and 1967-68; Florida Atlantic University, 1969-70 and 1970-71; and Arizona State University, 1971-72) during the period 1967-72 *showed that* Bowker indicated a 48.1% increase, while the libraries showed an 18.5% increase for this period. **(630)**

■ An Indiana University survey for the National Science Foundation reported in 1979 *showed that* library administrators in major academic libraries responded to shortages in the library materials serials budget primarily by canceling duplicates and shifting funds from monographic to serials accounts. The third most common tactic was to halt new subscriptions in order to renew old ones. **(016)**

Ibid. . . . *showed that* during the period 1969-76 large academic libraries increased the percentage of their budget spent on serials at the expense of monographs. In 1969 $2 was spent on serials for every $1 on monographs; by 1976 a steady decrease had reduced the ratio to $1.23 for serials for each $1 spent on monographs. **(016)**

■ A study reported in 1980 at the University of Rochester comparing costs of 1-year versus 3-year journal subscriptions based on a sample of 20 business administration and management science periodicals, *showed that* when 4 variables were considered (cost of capital, reorder costs, average inflation rate for 1-year subscriptions and ratio of 3-year to 1-year subscription costs), the 3-year subscription period was always the most advantageous in terms of cost. Specifically, the least projected savings for the 20 periodicals was 12%, while the most in projected savings which could be realized was 106%. The savings was due to locking in advantageous subscription rates for a 3-year period and to reduced staff costs caused by reduced renewal activity. **(627)**

■ A study reported in 1981 of the annual price indexes and average prices of academic periodicals reported in *Library Journal* for the 12-year period 1967-79 *showed that* the overall price increase of periodicals for this period was 250.7%. This compares to a price increase of 89.7% for the previous 12-year period, 1957-69. **(272)**

Ibid. . . . *showed that*, even if periodical budgets increased at the same rate as overall inflation as measured by the Consumer Price Index for the 1967-79 period, the overall periodical purchasing power of those budgets would have declined from 100% in 1967-69 (base years) to 62% in 1979.
(272)

Ibid. . . . *showed that*, even if periodical budgets increased at the same rate as overall inflation as measured by the Consumer Price Index for the 1967-79 period, the periodical purchasing power declined differentially by subject area from 100% in 1967-69 (base years) to the following figures in 1979: law (90%), history (89%), general interest (86%), literature and language (84%), zoology (72%), agriculture (72%), medicine (66%), library science (65%), chemistry and physics (45%), and labor/industrial relations (41%). **(272)**

Ibid. . . . *showed that*, if a library had the same acquisitions budget in 1979 that it had in 1967, it would be able to purchase overall only 29% of the periodicals in 1979 it could have purchased in 1967. **(272)**

■ A study reported in 1983 at Harvard University updating an earlier study and comparing the average periodical prices of the Widener price index (based on humanities and social science periodicals published in the U.S., France, Germany, Great Britain, and Italy) with the average periodical prices in comparable sections of 2 published indexes (an

Costs

international index compiled by John B. Merriam of Blackwell and published in the *Library Association Record*; and a domestic index compiled by Norman Brown and Jane Phillips and published in the *Library Journal*) *showed that*, while the average prices for all 3 indexes were quite different during the 12-year period 1970-82, the Widener index was nevertheless highly correlated with the 2 published indexes, so that the published indexes were effective tools to predict average periodical prices for the Widener humanities and social science collection. Specifically, in 1970 the average Widener periodical cost $9.45, the average Blackwell periodical cost $12.96, and the average LJ periodical cost $10.41; by 1982 these costs were $38.11, $46.58, and $44.80, respectively. On the other hand, the Widener and the Blackwell average periodical prices for the same 12-year period had a correlation coefficient of $r = .9971$, while the Widener and the LJ average periodical prices had a correlation coefficient of $r = .9662$ (Widener index for U.S. periodicals only had a correlation coefficient with LJ periodicals of $r = .9938$). **(777)**

Ibid. . . . *showed that* using the Blackwell published data to predict changes in the Widener index (based on at least 9 years of Widener average periodical data to establish the regression line) enabled Harvard to predict humanities and social science average periodical prices within at least 1.4% each year over a 4-year period. Over the 4-year period, the cumulative error in prediction was 1%. **(777)**

Special

■ A study reported in 1980 comparing the subscription rates as reported in *Ulrich's International Periodicals Directory* for 135 journals on the 1977 Brandon list (for the small hospital library) for the years 1958, 1963, 1968, 1973, and 1978 *showed that* the average cost per journal increased from $11.38 in 1958 to $36.16 in 1978. This represented a cost increase of 218% compared to a cost increase of 126% for the Consumer Price Index for the same period. **(729)**

Ibid. . . . *showed that*, for the 5 5-year periods, the lowest rate of increase was during the period 1958-63 (9% increase), while the highest rate of increase was during the 1973-78 period (56% increase). In all 5 periods the rate of journal increase exceeded the Consumer Price Index increase. **(729)**

Ibid. . . . *showed that*, without adjusting the increase in journal costs for inflation, 1978 dollars would only have bought 31% of the journal subscriptions they would have bought in 1958. If adjustments for inflation were made (using the Consumer Price Index), the 1978 dollars would still only have bought 70% of the journal subscriptions they would have bought in 1958. **(729)**

Ibid. . . . *showed that* the rate of increase in journal costs for the 135 journals on the 1977 Brandon list, while large, was nevertheless substantially lower than the increases generally for U.S. periodicals or generally for medical periodicals. For example, based on the Brown annual price surveys in *Library Journal* for the period 1968-78, the cost increases for the various groups of journals during this period can be shown as follows:

> for the 135 Brandon list journals, the 1968 dollars would have purchased only 46% of the 1978 journal subscriptions;

> for medical periodicals on the Brown list, the 1968 dollars would have purchased only 34% of the 1978 journal subscriptions;

> for U.S. periodicals on the Brown list, the 1968 dollars would have purchased only 31% of the 1978 journal subscriptions.

All of these drops in purchasing power were greater than the general rate of inflation for this period as measured by the Consumer Price Index. The CPI dollar dropped to 53% of its 1968 value by 1978. **(729)**

■ A study reported in 1983 concerning inflation of medical journal prices and based on prices of 111 journals listed on the 1983 Brandon list *showed that* the average costs of these journals at 5-year intervals between 1963 and 1983 were as follows:

> 1963 $11.81 average journal cost
> 1968 $14.00 average journal cost
> 1973 $21.16 average journal cost
> 1978 $33.35 average journal cost
> 1983 $59.67 average journal cost **(749)**

Ibid. . . . *showed that*, for the 20-year period, not only did the cost of the average journal subscription increase but that the rate of increase increased as well. Further, the increase in the average journal subscription was always greater than the increase in the Consumer Price Index. For example, the percentage increase in journal costs and in the Consumer Price Index by 5-year intervals for the period 1963-83 was as follows:

> 1963-68 19% journal/12% CPI increase
> 1968-73 51% journal/28% CPI increase

Costs

> 1973-78   58% journal/47% CPI increase
> 1978-83   79% journal/50% CPI increase

Further, for the overall period 1963-83, the journals increased a total of 405% while the Consumer Price Index increased a total of 219%. **(749)**

Ibid. . . . *showed that* during the period 1963-83 a journal budget that increased at the same rate as the Consumer Price Index would by 1983 only purchase 65% of the journal titles it could purchase in 1963. **(749)**

Ibid. . . . *showed that* a comparison of price increases for Brandon list journals, compared to price increases for medical journals and overall U.S. periodicals listed by Brown in *Library Journal*, indicated that, during each of the 3 5-year periods between 1968-83, the increases for overall U.S. periodicals and for medical journals were almost always larger than for the Brandon journals. For example:

> in 1968-73 U.S. periodicals increased 87%, medical periodicals increased by 73%, and the Brandon list journals increased by 51%;

> in 1973-78 U.S. periodicals and medical periodicals both increased by 70%, while Brandon list journals increased by 58%;

> in 1978-83 (data for U.S. periodicals and medical periodicals based on 1982 data) U.S. periodicals increased 63%, medical periodicals increased by 80%, and Brandon list journals increased by 79%. **(749)**

Costs—Vendor Discounts

Public

■ A 1979 study of vendor performance (Baker & Taylor, Brodart) over a 5-month period in 8 small- to medium-sized public libraries and 1 regional resource center on Maryland's eastern shore *showed that* the average discounts received from each vendor were as follows)

TYPE OF BOOK	BAKER & TAYLOR	BRODART
adult fiction	38.91%	37.6%
adult nonfiction	36.1%	33.2%

continued

TYPE OF BOOK   BAKER & TAYLOR   BRODART
juvenile discounts   28.15%   20.4%
paperbacks   37.5%   32.7%   **(385)**

Duplication of Copies

Academic

■ A 1968 survey of all law schools approved by the American Bar Association (population: 138; responding: 129 or 93.5%) *showed that* the average number of copies of all current state reports available ran from 0.1 copies for schools with student bodies under 200 to 1.1 copies for schools with student bodies of 800 or more, while the number of copies of home state reports had no relation to size of student body, with the smallest schools reporting 6.0 copies, the largest schools reporting 5.0 copies, and the medium-sized schools (500-599 students) reporting 10.5 copies.
(376)

Ibid. . . . *showed that* the combined average number of copies of U.S. Supreme Court reporters (including Supreme Court edition, U.S. edition, and Lawyers' edition) ranged from 3.8 copies for law schools with student bodies under 200 to 11.6 copies for law schools with student bodies of 800 or more. **(376)**

■ An international survey reported in 1972 of university librarians worldwide (sample size: 2,612; responding: 522) *showed that* purchase of multiple copies of a work was reported to be "always" or "often" the practice by 6% of the North American respondents and 12% of the respondents of the rest of the world when the work was a reference book; by 7% of the North American respondents and 14% of the rest of the world when the work was a monograph; by 6% of the North American respondents and 67% of the rest of the world when the work was a student text; and by 7% of the North American respondents and 9% of the rest of the world when the work was some other kind of book. **(320)**

Ibid. . . . *showed that* 1% of the North American respondents would purchase extra copies of a work in microfilm format rather than traditional book format if the price were 15% more, 8% would purchase the extra microfilm copies if the price were the same, and 25% would purchase the extra microfilm copies if the price were reduced by 15%; while for the rest

Duplication of Copies

of the world 2% of the respondents would purchase the extra microfilm copies rather than the traditional book format if they cost 15% more, 4% would purchase extra microfilm copies if they were the same price, and 16% would purchase extra microfilm copies if they were 15% cheaper.

(320)

■ A review in 1974-75 of faculty book requests in the Economics and Political Science Library of Indiana University *showed that* 24% of the books immediately available had multiple copies, while only 15.8% of those not immediately available had more than one copy. **(012)**

■ A 1980 survey of law school libraries with collections in excess of 175,000 volumes (sample size: 50; responding: 37 or 70%) *showed that* the degree to which periodical titles were duplicated in hard copy (rather than microform) in responding libraries was as follows:

less than 5% duplication	4 libraries
5-10% duplication	4 libraries
11-19% duplication	4 libraries
20-30% duplication	9 libraries
40-50% duplication	2 libraries
60% duplication	4 libraries
no answer	10 libraries	**(369)**

Ibid. . . . *showed that* the numbers of periodicals reported by respondents were as follows:

less than 500 periodicals	1 library
500-600 periodicals	2 libraries
700-900 periodicals	6 libraries
1,000-1,200 periodicals	4 libraries
1,300-1,500 periodicals	3 libraries
over 1,600 periodicals	4 libraries
no answer	17 libraries	**(369)**

Special

■ A 1968 survey of all law schools approved by the American Bar Association (population: 138; responding: 129 or 93.5%) *showed that* the average number of copies of all current state reports available ran from 0.1

copies for schools with student bodies under 200 to 1.1 copies for schools with student bodies of 800 or more, while the number of copies of home state reports had no relation to size of student body, with the smallest schools reporting 6.0 copies, the largest schools reporting 5.0 copies, and the medium-sized schools (500-599 students) reporting 10.5 copies.

(376)

Ibid. . . . *showed that* the combined average number of copies of U.S. Supreme Court reporters (including Supreme Court edition, U.S. edition, and Lawyers' edition) ranged from 3.8 copies for law schools with student bodies under 200 to 11.6 copies for law schools with student bodies of 800 or more. (376)

■ A 1972 survey of the 45 law libraries participating in the union list of foreign legal periodicals *showed that* only 4 titles from the *Index to Foreign Legal Periodicals* were common to all 45 libraries:

American Journal of Comparative Law
American Journal of International Law
International and Comparative Law Quarterly
International Lawyer (391)

■ A 1980 survey of law school libraries with collections in excess of 175,000 volumes (sample size: 50; responding: 37 or 70%) *showed that* the degree to which periodical titles were duplicated in hard copy (rather than microform) in responding libraries was as follows:

less than 5% duplication	4 libraries
5-10% duplication	4 libraries
11-19% duplication	4 libraries
20-30% duplication	9 libraries
40-50% duplication	2 libraries
60% duplication	4 libraries
no answer	10 libraries

(369)

Ibid. . . . *showed that* the numbers of periodicals reported by respondents were as follows:

less than 500 periodicals	1 library
500-600 periodicals	2 libraries
700-900 periodicals	6 libraries
1,000-1,200 periodicals	4 libraries
1,300-1,500 periodicals	3 libraries

continued

over 1,600 periodicals	4 libraries	
no answer	17 libraries	**(369)**

Estimating Size

Academic

■ A 1981 study in the science section of the University of Guelph Library (Canada) of the amount of shelf space an average item required, based on sampling "several thousand items in the monograph and serials collection," *showed that* an average size of 1.13 linear inches per monograph volume and 2.18 linear inches per periodical volume was required. **(531)**

Foreign Languages—General Issues

Public

■ A 1969 survey of Canadian public libraries serving populations of more than 10,000 people as well as all county and regional libraries belonging to the Canadian Library Association concerning holdings and use of non-English collections (survey size: 203; responding: 83 or 41%) *showed that* the demand for non-English material did not come from predominately French-speaking Canadians. Specifically, 37 (44%) of the libraries reported that their non-English material was primarily used by new Canadians, while only 19 (23%) libraries reported that their non-English material was used primarily by native Canadians. **(534)**

Ibid. . . . *showed that*, of 73 respondents, 31 (42.5%) reported non-English language collections of more than 500 volumes. **(534)**

Ibid. . . . *showed that*, of 81 respondents, 21 (25.9%) libraries reported they did not buy books in non-English languages. Further, of 78 respondents, 22 (28.2%) reported they did not borrow books in other languages. **(534)**

Foreign Languages—Patron Skills and Attitudes

Academic

■ A survey reported in 1979 of a large plant pathology department at the University of Minnesota concerning language skills (sample size: 100; responding: 43 or 42%) *showed that* only 27% of the respondents reported reading or speaking proficiency in any one foreign language. 39.5% reported proficiency in German; 25.5% reported proficiency in French; 18.6% reported proficiency in Spanish; and 6.2% reported proficiency in Russian. **(426)**

Ibid. . . . *showed that*, although *Translations Register Index* and *World Transindex* were readily available in the library, only 7% of the respondents were familiar with either index. **(426)**

■ A survey reported in 1981 of historians listed in the 1978 *Directory of American Scholars* concerning their use of and attitudes toward periodicals (survey size: 767 historians, although not all questionnaires could be delivered; responding: 360 or 46.9% with respondents tending to be younger and with a higher scholarly productivity record than nonrespondents) *showed that* 58% of the respondents "do not attempt to keep up with research published in foreign languages." Further, when asked if they felt their research was restricted in any way because of a language problem, 334 respondents reported as follows:

no restriction	138 (41.3%)	respondents
slight restriction	136 (40.7%)	respondents
moderate restriction	42 (12.6%)	respondents
substantial restriction	18 (5.4%)	respondents

Finally, when encountering a reference in a foreign language they did not read, respondents reported the following responses:

try to get article translated	30.3%	respondents
search for summary or abstract	21.7%	respondents
try to get gist on own	34.7%	respondents
ignore	13.3%	respondents **(780)**

Gift and Exchange Programs

General

■ A 1973 survey of all Duplicates Exchange Union (formerly Periodicals Exchange Union) members (survey size: 399 libraries; responding: 229 or 58%) *showed that*, of 228 respondents, 205 (89.5%) were college libraries; 15 (6.6%) were special libraries including hospital, art museum, and company libraries; and 8 (3.5%) were public libraries. **(635)**

Ibid. . . . *showed that* most of the Duplicates Exchange Union libraries were small. For example, the "approximate number of [periodical] subscriptions" per library was distributed as follows:

1-300 subscriptions	42 (18.3%)	libraries
301-600 subscriptions	78 (34.1%)	libraries
601-1,000 subscriptions	52 (22.7%)	libraries
over 1,000 subscriptions	45 (19.6%)	libraries
no response	12 (5.3%)	libraries

(635)

Ibid. . . . *showed that* respondents' estimates of the percentage of exchange lists received that proved useful were as follows (only 10 categories of usefulness were reported, e.g., 10%, 20%, etc., nothing in between):

30% or less of the lists received were useful to 65 (28.4%) of the respondents;

40-50% of the lists received were useful to 42 (18.3%) of the respondents;

60-80% of the lists received were useful to 66 (28.8%) of the respondents;

90% or more of the lists received were useful to 51 (22.2%) of the respondents

(5 or 2.3% of the respondents did not reply to this particular question). **(635)**

Ibid. . . . *showed that* the average number of items requested from a list was as follows: 22.7% of the libraries requested 4 or fewer items; 48.5% requested 8 or fewer items; and 70.8% requested 12 or fewer items. Further, 61.6% of the libraries estimated they received less than 30% of the items requested, while 87.4% estimated they received less than 50% of the items requested. **(635)**

Ibid. . . . *showed that*, although 24 (10.5%) libraries reported that use of the Duplicates Exchange Union resulted in a financial loss, most libraries considered it useful. Specifically, the libraries reported as follows:

very useful	98 (42.8%) libraries
useful	93 (40.6%) libraries
of some use	35 (15.3%) libraries
useless	3 (1.3%) libraries

(635)

Ibid. . . . *showed that* generally libraries supported the idea of continuing to include books and documents in the exchange program. Of 221 respondents, 160 (69.9%) favored the idea, while 61 (26.6%) did not.
(635)

Academic

■ A survey in 1979 of 119 major academic business libraries (89 responding or 75%, with 86 usable responses) *showed that*, of the 28 major academic business libraries collecting working papers, the selection criteria used were reputation of institution (20 libraries), faculty/patron request (18), available as gift (17), available through exchange (9), and reputation of the author (7). **(120)**

■ A survey reported in 1981 of a select group of American academic and research libraries known for their third world collections (45 libraries surveyed; 26 responding) *showed that* 35% of the responding libraries felt that most of the third world publications were only available through gift and exchange, while an additional 65% felt that some of the third world publications were only available through gift and exchange. 70% of responding libraries said that gift and exchange material was crucial to their collections. **(037)**

Gifts

Academic

■ A survey in 1979 of 119 major academic business libraries (89 responding or 75%, with 86 usable responses) *showed that*, of the 28 major academic business libraries collecting working papers, the selection criteria

Gifts

used were reputation of institution (20 libraries), faculty/patron request (18), available as gift (17), available through exchange (9), and reputation of the author (7). **(120)**

■ A study reported in 1981 at DePauw University of circulation patterns over a 5-year period (1973-77) for a group of newly acquired monographs (sample size: 1,904 books) *showed that* there was a statistically significant difference in the circulation rates of gift books and those books purchased on the recommendation of classroom instructors or librarians, with the gift books circulating less than the purchased books (significant at the .01 level). For example, of 189 gift books, 121 (64.0%) did not circulate at all [during the 5-year period]; while of 1,715 purchased books, 581 (33.8%) did not circulate at all [during the 5-year period]. **(573)**

■ A 1982 study at the University of Wisconsin, Milwaukee, concerning the use of gift books in 2 separate parts of the collection, both the PS 3537-PS 3545 section (American literature, 1,039 nongift books and 104 gift books) and the QC 6-QC 75 section (physics, 1,023 nongifts and 16 gift books) *showed that* the average use of gift books was considerably lower than the use of nongift books. Specifically, nongift books in the PS section averaged 5.30 uses since added to the collection, while gift books averaged 1.23 uses; nongift books in the QC section averaged 5.31 uses since added to the collection, while gift books averaged 2.25 uses. **(807)**

Ibid. . . . *showed that* a higher percentage of gift books than nongift books did not circulate at all and that of the books that circulated at least once gift books circulated much less on the average than nongift books. Specifically, in the PS section 343 (33.0%) of the nongift books did not circulate compared to 59 (56.7%) of the gift books, while in the QC section 272 (26.6%) of the nongift books did not circulate compared to 6 (60.0%) of the gift books. Further, of the books that did circulate, the average number of uses for PS nongifts was 7.92 since added to the collection compared to 2.84 uses for gifts, while the average number of uses for QC nongifts was 7.23 since added to the collection compared to 3.60 uses for gifts. **(807)**

Ibid. . . . *showed that* the use of gift books followed a Bradford-like distribution. For example, in the PS section, the 14 (13.5%) most frequently used books accounted for 80 (62.5%) of the uses. **(807)**

Ibid. . . . *showed that* gift books tended to be older than nongift books. For example, in the PS section 375 (36.1%) of the nongift books had been published after 1970 compared to 11 (10.6%) of the gift books; in the QC section 380 (37.1%) of the nongift books had been published after 1970 compared to 2 (12.5%) of the gift books. **(807)**

Ibid. . . . *showed that* gift books tended to be old when given to the library. For example, in the PS section 68 (65.4%) of the gift books were over 20 years old when given to the library, while of the PS and QC sections combined, 105 (87.5%) of the gifts were over 10 years old when given to the library. **(807)**

Holdings—General Issues

General

■ A survey published in 1966 of first-edition Polish publications (excluding children's literature, music, textbooks, translations, and reprints) published between April 15, 1957, and August 17, 1957 (882 titles) and shown to be available in U.S. libraries through the NUC 1958-62 *showed that* 332 (37.5%) of the 882 titles were available in U.S. libraries. Due to duplication the 332 titles are represented by 557 volumes. **(664)**

Ibid. . . . *showed that* 320 volumes were in the area of the humanities (and distributed in 23 libraries), 167 volumes in social sciences (19 libraries), 23 volumes in pure sciences (9 libraries), and 44 volumes in applied sciences (6 libraries). **(664)**

■ An analysis reported in 1974 of geographic centers in the U.S. of no more than a 50-mile radius that contained library holdings of 500,000 volumes or more *showed that* there was an increase in such centers from 77 in 1935 to 109 in 1955 to 265 in 1973. The number of volumes in these centers has increased from 138,867,606 in 1935 to 289,355,391 in 1955 to 724,945,043 in 1973. **(094)**

Ibid. . . . *showed that* California had the most such centers (21), followed by Ohio (18), New York and Texas (14 each), and Illinois (11), although the top 5 centers in terms of total volumes held were New York City (47,305,190), Washington, D.C. (39,728,774), Boston (30,467,291), Los Angeles (24,455,236), and Chicago (22,414,327). **(094)**

■ A study reported in 1978 of the 8th (1967) and 9th (1976) editions of *Guide to Reference Books showed that* the number of Canadian reference

Holdings 119

works had increased from a total of 113 to a total of 196 for an increase of 73.5%. **(550)**

■ A study reported in 1983 of 3 surveys made by the American Medical Association's Division of Library and Archival Services in 1969, 1973, and 1979 concerning the status of health sciences libraries in the U.S. (survey size for each survey ran between 12,000-14,000 health-related organizations with a response rate for each survey around 95%) *showed that*, during the period 1969-79, hospital health science libraries increased the average number of current serial titles received by 13% (from 115 titles per library on average to 130 titles per library on average). **(747)**

Academic

■ A survey reported in 1977 of moderate-sized (120,000-500,000 volumes) U.S. academic libraries listed in the 1972-73 *American Library Directory* (survey size: 200; responding: 147 or 74%) *showed that* these libraries had a median of 37,000 bound periodical volumes and a median of 2,181 periodical subscriptions. **(454)**

Ibid. . . . *showed that* 128 (87%) libraries reported subscribing to some periodical titles in microform instead of binding. Further, 53% of responding libraries reported 25 or fewer microform subscriptions, while 21% reported 100+ microform subscriptions. **(454)**

■ A study of 1977 survey information gathered by the National Center for Educational Statistics (U.S. Office of Education) concerning the degree to which 1,146 college and university libraries (Liberal Arts Colleges I and II; Comprehensive Universitites and Colleges I and II) met the 1975 Standards for College Libraries (ACRL), *showed that* the majority did not meet the minimum collection size for monographs. Although the standard for each library must be computed for each institutional situation, a collection size of at least 100,000 volumes is almost always required. Specifically, 43% had monograph collections under 100,000 volumes; 34% had collections 100,000-199,999 volumes; 13% had collections 200,000-299,999 volumes; and 10% had collections of 300,000 volumes or more. The average number of volumes was 151,700, volumes and the median was 112,800 volumes. **(486)**

Ibid. . . . *showed that* 27% of the libraries had less than 1,000 monograph volumes per faculty member; 50% had 1,000-1,999 volumes per faculty member; 17% had 2,000-2,999 volumes per faculty member; and 5% had

3,000 volumes or more per faculty member. The average number of volumes per faculty member was 1,670, while the median number of volumes per faculty member was 1,410. **(486)**

Ibid. . . . *showed that* the average number of monographic volumes per FTE student was 85, while the median number of monographic volumes per FTE student was 63. **(486)**

Ibid. . . . *showed that* 28% of the libraries received less than 500 periodical subscriptions; 22% received 500-749 periodical subscriptions; 27% received 750-1,499 periodical subscriptions; and 23% received 1,500 or more periodical subscriptions. The average number of periodical subscriptions was 1,170, while the median number of periodical subscriptions was 755. **(486)**

Ibid. . . . *showed that* 63% of the libraries did not meet the minimum standards for annual new monographic acquisitions in that the number of new books added annually to the collection was less than 5% of the collection. However, the average number of new annual acquisitions based on collection size was 5.3%, while the median number of new annual acquisitions based on collection size was 4.3%. Further, the average number of actual volumes added was 7,490, while the median was 4,770 volumes. **(486)**

■ A survey reported in 1978 of 31 Ph.D. dissertations in the field of business/management (13 from the State University of New York at Buffalo and 18 from SUNYAB incoming faculty but completed at other schools) *showed that* overall SUNYAB owned 85.7% of the cited materials, with ownership of 95.8% of the periodicals cited, 89.3% of the monographs cited, 81.2% of the serials cited, and 26.2% of the miscellaneous materials cited. Further, SUNYAB owned 88.2% of the materials cited in SUNYAB dissertations and 83.9% of the materials cited for non-SUNYAB dissertations. **(461)**

■ A 1979 survey of libraries in accredited North American veterinary schools (population: 25 libraries; responding: 23 or 92%) *showed that*, of the 18 separately housed veterinary libraries, the number of serials received ranged from a low of 193 at Tuskegee to a high of 1,105 at Cornell. The average number of serials received was 624. The number of bound serial volumes ranged from 2,844 volumes at Mississippi State University to 66,000 volumes at Cornell. The average number of bound volumes held was 26,274. **(740)**

Holdings

Ibid. . . . *showed that* 11 (47.8%) respondents reported no AV holdings other than microforms. **(740)**

■ A 1980 survey of law school libraries with collections in excess of 175,000 volumes (sample size: 50; responding: 37 or 70%) *showed that* the numbers of periodicals reported by respondents were as follows:

less than 500 periodicals	1 library
500-600 periodicals	2 libraries
700-900 periodicals	6 libraries
1,000-1,200 periodicals	4 libraries
1,300-1,500 periodicals	3 libraries
over 1,600 periodicals	4 libraries
no answer	17 libraries **(369)**

Ibid. . . . *showed that* the degree to which periodical titles were duplicated in hard copy (rather than microform) in responding libraries was as follows:

less than 5% duplication	4 libraries
5-10% duplication	4 libraries
11-19% duplication	4 libraries
20-30% duplication	9 libraries
40-50% duplication	2 libraries
60% duplication	4 libraries
no answer	10 libraries **(369)**

■ A survey reported in 1981 of bibliographic instruction in business school libraries (sample size: 120; responding: 65; usable: 61 or 50.8%) *showed that* 27% of the business school libraries have collections of 20,000 volumes or less, while 75% have collections of 80,000 volumes or less.
(436)

■ A study reported in 1981 of data on 1,146 2-year colleges as reported in the 1977 Higher Education General Information Surveys and compared to the 1979 Association of College and Research Libraries standards *showed that* in terms of periodical subscriptions the number of schools meeting minimum standards (by enrollment ranges of FTE students) was as follows:

less than 1,000 students
(200 titles minimum)   49% met standards

continued

1,000 to 2,999 students
(300 titles minimum)   48% met standards
3,000 to 4,999 students
(500 titles minimum)   29% met standards
5,000 to 6,999 students
(700 titles minimum)   13% met standards
7,000 to 8,999 students
(710 titles minimum)   25% met standards
9,000 to 10,999 students
(720 titles minimum)   53% met standards

The overall average number of periodicals held per school was 350 titles.
(500)

Ibid. . . . *showed that* in terms of book collection the number of schools meeting minimum standards (by enrollment ranges of FTE students) was as follows:

less than 1,000 students
(20,000 volumes minimum)   61% met standards
1,000 to 2,999 students
(30,000 volumes minimum)   39% met standards
3,000 to 4,999 students
(50,000 volumes minimum)   24% met standards
5,000 to 6,999 students
(70,000 volumes minimum)   12% met standards
7,000 to 8,999 students
(82,000 volumes minimum)   14% met standards
9,000 to 10,999 students
(94,000 volumes minimum)   32% met standards

The overall average number of volumes held per school was 33,900 volumes. **(500)**

■ A study reported in 1983 concerning costs among academic libraries based on data gathered by the National Center for Education Statistics for the year 1977 and various sources of institutional data (involving 3,057 institutions, including 2-year public, 2-year private, 4-year public, and 4-year private schools) *showed that* the strongest and most consistent correlation for all 4 types of libraries was between number of volumes held and number of items circulated. Specifically, the correlation coefficient by type of library was:

2-year public college libraries $r = .67$
2-year private college libraries $r = .68$
4-year public college and
university libraries $r = .88$

continued

Holdings

                    4-year private college and
                        university libraries   r = .84
(No significance level was reported.)   (800)

■ A study reported in 1983 of 3 surveys made by the American Medical Association's Division of Library and Archival Services in 1969, 1973, and 1979 concerning the status of health sciences libraries in the U.S. (survey size for each survey ran between 12,000-14,000 health-related organizations, with a response rate for each survey around 95%) *showed that*, during the period 1969-79, hospital health science libraries increased the average number of current serial titles received by 13% (from 115 titles per library on average to 130 titles per library on average).   (747)

Public

■ A 1969 survey of Canadian public libraries serving populations of more than 10,000 people as well as all county and regional libraries belonging to the Canadian Library Association concerning holdings and use of non-English collections (survey size: 203; responding: 83 or 41%) *showed that*, of 73 respondents, 31 (42.5%) reported non-English language collections of more than 500 volumes.   (534)

Ibid. . . . *showed that*, of 81 respondents, 21 (25.9%) libraries reported they did not buy books in non-English languages. Further, of 78 respondents, 22 (28.2%) reported they did not borrow books in other languages.   (534)

■ A survey reported in 1977 of public and elementary school libraries in the Regional Municipality of York (Ontario, Canada) concerning their holdings of Canadian juvenile fiction (survey size: 72 school libraries and 19 public libraries; responding: 29 or 40.3% school libraries and 17 or 89.5% public libraries) *showed that*, based on a total of 50 Canadian, U.S., and British titles, the responding public libraries had a higher percentage of quality Canadian titles than the national average but a lower percentage of quality U.S. and British titles than the national average. For example, the overall probability that any 1 of 8 award-winning Canadian titles would be found in a public library responding to this survey was 70% compared to 66% for the public libraries responding to an earlier national study. Further, the overall probability that any 1 of 10 award-winning U.S. or any 1 of 11 award-winning British titles would be found in a public library responding to this survey was 59% and 44%, respectively, compared to 76% and 50%, respectively, for the public libraries responding to the earlier national study.   (544)

Ibid. . . . *showed that* school libraries responding to this survey were less likely than the public libraries to have award-winning Canadian juvenile titles. For example, the overall probability that any 1 of 8 award-winning Canadian titles would be found in a school library responding to this survey was 36.6% compared to 70% for the public libraries responding to this survey. **(544)**

School

■ A survey reported in 1963 of principals of elementary schools in 50 states (sample size: 730; responding: 424 or 58%) *showed that* 326 (76.9%) of the respondents reported that their schools had a collection of professional periodicals and books. An additional 23 principals reported a professional collection of books but no periodicals, and 36 reported a professional collection of periodicals but no books. **(277)**

Ibid. . . . *showed that* the book collections ranged from 5 to 500 with the median between 46-50; the range of new books added each year was 0 to 32 with a median of 5. **(277)**

■ A survey reported in 1977 of public and elementary school libraries in the Regional Municipality of York (Ontario, Canada) concerning their holdings of Canadian juvenile fiction (survey size: 72 school libraries and 19 public libraries; responding: 29 or 40.3% school libraries and 17 or 89.5% public libraries) *showed that*, based on a total of 50 Canadian, U.S., and British titles, the responding public libraries had a higher percentage of quality Canadian titles than the national average but a lower percentage of quality U.S. and British titles than the national average. For example, the overall probability that any 1 of 8 award-winning Canadian titles would be found in a public library responding to this survey was 70% compared to 66% for the public libraries responding to an earlier national study. Further, the overall probability that any 1 of 10 award-winning U.S. or any 1 of 11 award-winning British title would be found in a public library responding to this survey was 59% and 44%, respectively, compared to 76% and 50%, respectively, for the public libraries responding to the earlier national study. **(544)**

Ibid. . . . *showed that* school libraries responding to this survey were less likely than the public libraries to have award-winning Canadian juvenile titles. For example, the overall probability that any 1 of 8 award-winning Canadian titles would be found in a school library responding to this survey was 36.6% compared to 70% for the public libraries responding to this survey. **(544)**

Holdings

- A 1980 survey of 310 public library children's specialists in 74 California library systems (all responding) *showed that*, while over 97% of the respondents reported circulating or noncirculating collections of hardbound books, paperback books, and magazines in their libraries, many of the libraries reported no collections of the following materials: records (17.1%), films (63.5%), filmstrips (71.3%), audiocassettes (46.5%), games/puzzles (44.2%), toys/puppets (59.7%), braille materials (85.8%), and materials for hearing-impaired (91.3%). **(163)**

- A 1983 survey of a systematic sample of school library media centers concerning data for fiscal year 1982-83 (survey size: 2,000 centers; responding: 1,297; usable: 1,251 or 62%) *showed that* a comparison of privately supported (72) and publicly supported (1,179) school library media centers revealed that media specialists in private schools served fewer students, had more money to spend on resources, administered smaller collections, and earned more modest salaries. Specifically:

    enrollment averaged 460 students for private schools and 669 for public schools;

    total materials expenditure per student averaged $12.55 for private schools and $9.62 for public schools;

    the number of books per student averaged 27.08 for private schools and 18.44 for public schools;

    the number of AV items per student averaged 3.2 for private schools and 3.26 for public schools;

    in private schools the media specialist averaged 8.92 years of experience with a salary of $13,880, while in public schools the media specialists averaged 11.08 years of experience with a salary of $20,389. **(056)**

Ibid. . . . *showed that* a comparison of schools with (666 schools) and without (597 schools) district level library media coordinators revealed that schools without district coordinators spent more money per student on resources and had more books per student than schools with district coordinators. However, schools with district coordinators paid media specialists higher salaries, had more AV items per student, had more clerical assistance, and used more adult volunteers than schools without district coordinators. Specifically:

    total materials expenditure per student in schools with coordinators averaged $8.80, and in schools without coordinators averaged $10.92;

    average books per student in schools with coordinators averaged 18, and in schools without coordinators averaged 20;

number of AV items per student in schools with coordinators averaged 3.45, and in schools without coordinators averaged 3.03;

media specialist salary in schools with coordinators averaged $20,699, and in schools without coordinators averaged $19,354;

the number of clerical assistants and adult volunteers in schools with coordinators averaged .83 and 2.46, respectively, and in schools without coordinators averaged .77 and 1.85, respectively. **(056)**

Ibid. . . . *showed that* the average number of books per pupil and average total volumes added in 1982-83 by type of library media center was as follows:

elementary school (587 schools): 20.42 books per student with an average of 295.8 volumes added;

junior high/middle school (308 schools): 16.29 books per student with an average of 393.01 volumes added;

senior high school (304 schools): 17.06 books per student with an average of 465.96 volumes added;

other (49 schools): 28.62 books per student with an average of 364.97 volumes added. **(056)**

Ibid. . . . *showed that* the average number of AV items per pupil and the average total AV items added in 1982-83 by type of library media center was as follows:

elementary school (587 schools): 3.71 items per student with an average of 61.13 items added;

junior high/middle school (308 schools): 2.97 items per student with an average of 68.56 items added;

senior high school (304 schools): 2.70 items per student with an average of 112.97 items added;

other (49 schools): 3.06 items per student with an average of 87.53 items added. **(056)**

Ibid. . . . *showed that* [in 1982-83] the average expenditure for microcomputer software reported by 81 elementary centers was $595; for 37 junior high/middle school centers was $322; for 46 senior high centers was $381; and for 5 combinations of the above schools was $523. **(056)**

Holdings

Special

■ A 1972 survey of prison law libraries (sample size: 90; responding: 68% [no number given, 62 assumed] *showed that* the 5 types of state legal materials reported most often present in prison law libraries were (multiple responses allowed): compiled statutes (51 or 82.3% respondents), Supreme Court reports (44 or 71.0% respondents), appellate court reports (33 or 53.2% respondents), criminal practice and procedure texts (32 or 51.6% respondents), and digests (31 or 50.0% respondents). **(389)**

Ibid. . . . *showed that* the 5 types of federal legal materials reported most often present in prison law libraries were (multiple responses allowed):

U.S. Code	52 (83.9%)	respondents
Federal Reporter, 2nd	43 (69.4%)	respondents
Supreme Court reports	41 (66.1%)	respondents
Federal Supplement	41 (66.1%)	respondents
Digest (Supreme Court)	29 (46.8%)	respondents

(389)

Ibid. . . . *showed that* the following 5 types of general legal materials were present to the degree shown in prison law libraries:

criminal procedure text	39 (62.9%)	respondents
legal dictionary	37 (59.7%)	respondents
criminal law text	33 (53.2%)	respondents
Criminal Law Reporter	32 (51.6%)	respondents
criminal law forms	27 (43.5%)	respondents

(389)

■ A 1973 survey of all county law libraries listed in the 1972 American Association of Law Libraries *Directory of Law Libraries* (population: 260; responding: 86 or 33.1%) *showed that* 75 (85%) respondents reported that the library book collection was adequate to meet the needs of those who use the library. Further, of 62 respondents, 38 (61.3%) reported that 1% or less of their material is unused or unneeded; 8 (12.9%) reported that unused and unneeded material ran 2 to 10% of the collection; and 6 (9.7%) reported that unused and unneeded material exceeded 11% of the collection. [No data was given for the remaining respondents.] **(392)**

■ A 1974 survey of a random sample of U.S. museum libraries (including history, art, and science museums) listed in the 1973 *Official Museum Directory* (population: 2,556; sample size: 856; responding: 374 or 43.7%) *showed that* 53% of the libraries reported 1,000 or fewer books, while 91%

reported 20,000 or fewer books. The average book collection was 8,924 titles with a median of 992 titles. Further, 69.7% of the respondents reported that their collection was cataloged, with 10% reporting that the collection was partially cataloged. **(412)**

■ A 1979 survey of libraries in accredited North American veterinary schools (population: 25 libraries; responding: 23 or 92%) *showed that*, of the 18 separately housed veterinary libraries, the number of serials received ranged from a low of 193 at Tuskegee to a high of 1,105 at Cornell. The average number of serials received was 624. The number of bound serial volumes ranged from 2,844 volumes at Mississippi State University to 66,000 volumes at Cornell. The average number of bound volumes held was 26,274. **(740)**

Ibid. . . . *showed that* 11 (47.8%) respondents reported no AV holdings other than microforms. **(740)**

■ A 1980 survey of law school libraries with collections in excess of 175,000 volumes (sample size: 50; responding: 37 or 70%) *showed that* the numbers of periodicals reported by respondents were as follows:

less than 500 periodicals	1 library	
500-600 periodicals	2 libraries	
700-900 periodicals	6 libraries	
1,000-1,200 periodicals	4 libraries	
1,300-1,500 periodicals	3 libraries	
over 1,600 periodicals	4 libraries	
no answer	17 libraries	**(369)**

Ibid. . . . *showed that* the degree to which periodical titles were duplicated in hard copy (rather than microform) in responding libraries was as follows:

Holdings

■ A study reported in 1983 of surveys of medical school libraries for the period 1960-61 through 1980-81, made by the American Medical Association, the Medical Library Association, the Association of Academic Health Sciences Library Directors, and the National Library of Medicine, *showed that* the average number of serial titles increased by 10.8% in the 5-year period ending in 1969-70, by 14.8% in the 5-year period ending in 1974-75, and by 9.4% in the 5-year period ending in 1979-80. Overall, between 1965-66 and 1980-81 the average number of current serial titles increased from 1,698 titles to 1,415 titles (42%).
(746)

■ A study reported in 1983 of 3 surveys made by the American Medical Association's Division of Library and Archival Services in 1969, 1973, and 1979 concerning the status of health sciences libraries in the U.S. (survey size for each survey ran between 12,000-14,000 health-related organizations, with a response rate for each survey around 95%) *showed that*, during the period 1969-79, hospital health science libraries increased the average number of current serial titles received by 13% (from 115 titles per library on average to 130 titles per library on average).
(747)

■ A survey reported in 1983 of Medical Library Association institutional members concerning their use of audiovisual materials (survey size: 300; responding: 201; usable: 198 or 66%) *showed that*, of 143 respondents (91 hospital, 29 medical school, and 13 "other" libraries) that did provide AV services, the numbers of libraries collecting the various types of AV materials were as follows:

> audiocassettes: collected by 91% of the hospital, 79% of the medical school, and 77% of the other libraries;

> videocassettes: collected by 88% of the hospital, 90% of the medical school, and 77% of the other libraries;

> filmstrips/cassettes: collected by 82% of the hospital, 76% of the medical school, and 77% of the other libraries;

> slide/cassettes: collected by 80% of the hospital, 86% of the medical school, and 85% of the other libraries;

> films (both 16 mm and super 8): collected by 62% of the hospital, 76% of the medical school, and 85% of the other libraries;

> color microfiche: collected by 52% of the hospital, 62% of the medical school, and 70% of the other libraries.
(750)

Holdings—Media

Academic

■ A 1972 survey of chief library administrators in public comprehensive community colleges (population: 586; usable responses: 75.9% [no raw number given]) *showed that* types of holdings were as follows:

slides, records, filmstrips, audiotapes, and microforms	90.0% respondents
transparencies	83.2% respondents
films	74.2% respondents
videotape	69.5% respondents
self-instructional carrels with media outlets	64.6% respondents

(452)

■ A survey reported in 1977 of moderate-sized (120,000-500,000 volumes) U.S. academic libraries listed in the 1972-73 *American Library Directory* (survey size: 200; responding: 147 or 74%) *showed that* 128 (87%) libraries reported subscribing to some periodical titles in microform instead of binding. Further, 53% of responding libraries reported 25 or fewer microform subscriptions, while 21% reported 100+ microform subscriptions. **(454)**

■ A 1979 survey of libraries in accredited North American veterinary schools (population: 25 libraries; responding: 23 or 92%) *showed that* 11 (47.8%) respondents reported no AV holdings other than microforms.
(740)

■ A survey reported in 1983 of Medical Library Association institutional members concerning their use of audiovisual materials (survey size: 300; responding: 201; usable: 198 or 66%) *showed that*, of 143 respondents (91 hospital, 29 medical school, and 13 "other" libraries) that did provide AV services, the numbers of libraries collecting the various types of AV materials were as follows:

audiocassettes: collected by 91% of the hospital, 79% of the medical school, and 77% of the other libraries;

videocassettes: collected by 88% of the hospital, 90% of the medical school, and 77% of the other libraries;

Holdings

filmstrips/cassettes: collected by 82% of the hospital, 76% of the medical school, and 77% of the other libraries;

slide/cassettes: collected by 80% of the hospital, 86% of the medical school, and 85% of the other libraries;

films (both 16 mm and super 8): collected by 62% of the hospital, 76% of the medical school, and 85% of the other libraries;

color microfiche: collected by 52% of the hospital, 62% of the medical school, and 70% of the other libraries. **(750)**

School

■ A 1980 survey of 310 public library children's specialists in 74 California library systems (all responding) *showed that*, while over 97% of the respondents reported circulating or noncirculating collections of hardbound books, paperback books, and magazines in their libraries, many of the libraries reported no collections of the following materials: records (17.1%), films (63.5%), filmstrips (71.3%), audiocassettes (46.5%), games/puzzles (44.2%), toys/puppets (59.7%), braille materials (85.8%), and materials for hearing-impaired (91.3%). **(163)**

■ A 1983 survey of a systematic sample of school library media centers concerning data for fiscal year 1982-83 (survey size: 2,000 centers; responding: 1,297; usable: 1,251 or 62%) *showed that* a comparison of privately supported (72) and publicly supported (1,179) school library media centers revealed that media specialists in private schools served fewer students, had more money to spend on resources, administered smaller collections, and earned more modest salaries. Specifically:

enrollment averaged 460 students for private schools and 669 for public schools;

total materials expenditure per student averaged $12.55 for private schools and $9.62 for public schools;

the number of books per student averaged 27.08 for private schools and 18.44 for public schools;

the number of AV items per student averaged 3.2 for private schools and 3.26 for public schools;

in private schools the media specialist averaged 8.92 years of experience with a salary of $13,880, while in public schools the media specialists averaged 11.08 years of experience with a salary of $20,389. **(056)**

Ibid. . . . *showed that* a comparison of schools with (666 schools) and without (597 schools) district level library media coordinators revealed that schools without district coordinators spent more money per student on resources and had more books per student than schools with district coordinators. However, schools with district coordinators paid media specialists higher salaries, had more AV items per student, had more clerical assistance, and used more adult volunteers than schools without district coordinators. Specifically:

    total materials expenditure per student in schools with coordinators averaged $8.80, and in schools without coordinators averaged $10.92;

    average books per student in schools with coordinators averaged 18, and in schools without coordinators averaged 20;

    number of AV items per student in schools with coordinators averaged 3.45, and in schools without coordinators averaged 3.03;

    media specialist salary in schools with coordinators averaged $20,699, and in schools without coordinators averaged $19,354;

    the number of clerical assistants and adult volunteers in schools with coordinators averaged .83 and 2.46, respectively, and in schools without coordinators averaged .77 and 1.85, respectively. **(056)**

Ibid. . . . *showed that* the average number of books per pupil and average total volumes added in 1982-83 by type of library media center was as follows:

    elementary school (587 schools): 20.42 books per student with an average of 295.8 volumes added;

    junior high/middle school (308 schools): 16.29 books per student with an average of 393.01 volumes added;

    senior high school (304 schools): 17.06 books per student with an average of 465.96 volumes added;

    other (49 schools): 28.62 books per student with an average of 364.97 volumes added. **(056)**

Ibid. . . . *showed that* the average number of AV items per pupil and the average total AV items added in 1982-83 by type of library media center was as follows:

    elementary school (587 schools): 3.71 items per student with an average of 61.13 items added;

Holdings

junior high/middle school (308 schools): 2.97 items per student with an average of 68.56 items added;

senior high school (304 schools): 2.70 items per student with an average of 112.97 items added;

other (49 schools): 3.06 items per student with an average of 87.53 items added. **(056)**

Ibid. . . . *showed that* [in 1982-83] the average expenditure for microcomputer software reported by 81 elementary centers was $595; for 37 junior high/middle school centers was $322; for 46 senior high centers was $381; and for 5 combinations of the above schools was $523. **(056)**

Special

■ A 1979 survey of libraries in accredited North American veterinary schools (population: 25 libraries; responding: 23 or 92%) *showed that* 11 (47.8%) respondents reported no AV holdings other than microforms.
(740)

■ A survey reported in 1983 of Medical Library Association institutional members concerning their use of audiovisual materials (survey size: 300; responding: 201; usable: 198 or 66%) *showed that*, of 143 respondents (91 hospital, 29 medical school, and 13 "other" libraries) that did provide AV services, the numbers of libraries collecting the various types of AV materials were as follows:

audiocassettes: collected by 91% of the hospital, 79% of the medical school, and 77% of the other libraries;

videocassettes: collected by 88% of the hospital, 90% of the medical school, and 77% of the other libraries;

filmstrips/cassettes: collected by 82% of the hospital, 76% of the medical school, and 77% of the other libraries;

slide/cassettes: collected by 80% of the hospital, 86% of the medical school, and 85% of the other libraries;

films (both 16 mm and super 8): collected by 62% of the hospital, 76% of the medical school, and 85% of the other libraries;

color microfiche: collected by 52% of the hospital, 62% of the medical school, and 70% of the other libraries. **(750)**

Lease Plans

Academic

■ A survey reported in 1976 of libraries using lease plans *showed that* the percentage of the lease collection usually in circulation ranged from 25% to 90%, with the majority of the libraries reporting 50% or more of the books in constant use. **(054)**

Ibid. . . . *showed that* the University of Colorado reported that 565 of its 600 lease titles had circulated 5 times or more in 1 year's time in 1974.
(054)

Method of Selection

Academic

■ A study reported in 1974 comparing the effectiveness of collection development of librarians, teaching faculty, and approval plans in 5 academic libraries (3 college, 2 university) by comparing books bought by each of these groups with the books' subsequent circulation records (7,213 books studied in total) *showed that* the circulation rates of the materials selected by each of the 3 groups were different to a statistically significant degree, with materials selected by librarians circulating most, materials selected by teaching faculty circulating next most often, and approval plan materials circulating the least (significance level not given). **(628)**

■ A survey reported in 1977 of moderate-sized (120,000-500,000 volumes) U.S. academic libraries listed in the 1972-73 *American Library Directory* (survey size: 200; responding: 147 or 74%) *showed that* faculty participated in the periodical selection process in 95% of the responding libraries, while students actively participated in only 9% of the libraries. Further, the library administrator was responsible for final approval of selections in 49% of the libraries; the serials librarian was responsible for final approval in 29% of the libraries; and in 17 (12%) of the libraries teaching faculty were responsible for final selection. **(454)**

■ A study reported in 1979 of faculty in the school of education at a medium-sized, state-supported midwestern university who were responsible for library book selection (2/3 of the library materials budget was allocated to the various academic departments, who selected books in their

Method of Selection 135

fields) (population: 82 faculty; responding: 66; usable: 64 or 78.0%) *showed that* of 10 variables the 3 most strongly associated with the number of books selected for the library were (based on Pearson product-moment correlation coefficients): number of graduate courses taught (r2 = .108), number of professional meetings attended (r2 = .093) and number of publications already completed (r2 = .090) (significant at the .05 level or better). All 10 factors together (based on multiple regression) accounted for 29.9% of the variance (significant at the .05 level). **(528)**

■ A study reported in 1981 at DePauw University of circulation patterns over a 5-year period (1973-77) for a group of newly acquired monographs (sample size: 1,904 books) *showed that* there was a statistically significant difference in the circulation rates of books selected by the classroom instructors (1,542 books) and those books selected by librarians (173 books) with the books selected by the librarians circulating more (significant at the .01 level). For example, 74% of the librarian-selected books were either lightly circulated or not circulated at all, compared to 87.3% of the books selected by classroom instructors, while 26% of the librarian-selected books were either moderately or heavily circulated, compared to 12.7% of the books selected by classroom instructors. **(573)**

Ibid. . . . *showed that* there was a statistically significant difference in the circulation rates of gift books and those books purchased on the recommendation of classroom instructors or librarians, with the gift books circulating less than the purchased books (significant at the .01 level). For example, of 189 gift books, 121 (64.0%) did not circulate at all [during the 5-year period], while of 1,715 purchased books 581 (33.8%) did not circulate at all [during the 5-year period]. **(573)**

■ A study during the 1981-82 academic year in the main library at Purdue concerning books undergraduates selected to read (involving interviews with 240 undergraduate borrowers and analysis of 598 of the mongraphic titles borrowed by both students and nonstudents) *showed that*, based on 364 items circulated to undergraduates, only 15.9% of the titles selected by undergraduates were based on instructor recommendation (direct recommendation or reading lists), while the remaining titles were selected without instructor direction. 86.6% were selected for subject matter relating to a specific course; 11.6% were selected for leisure reading; and 1.8% were selected for research in the student's major with no specific course in mind. **(530)**

Ibid. . . . *showed that* titles recommended by instructors and checked out by undergraduates were no more likely to fall within the core of highly circulating materials than outside it. For example, of 111 titles that

COLLECTION DEVELOPMENT

circulated less than 6 times, 16 or 14.4% had been recommended by faculty, while of 253 titles that had circulated 6 times or more, 42 (16.6%) had been recommended by faculty. **(530)**

Ibid. . . . *showed that* the "best and most critically acclaimed" books do not make up the majority of undergraduate reading. For example, of 252 books checked out by undergraduates that had been published before 1973, only 61 (24.2%) were listed in *Books for College Libraries*, while of 246 books published after 1963, only 74 (30.1%) were reviewed in *Choice*, and of these, only 35% were given top recommendations. **(530)**

Out-of-Print Materials

General

■ A survey reported in 1973 of out-of-print dealers concerning common dealer practices and preferences (survey size: 54 dealers; responding: 22 or 40.7%) *showed that* 13 (59.1%) reported a book stock of less than 25,000 volumes, while "nearly 30%" reported a book stock of 50,000 volumes or more. **(601)**

Ibid. . . . *showed that* (multiple responses allowed) the most commonly reported basis of assigning prices was book trade experience (reported by 19 or 86.4% respondents); "next in order" [no numbers given] were *Bookman's Price Index* and *American Book Prices Current*. Only 1 major retrospective guide to book prices was mentioned, Wright Howes's *U.S. iana* (reported by 50% of the respondents). **(601)**

Ibid. . . . *showed that* 4 categories of sales were ranked as follows by respondents from most important to least important:
 1. catalog sales
 2. want list sales
 3. specific title requests
 4. on-premises sales **(601)**

Ibid. . . . *showed that*, based on responses from 15 respondents, 53% of the want list quotes were filled; based on responses from 12 respondents, on the average 58% of the items listed in a catalog were sold. Further, 5 respondents advised ordering from catalogs within 2 weeks of receipt, while 4 reported that ordering within a month was acceptable if a library wanted to have a good chance of getting a desired item. **(601)**

Ibid. . . . *showed that*, based on responses from 5 respondents, 11.8% of the items in a catalog were sold within 1 week of issue; 26% of the items were sold within 2 weeks of issue; and 45% of the items were sold within 1 month of issue. **(601)**

Academic

■ A 1969 study at San Fernando Valley State College involving out-of-print acquisitions over a year's time *showed that*, of 17,689 titles ordered, 4,720 titles (27%) were received. Further, the average unit cost of in-print books (all subjects) for that year was $9.19, compared to the average unit cost of $10.18 for the 4,720 out-of-print books. **(593)**

■ A survey reported in 1973 of U.S. and foreign out-of-print dealers concerning their practices (survey size: 286; responding: 157 or 54.9%, including 108 U.S. and 49 foreign dealers) by the California State University, Northridge, *showed that* their methods for locating out-of-print books were as follows (multiple responses allowed):

supply from own stock	99 (92%) U.S.; 45 (92%) foreign
advertise	89 (82%) U.S.; 28 (57%) foreign
check other dealers' catalogs	82 (76%) U.S.; 38 (78%) foreign
visit other dealers	82 (76%) U.S.; 32 (65%) foreign
contact other dealers by letter	68 (63%) U.S.: 31 (63%) foreign

Further, the most effective method reported by both U.S. (34 or 35%) and foreign (22 or 52%) dealers was supplying from own stock. **(603)**

Ibid. . . . *showed that* 84 (82%) of the U.S. and 38 (83%) of the foreign dealers reported that they made more than 1 attempt to locate the titles on the university's list. Of these 84 dealers, the length of time they continued to search was as follows:

indefinitely	42 (54%) U.S.; 22 (59%) foreign
2-5 years	4 (5%) U.S.; 5 (14%) foreign
1 year	18 (23%) U.S.; 3 (8%) foreign
6 months	10 (13%) U.S.; 3 (8%) foreign
1-3 months	4 (5%) U.S.; 4 (11%) foreign

(603)

Outreach and Extension

Academic

■ A 1971-72 study of the articles supplied by the University of Oklahoma Health Sciences Center Library to state health professionals and institutions during a 4-month period, involving 1,756 articles (from 373 journals) sent to individual health professionals and 1,620 articles (from 527 journals) sent to health institutions, *showed that*, in terms of the publication dates of the articles sent to individuals, 28% of the information requests could have been filled with a journal backfile of 1 year, 57% could have been filled with a backfile of 2 years, 72% with a backfile of 3 years, 80% with a backfile of 4 years, 85% with a backfile of 5 years. **(409)**

Ibid. . . . *showed that*, of the 1,620 articles sent to institutions, 24.5% [no raw number given] of the articles were supplied by 26 titles, each contributing 10 or more articles, while 53% [no raw number given] of the articles were supplied by 100 titles, each contributing 5 or more articles. **(409)**

Ibid. . . . *showed that*, in terms of publication dates of the articles, 69.3% of the information requests could have been filled with a journal backfile of 5 years, while 85.5% of the information requests could have been filled with a journal backlog of 10 years. **(409)**

■ A study reported in 1977 by the University of Oklahoma Health Sciences Center Library of the literature searches performed during a 3-year period (1973-75) for physicians and fourth-year medical students serving a 5-week "preceptorship" with a rural physician (1,775 searches) *showed that* for both the physicians and students the subject category of most requests was "Diseases" (66% of the physicians' searches; 84% of the students' searches), while the subject category of the next most requests for both groups was "Chemicals and Drugs" (27.2% of the physicians' searches; 27.6% of the students' searches). **(716)**

Special

■ A 1971-72 study of the articles supplied by the University of Oklahoma Health Sciences Center Library to state health professionals and institutions during a 4-month period, involving 1,756 articles (from 373 journals) sent to individual health professionals and 1,620 articles (from 527

Overlap

journals) sent to health institutions, *showed that*, in terms of the publication dates of the articles sent to individuals, 28% of the information requests could have been filled with a journal backfile of 1 year, 57% could have been filled with a backfile of 2 years, 72% with a backfile of 3 years, 80% with a backfile of 4 years, 85% with a backfile of 5 years. **(409)**

Ibid. . . . *showed that*, of the 1,620 articles sent to institutions, 24.5% [no raw number given] of the articles were supplied by 26 titles, each contributing 10 or more articles, while 53% [no raw number given] of the articles were supplied by 100 titles, each contributing 5 or more articles. **(409)**

Ibid. . . . *showed that*, in terms of publication dates of the articles, 69.3% of the information requests could have been filled with a journal backfile of 5 years, while 85.5% of the information requests could have been filled with a journal backlog of 10 years. **(409)**

■ A study reported in 1977 by the University of Oklahoma Health Sciences Center Library of the literature searches performed during a 3-year period (1973-75) for physicians and fourth-year medical students serving a 5-week "preceptorship" with a rural physician (1,775 searches) *showed that* for both the physicians and students the subject category of most requests was "Diseases" (66% of the physicians' searches; 84% of the students' searches), while the subject category of the next most requests for both groups was "Chemicals and Drugs" (27.2% of the physicians' searches; 27.6% of the students' searches). **(716)**

Overlap

General

■ A survey published in 1966 of first-edition Polish publications (excluding children's literature, music, textbooks, translations, and reprints) published between April 15, 1957, and August 17, 1957 (882 titles) and shown to be available in U.S. libraries through the NUC 1958-62 *showed that* 332 (37.5%) of the 882 titles were available in U.S. libraries. Due to duplication the 332 titles were represented by 557 volumes. **(664)**

Academic

■ A study reported in 1968 of collection overlap in 6 New England state university libraries (Maine, New Hampshire, Vermont, Massachusetts, Rhode Island, and Connecticut) involving 2 samples from each library of 550 cards each (1 sample from the overall collection; 1 sample from current imprints only, i.e., 1964-65-66) *showed that* the overlap in the overall collections ranged from 28.1% (New Hampshire with Vermont) to 55.2% (Rhode Island with Connecticut), with an average overlap between libraries of 39.7%. The overlap in the current imprints ranged from 25.1% (Massachusetts with Vermont) to 70.6% (Vermont with Massachusetts), with an average overlap between libraries of 46.9%. These percentages were correct ±5% at the 99% confidence level. **(588)**

■ A 1971 survey of owners (primarily academics) of personal library collections (sample selected from authors of 300 single-author articles published during 1969-70 in one of 3 broad areas: humanities, social science, and science; 178 authors responding, of which 175 owned personal collections) *showed that* a physical check of the libraries reported used by 45 (25%) of the respondents indicated that the 244 (21%) of the cited materials they reported as in the library were in fact in the library as well as 592 (88%) of the personal collection works cited by this group. **(258)**

■ A study reported in 1974 investigating the degree of overlap in journal collections among U.S. academic health science libraries (survey size: 40 libraries; responding: 37 or 92.5%) *showed that* at least 60% of the surveyed libraries held 852 of the journal titles. A further breakdown was as follows (number of titles not cumulated):

60-69% of the libraries	149 titles
70-79% of the libraries	171 titles
80-89% of the libraries	163 titles
90-99% of the libraries	306 titles
100% of the libraries	63 titles

A title list was given for the 369 titles held by 90-100% of the libraries. **(702)**

■ A study reported in 1975 of the degree to which a sample of 845 titles were duplicated in the collections of 22 state-assisted senior colleges and universities of Texas *showed that* together the libraries held 783 (92%) of the titles, with an average acquisition rate of 8.9 copies per title. **(126)**

Overlap

Ibid. . . . *showed that* 91% of all titles in the sample that were acquired in any one of the libraries were duplicated in one or more of the other 22 libraries. **(126)**

Ibid. . . . *showed that*, both in total and in a breakdown of 19 subject areas, there was a pronounced tendency for holdings and duplication to rise progressively from low levels in schools with no degree program to the highest levels among those schools with doctoral-level programs, as follows:

LEVEL OF PROGRAM	AVERAGE DUPLICATION RANGE
doctoral	69-86%
master's	44-74%
bachelor's	34-65%
no degree	15-58%

(126)

Ibid. . . . *showed that* the average duplication rate for the 22 Texas academic libraries ranged from 45 to 64% and averaged 52.2%. This was compared to other studies, which indicated that the collection overlap of 6 New England state university libraries ranged from 38 to 67% and averaged 46.9%; for 9 Colorado academic libraries ranged from 23 to 44% with an average of 30.8%; for 5 Washington, D.C., university libraries ranged from 43 to 60% and averaged 48.8%. **(126)**

■ A study reported in 1982 of collection overlap among libraries on 11 University of Wisconsin campuses, based on 267,979 cataloging records created during fiscal years 1977-79, *showed that* 18.16% of the titles were held on 2 or more campuses, while 1.05% of the titles were held by 6 or more campuses. When only current imprints were considered, 31.99% of the titles were held on 2 or more campuses, while 2.24% of the titles were held on 6 or more campuses. **(504)**

Ibid. . . . *showed that* collection overlap was lowest with the larger libraries and greatest with the smaller libraries. Specifically, the largest library (UW, Madison) had the lowest overlap rate (38.09% of its current imprints duplicated elsewhere), while the 4 campuses that cataloged less than 14,000 titles each during this period had an average of 73.24% of their collection (current imprints) duplicated elsewhere. **(504)**

Ibid. . . . *showed that* comparison of a subsample of 249 unique titles and 84 of the "highly overlapped" titles (held by 6 or more libraries) revealed major differnces in language, publisher, and source of cataloging. Specifically, all high-overlap titles were in English, compared to 78% of the unique titles; 40% of the high-overlap titles were published by university presses, compared to 7% of the unique titles; and all but 1 of the high-overlap titles were originally cataloged by the Library of Congress, while 61 (24%) of the unique titles were originally cataloged by OCLC members. **(504)**

Public

■ A study reported in 1983 of collection overlap among 2 elementary school libraries and 1 public library in each of 4 Illinois communities of approximately 30,000 population *showed that* each elementary school had an average collection overlap with the other of "about 30%"; elementary school library collection overlap with public libraries averaged "about 50%"; and public library overlap with the elementary school libraries averaged "about 30%." **(223)**

School

■ A study reported in 1983 of collection overlap among 2 elementary school libraries and 1 public library in each of 4 Illinois communities of approximately 30,000 population (sample size: 200 titles from each of the 3 libraries) *showed that* each elementary school had an average collection overlap with the other of "about 30%"; elementary school library collection overlap with public libraries averaged "about 50%"; and public library overlap with the elementary school libraries averaged "about 30%." **(223)**

Special

■ A 1972 survey of the 45 law libraries participating in the union list of foreign legal periodicals *showed that* only 4 titles from the *Index to Foreign Legal Periodicals* were common to all 45 libraries:
American Journal of Comparative Law
American Journal of International Law
International and Comparative Law Quarterly
International Lawyer **(391)**

■ A study reported in 1974 investigating the degree of overlap in journal collections among U.S. academic health science libraries (survey size: 40 libraries; responding: 37 or 92.5%) *showed that* at least 60% of the surveyed libraries held 852 of the journal titles. A further breakdown was as follows (number of titles not cumulated):

> 60-69% of the libraries   149 titles
> 70-79% of the libraries   171 titles
> 80-89% of the libraries   163 titles
> 90-99% of the libraries   306 titles
> 100% of the libraries   63 titles

A title list was given for the 369 titles held by 90-100% of the libraries. **(702)**

■ A study reported in 1979 of collection overlap among 8 Canadian addictions libraries using a random sample of 71 monographs with an imprint of 1970 or later *showed that* 55 (77.5%) were found in 1 or more of the other addictions libraries. Of those so found, 64% were held in 1-3 libraries; 31% were held in 4-6 libraries; and 5% were held in 7-8 libraries. **(427)**

Practices and Procedures

Academic

■ A 1967 survey of medical school libraries concerning reference services (survey size: 93 libraries; responding: 85 or 91.4%) *showed that* 65 (76.5%) libraries reported that the reference department assumed "some degree of responsibility for book selection," while 20 (23.5%) libraries reported no such responsibility. **(682)**

■ A study reported in 1970 of 3 types of book selection procedures in 4 midwestern 4-year institutions of higher education with graduate programs who had used at least 2 methods of book selection for current-imprint, English-language titles (sample size: 6,891 books, including 2,559 selected on approval plan, 2,196 selected by faculty, and 2,136 selected by librarians) *showed that* on the basis of subsequent book circulation (at least once in the 12 months following public availability) the librarians were the best selectors, faculty the next best, and approval plans the worst. 80.4% of librarians' books circulated; 69.7% of the faculty books circulated; and 61.8% of the approval plan books circulated. These differences were statistically significant at the .05 level. **(246)**

■ A 1976 study at the Health Sciences Library of the University of Iowa involving 1,288 books received during a 6-month period showed that 730 (57%) books were received on the approval plan; 330 (25%) were received due to orders placed on the basis of book reviews or publishers fliers; 131 (10%) were received due to orders generated as a result of patron request; and 97 (8%) were received due to standing order. **(467)**

■ A 1978 survey of law school libraries listed in the 1977 *AALS Directory of Law Teachers* (population: 167; responding: 158 or 95%) *showed that* law-related acquisitions or titles requested by the law library were arbitrarily assigned to other departmental libraries on the basis of a classification scheme or some other means. **(362)**

■ A 1978-79 study underwritten by the NSF Division of Information Science and Technology of academic and research journal subscription and cancellation for both individuals and libraries (individual questionnaires: 2,817; usable responses: 1,190; library questionnaires: 4,997; usable responses: 1,905) of journals at least 5 years old *showed that* publisher information about library subscriptions was suspect. In 514 or 42.4% of the cases libraries disputed publisher claims that they had entered new subscriptions for a journal, while in 853 or 50.9% of the cases they disputed publisher claims that they had canceled a journal subscription. **(264)**

Ibid. . . . *showed that* 152 (58%) of the libraries planned to review their new subscriptions upon renewal. Of these libraries (multiple responses possible), 98 (64.5%) report the review will involve user evaluations, 84 (55.3%) staff evaluations, 67 (44.1%) usage statistics, 17 (11.2%) rank ordering with other titles, 11 (7.2%) acquisitions decisions of other libraries, 8 (5.3%) network or consortium policies, and 2 (1.3%) did not specify procedures. **(264)**

Ibid. . . . *showed that*, of 296 new subscriptions placed, 182 (61.5%) were to titles not previously held; 78 (26.4%) were reinstatements of previously held titles; 19 (6.4%) were additional subscriptions for a title already held; 12 (4.1%) were formerly free, i.e., exchange or gift, subscriptions; and 5 (1.7%) were for miscellaneous other reasons. **(264)**

Ibid. . . . *showed that* reasons for library subscriptions were as follows (multiple responses possible; N = 296): 93 (31.4%) subscriptions were due to user group or departmental evaluation; 76 (25.7%) were recommended by library staff; 70 (23.6%) were specifically requested by a continuing user; 63 (21.3%) were due to development of new areas of specialization; 55 (18.6%) were specifically requested by a new user; 31 (10.5%) were due to easing of budgetary restrictions. **(264)**

Practices and Procedures 145

Ibid. . . . *showed that*, of 419 responding libraries, the top 5 factors for journal subscription cancellations were as follows (multiple responses possible): 238 (56.8%) cancellations were due to budget curtailments, 192 (45.8%) due to staff evaluation, 148 (35.3%) due to shifting priorities, 117 (27.9%) due to user recommendations, and 36 (8.6%) due to high price. **(264)**

Ibid. . . . *showed that*, of 358 libraries, 329 (91.9%) reported that journal subscription cancellations were not due in any degree to membership in a consortium or network whose policies formally encouraged cancellation of titles elsewhere, while 29 (8.1%) reported that such membership did play a role in the cancellation decision. **(264)**

Ibid. . . . *showed that*, of 362 libraries who had canceled a journal subscription, only 13 (3.6%) reported they had had any request for the title since cancellation; 269 (74.3%) reported they had not had such a request; and 80 (22.1%) reported they were uncertain. **(264)**

Ibid. . . . *showed that*, of 362 libraries who had canceled a journal subscription, only 56 (15.5%) planned any sort of formal review of the cancellation decision, and of these 56 only 9 (16.1%) "estimated the possibility of resubscription as good." **(264)**

■ An Indiana University survey for the National Science Foundation reported in 1979 *showed that* library administrators responded to shortages in the library materials serials budget primarily by canceling duplicates and shifting funds from monographic to serials accounts. The third most common tactic was to halt new subscriptions in order to renew old ones. **(016)**

■ A survey in 1979 of 119 major academic business libraries (89 responding or 75%, with 86 usable responses) *showed that* 28 (33%) actively collected business/economic working papers. 0f the 28, 9 (32%) selected only single numbers of working paper series; 7 (25%) collected complete runs; and 12 (43%) used both methods. **(120)**

Ibid. . . . *showed that*, of the 28 major academic business libraries collecting working papers, the selection criteria used were reputation of institution (20 libraries), faculty/patron request (18), available as gift (17), available through exchange (9), and reputation of the author (7). **(120)**

■ A study reported in 1980 at the University of Rochester comparing costs of 1-year versus 3-year journal subscriptions, based on a sample of 20 business administration and management science periodicals, *showed that*, when 4 variables were considered (cost of capital, reorder costs, average inflation rate for 1-year subscriptions, and ratio of 3-year to 1-year subscription costs), the 3-year subscription period was always the most advantageous in terms of cost. Specifically, the least projected savings for the 20 periodicals was 12%, while the most in projected savings that could be realized was 106%. The savings was due to locking in advantageous subscription rates for a 3-year period and to reduced staff costs caused by reduced renewal activity. **(627)**

■ A survey reported in 1983 of Medical Library Association institutional members concerning their use of audiovisual materials (survey size: 300; responding: 201; usable: 198 or 66%) *showed that*, of 143 respondents (91 hospital, 29 medical school, and 13 "other" libraries) that did provide AV services, 71% of the hospital and 50% of the medical school libraries reported previewing less than 25% of the AV materials before purchase. **(750)**

School

■ A survey reported in 1978 of factors influencing selection of school media materials, involving 107 wholesaler/distributors (25 responses or 27%), 106 publishers/producers (46 responses or 49%), and 516 media program personnel (222 responses or 44%), *showed that* media program personnel reported final responsibility for selecting books resided as follows: media specialists (63%), acquisitions or order librarians (17%), district media coordinator (10%), other (6%), principal (2%), teachers and reviewing group (1% each), students (0%). **(217)**

Ibid. . . . *showed that* media program personnel reported final responsibility for selecting nonprint materials resided as follows: media specialists (64%), district media coordinator (13%), acquisitions or order librarian (12%), other (6%), principals and teachers (2% each), reviewing group (1%), students (0%). **(217)**

Ibid. . . . *showed that* publishers and producers rated the following individuals or groups as "very important" in selecting books for school media

Practices and Procedures

centers (multiple responses allowed): reviewing group (58%), media specialists (57%), acquisitions or order librarian (48%), district media coordinator (36%), teachers (29%), curriculum coordinators (21%), principals (13%), and students (0%). **(217)**

Ibid. . . . *showed that* publishers and producers rated the following individuals or groups as "very important" in selecting nonprint materials for school media centers (multiple responses allowed): media specialists (62%), reviewing group (54%), teachers (52%), district media coordinator (50%), curriculum coordinators (42%), acquisitions or order librarian (35%), principal (28%), and students (4%). **(217)**

Ibid. . . . *showed that* school media personnel reported the following teacher roles in selecting materials (multiple responses allowed): requests from teachers to media staff (92%), exhibits of new materials for teacher preview (42%), requests from media staff to subject area teachers (39%), demonstrations of new materials by publisher/distributor representatives (35%), selection committee (17%), and other (10%). **(217)**

Ibid. . . . *showed that* school media personnel reported that 37% had access to a book examination center. Of those so responding, 46% had access to a local center; 31% had access to a regional center; and 23% had access to a state center. **(217)**

Ibid. . . . *showed that* school media personnel reported that 24% had access to a nonprint materials center. Of those so responding, "more than half" had access to a local center; "one-third" reported access to a regional center; and "the remainder" had access to a state center. **(217)**

Ibid. . . . *showed that* 37% of the school media personnel reported a systematic plan in their school for previewing, but 59% of those so responding reported that use of the plan was not required. **(217)**

Ibid. . . . *showed that* publishers/producers reported the following methods of materials preview: sent when requested by reviewers for publication (books: 46%; nonprint: 41%), sent automatically to reviewers for publicton (books: 46%; nonprint: 30%), sent to media programs on request (books: 35%; nonprint: 37%), sent automatically to school systems of specified size and budget (books: 30%; nonprint: 2%). **(217)**

Ibid. ... *showed that* 16% of the school media personnel reported the importance of the teacher's guide packaged with school media center materials as essential; 65% reported them helpful; 13% reported them as of little use; and 6% reported them never used. **(217)**

Ibid. ... *showed that* publishers/producers reported the following dollar sales volume for various media: books (54%); sound filmstrips (16%); 16mm film (6%); kits (4%); audiocassettes (2%); super 8 loops, filmstrips, records, reel-to-reel tapes, videotapes, and study prints (approximately 1% each). **(217)**

Special

■ A 1967 survey of medical school libraries concerning reference services (survey size: 93 libraries; responding: 85 or 91.4%) *showed that* 65 (76.5%) libraries reported that the reference department assumed "some degree of responsibility for book selection," while 20 (23.5%) libraries reported no such responsibility. **(682)**

■ A 1976 study at the Health Sciences Library of the University of Iowa, involving 1,288 books received during a 6-month period, *showed that* 730 (57%) books were received on the approval plan; 330 (25%) were received due to orders placed on the basis of book reviews or publishers' fliers; 131 (10%) were received due to orders generated as a result of patron request; and 97 (8%) were received due to standing order. **(467)**

■ A 1978 survey of law school libraries listed in the 1977 *AALS Directory of Law Teachers* (population: 167; responding: 158 or 95%) *showed that* law-related acquisitions or titles requested by the law library were arbitrarily assigned to other departmental libraries on the basis of a classification scheme or some other means. **(362)**

■ A survey reported in 1983 of Medical Library Association institutional members concerning their use of audiovisual materials (survey size: 300; responding: 201; usable: 198 or 66%) *showed that*, of 143 respondents (91 hospital, 29 medical school, and 13 "other" libraries) that did provide AV services, 71% of the hospital and 50% of the medical school libraries reported previewing less than 25% of the AV materials before purchase. **(750)**

Retrenchment

Academic

■ An Indiana University survey for the National Science Foundation *showed that* during the period 1969-76 large academic libraries reduced the percentage of their budget spent on serials vs. monographs. In 1969 $2 was spent on serials for every $1 on monographs; by 1976 it had been steadily reduced to $1.23 for serials for each $1.00 spent on monographs. **(016)**

Ibid. . . . *showed that* library administrators responded to shortages in the library materials serials budget primarily by canceling duplicates and shifting funds from monographic to serials accounts. The third most common tactic was to halt new subscriptions in order to renew old ones. **(016)**

Ibid. . . . *showed that* major academic libraries increased their materials budget by an average of 9.4% in the period 1973-76; a 15-18% increase was reported necessary to maintain equivalent coverage. **(016)**

■ A review of various indicators for the 1970-75 period *showed that*, while the U.S. Consumer Price Index showed an increase of 38.6%, the average price of U.S. periodicals increased by 92% compared to an increase in Association for Research Libraries materials expenditures of 36.5% and a decrease in gross volumes added to ARL collections of 14.3%. **(111)**

■ A 1978-79 study underwritten by the NSF Division of Information Science and Technology of academic and research journal subscription and cancellation for both individuals and libraries (individual questionnaires: 2,817; usable responses: 1,190; library questionnaires: 4,997; usable responses: 1,905) of journals at least 5 years old *showed that* of 419 responding libraries the top 5 factors for journal subscription cancellations were as follows (multiple responses possible): 238 (56.8%) cancellations were due to budget curtailments, 192 (45.8%) due to staff evaluation, 148 (35.3%) due to shifting priorities, 117 (27.9%) due to user recommendations, and 36 (8.6%) due to high price. **(264)**

Ibid. . . . *showed that*, of 358 libraries, 329 (91.9%) reported that journal subscription cancellations were not due in any degree to membership in a consortium or network whose policies formally encouraged cancellation of titles elsewhere, while 29 (8.1%) reported that such membership did play a role in the cancellation decision. **(264)**

Ibid. . . . *showed that*, of 362 libraries who had canceled a journal subscription, only 13 (3.6%) reported they had had any request for the title since cancellation; 269 (74.3%) reported they had not had such a request; and 80 (22.1%) reported they were uncertain. **(264)**

Ibid. . . . *showed that*, of 362 libraries who had canceled a journal subscription, only 56 (15.5%) planned any sort of formal review of the cancellation decision, and of these 56 only 9 (16.1%) "estimated the possibility of resubscription as good." **(264)**

■ A 1979 study at the University of North Dakota of faculty willingness to cancel journal titles and rely on interlibrary loan (3,030 periodical titles considered; responses from 32 of 47 departments) *showed that* teaching faculty were willing to cancel not only periodicals they rated as marginally important but even substantial numbers of periodicals they rated as moderately important and a few they rated as essential. Specifically, of 1,721 periodical titles rated "essential," of 832 periodical titles rated "of moderate value," and of 418 periodical titles rated "of marginal value" by the faculty respondents, the average number of subscriptions faculty would be willing to cancel in each group (weighted to reflect the different number of journals considered by each responding department) was 1.2% of the "essential" journal titles, 17.9% of the "of moderate value" journal titles, and 82.8% of the "of marginal value" titles. **(645)**

Selection—General Issues

Academic

■ A survey reported in 1966 of 68 libraries in colleges related to a church and having church historical materials in their collection (57 or 83.8% responding; usable replies: 48 or 70.6%) *showed that* 95.8% of respondents collected periodicals published by the denomination; 89.6% collected denominational/district yearbooks; 87.5% collected books by church authors; 85.4% collected various official minutes; 77.1% collected disciplines/church manuals; 72.9% collected some form of institutional records; 60.4% collected pictures; 54.2% collected directories of members; 43.7% collected various kinds of correspondence; and 39.8% collected some form of AV material. **(176)**

Selection

■ A study reported in 1983 investigating the relationship between the scholarliness of academic papers and their impact by comparing the number of references in each of 110 papers (taken from the *American Sociological Review* and the *American Journal of Sociology* during the years 1972-73) to the number of citations listed for each of the papers in *Social Science Citation Index*, 1972-81, *showed that* there was a very modest but statistically significant relationship between scholarliness and impact. Specifically, the correlation coefficient (partial gamma coefficient) was .26 and significant at the .03 level. **(659)**

Public

■ An analysis reported in 1973 of 154 picture books with imprints ranging from 1903 to 1971, representing 78 authors and selected from a university education department library collection of 957 such books, *showed that* 65% pictured women in some role. 87% of these depictions of women portrayed them in homemaking roles, while 17% portrayed them in professional roles. **(279)**

Ibid. . . . *showed that* the most common professional roles women portrayed in the books were teacher (30%), maid (15%), and nun (12%).
(279)

School

■ An analysis reported in 1973 of 154 picture books with imprints ranging from 1903 to 1971, representing 78 authors and selected from a university education department library collection of 957 such books, *showed that* 65% pictured women in some role. 87% of these depictions of women portrayed them in homemaking roles, while 17% portrayed them in professional roles. **(279)**

Ibid. . . . *showed that* the most common professional roles women portrayed in the books were teacher (30%), maid (15%), and nun (12%).
(279)

Selection, Monographs—General Issues

Academic

■ A study reported in 1976 of the bibliographic coverage of 1,972 social science (psychology, sociology, political science, and economics) books and government publications (primarily 1971 and 1972 imprints searched in the bibliographic sources for the subsequent 3-4 years) *showed that* books reviewed in a discipline's journals are more likely than nonreviewed books to be cited in the bibliographic services. For example:

in psychology, 115 of 170 books (68%) were reviewed overall, while 57 of 77 (74%) cited books were reviewed;

in sociology, 108 of 270 books (40%) were reviewed overall, while 72 of 136 (53%) cited books were reviewed;

in political science, 44 of 105 (42%) books were reviewed overall, while 42 of 86 (49%) cited books were reviewed;

in economics, 44 of 149 (30%) books were reviewed overall, while 43 of 116 (37%) cited books were reviewed. **(410)**

■ A study reported in 1978 at the West Virginia University College of Engineering of the citations found in the master's theses accepted over a 4-year period (126 theses between 1971-74) *showed that* nonjournal (i.e. book) literature was more important in the engineering sciences than previously thought by showing that, of 3,002 references overall, only 1,000 (33.3%) were journal citations, with the proportion of journal citations by department ranging from 11.4% of the references in aerospace theses to 49.4% of the references in chemical theses. **(460)**

■ A survey reported in 1978 of 31 Ph.D. dissertations in the field of business/management (13 from the State University of New York at Buffalo and 18 from SUNYAB incoming faculty but completed at other schools) *showed that* the overall distribution of 2,805 citations by form was:

periodicals	1,377 (49.1%) citations
monographs	895 (31.9%) citations
serials	266 (9.5%) citations
miscellaneous	267 (9.5%) citations

(461)

■ A study during the 1981-82 academic year in the main library at Purdue concerning books undergraduates selected to read (involving interviews

Selection, Monographs 153

with 240 undergraduate borrowers and analysis of 598 of the mongraphic titles borrowed by both students and nonstudents) *showed that* undergraduates (and surprisingly) graduate students tended to use a core of heavily used titles, while faculty tended to use materials that had never before circulated. For example, of 67 items circulated to faculty, 18 (26.9%) had circulated 6 or more times, while of 131 items circulated to graduate students, 77 (58.8%) had been circulated 6 or more times, and of 364 items circulated to undergraduates, 253 (69.5%) had been circulated 6 or more times. (There were 36 missing cases.) (530)

Ibid. . . . *showed that*, based on 364 items circulated to undergraduates, only 15.9% of the titles selected by undergraduates were based on instructor recommendation (direct recommendation or reading lists), while the remaining titles were selected without instructor direction. 86.6% were selected for subject matter relating to a specific course; 11.6% were selected for leisure reading; and 1.8% were selected for research in the student's major with no specific course in mind. (530)

Ibid. . . . *showed that* titles recommended by instructors and checked out by undergraduates were no more likely to fall within the core of highly circulating materials than outside it. For example, of 111 titles that circulated less than 6 times, 16 or 14.4% had been recommended by faculty, while of 253 titles that had circulated 6 times or more, 42 (16.6%) had been recommended by faculty. (530)

Ibid. . . . *showed that* the "best and most critically acclaimed" books do not make up the majority of undergraduate reading. For example, of 252 books checked out by undergraduates that had been published before 1973, only 61 (24.2%) were listed in *Books for College Libraries*, while of 246 books published after 1963, only 74 (30.1%) were reviewed in *Choice*, and of these, only 35% were given top recommendations.
(530)

Selection, Monographs—Hardback versus Paperback

General

■ A study reported in 1968 of Book Trade Statistics sections of the *Bowker Annual*, 1960-67, *showed that* the increase of sales of hardbound books rose from 32,298,000 in 1958 to 40,213,000 in 1963 (increase of

24.2%), while sales of paperbound books rose in the same period from 5,661,000 to 48,874,000 (for an increase of 763.3%). **(189)**

Academic

■ A 1967 survey by the Institute of Higher Education at Teachers College, Columbia University, of innovative programs in libraries in academic institutions with liberal arts programs (sample size: 1,193; responding: 781 or 65%) *showed that* 71 responding libraries (9%) reported that they did not use paperbound books in their collections.
(190)

■ A study reported in 1968 of monographic acquisitions during the last 7 months of 1966 at the University of North Carolina *showed that* 29.6% of all books acquired were paperbound, while for the same period in 1967 the figure had risen to 46.7%. **(189)**

Public

■ A study reported in 1979 at the Oklahoma City/County Metropolitan Library System *showed that* during FY 1978-79, for an uncataloged paperback collection of 76,862 items, each item circulated an average of 4.75 times during the year. This compared to an average circulation of 2.31 times per item during the same period for a collection of 465,326 cataloged hardback books. **(231)**

Ibid. . . . *showed that*, for 18,996 adult hardback books and 19,126 adult paperback books purchased in FY 1976-77, the cost ratio based on purchase price alone of hardback to paperback was 4.1 to 1, while the cost per circulation (again based on purchase price only) of hardback to paperback was 4.2 to 1. For slightly more materials in FY 1977-78, the cost ratio of hardbound to paperback was 3.7 to 1, and the cost per circulation was 3.89 to 1. **(231)**

Ibid. . . . *showed that*, for 5,624 juvenile hardback books and 6,031 paperback books purchased in FY 1976-77, the cost ratio based on purchase price alone of hardback to paperback was 5.9 to 1, while the cost per circulation (again based on purchase price only) of hardback to paperback was 2.7 to 1. For approximately the same number of materials purchased in FY 1977-78, the cost ratio of hardbound to paperback was 4.8 to 1, and the cost per circulation was 2.6 to 1. **(231)**

Selection, Monographs 155

Ibid. . . . *showed that*, during the month of July 1979, the average number of circulations per volume for 15,784 cataloged adult hardback volumes purchased in FY 1976-77 was .25, for 18,163 volumes purchased in FY 1977-78 was .33, and for 18,569 volumes purchased in FY 1978-79 was .64. This compares to the average number of circulations per volume for adult uncataloged paperbacks of .32 for a group of 6,743 volumes purchased in FY 1976-77, .54 for a group of 11,760 volumes purchased in FY 1977-78, and .87 for 19,138 volumes purchased in FY 1978-79. (231)

Ibid. . . . *showed that*, during the month of July 1979, the average number of circulations per volume for 4,723 juvenile cataloged hardback volumes purchased in FY 1976-77 was 1.20; for 4,777 volumes purchased in FY 1977-78 was 1.18; and for 4,771 volumes purchased in 1978-79 was 1.28. This compares to the average number of circulations per volume for juvenile uncataloged paperbacks of .79 for 2,973 volumes purchased in FY 1976-77, 1.06 for 3,349 volumes purchased in 1977-78, and 1.09 for 3,037 volumes purchased in FY 1978-79. (231)

■ A 1982 survey of American and Canadian public libraries (sample size: 279; responding: 68 or 24%) *showed that* approximately 10.5% (±3.2%, representing a 95% confidence interval for the population at large) of respondents' current book acquisitions budgets had been allocated for the purchase of mass market paperbacks, while about 9.2% (±3.1%, representing a 95% confidence interval for the population at large) of their last year's book budget was spent on mass market paperbacks. There was a small statistical correlation ("y's = .26 and .30 respectively") between the book budget percentages and size of populations served, with the libraries serving larger populations tending to allocate more money for the purchase of paperbacks (significance level not given). (273)

Ibid. . . . *showed that* approximately 27.4% (±5.9%, representing a 95% confidence interval for the population at large) of the books purchased by responding libraries were mass market paperbacks, while approximately 11% (±6.3%, representing 95% confidence interval for the population at large) of the circulating collections were mass market paperbacks. These percentages of books purchased were statistically independent of the institutional characteristics (e.g., size of population served) of the libraries. (273)

Ibid. . . . *showed that*, while approximately 11% of the circulating collections consisted of mass market paperbacks, these books accounted for approximately 18.2% of the book circulation, with hardcover books accounting for the rest. (273)

Ibid. . . . *showed that* the top 3 types of 86 problems indentified by responding libraries were lack of adequate reviewing media for paperbacks (24%), backlist ordering (13%), and partial order fulfillment (12%). **(273)**

Selection, Monographs—Subject Area (African Studies)

Academic

■ A 1971 study at Indiana University, Bloomington during a 3-month period concerning the bibliographic tools used by 6 professional staff members responsible for different areas of collection development *showed that*, for 566 monographic titles selected by the African studies specialist, 39 bibliographic sources were used. The 6 most important sources were as follows:

LC proof slips	124 (21.9%) titles	
publishers' blurbs	83 (14.7%) titles	
Oxford Books for East Africa	49 (8.7%) titles	
British National Bibliography	48 (8.5%) titles	
LC Accessions List: East Africa	29 (5.1%) titles	
Bibliographie de la France	29 (5.1%) titles	**(631)**

Selection, Monographs—Subject Area (Anthropology)

Academic

■ A 1971 study at Indiana University, Bloomington during a 3-month period concerning the bibliographic tools used by 6 professional staff members responsible for different areas of collection development *showed that*, for the 744 monographic titles selected by the specialist for anthropology, folklore, and sociology, 24 bibliographic sources were used. The 6 most important sources were as follows:

Selection, Monographs

LC proof slips	147 (19.8%) titles	
Publishers' Weekly	68 (9.1%) titles	
Blackwell	62 (8.3%) titles	
publishers' blurbs	58 (7.8%) titles	
American Sociological Review	50 (6.7%) titles	
American Journal of Sociology	24 (3.2%) titles	**(631)**

Selection, Monographs—Subject Area (Business)

Academic

■ A 1971 study at Indiana University, Bloomington during a 3-month period concerning the bibliographic tools used by 6 professional staff members responsible for different areas of collection development *showed that*, for 364 titles selected by the business specialist, 20 bibliographic sources were used. The 6 most important sources were as follows:

American Book Publishing Record	133 (36.5%) titles	
publishers' blurbs	73 (20.1%) titles	
Library Journal	40 (11.0%) titles	
Blackwell	10 (2.7%) titles	
Books in Print	6 (1.6%) titles	
Business and Technology Sources	6 (1.6%) titles	**(631)**

■ A survey reported in 1978 of 31 Ph.D. dissertations in the field of business/management (13 from the State University of New York at Buffalo and 18 from SUNYAB incoming faculty but completed at other schools) *showed that* the overall distribution of 2,805 citations by form was:

periodicals	1,377 (49.1%) citations	
monographs	895 (31.9%) citations	
serials	266 (9.5%) citations	
miscellaneous	267 (9.5%) citations	**(461)**

Ibid. . . . *showed that* the 7 most frequently cited subject areas (based on 1,161 citations to monographs and serials) were:

business (HF 5001-6351)	14.7% citations	
economics: labor (HD 4801-8942)	11.5% citations	
economics: production (HD 1-100)	10.8% citations	
psychology (BF)	8.2% citations	
sociology (HM-HX)	7.3% citations	
finance (HG)	6.4% citations	
economic theory	6.0% citations	**(461)**

Selection, Monographs—Subject Area (Engineering)

Academic

■ A study reported in 1978 at the West Virginia University College of Engineering of the citations found in the master's theses accepted over a 4-year period (126 theses between 1971-74) *showed that* nonjournal (i.e., book) literature was more important in the engineering sciences than previously thought by showing that, of 3,002 references overall, only 1,000 (33.3%) were journal citations, with the proportion of journal citations by department ranging from 11.4% of the references in aerospace theses to 49.4% of the references in chemical theses. **(460)**

Selection, Monographs—Subject Area (History)

Academic

■ A 1971 study at Indiana University, Bloomington during a 3-month period concerning the bibliographic tools used by 6 professional staff members responsible for different areas of collection development *showed that*, for 220 titles selected by the specialist for philosophy, history and philosophy of science, and classics, 29 bibliographic sources were used. The 6 most important sources were as follows:

publishers' blurbs	38 (17.3%) titles	
Repertoire Bibliographique de la Philosophie	26 (11.8%) titles	
Gnomon	15 (6.8%) titles	
Classical Review	15 (6.8%) titles	
Choice	14 (6.4%) titles	
American Book Publishing Record	12 (5.5%) titles	**(631)**

Ibid. . . . *showed that*, for 546 titles selected by the history specialist, 21 bibliographic sources were used. The 6 most important sources were as follows:

Library Journal	97 (17.8%) titles	
British National Bibliography	92 (16.8%) titles	
publishers' blurbs	87 (15.9%) titles	
Publishers' Weekly	83 (15.2%) titles	
LC proof slips	46 (8.4%) titles	
Bibliographie de la France	22 (4.0%) titles	**(631)**

■ A survey reported in 1981 of historians listed in the 1978 *Directory of American Scholars* concerning their use of and attitudes toward periodicals (survey size: 767 historians, although not all questionnaires could be delivered; responding: 360 or 46.9%, with respondents tending to be younger and with a higher scholarly productivity record than nonrespondents) *showed that* historians tended not to use the invisible college for discovering relevant published information for research. Specifically, the 3 most highly rated methods (out of 10) of discovering relevant published information for research (based on a rating scale of 1 to 5 where 5 was most highly rated) were:

bibliographies or references in books or journals	4.36 rating
specialized bibliographies	4.01 rating
book reviews	3.85 rating

While "discussion or correspondence with acquaintances elsewhere" ranked 6th with a rating of 3.14, "consulting a known expert" ranked 8th (2.87 rating), and "discussion with colleague at own institution" ranked 9th

(2.6 rating). "Consulting librarian" ranked 10th (2.16 rating). **(780)**

Ibid. . . . *showed that* respondents clearly preferred bibliographic tools providing abstracts over those providing simple author and title entries. Specifically, when asked to compare the value of bibliographic tools providing abstracts in contrast to simple author and title entries, 23.7% reported the abstracts "about the same"; 46.4% reported the abstracts "somewhat more satisfactory"; and 29.9% reported the abstracts "much more satisfactory." **(780)**

Ibid. . . . *showed that* the degree of importance to their research of knowing as soon as possible after publication what had been published was as follows:

very important	40.7% respondents	
moderately important	47.8% respondents	
not very important	11.5% respondents	**(780)**

Ibid. . . . *showed that* the 3 most used formats (out of 14) in their current research were (based on a rating scale of 1 to 5 where 5 was the most used) as follows: periodicals (4.26 rating), books (4.47 rating), and manuscripts (3.66 rating). **(780)**

Selection, Monographs—Subject Area (Library Science)

Academic

■ A study reported in 1979 of the English-language literature of library administration (2,877 citations to materials cited in 364 refereed articles indexed in *Library Literature* between 1961-70) *showed that* the distribution of cited works by type was as follows:

monographs	1,247 (43.3%) cited works	
journals	1,149 (39.9%) cited works	
governmental publications	338 (11.7%) cited works	
miscellaneous	143 (4.9%) cited works	**(566)**

Selection, Monographs—Subject Area (Music)

Academic

■ A study reported in 1972 of the 1967 *RILM Abstracts (Repertoire International de la Litterature Musicale)* involving every tenth entry from the subject index (158 items) *showed that* the 3 most popular languages were English (72.5 or 46% articles), German (20 or 12.5% articles), and French (15 or 9.5% articles). Articles published in 2 languages were counted as .5 in each language. **(401)**

Ibid. . . . *showed that* an examination of every twelfth entry in the 1967 cumulative index (1,125 entries) indicated that the 4 most common publication forms were articles from periodicals (612 or 54.4%), monographs (145 or 13.7%), articles from Festschriften (75 or 6.7%), and book reviews (72 or 6.4%). **(401)**

Special

■ A study reported in 1972 of the 1967 *RILM Abstracts (Repertoire International de la Litterature Musicale)* involving every tenth entry from the subject index (158 items) *showed that* the 3 most popular languages were English (72.5 or 46% articles), German (20 or 12.5% articles), and French (15 or 9.5% articles). Articles published in 2 languages were counted as .5 in each language. **(401)**

Ibid. . . . *showed that* an examination of every twelfth entry in the 1967 cumulative index (1,125 entries) indicated that the 4 most common publication forms were articles from periodicals (612 or 54.4%), monographs (145 or 13.7%), articles from Festschriften (75 or 6.7%), and book reviews (72 or 6.4%). **(401)**

Selection, Monographs—Subject Area (Philosophy)

Academic

■ A 1971 study at Indiana University, Bloomington during a 3-month period concerning the bibliographic tools used by 6 professional staff members responsible for different areas of collection development *showed that*, for 220 titles selected by the specialist for philosophy, history and philosophy of science, and classics, 29 bibliographic sources were used. The 6 most important sources were as follows:

publishers' blurbs	38 (17.3%) titles	
Repertoire Bibliographique de la Philosophie	26 (11.8%) titles	
Gnomon	15 (6.8%) titles	
Classical Review	15 (6.8%) titles	
Choice	14 (6.4%) titles	
American Book Publishing Record	12 (5.5%) titles	**(631)**

Selection, Monographs—Subject Area (Political Science)

Academic

■ A summary of a study of 46 political science books published in 1948 and 1949 *showed that* 30.9% of the books' citations were from other political science works and 69.1% of the citations came from other disciplines. **(053)**

■ A 1971 study at Indiana University, Bloomington during a 3-month period concerning the bibliographic tools used by 6 professional staff members responsible for different areas of collection development *showed that*, for 1,082 titles selected by the political science specialist, 40 bibliographic sources were used. The 6 most important sources were as follows:

LC proof slips	364 (33.6%) titles	
publishers' blurbs	148 (13.7%) titles	
Publishers' Weekly	139 (12.8%) titles	
British National Bibliography	69 (6.4%) titles	
Blackwell	64 (5.9%) titles	
Public Affairs Information Service Bulletin	49 (4.5%) titles	**(631)**

Selection, Monographs—Subject Area (Sociology)

Academic

■ A 1971 study at Indiana University, Bloomington during a 3-month period concerning the bibliographic tools used by 6 professional staff members responsible for different areas of collection development *showed that*, for the 744 monographic titles selected by the specialist for anthropology, folklore, and sociology, 24 bibliographic sources were used. The 6 most important sources were as follows:

LC proof slips	147 (19.8%) titles	
Publishers' Weekly	68 (9.1%) titles	
Blackwell	62 (8.3%) titles	
publishers' blurbs	58 (7.8%) titles	
American Sociological Review	50 (6.7%) titles	
American Journal of Sociology	24 (3.2%) titles	**(631)**

Selection, Other—General Issues

Academic

■ A survey in 1979 of faculty members and graduate students at the School of Management at Purdue and the School of Commerce at the University of Illinois, Urbana (sample size: 567, responding: 213) *showed that*, of the faculty responding, 39 at Purdue (90.7%) and 57 at Illinois (72.2%) felt that the library should collect working papers. The majority of both faculties (59% at Illinois; 74% at Purdue) felt the library should collect all papers in a series rather than selected papers. **(120)**

Ibid. . . . *showed that*, of the faculty responding, 23 at Illinois (28.4%) and 17 at Purdue (44.7%) felt that working papers had lasting research value rather than current awareness value only. This compared to 53% of the responding librarians in major academic business libraries who felt that working papers had lasting research value. **(120)**

164   COLLECTION DEVELOPMENT

■ A 1980 survey of law school libraries with collections in excess of 175,000 volumes (sample size: 50; responding: 37 or 70%) *showed that* the demand for old case books was:

for faculty, frequent (1 library), occasional (18 libraries), almost none (17 libraries), and no answer (1 library);

for students, frequent (2 libraries), occasional (8 libraries), almost none (24 libraries), and no answer (3 libraries);

for other patrons, frequent (1 library), occasional (6 libraries), almost none (27 libraries), and no answer (3 libraries). **(369)**

■ A survey reported in 1981 of a select group of American academic and research libraries known for their third world collections (45 libraries surveyed; 26 responding) *showed that* 35% of the responding libraries felt that most of the third world publications were only available through gift and exchange, while an additional 65% felt that some of the third world publications were only available through gift and exchange. 70% of responding libraries said that gift and exchange material was crucial to their collections. **(037)**

Public

■ A survey reported in 1977 based on a stratified random sample of 300 households (response rate: 251 or 83%) in the Piedmont area of North Carolina *showed that* library users (135) and library nonusers (115), with one respondent not reporting, had the following musical preferences: gospel (nonusers 83%, users 55%); country (nonusers 53%, users 53%); rock (nonusers 37%, users 41%); popular (nonusers 30%, users 67%); soul (nonusers 30%, users 29%), classical (nonusers 11%, users 43%); Broadway (nonusers 10%, users 29%). **(225)**

Special

■ A 1980 survey of law school libraries with collections in excess of 175,000 volumes (sample size: 50; responding: 37 or 70%) *showed that* the demand for old case books was:

for faculty, frequent (1 library), occasional (18 libraries), almost none (17 libraries), and no answer (1 library);

Selection, Other

for students, frequent (2 libraries), occasional (8 libraries), almost none (24 libraries), and no answer (3 libraries);

for other patrons, frequent (1 library), occasional (6 libraries), almost none (27 libraries), and no answer (3 libraries). **(369)**

Selection, Other—Dissertations

Academic

■ A study reported in 1972 of the bibliographic control of doctoral dissertations in the areas of sociology, psychology, biology, and education, involving 3,012 dissertations selected from *American Doctoral Dissertations*, showed that 1,665 (55.3%) dissertations were abstracted in either *Microfilm Abstracts* or the following *Dissertation Abstracts* during the period 1934-69. **(400)**

Ibid. . . . *showed that*, of those dissertations abstracted in *Dissertation Abstracts* and available on microfilm, 1,604 (90.5%) were abstracted within 2 years of the date of degree issuance. However, this comprised only 53.4% of the total number of dissertations issued. **(400)**

Ibid. . . . *showed that* 2,452 (81.4%) dissertations were never published; 457 (15.2%) resulted in journal articles; 62 (2.0%) resulted in books; and 41 (1.4%) resulted in chapters in books. **(400)**

Ibid. . . . *showed that* the subject of the dissertation as determined by the author for *Dissertation Abstracts* and the subject field assigned in *American Doctoral Dissertations* varied in their degree of agreement from a high of 88.9% agreement in psychology to a low of 45.1% agreement in health sciences. **(400)**

Selection, Other—Encyclopedias

Public

■ A 1978 survey of 100 (77 or 77% responding) U.S. public libraries of varying sizes concerning 37 general English-language encyclopedias

showed that the following 5 encyclopedias were reported to be in "constant and heavy demand" by at least a third of the respondents: *World Book Encyclopedia* (76 respondents); *Encyclopedia Americana* (66 respondents); *New Encyclopedia Britannica* (30 respondents); *Collier's Encyclopedia* (28 respondents); and *Compton's Encyclopedia* (26 respondents).
(232)

Ibid. . . . *showed that* the 3 "most effective all-around" encyclopedias were reported to be *World Book Encyclopedia* by 56 (75%) respondents, *Encyclopedia Americana* by 25 (32%), and *Collier's Encyclopedia* by 5 (6%).
(232)

Ibid. . . . *showed that*, of 3 major multivolume adult encyclopedias, *Encyclopedia Americana* was rated most effective (i.e., reliable, easy to use, clearly written, etc.) by 54 (70%) respondents, *Collier's Encyclopedia* by 17 (22%), and *Encyclopedia Britannica* by 5 (6%).
(232)

Ibid. . . . *showed that*, of 6 small-volume adult encyclopedias *New Columbia* was rated most effective (i.e., reliable, easy to use, clearly written, etc.) by 29 (38%) respondents, *Lincoln Library* by 19 (25%) respondents, and *Random House* by 13 (17%) respondents.
(232)

Ibid. . . . *showed that*, of 4 young adult encyclopedias, *World Book* was rated most effective (i.e., reliable, easy to use, clearly written, etc.) by 71 (92%) respondents, *Compton's Encyclopedia* by 5 (6%) respondents, and *Merit Students Encyclopedia* by 4 (5%) respondents.
(232)

Ibid. . . . *showed that*, of 3 multivolume children's encyclopedias, *New Book of Knowledge* was rated most effective (i.e., reliable, easy to use, clearly written, etc.) by 41 (53%) respondents and *Britannica Junior Encyclopedia* by 19 (25%).
(232)

Ibid. . . . *showed that* the general encyclopedia most commonly included in a ready reference collection was *World Book Encyclopedia* (29 or 38% respondents), followed by *Encyclopedia Americana* (11 or 14% respondents), and *New Encyclopedia Britannica* (6 or 8% respondents).
(232)

Selection, Other—Government Documents

Academic

▪ A 1977 survey of academic depository libraries (sample size: 200; responding: 160 or 80%) concerning the impact of commercially produced microforms *showed that* 93 (58%) respondents indicated that they "systematically" collected state government documents; that 33 (21%) reported that they made an effort to systematically collect municipal government documents; and that 33 (21%) reported collecting county or regional government publications in an organized way. **(318)**

Ibid. . . . *showed that* 73 (46%) respondents reported purchasing microforms of governmental publications from commercial publishers. Of these 73, 52 (71%) reported that they systematically consult reviewing sources related to microforms. **(318)**

Ibid. . . . *showed that* the top 6 sources consulted by the 73 respondents for information concerning commercially produced microforms were (multiple responses allowed): publishers' brochures (50 respondents), *Documents to the People* (42 respondents), *Government Publications Review* (39 respondents), advice from colleagues (36 respondents), faculty recommendations (34 respondents), and *Microform Review* (33 respondents).
(318)

Ibid. . . . *showed that* the top 3 types of federal publications collected in microform were (multiple responses allowed): congressional hearings (39 respondents), documents from executive departments and agencies (39 respondents), and the Serial Set (38 respondents). Number of respondents not given. **(318)**

Ibid. . . . *showed that* the top 3 reasons for purchasing documents on microform were (multiple responses allowed): to save space (60 or 82%), to acquire needed research material (57 or 78%), and to fill gaps in the collection (77 or 56%). Number of respondents was 73. **(318)**

Ibid. . . . *showed that* the top 3 reasons given by the 73 respondents who reported purchasing commercially produced documents for selecting a particular publisher were (multiple responses allowed): cost (64 or 88%); format, i.e., fiche, card, or film (57 or 78%); and reputation of company (43 or 59%). (318)

Ibid. . . . *showed that* 12 (16%) of the responding librarians (N = 73) reported having significant problems with commercial publishers of document microforms. The 2 most frequent complaints were poor production quality, including defective microfiche, and delays in the shipment of orders. (318)

■ An international survey reported in 1972 of university librarians worldwide (sample size: 2,612; responding: 522) *showed that* purchase of multiple copies of a work was reported to be "always" or "often" the practice by 6% of the North American respondents and 12% of the respondents of the rest of the world when the work was a reference book; by 7% of the North American respondents and 14% of the rest of the world when the work was a monograph; by 6% of the North American respondents and 67% of the rest of the world when the work was a student text; and by 7% of the North American respondents and 9% of the rest of the world when the work was some other kind of book. (320)

Ibid. . . . *showed that* 1% of the North American respondents would purchase extra copies of a work in microfilm format rather than traditional book format if the price were 15% more, 8% would purchase the extra microfilm copies if the price were the same, and 25% would purchase the extra microfilm copies if the price were reduced by 15%, while for the rest of the world 2% of the respondents would purchase the extra microfilm copies rather than the traditional book format if they cost 15% more, 4% would purchase extra microfilm copies if they were the same price, and 16% would purchase extra microfilm copies if they were 15% cheaper. (320)

■ A 1981 survey of U.S. depository libraries, both academic and public (sample size: 221; responding: 171 or 77%) concerning their use of online data bases (DIALOG, ORBIT, and BRS), particularly with regard to government documents, *showed that* the top 3 reasons given by respondents for not ordering government documents microfiche as the result of an online search were library does not have computer terminals (academic depositories, 33%; public depositories, 59%), didn't know that microfiche government documents could be ordered online (academic depositories, 24%; public depositories, 25%), and prefer hard copy to microfiche copy (academic depositories, 27%; public depositories, 20%). (317)

Ibid. . . . *showed that* none of the public depositories had ever ordered microfiche online as the result of a government document search, while only 3% of the academic libraries had ever done so. **(317)**

Public

■ A 1981 survey of U.S. depository libraries, both academic and public (sample size: 221; responding: 171 or 77%) concerning their use of online data bases (DIALOG, ORBIT, and BRS), particularly with regard to government documents, *showed that* the top 3 reasons given by respondents for not ordering government documents microfiche as the result of an online search were library does not have computer terminals (academic depositories, 33%; public depositories, 59%), didn't know that microfiche government documents could be ordered online (academic depositories, 24%; public depositories, 25%), and prefer hard copy to microfiche copy (academic depositories, 27%; public depositories, 20%). **(317)**

Selection, Other—Media

Academic

■ A 1972 study of audiovisual use in U.S. law schools undertaken by the American Association of Law Libraries Audio-Visual Committee (population: 149 law schools taken from the 1970 edition of the *Directory of Law Libraries*; responding: 142 or 95.3%) *showed that* the 4 types of AV media most commonly reported as heavily used (i.e., more than several times a year) were standard TV receiver (20.59% respondents), television camera (16.28% respondents), videotape recorder (14.00% respondents), and cassette tape recorder (12.93% respondents). **(387)**

■ A study reported in 1977 of audiovisual catalogs in the Learning Resources Center of the University of Connecticut Health Center Library (64 catalogs selected randomly from a total collection of 640 domestic and foreign catalogs) *showed that*:

> the catalogs provided a title 100% of the time and a summary and physical description at least 75% of the time;

> the catalogs provided information about intended audience 44-47% of the time, date of production 31-53% of the time, and producer 47-53% of the time;

the catalogs provided a title index 25% of the time and a
subject index 16-22% of the time. **(713)**

■ A survey reported in 1983 of Medical Library Association institutional members concerning their use of audiovisual materials (survey size: 300; responding: 201; usable: 198 or 66%) *showed that*, of 143 respondents (91 hospital, 29 medical school, and 13 "other" libraries) that did provide AV services, 71% of the hospital and 50% of the medical school libraries reported previewing less than 25% of the AV materials before purchase.
(750)

School

■ A survey reported in 1978 of factors influencing selection of school media materials, involving 107 wholesaler/distributors (25 responses or 27%), 106 publisher/s producers (46 responses or 49%), and 516 media program personnel (222 responses or 44%), *showed that* 16% of the school media personnel reported the importance of the teacher's guide packaged with school media center materials as essential; 65% reported them helpful; 13% reported them as of little use; and 6% reported them never used. **(217)**

Special

■ A 1972 study of audiovisual use in U.S. law schools undertaken by the American Association of Law Libraries Audio-Visual Committee (population: 149 law schools taken from the 1970 edition of the *Directory of Law Libraries*; responding: 142 or 95.3%) *showed that* the 4 types of AV media most commonly reported as heavily used (i.e., more than several times a year) were standard TV reciever (20.59% respondents), television camera (16.28% respondents), videotape recorder (14.00% respondents), and cassette tape recorder (12.93% respondents). **(387)**

■ A study reported in 1977 of audiovisual catalogs in the Learning Resources Center of the University of Connecticut Health Center Library (64 catalogs selected randomly from a total collection of 640 domestic and foreign catalogs) *showed that*:

the catalogs provided a title 100% of the time and a summary
and physical description at least 75% of the time;

the catalogs provided information about intended audience
44-47% of the time, date of production 31-53% of the time,
and producer 47-53% of the time;

the catalogs provided a title index 25% of the time and a subject index 16-22% of the time. **(713)**

■ A survey reported in 1983 of Medical Library Association institutional members concerning their use of audiovisual materials (survey size: 300; responding: 201; usable: 198 or 66%) *showed that*, of 143 respondents (91 hospital, 29 medical school, and 13 "other" libraries) that did provide AV services, 71% of the hospital and 50% of the medical school libraries reported previewing less than 25% of the AV materials before purchase.
(750)

Selection, Other—Microforms

Academic

■ A 1977 survey of academic depository libraries (sample size: 200; responding: 160 or 80%) concerning the impact of commercially produced microforms *showed that* 73 (46%) respondents reported purchasing microforms of governmental publications from commercial publishers. Of these 73, 52 (71%) reported that they systematically consult reviewing sources related to microforms. **(318)**

Ibid. . . . *showed that* the top 6 sources consulted by the 73 respondents for information concerning commercially produced microforms were (multiple responses allowed): publishers' brochures (50 respondents), *Documents to the People* (42 respondents), *Government Publications Review* (39 respondents), advice from colleagues (36 respondents), faculty recommendations (34 respondents), and *Microform Review* (33 respondents).
(318)

Ibid. . . . *showed that* the top 3 types of federal publications collected in microform were (multiple responses allowed): congressional hearings (39 respondents), documents from executive departments and agencies (39 respondents), and the Serial Set (38 respondents). Number of respondents not given. **(318)**

Ibid. . . . *showed that* the top 3 reasons for purchasing documents on microform were (multiple responses allowed): to save space (60 or 82%), to acquire needed research material (57 or 78%), and to fill gaps in the collection (56 or 77%). Number of respondents was 73. **(318)**

Ibid. . . . *showed that* the top 3 reasons given by the 73 respondents who reported purchasing commercially produced documents for selecting a particular publisher were (multiple responses allowed): cost (64 or 88%); format, i.e., fiche, card, or film (57 or 78%); and reputation of company (43 or 59%). **(318)**

Ibid. . . . *showed that* 12 (16%) of the responding librarians (N = 73) reported having significant problems with commercial publishers of document microforms. The 2 most frequent complaints were poor production quality, including defective microfiche, and delays in the shipment of orders. **(318)**

■ An international survey reported in 1972 of university librarians worldwide (sample size: 2,612; responding: 522) *showed that* purchase of multiple copies of a work was reported to be "always" or "often" the practice by 6% of the North American respondents and 12% of the respondents of the rest of the world when the work was a reference book; by 7% of the North American respondents and 14% of the rest of the world when the work was a monograph; by 6% of the North American respondents and 67% of the rest of the world when the work was a student text; and by 7% of the North American respondents and 9% of the rest of the world when the work was some other kind of book. **(320)**

Ibid. . . . *showed that* 1% of the North American respondents would purchase extra copies of a work in microfilm format rather than traditional book format if the price were 15% more, 8% would purchase the extra microfilm copies if the price were the same, and 25% would purchase the extra microfilm copies if the price were reduced by 15%, while for the rest of the world 2% of the respondents would purchase the extra microfilm copies rather than the traditional book format if they cost 15% more, 4% would purchase extra microfilm copies if they were the same price, and 16% would purchase extra microfilm copies if they were 15% cheaper.
(320)

■ A 1981 survey of U.S. depository libraries, both academic and public (sample size: 221; responding: 171 or 77%) concerning their use of online data bases (DIALOG, ORBIT, and BRS), particularly with regard to government documents, *showed that* the top 3 reasons given by respondents for not ordering government documents microfiche as the result of an online search were library does not have computer terminals (academic

Selection, Other

depositories, 33%; public depositories, 59%), didn't know that microfiche government documents could be ordered online (academic depositories, 24%; public depositories, 25%), and prefer hard copy to microfiche copy (academic depositories, 27%; public depositories, 20%). (317)

Ibid. . . . *showed that* none of the public depositories had ever ordered microfiche online as the result of a government document search, while only 3% of the academic libraries had ever done so. (317)

Public

■ A 1981 survey of U.S. depository libraries, both academic and public (sample size: 221; responding: 171 or 77%) concerning their use of online data bases (DIALOG, ORBIT, and BRS), particularly with regard to government documents, *showed that* the top 3 reasons given by respondents for not ordering government documents microfiche as the result of an online search were library does not have computer terminals (academic depositories, 33%; public depositories, 59%), didn't know that microfiche government documents could be ordered online (academic depositories, 24%; public depositories, 25%), and prefer hard copy to microfiche copy (academic depositories, 27%; public depositories, 20%). (317)

School

■ A 1971-72 study of the effect of microfiche copies of children's trade books on fourth graders' attitudes toward reading and on reading achievement, conducted in the Oglethorpe County Elementary School (near Athens, Georgia) and involving 142 pupils divided into control (no access to microfiche materials) and experimental groups (access to microfiche materials and readers), *showed that* attitudes toward reading were not statistically significantly different for the 2 groups by treatment, race, or sex (significant at the .05 level). (319)

Ibid. . . . *showed that*, although there was no statistically significant difference between the full control and experimental groups in vocabulary and reading comprehension, there was a statistically significant difference for the black subgroups in the control and experimental groups, with an increase in vocabulary and reading comprehension for the experimental subgroup using the microfiche materials and readers (significant at the .05 level). (319)

Selection, Other—Reprints

General

■ A 1969 survey of U.S. reprint publishers (population: 274; survey size: 250; responding: 157 or 62.8%) *showed that*, of 216 firms for which data was available (some firms were interviewed directly rather than being sent a questionnaire), reprints were reported available in the following formats from the following numbers of firms:

hardcovered books	183 (85.1%) firms
paperbound books	103 (47.7%) firms
microfilm	31 (14.4%) firms
microfiche	15 (6.9%) firms
xerographic	12 (5.6%) firms
microcards	8 (3.7%) firms
micro-opaques	3 (1.4%) firms
ultramicrofiche	3 (1.4%) firms

(592)

Selection, Other—Working Papers

Academic

■ A survey in 1979 of 119 major academic business libraries (89 responding or 75%, with 86 usable responses) *showed that* 28 (33%) actively collect business/economic working papers. 0f the 28, 9 (32%) select only single numbers of working paper series; 7 (25%) collect complete runs; and 12 (43%) use both methods. **(120)**

Ibid. . . . *showed that*, of the 28 major academic business libraries collecting working papers, the selection criteria used were reputation of institution (20 libraries); faculty/patron request (18); available as gift (17); available through exchange (9); and reputation of the author (7). **(120)**

■ A 1979 survey of faculty members and graduate students at the School of Management at Purdue and the School of Commerce at the University of Illinois, Urbana (sample size: 567; responding: 213) *showed that* 85.5%

Selection, Periodicals

used working papers from institutions other than their own. **(120)**

Ibid. . . . *showed that*, of the faculty responding, 39 at Purdue (90.7%) and 57 at Illinois (72.2%) felt that the library should collect working papers. The majority of both faculties (59% at Illinois; 74% at Purdue) felt the library should collect all papers in a series rather than selected papers.
(120)

Ibid. . . . *showed that*, of the faculty responding, 23 at Illinois (28.4%) and 17 at Purdue (44.7%) felt that working papers had lasting research value rather than current awareness value only. This compared to 53% of the responding librarians in major academic business libraries who felt that working papers had lasting research value. **(120)**

Selection, Periodicals—General Issues

General

■ A review in 1967 of variant editions of periodicals listed in the *Reader's Guide to Periodical Literature* by the Special Committee to Study the Indexing of Variant Editions of Periodicals (ALA, Reference Service Division) *showed that* there were 3 main categories of variations: (1) international editions, (2) special interest editions, and (3) U.S. regional editions. Of the 126 periodicals indexed in the *Reader's Guide*, 28 published 1 or more variant editions. **(078)**

■ A study reported in 1979 of the English-language literature of library administration (2,877 citations to materials cited in 364 refereed articles indexed in *Library Literature* between 1961-70) *showed that*, of 254 journal titles containing 1,149 article citations; 2 (.8%) journal titles contained 289 (25%) of the articles; 8 (3.15%) journal titles contained 575 (50%) of the articles; and 246 journal titles contained the remaining 574 articles.
(566)

Ibid. . . . *showed that* the 8 most frequently cited journals in the area of library administration were as follows:

Library Journal	165 (14.4%) citations
College and Research Libraries	124 (10.8%) citations
ALA Bulletin [American Libraries]	94 (8.2%) citations

continued

Library Quarterly	50 (4.4%) citations
Library Trends	48 (4.2%) citations
Special Libraries	36 (3.1%) citations
Wilson Library Bulletin	29 (2.5%) citations
Medical Library Association Bulletin	28 (2.4%) citations **(566)**

■ A 1979 report of the serials acquired through exchange in the British Library Lending Division *showed that* 3,712 titles were received on exchange from Eastern Europe (58% of all the serials received from that region), 838 titles from South America (58% of all the titles received from that region), 490 titles from Africa (49% of all titles received from that region), 494 titles from Austrialia/New Zealand (42% of all titles from the region), 1,750 titles from Asia (38% of all titles from the region), 2,102 titles from USA/Canada (20% of all titles from the region), and 2,311 titles from Western Europe (16% of all titles from the region). **(306)**

Academic

■ A study reported in 1969 at Washington University School of Medicine where medical faculty members reviewed a group of articles that cited an article of theirs (survey size: 25 faculty members reviewing 230 citing works; responding: 18 or 72% faculty members reviewing 161 citing works) *showed that* cited and citing articles were generally related in terms of the subject considered. Specifically, faculty rated 72.0% of the citing works as "very closely" or "directly related" to the cited work in terms of subject content. A further 22.4% of the citing works were rated as "slightly" or "indirectly related" to the cited article, while 4.9% were rated as "not related at all." **(680)**

■ A 1972 study comparing the rates of intergenerational information transfer in different scientific fields by reviewing citations in approximately 100 articles taken from a single representative journal in each of 15 biomedical scientific speciality fields (articles cited that were at least 25 years old were considered to be evidence of intergenerational information transfer) *showed that* the rates of intergenerational information transfer varied considerably among the various fields. Physiology had the highest rate of intergenerational information transfer with 87 papers cited that were 25 years old or older in 128 articles reviewed (68% rate), while molecular biology had the lowest rate of intergenerational information transfer, with 14 papers cited that were 25 years old or older in 97 articles reviewed (14.4% rate). **(707)**

Selection, Periodicals

Ibid. . . . *showed that* the amount of intergenerational information transfer may change over time in a field. A comparison of physiology and microbiology showed changes in different directions, with physiology citing an increasing amount of older literature in the past 50 years and microbiology citing a decreasing amount of older literature in the past 50 years. Specifically, the transfer rate in physiology (number of cited papers 25 years old or older/number of articles reviewed) was 68.0% in 1972, 50% in 1947, and 40.2% in 1922. The transfer rate in microbiology was 19.4% in 1972, 30.1% in 1947, and 34.3% in 1922. **(707)**

■ A study reported in 1974 investigating the materials used by master's and doctoral candidates completing theses after 1966 in public health at 5 universities (Yale; Harvard; University of California, Los Angeles; University of California, Berkeley; and California State University, Northridge), involving 3,456 citations taken from 44 theses, *showed that* doctoral theses had a higher proportion of journal citations than masters' theses to a statistically significant degree (significant at the .02 level). However, in terms of overall number of citations per thesis, there was no statistically significant difference between doctoral and masters' theses when method of investigation was considered. **(698)**

Ibid. . . . *showed that* 50% of the citations were accounted for by 40 different journal titles, while 63% of the citations were accounted for by 115 different journal titles. **(698)**

■ A study reported in 1974 investigating the degree of overlap in journal collections among U.S. academic health science libraries (survey size: 40 libraries; responding: 37 or 92.5%) *showed that* at least 60% of the surveyed libraries held 852 of the journal titles. A further breakdown was as follows (number of titles not cumulated):

60-69% of the libraries	149 titles
70-79% of the libraries	171 titles
80-89% of the libraries	163 titles
90-99% of the libraries	306 titles
100% of the libraries	63 titles

A title list was given for the 369 titles held by 90-100% of the libraries. **(702)**

■ A survey reported in 1977 of moderate-sized (120,000-500,000 volumes) U.S. academic libraries listed in the 1972-73 *American Library Directory* (survey size: 200; responding: 147 or 74%) *showed that* these libraries had a median of 37,000 bound periodical volumes and a median of 2,181 periodical subscriptions. **(454)**

COLLECTION DEVELOPMENT

■ A study of 1977 survey information gathered by the National Center for Educational Statistics (U.S. Office of Education), concerning the degree to which 1,146 college and university libraries (Liberal Arts Colleges I and II; Comprehensive Universitites and Colleges I and II) met the 1975 Standards for College Libraries (ACRL), *showed that* 28% of the libraries received less than 500 periodical subscriptions; 22% received 500-749 periodical subscriptions; 27% received 750-1,499 periodical subscriptions; and 23% received 1,500 or more periodical subscriptions. The average number of periodical subscriptions was 1,170, while the median number of periodical subscriptions was 755. **(486)**

■ A study reported in 1978 at the West Virginia University College of Engineering of the citations found in the master's theses accepted over a 4-year period (126 theses between 1971-74) *showed that* nonjournal (i.e., book) literature was more important in the engineering sciences than previously thought by showing that, of 3,002 references overall, only 1,000 (33.3%) were journal citations, with the proportion of journal citations by department ranging from 11.4% of the references in aerospace theses to 49.4% of the references in chemical theses. **(460)**

■ A survey reported in 1978 of a stratified random sample of 811 sociologists from 183 graduate departments (response rate: 526 or 64.86%) reporting which social science journals they regularly read *showed that*, comparing the rank order list of regularly read journals with the rank order of sociology journals by citation, 55% of the 20 most reported regularly read journals were found on the list of the 20 most cited journals. However, the citation list tended to focus on interdisciplinary and non-sociological journals, whereas the regularly read list had a "distinctive, disciplinary focus." **(261)**

■ A 1978-79 study underwritten by the NSF Division of Information Science and Technology of academic and research journal subscription and cancellation for both individuals and libraries (individual questionnaires: 2,817; usable responses: 1,190; library questionnaires: 4,997; usable responses: 1,905) of journals at least 5 years old *showed that* the top 5 reasons for subscribing to a journal given by individuals out of a group of 705 respondents were as follows (multiple responses allowed): relatively new to this professional activity (255 responses or 36.2%); now can afford to subscribe (234 or 33.2%); formerly used a library copy but that is no longer practical (142 or 20.1%); recently changed to this area of specialization (116 or 16.5%); and recently joined a society that supplies the subscription as part of the membership (105 or 14.9%). **(264)**

Selection, Periodicals 179

Ibid. . . . *showed that* the top 5 means through which individuals reported learning about a journal (multiple responses permitted; N = 705) were as follows: 254 individuals (36%) became aware of the journal while in school, 241 (34.2%) through professional contacts, 225 (31.9%) through references in the literature, 116 (16.5%) through browsing in the library, and 24 (3.4%) through promotional activity by publisher. **(264)**

Ibid. . . . *showed that* the top 6 reasons individuals reported for canceling journal subscriptions (multiple responses permitted; N = 705) were as follows: 200 individuals (41.2%) canceled journal subscriptions because of changed focus of interest, 91 (18.8%) because it did not contain the kind of information expected, 81 (16.7%) substituted a more appropriate journal, 71 (14.6%) were no longer a member of the society through which they received the journal, 65 (13.4%) due to financial reasons, 53 (10.9%) because library purchased a subscription they could use. **(264)**

Ibid. . . . *showed that* only 6% of the individual respondents reported that the availability of a library copy was the only reason they canceled their personal subscription, while only 5.1% reported that they might resubscribe if they lost access to the library's copy. **(264)**

■ A 1979 survey of libraries in accredited North American veterinary schools (population: 25 libraries; responding: 23 or 92%) *showed that*, of the 18 separately housed veterinary libraries, the number of serials received ranged from a low of 193 at Tuskegee to a high of 1,105 at Cornell. The average number of serials received was 624. The number of bound serial volumes ranged from 2,844 volumes at Mississippi State University to 66,000 volumes at Cornell. The average number of bound volumes held was 26,274. **(740)**

■ A study reported in 1981 of data on 1,146 2-year colleges, as reported in the 1977 Higher Education General Information Surveys and compared to the 1979 Association of College and Research Libraries standards, *showed that* in terms of periodical subscriptions the number of schools meeting minimum standards (by enrollment ranges of FTE students) was as follows:

less than 1,000 students (200 titles minimum)	49% met standards
1,000 to 2,999 students (300 titles minimum)	48% met standards
3,000 to 4,999 students (500 titles minimum)	29% met standards
5,000 to 6,999 students (700 titles minimum)	13% met standards

continued

7,000 to 8,999 students
(710 titles minimum)   25% met standards
9,000 to 10,999 students
(720 titles minimum)   53% met standards

The overall average number of periodicals held per school was 350 titles.
(500)

■ A study reported in 1981 at the St. Lawrence College of Applied Arts and Technology (a community college in southeastern Ontario), comparing their 801 periodical titles with 7 main indexes owned by the library and covering subject areas reflecting college course offerings, *showed that*, of the 801 periodical titles, 473 (59%) were indexed in the indexes. Of the remaining 328 titles, 86 (11%) were not reported in *Ulrich's*; 189 (23%) were reported in *Ulrich's* but no indexing was given; and 53 (7%) were reported in *Ulrich's* with indexes given that the library did not own.
(358)

■ A survey reported in 1981 of historians listed in the 1978 *Directory of American Scholars* concerning their use of and attitudes toward periodicals (survey size: 767 historians, although not all questionnaires could be delivered; responding: 360 or 46.9%, with respondents tending to be younger and with a higher scholarly productivity record than nonrespondents) *showed that* the 3 most used formats (out of 14) in their current research were (based on a rating scale of 1 to 5 where 5 was the most used) as follows: periodicals (4.26 rating), books (4.47 rating), and manuscripts (3.66 rating).
(780)

■ A study reported in 1982 of publication and citation patterns in *College and Research Libraries* during the 40 years between 1939-79, involving 1,775 articles, *showed that* the 3 most frequently cited journals by articles in *College and Research Libraries* were (5,205 citations):

College and Research Libraries   1,001 (19.23%) citations
Library Journal   550 (10.57%) citations
Library Quarterly   379 (7.28%) citations

10 journals (1.6% of the total number of journals cited) provided almost 55% of the total journal citations.
(511)

Public

■ A survey reported in 1968 of Michigan public libraries (559 libraries or branches queried; 462 [82%] responding) receiving periodicals from the state *showed that* the larger the library, the longer the periodicals were

Selection, Periodicals

retained, with 4 years being the most common retention period for all sizes of libraries. **(133)**

■ An attempt reported in 1982 to establish 4 input measures and 4 output measures for public libraries, based on published statistical reports for 301 New Jersey public libraries over a 6-year period (1974-79) and survey data for 96 public libraries in New Jersey, *showed that* (where "per capita" is based on the number of residents in the library's service area):

INPUT MEASURES

The proportion of budget spent on materials averaged 19.9%, with a standard deviation of .081 (based on 301 libraries).

The new volumes per capita averaged .181, with a standard deviation of .097 (based on 301 libraries).

The periodical titles per capita averaged .0094, with a standard deviation of .0054 (based on 301 libraries).

The circulation per volume averaged 1.79, with a standard deviation of .77 (based on 301 libraries).

OUTPUT MEASURES

The circulation per capita averaged 5.04, with a standard deviation of 3.07 (based on 301 libraries).

The patron visits per capita averaged 2.82, with a standard deviation of 1.82 (based on 96 libraries).

The reference questions per capita averaged 1.12, with a standard deviation of .79 (based on 96 libraries).

The in-library uses of materials per capita averaged 2.29, with a standard deviation of 2.02 (based on 96 libraries). **(576)**

School

■ A study reported in 1978 of 19 bibliographic tools listing materials for young adults, involving a total of 19,405 titles in conjunction with a purposeful sample of 270 papers collected from college-bound high school students (grades 10 through 12) in a large metropolitan area from a wide variety of schools, *showed that*, of the 602 journal citations made in the 270 student papers, 6 journal titles supplied 32% of the citations; 16 titles supplied 50% of the citations; 52 titles supplied 75% of the citations; and 170 titles were required to supply 100% of the citations.
(523)

Ibid. . . . *showed that* the 3 most frequently cited journal titles in the 270 student papers were:

Newsweek	54 (8.9%) citations	
Time	48 (8.0%) citations	
Scientific American	29 (4.8%) citations	**(523)**

■ A study reported in 1979 of term paper bibliographies of high school students (270 students/papers from 6 high schools, involving 3,165 identifiable references) *showed that* 426 (68%) of 624 journal citations were indexed in *Readers' Guide*. Nevertheless, 43% of the students citing journals selected journals not covered by *Readers' Guide*. **(564)**

Ibid. . . . *showed that* the 6 most frequently cited journals were as follows:

Newsweek	54 (8.9%) total citations	
Time	48 (7.9%) total citations	
Scientific American	29 (4.8%) total citations	
American Heritage	23 (3.8%) total citations	
New Republic	20 (3.3%) total citations	
US News and World Report	19 (3.1%) total citations	**(564)**

Ibid. . . . *showed that*, of 602 periodical citations, 6 journal titles accounted for 193 (32%) periodical citations; 16 titles accounted for 301 (50%) periodical citations; 52 titles accounted for 457 (75.9%) citations; and 170 titles accounted for 602 (100%) citations. **(564)**

■ A 1981 study of 53 ninth-grade honors students in science in a suburban Philadelphia public high school *showed that*, out of 189 magazine citations in 47 bibliographies, 50% of all citations were from 8 magazines. These were *Newsweek* (9%), *Time* (8%), *National Geographic* (7%), *U.S. News* (6%), *Business Week* (6%), *Forbes* (5%), *Science* (5%), and *Fortune* (4%). (Taken from a list of 13 magazines in rank order.) **(222)**

Special

■ A 1964 study at the Air Force Cambridge Research Laboratories (Bedford, Massachusetts) over a 6-month period, involving use of 4,579 articles from 552 journal titles by 382 patrons, *showed that* even low-use

Selection, Periodicals 183

journals were an important part of the collection for a substantial number of patrons. Specifically, while 281 (51%) titles had only 1 patron using them during this period and accounted for only 598 (13%) of the total articles requested, this group of titles was nevertheless requested by 144 (38% of the total) different patrons. **(586)**

■ A study reported in 1969 at Washington University School of Medicine where medical faculty members reviewed a group of articles that cited an article of theirs (survey size: 25 faculty members reviewing 230 citing works; responding: 18 or 72% faculty members reviewing 161 citing works) *showed that* cited and citing articles were generally related in terms of the subject considered. Specifically, faculty rated 72.0% of the citing works as "very closely" or "directly related" to the cited work in terms of subject content. A further 22.4% of the citing works were rated as "slightly" or "indirectly related" to the cited article, while 4.9% were rated as "not related at all." **(680)**

■ A 1971-72 study of the articles supplied by the University of Oklahoma Health Sciences Center Library to state health professionals and institutions during a 4-month period, involving 1,756 articles (from 373 journals) sent to individual health professionals and 1,620 articles (from 527 journals) sent to health institutions, *showed that*, of the 1,620 articles sent to institutions, 24.5% [no raw number given] of the articles were supplied by 26 titles, each contributing 10 or more articles, while 53% [no raw number given] of the articles were supplied by 100 titles, each contributing 5 or more articles. **(409)**

■ A 1972 study comparing the rates of intergenerational information transfer in different scientific fields by reviewing citations in approximately 100 articles taken from a single representative journal in each of 15 biomedical scientific speciality fields (articles cited that were at least 25 years old were considered to be evidence of intergenerational information transfer) *showed that* the rates of intergenerational information transfer varied considerably among the various fields. Physiology had the highest rate of intergenerational information transfer with 87 papers cited that were 25 years old or older in 128 articles reviewed (68% rate), while molecular biology had the lowest rate of intergenerational information transfer, with 14 papers cited that were 25 years old or older in 97 articles reviewed (14.4% rate). **(707)**

Ibid. . . . *showed that* the amount of intergenerational information transfer may change over time in a field. A comparison of physiology and microbiology showed changes in different directions, with physiology citing an increasing amount of older literature in the past 50 years and microbiol-

184   **COLLECTION DEVELOPMENT**

ogy citing a decreasing amount of older literature in the past 50 years. Specifically, the transfer rate in physiology (number of cited papers 25 years old or older/number of articles reviewed) was 68.0% in 1972, 50% in 1947, and 40.2% in 1922. The transfer rate in microbiology was 19.4% in 1972, 30.1% in 1947, and 34.3% in 1922. **(707)**

■ A study reported in 1974 investigating the degree of overlap in journal collections among U.S. academic health science libraries (survey size: 40 libraries; responding: 37 or 92.5%) *showed that* at least 60% of the surveyed libraries held 852 of the journal titles. A further breakdown was as follows (number of titles not cumulated):

          60-69% of the libraries   149 titles
          70-79% of the libraries   171 titles
          80-89% of the libraries   163 titles
          90-99% of the libraries   306 titles
          100% of the libraries   63 titles

A title list was given for the 369 titles held by 90-100% of the libraries.
(702)

■ A study reported in 1975 of interlibrary loan requests submitted to the Information Dissemination Service (serving the information needs of health professionals in a surrounding 9-county area) located in the Health Sciences Library of the State University of New York, Buffalo, broken down into 2 samples (sample A: all requests during a 3-month period in 1972 from 4 major teaching hospitals, 1,802 interlibrary loan requests; sample B: a 10% random sample of all requests from a broad group of health professionals over a 3-year period, 1970-73, 2,280 interlibrary loan requests), *showed that* for both samples 3% of the journal titles satisfied "approximately 20%" of the journal requests. **(708)**

■ A 1975 study of interlibrary loan requests initiated by 21 hospitals in central and western Massachusetts for their patrons during 1975 (4,368 requests for copies of periodical articles from 1,071 different journals) *showed that*:

12 (1.12%) journal titles accounted for 439 (10.05%) requested articles;

47 (4.39%) journal titles accounted for 1,059 (24.24%) requested articles;

160 (14.94%) journal titles accounted for 2,227 (50.98%) requested articles;

1,071 (100%) journal titles accounted for 4,368 (100%) requested articles. **(718)**

Selection, Periodicals

Ibid. . . . *showed that* the age of requested items was as follows:

5 years old or less	2,729 (62.48%) items
10 years old or less	3,501 (80.15%) items
20 years old or less	4,086 (93.54%) items
30 years old or less	4,262 (97.57%) items

This compared to the number of items 5 years old or less in 4 other studies reported in the literature, which ranged from 50-65%, and the number of items in 3 other studies reported in the literature which were 10 years old or less, which ranged from 69-85%. **(718)**

■ A 1977 study at the Treadwell Library of the Massachusetts General Hospital investigating all requests for journals (both circulation use and interlibrary loan requests) over a year's time (79,369 requests) *showed that* the 647 journal titles held in the library satisfied 75,039 (94.5%) of the requests, while interlibrary loan had to be used to satisfy the remaining 4,330 (5.5%) requests. To satisfy these interlibrary loan requests itself the library would have had to subscribe to an additional 1,352 journals.
(733)

■ A 1979 survey of libraries in accredited North American veterinary schools (population: 25 libraries; responding: 23 or 92%) *showed that*, of the 18 separately housed veterinary libraries, the number of serials received ranged from a low of 193 at Tuskegee to a high of 1,105 at Cornell. The average number of serials received was 624. The number of bound serial volumes ranged from 2,844 volumes at Mississippi State University to 66,000 volumes at Cornell. The average number of bound volumes held was 26,274. **(740)**

■ A 1980 survey of law school libraries with collections in excess of 175,000 volumes (sample size: 50; responding: 37 or 70%) *showed that* the numbers of periodicals reported by respondents were as follows:

less than 500 periodicals	1 library
500-600 periodicals	2 libraries
700-900 periodicals	6 libraries
1,000-1,200 periodicals	4 libraries
1,300-1,500 periodicals	3 libraries
over 1,600 periodicals	4 libraries
no answer	17 libraries

(369)

Ibid. . . . *showed that* the degree to which periodical titles were duplicated in hard copy (rather than microform) in responding libraries was as follows:

less than 5% duplication	4 libraries
5-10% duplication	4 libraries
11-19% duplication	4 libraries
20-30% duplication	9 libraries
40-50% duplication	2 libraries
60% duplication	4 libraries
no answer	10 libraries

(369)

Selection, Periodicals—Bradford Distribution, Explicit

General

■ A study reported in 1978 comparing top-ranked journals in a Bradford distribution (i.e., journals contributing the most articles in a subject field) with the top-ranked journals in terms of quality of articles in a subject field (i.e., journals whose articles are cited most heavily on the average) and involving 18 journals (452 articles) in the area of "experimental extinction" (i.e., "removal of a conditioned response to a stimulus") *showed that* there was no statistically significant correlation between the 2 groups. The journals that provided the most subject coverage were not the journals that published the most important articles. **(642)**

■ A study reported in 1978 reviewing the distribution of relevant papers published in scientific journals in 23 data sets reported in the literature *showed that* in all cases the correlation between the individual distribution and Bradford's law exceeded r = .96. Further, investigations into the slope and intercept indicated that "Bradford's law is the reflection of some underlying process not related to the characteristics of the search mechanism or the nature of the literature." Specifically, the slope was shown to be "almost entirely determined by the total number of articles retrieved" (these accounted for 98+% of the variance), while 67% of the variance of the intercept was accounted for by the total number of journal titles retrieved. **(620)**

Academic

■ A study reported in 1978 comparing top-ranked journals in a Bradford distribution (i.e., journals contributing the most articles in a subject field)

Selection, Periodicals 187

with the top-ranked journals in terms of quality of articles in a subject field (i.e., journals whose articles are cited most heavily on the average), involving 18 journals (452 articles) in the area of "experimental extinction" (i.e. "removal of a conditioned response to a stimulus"), *showed that* there was no statistically significant correlation between the 2 groups. The journals that provided the most subject coverage were not the journals that published the most important articles. **(642)**

■ A study reported in 1978 reviewing the distribution of relevant papers published in scientific journals in 23 data sets reported in the literature *showed that* in all cases the correlation between the individual distribution and Bradford's law exceeded r = .96. Further, investigations into the slope and intercept indicated that "Bradford's law is the reflection of some underlying process not related to the characteristics of the search mechanism or the nature of the literature." Specifically, the slope was shown to be "almost entirely determined by the total number of articles retrieved" (these accounted for 98+% of the variance), while 67% of the variance of the intercept was accounted for by the total number of journal titles retrieved. **(620)**

Selection, Periodicals—Bradford Distribution, Implicit

General

■ A study reported in 1973 based on the journal articles listed in the 1967 volume of *Library Literature* (4,418 journal articles in 247 journals) *showed that*, of both total and selected articles, 5% of the journals produced "about 50% of the articles," while 20% of the journals produced 80% of the articles. The bottom 50% of the journals contributed only 5% of the articles. **(610)**

■ A study reported in 1979 of the English-language literature of library administration (2,877 citations to materials cited in 364 refereed articles indexed in *Library Literature* between 1961-70) *showed that*, of 254 journal titles containing 1,149 article citations, 2 (.8%) journal titles contained 289 (25%) of the articles; 8 (3.15%) journal titles contained 575 (50%) of the articles; and 246 journal titles contined the remaining 574 articles. **(566)**

■ A study reported in 1982 of publication and citation patterns in *College and Research Libraries* during the 40 years between 1939-79, involving 1,775 articles, *showed that* the 3 most frequently cited journals by articles in *College and Research Libraries* were (5,205 citations):

>   College and Research Libraries 1,001 (19.23%) citations
>   Library Journal   550 (10.57%) citations
>   Library Quarterly   379 (7.28%) citations

10 journals (1.6% of the total number of journals cited) provided almost 55% of the total journal citations. **(511)**

Academic

■ A 1965 survey of the recommended reading lists for psychiatry residents from AMA-approved training programs (survey size: 204 programs; usable responses: 140 or 69% programs) *showed that* a composite list included 2,800 books. 87 programs reported that their reading lists included the basic literature of the field; these lists included 2,447 books, which received a total of 9,868 recommendations. A core of 104 books received 1/3 of the recommendations, the next 349 books likewise accounted for 1/3 of the recommendations, and the remaining 1/3 recommendations were distributed among the remaining 1,994 books. The 104 core books were listed. **(677)**

■ A 1965 survey of the recommended reading lists for psychiatry residents from AMA-approved training programs (survey size: 204 programs; usable responses: 140 or 69% programs) *showed that* it was possible to generate a composite list of 3,932 verifiable articles, which received a total of 7,594 recommendations. 33 articles accounted for 10% of the recommendations (receiving 14 or more recommendations each); 111 articles accounted for 20% of the recommendations (receiving 8 or more recommendations each); and 307 articles accounted for 35% of the recommendations (receiving 5 or more recommendations each). These 307 core articles were listed. **(678)**

■ A citation study reported in 1969 of a sample of article citations from 10 major journals in geology published in 1960 and 1965 (400 citations chosen for each year) *showed that*, for the 1960 citations, 46 journals accounted for just over 50% of the cited literature, while 145 journal titles were required to cover 75% of the cited literature. For the 1965 citations,

Selection, Periodicals 189

37 journals accounted for 50% of the cited literature, while 127 titles were required to cover 75% of the cited literature. **(193)**

■ A study reported in 1970 of the cardiovascular literature involving 78 journals "solely concerned with publishing papers dealing with some aspect of the heart and/or blood vessels, i.e. c-v speciality journals" plus 789 journals that published the findings of National Heart Institute grantees in fiscal 1967 (5,860 papers) *showed that* of the 789 journals the distribution of the NHI articles was as follows:

             13 journals   33.3% of total papers
             33 journals   50.0% of total papers
             75 journals   66.6% of total papers
           116 journals   75.0% of total papers   **(607)**

■ A 1971 study at the MIT Science Library of in-room use (journals do not circulate) of 220 physics journals over a 3.5-month period *showed that* of 4,292 uses the number of titles involved was as follows:

3 (1.4%) of the titles accounted for 1,384 (32.2%) of the uses;

14 (6.4%) of the titles accounted for 2,502 (58.3%) of the uses;

55 (25.0%) of the titles accounted for 3,949 (91.2%) of the uses;

138 (62.7%) of the titles accounted for 4,292 (100%) of the uses. **(608)**

■ A 1972 study at the University of Minnesota Bio-Medical Library concerning in-house use of periodicals during 2 1-week periods (1st period: 727 uses involving 269 different titles; 2nd period: 533 uses involving 209 different titles) *showed that* the numbersof titles accounting for different levels of use were as follows (2nd-period figures reported in parentheses):

        4% (5%) of the titles   27% (26%) of total use
        8% (9%) of the titles   38% (37%) of total use
       28% (29%) of the titles   68% (64%) of total use   **(697)**

■ A study reported in 1973 based on the journal articles listed in the 1967 volume of *Library Literature* (4,418 journal articles in 247 journals) *showed that*, of both total and selected articles, 5% of the journals produced "about 50% of the articles," while 20% of the journals produced 80% of the articles. The bottom 50% of the journals contributed only 5% of the articles. **(610)**

■ A study reported in 1974 investigating the materials used by master's and doctoral candidates completing theses after 1966 in public health at 5 universities (Yale; Harvard; University of California, Los Angeles; University of California, Berkeley; and California State University, Northridge), involving 3,456 citations taken from 44 theses, *showed that* 50% of the citations were accounted for by 40 different journal titles, while 63% of the citations were accounted for by 115 different journal titles. **(698)**

■ A study reported in 1974 using 52 sociological subject headings in *Social Science and Humanities Index* (1970-71) to identify 446 different journal articles, which in turn produced 8,926 citations to different publications (3,651 serial publications; 5,275 nonserial publications), *showed that*, of the 612 journals carrying the 3,521 journal citations, 25 titles contained 53.47% of the total articles cited, while 10 titles contained 38.76% of the total articles cited. Of the 84 journals that contained articles with 2 or more citations, the top 10 journals contained 66.99% of those articles, while the top 5 journals contained 58.01% of those articles. **(252)**

■ A survey reported in 1975 of University of North Carolina freshmen English papers *showed that* 60% of the articles cited were provided by 20 (8.3%) of the journal titles in the collection; 80% of the articles by 48 (20%) of the titles; and 90% of the articles by 120 (50%) of the titles. This is a standard Yule curve. **(060)**

■ A 1978 study in the Biology Library of Temple University involving a citation analysis of publications by full-time Temple biology faculty, doctoral dissertations of Temple biology Ph.D.'s, and preliminary doctoral qualifying briefs written by second-year graduate biology students at Temple during the 3-year period 1975-77 (153 source items with 4,155 citations) *showed that*, of 3,739 citations in 336 journals, the cumulative number of citations by journal rank was as follows:

top 5 journals	1,033 (28%) citations
top 10 journals	1,585 (42%) citations
top 60 journals	3,013 (81%) citations
top 100 journals	3,228 (89%) citations
top 300 journals	3,703 (99%) citations

(650)

Selection, Periodicals

- A study reported in 1978 of all articles indexed in 48 issues (1972-75) of the *Tropical Diseases Bulletin* (11,174 articles taken from 611 different journals) *showed that*:

    10 (1.6%) journal titles accounted for 2,765 (24.7%) articles;

    33 (5.1%) journal titles accounted for 5,452 (48.8%) articles;

    121 (18.9%) journal titles accounted for 8,707 (77.9%) articles;

    279 (43.5%) journal titles accounted for 10,378 (92.9%) articles. **(719)**

- A study reported in 1979 of the English-language literature of library administration (2,877 citations to materials cited in 364 refereed articles indexed in *Library Literature* between 1961-70) *showed that*, of 254 journal titles containing 1,149 article citations, 2 (.8%) journal titles contained 289 (25%) of the articles; 8 (3.15%) journal titles contained 575 (50%) of the articles; and 246 journal titles contined the remaining 574 articles. **(566)**

- A study reported in 1982 of publication and citation patterns in *College and Research Libraries* during the 40 years between 1939-79, involving 1,775 articles, *showed that* the 3 most frequently cited journals by articles in *College and Research Libraries* were (5,205 citations):

    College and Research Libraries   1,001 (19.23%) citations
    Library Journal   550 (10.57%) citations
    Library Quarterly   379 (7.28%) citations

    10 journals (1.6% of the total number of journals cited) provided almost 55% of the total journal citations. **(511)**

School

- A study reported in 1978 of 19 bibliographic tools listing materials for young adults, involving a total of 19,405 titles in conjunction with a purposeful sample of 270 papers collected from college-bound high school students (grades 10 through 12) in a large metropolitan area from a wide variety of schools, *showed that*, of the 602 journal citations made in the 270 student papers, 6 journal titles supplied 32% of the citations; 16 titles supplied 50% of the citations; 52 titles supplied 75% of the citations; and 170 titles were required to supply 100% of the citations. **(523)**

- A study reported in 1979 of term paper bibliographies of high school students (270 students/papers from 6 high schools, involving 3,165 identifiable references) *showed that*, of 602 periodical citations, 6 journal titles accounted for 193 (32%) periodical citations; 16 titles accounted for 301 (50%) periodical citations; 52 titles accounted for 457 (75.9%) citations;

and 170 titles accounted for 602 (100%) citations. **(564)**

■ A 1981 study of 53 ninth-grade honors students in science in a suburban Philadelphia public high school *showed that*, out of 189 magazine citations in 47 bibliographies, 50% of all citations were from 8 magazines. These were *Newsweek* (9%), *Time* (8%), *National Geographic* (7%), *U.S. News* (6%), *Business Week* (6%), *Forbes* (5%), *Science* (5%), and *Fortune* (4%). (Taken from a list of 13 magazines in rank order.) **(222)**

Special

■ A 1964 study at the Air Force Cambridge Research Laboratories (Bedford, Massachusetts) over a 6-month period, involving use of 4,579 articles from 552 journal titles by 382 patrons, *showed that* even low-use journals were an important part of the collection for a substantial number of patrons. Specifically, while 281 (51%) titles had only 1 patron using them during this period and accounted for only 598 (13%) of the total articles requested, this group of titles was nevertheless requested by 144 (38% of the total) different patrons. **(586)**

■ A 1965 survey of the recommended reading lists for psychiatry residents from AMA-approved training programs (survey size: 204 programs; usable responses: 140 or 69% programs) *showed that* a composite list included 2,800 books. 87 programs reported that their reading lists included the basic literature of the field; these lists included 2,447 books, which received a total of 9,868 recommendations. A core of 104 books received 1/3 of the recommendations, the next 349 books likewise accounted for 1/3 of the recommendations, and the remaining 1/3 recommendations were distributed among the remaining 1,994 books. The 104 core books were listed. **(677)**

■ A 1965 survey of the recommended reading lists for psychiatry residents from AMA-approved training programs (survey size: 204 programs; usable responses: 140 or 69% programs) *showed that* it was possible to generate a composite list of 3,932 verifiable articles, which received a total of 7,594 recommendations. 33 articles accounted for 10% of the recommendations (receiving 14 or more recommendations each); 111 articles accounted for 20% of the recommendations (receiving 8 or more recommendations each); and 307 articles accounted for 35% of the recommendations (receiving 5 or more recommendations each). These 307 core articles were listed. **(678)**

Selection, Periodicals

■ A study reported in 1970 of the cardiovascular literature involving 78 journals "solely concerned with publishing papers dealing with some aspect of the heart and/or blood vessels, i.e. c-v speciality journals" plus 789 journals that published the findings of National Heart Institute grantees in fiscal 1967 (5,860 papers) *showed that* of the 789 journals the distribution of the NHI articles was as follows:

13 journals	33.3% of total papers
33 journals	50.0% of total papers
75 journals	66.6% of total papers
116 journals	75.0% of total papers

(607)

■ A 1972 study at the University of Minnesota Bio-Medical Library concerning in-house use of periodicals during 2 1-week periods (1st period: 727 uses involving 269 different titles; 2nd period: 533 uses involving 209 different titles) *showed that* the numbers of titles accounting for different levels of use were as follows (2nd period figures reported in parentheses):

4% (5%) of the titles	27% (26%) of total use
8% (9%) of the titles	38% (37%) of total use
28% (29%) of the titles	68% (64%) of total use

(697)

■ A 1975 study of interlibrary loan requests initiated by 21 hospitals in central and western Massachusetts for their patrons during 1975 (4,368 requests for copies of periodical articles from 1,071 different journals) *showed that*:

12 (1.12%) journal titles accounted for 439 (10.05%) requested articles;

47 (4.39%) journal titles accounted for 1,059 (24.24%) requested articles;

160 (14.94%) journal titles accounted for 2,227 (50.98%) requested articles;

1,071 (100%) journal titles accounted for 4,368 (100%) requested articles. **(718)**

■ A study reported in 1978 of all articles indexed in 48 issues (1972-75) of the *Tropical Diseases Bulletin* (11,174 articles taken from 611 different journals) *showed that*:

10 (1.6%) journal titles accounted for 2,765 (24.7%) articles;

33 (5.1%) journal titles accounted for 5,452 (48.8%) articles;

121 (18.9%) journal titles accounted for 8,707 (77.9%) articles;

279 (43.5%) journal titles accounted for 10,378 (92.9%)
articles. **(719)**

Selection, Periodicals—ISSN

General

■ A study reported in 1977 at Brock University Library (Canada) of 532 titles from the university serials list that had International Standard Serial Numbers (ISSNs) reported both in *Irregular Serials and Annuals: An International Directory* (2nd edition) and in *New Serial Titles* showed that 32 (6.01%) titles did not have the same ISSN listed both places but instead had 2 different numbers listed. Of these 32, 30 (93.8%) had the "05" factor, i.e., the ISSN began with "05." **(546)**

Ibid. . . . *showed that* of 497 serial titles taken from 10 "representative" publishers' lists and searched in all the Bowker publications providing ISSNs (including *Irregular Serials and Annuals: An International Directory*, 2nd edition) and in *New Serial Titles* showed that 428 (86.1%) had ISSNs, of which 398 titles had ISSNs reported in more than 1 publication. Of these 398 titles, 31 (7.79%) titles did not have the same ISSN listed in all publications but instead had different ISSN numbers listed. Of these 31, the "05" factor, i.e., the ISSN began with "05," figured in 58.06% [no raw number given] of the cases. **(546)**

■ A study reported in 1977 of "Corrections to Previous ISSN Assignments" listed in *Ulrich's International Periodicals Directory*, 15th edition, and in *Irregular Serials and Annuals: An International Directory*, 3rd edition *showed that* using the "lower/lowest" ISSN is not a reliable practice. Specifically, of 67 ISSNs listed in *Ulrich's*, 57 (85.1%) were the lower of the 2 assigned numbers, while of 44 ISSNs listed in *Irregular*, 25 (56.82%) were the lower of the 2 assigned numbers. **(546)**

Selection, Periodicals—Subject Area (Biology)

Academic

■ A 1978 study in the Biology Library of Temple University involving a citation analysis of publications by full-time Temple biology faculty, doctoral dissertations of Temple biology Ph.D.'s, and preliminary doctoral

Selection, Periodicals

qualifying briefs written by second-year graduate Biology students at Temple during the 3-year period 1975-77 (153 source items with 4,155 citations) *showed that* 3,739 (90.0% [91% reported]) citations were to journal articles in 336 journals. **(650)**

Ibid. . . . *showed that*, of 3,739 citations in 336 journals, the cumulative number of citations by journal rank was as follows:

top 5 journals	1,033 (28%) citations
top 10 journals	1,585 (42%) citations
top 60 journals	3,013 (81%) citations
top 100 journals	3,228 (89%) citations
top 300 journals	3,703 (99%) citations **(650)**

Ibid. . . . *showed that* the 5 most frequently cited journals (out of 60 listed) were:

Proceedings of the National Academy of Science (USA)	307 (8.2%) citations
Journal of Cellular Biology	198 (5.3%) citations
Nature	185 (4.9%) citations
Science	177 (4.7%) citations
Journal of Molecular Biology	166 (4.4%) citations **(650)**

Selection, Periodicals—Subject Area (Business)

General

■ A 1982 investigation to identify a core group of business journals by selecting those periodicals that were listed in at least 3 of 4 business reference tools (*ABI/Inform, Business Index, Business Periodicals Index,* and *F and S Index United States*) or which were cited more than the median number of times business and business-related journals were cited in the 1981 *Social Sciences Citation Index Journal Reports showed that* a core of 283 business journals could be identified. (List given.) **(561)**

Ibid. . . . *showed that* the percentage of the 283 business periodicals indexed in each of the 4 tools was as follows:

Business Index	91% of the core periodicals
Business Periodicals Index	84% of the core periodicals
ABI/Inform	81% of the core periodicals
F and S Index United States	43% of the core periodicals **(561)**

Ibid. . . . *showed that* the number of the core periodicals as a percentage of the total periodicals indexed in each of the 4 tools was as follows:

Business Periodicals Index	78% of total periodicals indexed
Business Index	46% of total periodicals indexed
ABI/Inform	42% of total periodicals indexed
F and S Index United States	22% of total periodicals indexed **(561)**

Academic

■ A survey reported in 1978 of 31 Ph.D. dissertations in the field of business/management (13 from the State University of New York at Buffalo and 18 from SUNYAB incoming faculty but completed at other schools) *showed that* the overall distribution of 2,805 citations by form was:

periodicals	1,377 (49.1%) citations
monographs	895 (31.9%) citations
serials	266 (9.5%) citations
miscellaneous	267 (9.5%) citations **(461)**

Ibid. . . . *showed that* the 7 most frequently cited subject areas (based on 1,161 citations to monographs and serials) were:

business (HF 5001-6351)	14.7% citations
economics: labor (HD 4801-8942)	11.5% citations
economics: production (HD 1-100)	10.8% citations
psychology (BF)	8.2% citations
sociology (HM-HX)	7.3% citations
finance (HG)	6.4% citations
economic theory	6.0% citations **(461)**

Selection, Periodicals—Subject Area (Economics)

Academic

■ A study reported in 1978 at Indiana University, Bloomington, of materials requested through a delivery service to faculty in the political science and economics departments during a 32-month period (October 1972-June 1975), involving 39 political scientists and 14 economists (40-50% of the faculty in the departments) and 5,478 articles from 620 different journals and newspapers, *showed that* the 5 most requested journals by economists were as follows:

Journal of Economic Theory	48 (8.0%)	requests
Economic Journal	33 (5.6%)	requests
Quarterly Journal of Economics	26 (4.3%)	requests
American Economic Review	23 (3.9%)	requests
Science	22 (3.7%)	requests

(421)

Selection, Periodicals—Subject Area (English)

Academic

■ A survey reported in 1975 of University of North Carolina freshmen English papers *showed that* 60% of the articles cited were provided by 20 (8.3%) of the journal titles in the collection; 80% of the articles by 48 (20%) of the titles; and 90% of the articles by 120 (50%) of the titles. This is a standard Yule curve. **(060)**

Selection, Periodicals—Subject Area (Geology)

Academic

■ A citation study reported in 1969 of a sample of article citations from 10 major journals in geology published in 1960 and 1965 (400 citations chosen for each year) *showed that* 87.5% of the 1965 citations were to materials published in English, while 87.3% of the 1960 citations were to English-language materials. **(193)**

Ibid. . . . *showed that* of the 1965 citations 75.5% were to periodicals, 21.5% to books, and the remainder (3%) divided among maps, theses, and other unpublished papers. The data for 1960 were similar. **(193)**

Ibid. . . . *showed that* on the average researchers in geology would have to go back 15 years to find approximately 70% of the useful literature and about 25 years to find approximately 80% of the useful literature. **(193)**

Ibid. . . . *showed that*, for the 1960 citations, 46 journals accounted for just over 50% of the cited literature, while 145 journal titles were required to cover 75% of the cited literature. For the 1965 citations, 37 journals accounted for 50% of the cited literature, while 127 titles were required to cover 75% of the cited literature. **(193)**

Ibid. . . . *showed that* subject areas other than geology accounted for 43% of the cited literature in the 1960 citations, while 40.8% of the 1965 citations were to subject areas other than geology. **(193)**

Selection, Periodicals—Subject Area (History)

Academic

■ A survey reported in 1981 of historians listed in the 1978 *Directory of American Scholars* concerning their use of and attitudes toward periodicals (survey size: 767 historians, although not all questionnaires could be delivered; responding: 360 or 46.9%, with respondents tending to be younger and with a higher scholarly productivity record than nonrespondents) *showed that* historians tended not to use the invisible college for discovering relevant published information for research. Specifically, the 3 most highly rated methods (out of 10) of discovering relevant published information for research (based on a rating scale of 1 to 5 where 5 was most highly rated) were:

bibliographies or references in books or journals	4.36 rating
specialized bibliographies	4.01 rating
book reviews	3.85 rating

Selection, Periodicals

While "discussion or correspondence with acquaintances elsewhere" ranked 6th with a rating of 3.14, "consulting a known expert" ranked 8th (2.87 rating), and "discussion with colleague at own institution" ranked 9th (2.6 rating). "Consulting librarian" ranked 10th (2.16 rating). **(780)**

Ibid. . . . *showed that* respondents clearly preferred bibliographic tools providing abstracts over those providing simple author and title entries. Specifically, when asked to compare the value of bibliographic tools providing abstracts in contrast to simple author and title entries, 23.7% reported the abstracts "about the same"; 46.4% reported the abstracts "somewhat more satisfactory"; and 29.9% reported the abstracts "much more satisfactory." **(780)**

Ibid. . . . *showed that* the degree of importance to their research of knowing as soon as possible after publication what had been published was as follows:

very important	40.7%	respondents
moderately important	47.8%	respondents
not very important	11.5%	respondents

(780)

Ibid. . . . *showed that* the 3 most used formats (out of 14) in their current research were (based on a rating scale of 1 to 5 where 5 was the most used) as follows: periodicals (4.26 rating), books (4.47 rating), and manuscripts (3.66 rating). **(780)**

Selection, Periodicals—Subject Area (Library Science)

Academic

■ A study reported in 1973 based on the journal articles listed in the 1967 volume of *Library Literature* (4,418 journal articles in 247 journals) *showed that*, of 3,420 selected articles in 242 journals (excluding news and announcements about people and conferences, etc.), the 6 most frequently cited journals were as follows:

Library Journal (incl. *School Library Journal*)	575 (16.8%) articles
Publisher's Weekly	149 (4.4%) articles

continued

Wilson Library Bulletin	131 (3.8%) articles
Medical Library Association Bulletin	94 (2.7%) articles
ALA Bulletin (American Libraries)	88 (2.6%) articles
Library of Congress Information Bulletin	86 (2.5%) articles **(610)**

Ibid. . . . *showed that*, of both total and selected articles, 5% of the journals produced "about 50% of the articles," while 20% of the journals produced 80% of the articles. The bottom 50% of the journals contributed only 5% of the articles. **(610)**

Ibid. . . . *showed that*, of the 3,420 articles, the 3 most frequently occurring subject areas were: administration (625 or 18.3% articles), literatures (401 or 11.7% articles), and professional education (290 or 8.5% articles). **(610)**

■ 2 surveys, 1 conducted in 1973 (sample size: 300; responding: 259 or 86.3%) and then repeated in 1978 (sample size: 429; responding: 357 or 83.2%) of ACRL (Association of College and Research Libraries) academic librarians concerning professional reading *showed that* in 1973 the average number of library journals read regularly in the preceeding 12-month period was 5.78 (95% confidence interval was 5.4 to 6.2 journals), while in 1978 the average number of library journals read regularly in the preceeding 12-month period was 5.9 (95% confidence interval was 5.6 to 6.2 journals). The average number of nonlibrary professional journals read regularly in the preceeding 12-month period was 1.0 for 1973 and 1.3 for 1978. **(508)**

Ibid. . . . *showed that* the 4 most frequently read journals in each of the 2 surveys were as follows:

IN 1973	READ BY
American Libraries	90.0% of sample
College and Research Libraries	86.1% of sample
Library Journal	69.9% of sample
Library Resources and Technical Services	57.9% of sample
IN 1978	READ BY
American Libraries	92.2% of sample
College and Research Libraries	88.6% of sample

continued

Selection, Periodicals

IN 1978	READ BY
Library Journal	69.3% of sample
Journal of Academic Librarianship	44.0% of sample

(508)

■ A 1977 analysis of journal citations in the automation chapter of the *Annual Review of Information Science and Technology* for the 10 previous years (1,263 citations, 800 journal citations) *showed that* the 3 most cited journals were *Journal of Library Automation* (114 citations), *Program* (56 citations), and *Library Resources and Technical Services* (55 citations).

(330)

■ A study reported in 1979 of the English-language literature of library administration (2,877 citations to materials cited in 364 refereed articles indexed in *Library Literature* between 1961-70) *showed that*, of 254 journal titles containing 1,149 article citations, 2 (.8%) journal titles contained 289 (25%) of the articles; 8 (3.15%) journal titles contained 575 (50%) of the articles; and 246 journal titles contined the remaining 574 articles. **(566)**

Ibid. . . . *showed that* the distribution of cited works by type was as follows:

monographs	1,247 (43.3%) cited works
journals	1,149 (39.9%) cited works
governmental publications	338 (11.7%) cited works
miscellaneous	143 (4.9%) cited works **(566)**

Ibid. . . . *showed that* the 8 most frequently cited journals in the area of library administration were as follows:

Library Journal	165 (14.4%) citations
College and Research Libraries	124 (10.8%) citations
ALA Bulletin [American Libraries]	94 (8.2%) citations
Library Quarterly	50 (4.4%) citations
Library Trends	48 (4.2%) citations
Special Libraries	36 (3.1%) citations
Wilson Library Bulletin	29 (2.5%) citations
Medical Library Association Bulletin	28 (2.4%) citations **(566)**

■ A study reported in 1982 of publication and citation patterns in *College and Research Libraries* during the 40 years between 1939-79 and involving 1,775 articles *showed that* the 3 most frequently cited journals by articles in *College and Research Libraries* were (5,205 citations):

    College and Research Libraries 1,001 (19.23%) citations
    Library Journal 550 (10.57%) citations
    Library Quarterly 379 (7.28%) citations

10 journals (1.6% of the total number of journals cited) provided almost 55% of the total journal citations. **(511)**

Ibid. . . . *showed that*, of 11,658 citations to materials in *College and Research Libraries* articles, periodicals accounted for 5,205 (44.65%) citations; monographs accounted for 4,245 (36.41%) citations; and U.S. government publications accounted for 464 (3.98%) citations. **(511)**

Selection, Periodicals—Subject Area (Medicine, General)

Academic

■ A study reported in 1964 of journal circulation in the Columbia and Yale Medical libraries during a 6-month period for Columbia and a 1-year period for Yale [total circulation not given] *showed that* the number of journals needed to supply various use levels was as follows:

    4 journal titles   10% of total journal use
    10 journal titles   20% of total journal use
    63 journal titles   50% of total journal use
    262 journal titles   80% of total journal use
    920 journal titles   100% of total journal use   **(670)**

Ibid. . . . *showed that* the 6 most frequently used journal titles were:

    Biochimica et Biophysica Acta 238 uses
    Journal of Biological Chemistry 206 uses
    American Journal of Medicine 169 uses
    Nature 167 uses
    Lancet 157 uses
    New England Journal of Medicine 145 uses

(670)

Selection, Periodicals

■ A study reported in 1972 of the citations listed in articles presented in the *Annual Review of Medicine* (international coverage) for the years 1965-69 (975 periodical titles; 14,201 periodical citations) *showed that* the 9 most cited periodicals were:

Journal of Clinical Investigation. Baltimore. (618 citations; 4.35% of total)

Lancet. London. (511 citations; 3.60% of total)

New England Journal of Medicine. Boston. (415 citations; 2.92% of total)

American Journal of Physiology. Boston. (391 citations; 2.75% of total)

Journal of Experimental Medicine. New York. (357 citations; 2.51% of total)

American Journal of Medicine. New York. (323 citations; 2.27% of total)

Nature. London. (310 citations; 2.18% of total)

Journal of the American Medical Association. Chicago. (291 citations; 2.05% of total)

Proceedings of the Society for Experimental Biology and Medicine. New York. (280 citations; 1.97% of total) **(351)**

Ibid. . . . *showed that* of the 275 most cited journals (13,023 citations) the top 4 subject areas (out of 17) represented by the citations were clinical medicine—specialities (34.02% citations), clinical medicine—general (21.58% citations), physiology (12.88% citations), and experimental medicine (7.33% citations). **(351)**

Ibid. . . . *showed that* of the 275 most cited journals (13,023 citations) the top 5 countries of publication were United States (150 or 54.55% of total journals), Britain (48 or 17.45% of total journals), Germany (18 or 6.55% of total journals), Switzerland (14 or 5.09% of total journals), and France (13 or 4.73% of total journals). **(351)**

Ibid. . . . *showed that* of the 275 most cited journals (13,023 citations) 217 (78.91%) journals were published in English; 35 (12.73%) were published in multilingual text using a combination of English, French, or German; 11 (4%) were published in French; 6 (2.18%) were published in German; and 6 (2.18%) were published in some other language or combination of languages. **(351)**

■ A 1975-76 study of journal title usage through the extension services of the University of Oklahoma Health Sciences Center Library (Oklahoma City) to hospital clients (4,216 articles from 1,055 journal titles requested) *showed that* the 4 most requested titles were:

British Medical Journal	81 requests; 49 requesters
Lancet	73 requests; 36 requesters
New England Journal of Medicine	67 requests; 39 requesters
Journal of the American Medical Association	53 requests; 35 requesters **(429)**

Ibid. . . . *showed that* ranking journal use by number of requesters was not the same as ranking journal use by number of requests. Although the 4 titles with the most requests were also the 4 titles with the most requesters (though the ranked order differs slightly), the 20 titles with the most requests included 6 titles that were not among the 20 titles with the most requesters. **(429)**

Ibid. . . . *showed that* the journal titles requested by individuals in hospitals without libraries were different from the journal titles requested by libraries with hospitals. Of 27 journal titles requested 15 times or more by individuals and 7 journal titles requested 15 times or more by libraries, only 1 title appeared in common—the *British Medical Journal*. **(429)**

■ A 1976 survey of physicians associated with hospitals in a 17-county region of upstate New York (Health Service Area V) based on a systematic sample of "approximately 40%" of the physicians in each county (survey size: 592 physicians; responding: 258 or 45.6%) *showed that* respondents personally subscribed to an average of 4.1 professional journals, with "nearly 40% claiming five or more subscriptions." The 4 most frequently reported journals were (multiple responses allowed):

Journal of the American Medical Association	26.0% physicians	
New England Journal of Medicine	24.4% physicians	
Annals of Internal Medicine	13.6% physicians	
New York State Journal of Medicine	12.8% physicians	**(720)**

■ A study reported in 1979 comparing 5 core lists of medical journals *showed that* a composite list of 450 titles resulted. 37 titles appeared on all 5

Selection, Periodicals

lists, while 72 titles appeared on 4 or more lists. There was no clear relationship between the number of lists on which a journal appeared and the citation frequency to articles in the journal as reported in *Journal Citation Reports*. A list of the 72 journals appearing on 4 or more lists was given. **(725)**

Special

■ A study reported in 1964 of journal circulation in the Columbia and Yale Medical libraries during a 6-month period for Columbia and a 1-year period for Yale [total circulation not given] *showed that* the number of journals needed to supply various use levels was as follows:

4 journal titles	10% of total journal use
10 journal titles	20% of total journal use
63 journal titles	50% of total journal use
262 journal titles	80% of total journal use
920 journal titles	100% of total journal use

(670)

Ibid. . . . *showed that* the 6 most frequently used journal titles were:

Biochimica et Biophysica Acta	238 uses
Journal of Biological Chemistry	206 uses
American Journal of Medicine	169 uses
Nature	167 uses
Lancet	157 uses
New England Journal of Medicine	145 uses

(670)

■ A survey reported in 1969 of selected physicians in Virginia concerning the development of a basic journal list for small hospital libraries (hospitals of 100-300 beds) (survey size: [no number given]; responding: 23 physicians) *showed that* an average of 42 journal titles was recommended per respondent. 5 respondents felt that less than 20 journal titles would be sufficient, while 3 respondents recommended collections "of over 70 titles." A list of 48 basic journal titles was given. **(681)**

■ A study reported in 1972 of the citations listed in articles presented in the *Annual Review of Medicine* (international coverage) for the years 1965-69 (975 periodical titles; 14,201 periodical citations) *showed that* the 9 most cited periodicals were:

Journal of Clinical Investigation. Baltimore. (618 citations; 4.35% of total)

Lancet. London. (511 citations; 3.60% of total)

New England Journal of Medicine. Boston. (415 citations; 2.92% of total)

American Journal of Physiology. Boston. (391 citations; 2.75% of total)

Journal of Experimental Medicine. New York. (357 citations; 2.51% of total)

American Journal of Medicine. New York. (323 citations; 2.27% of total)

Nature. London. (310 citations; 2.18% of total)

Journal of the American Medical Association. Chicago. (291 citations; 2.05% of total)

Proceedings of the Society for Experimental Biology and Medicine. New York. (280 citations; 1.97% of total) **(351)**

Ibid. . . . *showed that* of the 275 most cited journals (13,023 citations) the top 4 subject areas (out of 17) represented by the citations were clinical medicine—specialities (34.02% citations), clinical medicine—general (21.58% citations), physiology (12.88% citations), and experimental medicine (7.33% citations). **(351)**

Ibid. . . . *showed that* of the 275 most cited journals (13,023 citations) the top 5 countries of publication were United States (150 or 54.55% of total journals), Britain (48 or 17.45% of total journals), Germany (18 or 6.55% of total journals), Switzerland (14 or 5.09% of total journals), and France (13 or 4.73% of total journals). **(351)**

Ibid. . . . *showed that* of the 275 most cited journals (13,023 citations) 217 (78.91%) journals were published in English; 35 (12.73%) were published in multilingual text using a combination of English, French, or German; 11 (4%) were published in French; 6 (2.18%) were published in German; and 6 (2.18%) were published in some other language or combination of languages. **(351)**

■ A 1975-76 study of journal title usage through the extension services of the University of Oklahoma Health Sciences Center Library (Oklahoma City) to hospital clients (4,216 articles from 1,055 journal titles requested) *showed that* the 4 most requested titles were:

Selection, Periodicals

British Medical Journal	81 requests; 49 requesters
Lancet	73 requests; 36 requesters
New England Journal of Medicine	67 requests; 39 requesters
Journal of the American Medical Association	53 requests; 35 requesters

(429)

Ibid. . . . *showed that* ranking journal use by number of requesters was not the same as ranking journal use by number of requests. Although the 4 titles with the most requests were also the 4 titles with the most requesters (though the ranked order differs slightly), the 20 titles with the most requests included 6 titles that were not among the 20 titles with the most requesters. **(429)**

Ibid. . . . *showed that* the journal titles requested by individuals in hospitals without libraries were different from the journal titles requested by libraries with hospitals. Of 27 journal titles requested 15 times or more by individuals and 7 journal titles requested 15 times or more by libraries, only 1 title appeared in common—the *British Medical Journal*. **(429)**

Ibid. . . . *showed that* health professionals in hospitals without libraries needed more recent information than their counterparts in hospitals with libraries. 82.3% of the journal articles requested by individuals had been published within the last 5 years, and 91.8% of the journal articles requested by individuals had been published within the last 10 years, while 74.6% of the articles requested by libraries had been published within the last 5 years, and 86.7% had been published within the last 10 years.
(429)

■ A 1976 survey of physicians associated with hospitals in a 17-county region of upstate New York (Health Service Area V) based on a systematic sample of "approximately 40%" of the physicians in each county (survey size: 592 physicians; responding: 258 or 45.6%) *showed that* respondents personally subscribed to an average of 4.1 professional journals, with "nearly 40% claiming five or more subscriptions." The 4 most frequently reported journals were (multiple responses allowed):

Journal of the American Medical Association	26.0% physicians

continued

New England Journal of Medicine	24.4% physicians	
Annals of Internal Medicine	13.6% physicians	
New York State Journal of Medicine	12.8% physicians	**(720)**

■ A study reported in 1979 comparing 5 core lists of medical journals *showed that* a composite list of 450 titles resulted. 37 titles appeared on all 5 lists, while 72 titles appeared on 4 or more lists. There was no clear relationship between the number of lists on which a journal appeared and the citation frequency to articles in the journal as reported in *Journal Citation Reports*. A list of the 72 journals appearing on 4 or more lists was given. **(725)**

Selection, Periodicals—Subject Area (Medicine, Cardiology)

Academic

■ A study reported in 1970 of the cardiovascular literature involving 78 journals "solely concerned with publishing papers dealing with some aspect of the heart and/or blood vessels, i.e. c-v speciality journals" plus 789 journals that published the findings of National Heart Institute grantees in fiscal 1967 (5,860 papers) *showed that* of the 789 journals the distribution of the NHI articles was as follows:

13 journals	33.3% of total papers	
33 journals	50.0% of total papers	
75 journals	66.6% of total papers	
116 journals	75.0% of total papers	**(607)**

Ibid. . . . *showed that* the 5 journals with the most papers published by National Heart Institute grantees were:

Federation Proceedings	419 papers	
Circulation	280 papers	
Clinical Research	180 papers	
American Journal of Physiology	151 papers	
Circulation Research	140 papers	**(607)**

Selection, Periodicals

Ibid. . . . *showed that* the coverage given to the 78 cardiovascular speciality journals by the major indexing and abstracting services was as follows:

Index Medicus	48 (62%) journals	
Excerpta Medica	47 (60%) journals	
Biological Abstracts	35 (45%) journals	
Chemical Abstracts	33 (42%) journals	
Science Citation Index	15 (19%) journals	**(607)**

Ibid. . . . *showed that*, based on the publication pattern of National Heart Institute grantees, the 78 cardiovascular speciality journals were not the most "quantitatively fertile" sources of cardiovascular information. Specifically, only "about 14%" of the American c-v papers were published in the 78 speciality journals, while the remaining 86% were widely dispersed among the 766 nonspeciality c-v journals. **(607)**

Special

■ A study reported in 1970 of the cardiovascular literature involving 78 journals "solely concerned with publishing papers dealing with some aspect of the heart and/or blood vessels, i.e. c-v speciality journals" plus 789 journals that published the findings of National Heart Institute grantees in fiscal 1967 (5,860 papers) *showed that* of the 789 journals the distribution of the NHI articles was as follows:

13 journals	33.3% of total papers	
33 journals	50.0% of total papers	
75 journals	66.6% of total papers	
116 journals	75.0% of total papers	**(607)**

Ibid. . . . *showed that* the 5 journals with the most papers published by National Heart Institute grantees were:

Federation Proceedings	419 papers	
Circulation	280 papers	
Clinical Research	180 papers	
American Journal of Physiology	151 papers	
Circulation Research	140 papers	**(607)**

Ibid. . . . *showed that* the coverage given to the 78 cardiovascular speciality journals by the major indexing and abstracting services was as follows:

Index Medicus	48 (62%) journals	
Excerpta Medica	47 (60%) journals	
Biological Abstracts	35 (45%) journals	
Chemical Abstracts	33 (42%) journals	
Science Citation Index	15 (19%) journals	**(607)**

Ibid. . . . *showed that*, based on the publication pattern of National Heart Institute grantees, the 78 cardiovascular speciality journals were not the most "quantitatively fertile" sources of cardiovascular information. Specifically, only "about 14%" of the American c-v papers were published in the 78 speciality journals, while the remaining 86% were widely dispersed among the 766 nonspeciality c-v journals. **(607)**

Selection, Periodicals—Subject Area (Medicine, Physiology)

Academic

■ A study reported in 1975 of the research literature of physiology over the 3-year period 1970-72 involving citation counting (first 3 months of each year) in 8 internationally known journals (31,669 citations) *showed that* serial titles accounted for 28,714 (90.67%) citations, while monographs accounted for 2,955 (9.3%) citations. **(355)**

Ibid. . . . *showed that* the 3 most cited serial titles accounted for 24.633% of the total serial citations; that the top 14 serial titles accounted for 50.968% of the total serial citations; and the top 176 serial titles accounted for 90.008% of the total serial citations. **(355)**

Ibid. . . . *showed that* the 10 most cited serial titles in physiology were:

Journal of Physiology (London)
American Journal of Physiology (Bethesda)
Journal of Applied Physiology (Bethesda)
Acta Physiologica Scandinavica (Stockholm)
Journal of Clinical Investigation (Boston)

Circulation Research (New York)
Journal of Biological Chemistry (Baltimore)
Journal of General Physiology (Baltimore)
Nature (London)
Pfleugers Archiv (Berlin) (355)

Ibid. . . . *showed that*, of the 2,955 citations to monographs, 1,586 (54.672%) citations referred to titles published within 8 years of the citation, and 2,335 citations (79.018%) referred to titles published within 13 years of citation. (355)

Ibid. . . . *showed that*, of the 28,714 serial citations, 7,992 (27.833%) were to articles published within 5 years of citation; 15,077 (52.507%) were to articles published within 8 years of citation; and 21,248 (73.767%) were to articles published within 13 years of citation. (355)

Ibid. . . . *showed that*, of the 909 serial titles identified as containing at least 1 of the 28,714 serial citations, 40 titles (4.4%) were classed by *Ulrich's* in the physiology subject area. 361 (39.71%) additional titles were classed in 5 other main subject areas: general medical sciences, general science, biology, pharmacy/pharmacology, and biochemistry. (355)

Ibid. . . . *showed that*, of the 28,714 serial citations themselves, 11,108 citations (38.69%) came from serials classed by *Ulrich's* in the subject area of physiology. 10,475 additional citations (36.49%) came from 5 main related subject areas: general medical sciences, biochemistry, general science, internal medicine, and pharmacy/pharmacology. (355)

Ibid. . . . *showed that*, of the 909 serial titles identified as containing at least 1 of the 28,714 serial citations, the top 3 countries of origin were United States (355 titles accounting for 57.37% of total citations), England (135 titles accounting for 22.54% of total citations), and Germany (96 titles accounting for 5.09% of total citations). (355)

Ibid. . . . *showed that* 23,118 (80.52%) of the serial citations referred to articles in English, while 4,696 (16.36%) of the citations referred to polylingual articles. Of the 909 serial titles identified as containing at least 1 of the 28,714 serial citations, 535 (58.85%) were English-language titles, while 237 (26.08%) were polylingual in format. **(355)**

Special

■ A study reported in 1975 of the research literature of physiology over the 3-year period 1970-72 involving citation counting (first 3 months of each year) in 8 internationally known journals (31,669 citations) *showed that* serial titles accounted for 28,714 (90.67%) citations, while monographs accounted for 2,955 (9.3%) citations. **(355)**

Ibid. . . . *showed that* the 3 most cited serial titles accounted for 24.633% of the total serial citations; that the top 14 serial titles accounted for 50.968% of the total serial citations; and the top 176 serial titles accounted for 90.008% of the total serial citations. **(355)**

Ibid. . . . *showed that* the 10 most cited serial titles in physiology were:
Journal of Physiology (London)
American Journal of Physiology (Bethesda)
Journal of Applied Physiology (Bethesda)
Acta Physiologica Scandinavica (Stockholm)
Journal of Clinical Investigation (Boston)
Circulation Research (New York)
Journal of Biological Chemistry (Baltimore)
Journal of General Physiology (Baltimore)
Nature (London)
Pfleugers Archiv (Berlin) **(355)**

Ibid. . . . *showed that*, of the 2,955 citations to monographs, 1,586 (54.672%) of the citations referred to titles published within 8 years of the citation, and 2,335 citations (79.018%) referred to titles published within 13 years of citation. **(355)**

Ibid. . . . *showed that*, of the 28,714 serial citations, 7,992 (27.833%) were to articles published within 5 years of citation; 15,077 (52.507%) were to articles published within 8 years of citation; and 21,248 (73.767%) were to articles published within 13 years of citation. **(355)**

Ibid. . . . *showed that*, of the 909 serial titles identified as containing at least 1 of the 28,714 serial citations, 40 titles (4.4%) were classed by *Ulrich's* in the physiology subject area. 361 (39.71%) additional titles were classed in 5 other main subject areas: general medical sciences, general

Selection, Periodicals

science, biology, pharmacy/pharmacology, and biochemistry. **(355)**

Ibid. . . . *showed that*, of the 28,714 serial citations themselves, 11,108 citations (38.69%) came from serials classed by *Ulrich's* in the subject area of physiology. 10,475 additional citations (36.49%) came from 5 main related subject areas: general medical sciences, biochemistry, general science, internal medicine, and pharmacy/pharmacology. **(355)**

Ibid. . . . *showed that*, of the 909 serial titles identified as containing at least 1 of the 28,714 serial citations, the top 3 countries of origin were United States (355 titles accounting for 57.37% of total citations), England (135 titles accounting for 22.54% of total citations), and Germany (96 titles accounting for 5.09% of total citations). **(355)**

Ibid. . . . *showed that* 23,118 (80.52%) of the serial citations referred to articles in English, while 4,696 (16.36%) of the citations referred to polylingual articles. Of the 909 serial titles identified as containing at least 1 of the 28,714 serial citations, 535 (58.85%) were English-language titles, while 237 (26.08%) were polylingual in format. **(355)**

Selection, Periodicals—Subject Area (Medicine, Tropics)

Academic

■ A study reported in 1978 of all articles indexed in 48 issues (1972-75) of the *Tropical Diseases Bulletin* (11,174 articles taken from 611 different journals) *showed that*:
  10 (1.6%) journal titles accounted for 2,765 (24.7%) articles;
  33 (5.1%) journal titles accounted for 5,452 (48.8%) articles;
  121 (18.9%) journal titles accounted for 8,707 (77.9%) articles;
  279 (43.5%) journal titles accounted for 10,378 (92.9%) articles. **(719)**

Ibid. . . . *showed that* the distribution of journal titles (and articles) by language was as follows for the 4 most frequently used languages:

English (439 titles)	8,963 (80.21%) articles
French (48 titles)	724 (6.48%) articles
Spanish (61 titles)	395 (3.53%) articles
Portuguese (27 titles)	361 (3.23%) articles **(719)**

Ibid. . . . *showed that* the 4 journals (out of 61 listed) accounting for the most articles were as follows:

Transactions of the Royal Society of Tropical Medicine and Hygiene	429 (3.8%) articles
American Journal of Tropical Medicine and Hygiene	427 (3.8%) articles
Journal of Parasitology	333 (3.0%) articles
Bulletin of the World Health Organization	309 (2.8%) articles **(719)**

Special

■ A study reported in 1978 of all articles indexed in 48 issues (1972-75) of the *Tropical Diseases Bulletin* (11,174 articles taken from 611 different journals) *showed that*:

10 (1.6%) journal titles accounted for 2,765 (24.7%) articles;

33 (5.1%) journal titles accounted for 5,452 (48.8%) articles;

121 (18.9%) journal titles accounted for 8,707 (77.9%) articles;

279 (43.5%) journal titles accounted for 10,378 (92.9%) articles. **(719)**

Ibid. . . . *showed that* the distribution of journal titles (and articles) by language was as follows for the 4 most frequently used languages:

English (439 titles)	8,963 (80.21%) articles
French (48 titles)	724 (6.48%) articles
Spanish (61 titles)	395 (3.53%) articles
Portuguese (27 titles)	361 (3.23%) articles **(719)**

Ibid. . . . *showed that* the 4 journals (out of 61 listed) accounting for the most articles were as follows:

Transactions of the Royal Society of Tropical Medicine and Hygiene	429 (3.8%) articles
American Journal of Tropical Medicine and Hygiene	427 (3.8%) articles
Journal of Parasitology	333 (3.0%) articles
Bulletin of the World Health Organization	309 (2.8%) articles **(719)**

Selection, Periodicals—Subject Area (Microbiology)

Academic

■ A study reported in 1974 of the *World List of Scientific Periodicals* (4th edition and 1968 supplement) *showed that* the number of journals in the field of microbiology increased as follows:

1900	19 journals
1920	68 journals
1940	160 journals
1960	286 journals
1968	327 journals

(353)

■ A study reported in 1974 of citations in articles listed in the *Annual Review of Microbiology* (vols. 22-24, 1968-70) involving 624 titles and 10,408 citations *showed that* the 10 most cited journals were:

Journal of Bacteriology
Proceedings of the National Academy of Sciences, U.S.A.
Virology
Nature (London)
Journal of Molecular Biology
Journal of Biological Chemistry
Biochimica et Biophysica Acta
Journal of General Microbiology
Biochemical and Biophysical Research Communications
Science (New York) (353)

Ibid. . . . *showed that* the 8,051 citations of the 141 most cited periodicals fell into 4 main subject areas (out of 23 categories): biochemistry (23.6%), microbiology (22.4%), science—general (18.1%), and virology (10%).

(353)

Ibid. . . . *showed that*, of the 141 most cited journals, the top 3 language formats were English (83 or 58.87% of total journals); multilingual, involving English, French, or German (27 or 19.15% of total); and multilingual, involving 4 languages of which English, French, and German were 3 of the languages (9 or 6.38% of total). (353)

Ibid. . . . *showed that* the 3 main countries of origin of the 141 most cited journals were United States (54 journals accounting for 58.03% of total citations), United Kingdom (29 journals accounting for 22.24% of total citations), and Germany (11 journals accounting for 4.16% of total citations). However, the Netherlands with only 5 journals accounted for 4.92% of the total citations. (353)

Special

■ A study reported in 1974 of the *World List of Scientific Periodicals* (4th edition and 1968 supplement) *showed that* the number of journals in the field of microbiology increased as follows:

1900	19 journals
1920	68 journals
1940	160 journals
1960	286 journals
1968	327 journals

(353)

■ A study reported in 1974 of citations in articles listed in the *Annual Review of Microbiology* (vols. 22-24, 1968-70) involving 624 titles and 10,408 citations *showed that* the 10 most cited journals were:

Journal of Bacteriology
Proceedings of the National Academy of Sciences, U.S.A.
Virology
Nature (London)
Journal of Molecular Biology
Journal of Biological Chemistry
Biochimica et Biophysica Acta
Journal of General Microbiology
Biochemical and Biophysical Research Communications
Science (New York) (353)

Ibid. . . . *showed that* the 8,051 citations of the 141 most cited periodicals fell into 4 main subject areas (out of 23 categories): biochemistry (23.6%), microbiology (22.4%), science—general (18.1%), and virology (10%).
(353)

Ibid. . . . *showed that*, of the 141 most cited journals, the top 3 language formats were English (83 or 58.87% of total journals); multilingual, involving English, French, or German (27 or 19.15% of total); and multilingual, involving 4 languages of which English, French, and German were 3 of the languages (9 or 6.38% of total). (353)

Ibid. . . . *showed that* the 3 main countries of origin of the 141 most cited journals were United States (54 journals accounting for 58.03% of total citations), United Kingdom (29 journals accounting for 22.24% of total citations), and Germany (11 journals accounting for 4.16% of total citations). However, the Netherlands with only 5 journals accounted for 4.92% of the total citations. (353)

Selection, Periodicals—Subject Area (Music)

General

■ A study reported in 1972 of the 1967 *RILM Abstracts (Repertoire International de la Litterature Musicale)*, involving every tenth entry from the subject index (158 items), *showed that* the 3 most popular languages were English (72.5 or 46% articles), German (20 or 12.5% articles), and French (15 or 9.5% articles). Articles published in 2 languages were counted as .5 in each language. (401)

Ibid. . . . *showed that* an examination of every twelfth entry in the 1967 cumulative index (1,125 entries) indicated that the 4 most common publication forms were articles from periodicals (612 or 54.4%), monographs (145 or 13.7%), articles from Festschriften (75 or 6.7%), and book reviews (72 or 6.4%). (401)

Selection, Periodicals—Subject Area (Pharmaceuticals)

Special

■ A study reported in 1974 of journal titles and articles appearing on the product bibliographies of 15 industrial libraries in the pharmaceutical industry during the 3-year period 1969-71 (2,017 journal titles; 33,119 articles) *showed that* 572 journal titles were required to account for 90% of the citations. This compares to an earlier study of biochemistry in which 80 journal titles accounted for 90% of the citations in a 3-year run of *Annual*

Review of Biochemistry, an earlier study at Edinburgh University's Central Medical Library in which medical school staff identified 523 journal titles that met 90% of their needs, and an earlier study at the Columbia and Yale Medical Libraries in which a use study indicated that 423 journal titles satisfied 90% of the demand. **(405)**

Ibid. . . . *showed that* the 4 most frequently cited journal titles were (in descending order of importance):
> British Medical Journal
> Journal of the American Medical Association
> Lancet
> New England Journal of Medicine **(405)**

Selection, Periodicals—Subject Area (Pharmacology)

Academic

■ A study reported in 1974 of the citations listed in the 1968-70 volumes of the *Annual Review of Pharmacology,* involving 11,424 citations, *showed that* journals accounted for 9,596 citations (84.00% of the total); nonprimary serial publications (e.g., annual review articles, recent advances, etc.) accounted for 714 citations (6.25% of total); and nonserial publications accounted for 1,114 citations (9.75% of total). **(354)**

Ibid. . . . *showed that* the 9,596 journal citations referred to a total of 781 titles, of which only 229 were cited 6 or more times. **(354)**

Ibid. . . . *showed that* the 10 most cited journals in pharmacology were:
> Journal of Pharmacology and Experimental Therapeutics
> Nature (London)
> British Journal of Pharmacology (formerly *British Journal of Pharmacology and Chemotherapy*)
> Journal of Physiology (London)
> Science (New York)
> Biochemical Pharmacology
> Proceedings of the Society for Experimental Biology and Medicine
> Annals of the New York Academy of Sciences

Selection, Periodicals

> *Federation Proceedings. Federation of American Societies for Experimental Biology*
> *Journal of Biological Chemistry* (354)

Ibid. . . . *showed that* the 229 most cited journals (8,571 citations) fell into 5 main subject areas (out of 22): pharmacology (22.7%), medicine—specialities (14.7%), physiology (13.4%), science—general (12.8%), and biochemistry (10.9%). (354)

Ibid. . . . *showed that*, of the 229 most cited journals, the 3 main language formats used were English (167 or 72.93% journals), multilingual involving various combinations of English, French, or German (36 or 15.72%), and French (7 or 3.06%). (354)

Ibid. . . . *showed that*, of the 229 most cited journals, the 3 main countries of publication were United States (125 journals accounting for 57.33% of total citations), United Kingdom (39 journals accounting for 26.36% of total citations), and Germany (11 journals accounting for 3.85% of total citations). (354)

Special

■ A study reported in 1974 of the citations listed in the 1968-70 volumes of the *Annual Review of Pharmacology*, involving 11,424 citations, *showed that* journals accounted for 9,596 citations (84.00% of the total); nonprimary serial publications (e.g., annual review articles, recent advances, etc.) accounted for 714 citations (6.25% of total); and nonserial publications accounted for 1,114 citations (9.75% of total). (354)

Ibid. . . . *showed that* the 9,596 journal citations referred to a total of 781 titles, of which only 229 were cited 6 or more times. (354)

Ibid. . . . *showed that* the 10 most cited journals in pharmacology were:
> *Journal of Pharmacology and Experimental Therapeutics*
> *Nature* (London)
> *British Journal of Pharmacology* (formerly *British Journal of Pharmacology and Chemotherapy*)
> *Journal of Physiology* (London)
> *Science* (New York)
> *Biochemical Pharmacology*
> *Proceedings of the Society for Experimental Biology and Medicine*

Annals of the New York Academy of Sciences
Federation Proceedings. Federation of American Societies for Experimental Biology
Journal of Biological Chemistry (354)

Ibid. . . . *showed that* the 229 most cited journals (8,571 citations) fell into 5 main subject areas (out of 22): pharmacology (22.7%), medicine—specialities (14.7%), physiology (13.4%), science—general (12.8%), and biochemistry (10.9%). (354)

Ibid. . . . *showed that*, of the 229 most cited journals, the 3 main language formats used were English (167 or 72.93% journals), multilingual involving various combinations of English, French, or German (36 or 15.72%), and French (7 or 3.06%). (354)

Ibid. . . . *showed that*, of the 229 most cited journals, the 3 main countries of publication were United States (125 journals accounting for 57.33% of total citations), United Kingdom (39 journals accounting for 26.36% of total citations), and Germany (11 journals accounting for 3.85% of total citations). (354)

Selection, Periodicals—Subject Area (Physics)

Academic

■ A 1971 study at the MIT Science Library of in-room use (journals do not circulate) of 220 physics journals over a 3.5-month period *showed that* of 4,292 uses the number of titles involved was as follows:

3 (1.4%) of the titles accounted for 1,384 (32.2%) of the uses;

14 (6.4%) of the titles accounted for 2,502 (58.3%) of the uses;

55 (25.0%) of the titles accounted for 3,949 (91.2%) of the uses;

138 (62.7%) of the titles accounted for 4,292 (100%) of the uses. (608)

Ibid. . . . *showed that* journals receiving heavy use had a later "point of obsolescence" than journals receiving light use. For example, for *Physical Review* (a heavy use item), volumes more than 10 years old accounted for 33.2% of its total use compared to the overall group of 220 journals, whose

volumes more than 10 years old accounted for only 26% of their use.
(608)

■ A 1973 survey of physicists in 6 universities of the greater Boston area (Boston University, Brandeis, Brown, Harvard, MIT, and Northeastern) to determine how they meet their information needs (sample size: 339; responding: 179 or 52.8%) *showed that* of 185 respondents (Harvard chemistry respondents included) the numbers of journals scanned per week by physicists were:

0 journals	4 (2.16%) respondents	
1-3 journals	105 (56.76%) respondents	
4-6 journals	62 (33.51%) respondents	
7-9 journals	10 (5.41%) respondents	
10+ journals	4 (2.16%) respondents	**(404)**

Ibid. . . . *showed that* the 3 most frequently reported journals scanned weekly by 179 responding physicists were: *Physics Review Letters* (73 or 40.8% respondents), *Physics Reviews* (66 or 36.9% respondents), and *Physics Letters* (30 or 16.8% respondents). Although in a different order, these were also the 3 journals physicists ranked most important. **(404)**

Selection, Periodicals—Subject Area (Political Science)

Academic

■ A study reported in 1970 of 3,610 citations in the area of political science taken from a book of readings (Harry Eckstein and David E. Apter, *Comparative Politics*, 1963), *American Political Science Review* (1963-66), and 2 British journals, *Political Studies* and *Political Quarterly* (1958-66), *showed that*, of the citations in the book alone (1,700 citations), 66% (1,124 citations) were to monographs; 23% (398 citations) were to periodicals; 3% (56 citations) were to newspapers; and 8% were to other sources. **(352)**

Ibid. . . . *showed that*, of the citations in the book alone (1,700 citations), 967 (86.0%) of the monographic citations, 65 (16.3%) of the periodical citations, and 12 (21.4%) of the newspaper citations were to English-language materials. **(352)**

Ibid. . . . *showed that*, of the 201 periodicals (1,910 citations) cited more than once, the 6 most cited journals were *American Political Science Review* (277 or 14.5% of the 1,910 citations), *Journal of Politics* (87 or 4.6% citations), *Western Political Quarterly* (61 or 3.2% citations), *Political Studies* (47 or 2.5% citations), *World Politics* (45 or 2.4% citations), and *Public Opinion Quarterly* (41 or 2.1% citations). **(352)**

Ibid. . . . *showed that*, of the 103 periodicals (1,493 citations) cited more than 4 times, 89% of the citations were after 1950, while 1955-67 provided 63% of the citations. **(352)**

■ A study reported in 1978 at Indiana University, Bloomington of materials requested through a delivery service to faculty in the political science and economics departments during a 32-month period (October 1972-June 1975), involving 39 political scientists and 14 economists (40-50% of the faculty in the departments) and 5,478 articles from 620 different journals and newspapers, *showed that* the 5 most requested journals by political scientists were as follows:

Journal of Politics	123 (3.2%) requests
American Political Science Review	118 (3.1%) requests
World Politics	115 (3.0%) requests
American Sociological Review	110 (2.9%) requests
Western Political Quarterly	104 (2.7%) requests **(421)**

Selection, Periodicals—Subject Area (Social Work)

Academic

■ A study reported in 1982 comparing journal rankings on the basis of local vs. national citations to determine the value of national citation studies for local collection development that used 3 sources of national social work citation data (1971 volume of *Social Work* [272 citations to 120 journals]; 16th edition of *Encyclopedia of Social Work* [1,006 citations to 252 journals]; and the 1971 volumes of *Social Casework, Social Service Review*, and (again) *Social Work* [756 citations to 237 journals]) vs. 2 journal rankings (local) derived from the citations in the articles published by the faculty of 1 school of social work (1971-74 period involving 376 citations to 118 journals and 1975-78 period involving 875 citations to 220 journals) *showed that*, of the 9 most cited journals locally 1971-74 and the 10 most cited journals locally 1975-78, 4 journals were in common; of the 9 most cited journals in *Social Work* both local rankings had 4 journals in common; of the 11 most cited journals in *Social Casework, Social Service Review*, and *Social Work*, the 1971-74 local ranking had 5 journals in common, and the 1975-78 ranking had 6 journals in common; of the 10 most cited journals in the *Encyclopedia of Social Work*, the 1971-74 local ranking had 3 in common, and the 1975-78 local ranking had 4 in common. **(269)**

Ibid. . . . *showed that*, of the titles cited 3 times or more locally, 9 (82%) from 1971-74 and 11 (100%) from 1975-78 appeared also on the top 11 ranking established by citations from *Social Casework, Social Service Review*, and *Social Work*; 12 (67%) from 1971-74 and 15 (83%) from 1975-78 appeared also on that national rankings list of 18 most cited journals; and 16 (48%) from 1971-74 and 24 (73%) from 1975-78 appeared also on that national rankings list of 33 most cited journals. Of the national rankings established by the *Encyclopedia of Social Work* and compared to titles cited 3 times or more locally, 4 (40%) from 1971-74 and 8 (80%) from 1975-78 appeared on that national rankings 10 most cited list; 11 (61%) from 1971-74 and 15 (83%) from 1975-78 appeared on that national rankings 18 most cited list; and 15 (42%) from 1971-74 and 25 (69%) from 1975-78 appeared on that national rankings 36 most cited list. **(269)**

Ibid. . . . *showed that* 8 (89%) of the titles cited 3 or more times locally in 1975-78 were among the 9 most cited titles locally in 1971-74; 15 (91%) were among the 17 most cited titles locally in 1971-74; and 27 (78%) were among the 34 most cited titles locally in 1971-74. This suggested that local citation rankings of journals may be slightly better predictors of the locally most heavily cited journals than the national rankings (see above). **(269)**

Selection, Periodicals—Subject Area (Sociology)

Academic

■ A study reported in 1974 using 52 sociological subject headings in *Social Science and Humanities Index* (1970-71) to identify 446 different journal articles, which in turn produced 8,926 citations to different publications (3,651 serial publications; 5,275 nonserial publications), *showed that* the serial publications had only 409 items (11.2%) cited 2 or more times and the monographic publications had only 759 (14.38%) items cited 2 or more times. **(252)**

Ibid. . . . *showed that* only 4.78% of the total citations (2.99% of the serial citations and 6.03% of the nonserial citations) referred to non-English language publications. **(252)**

Ibid. . . . *showed that*, of 84 journals cited 2 or more times, the top 10 were (in rank order with the last 3 journals tied):
American Sociological Review
American Journal of Sociology
Journal of Marriage and the Family
Social Forces
American Political Science Review
American Anthropologist
Human Relations
Journal of Personality and Social Psychology
Public Opinion Quarterly
Sociology and Social Research **(252)**

Ibid. . . . *showed that*, of the 612 journals carrying the 3,521 journal citations, 25 titles contained 53.47% of the total articles, while 10 titles contained 38.76% of the total articles cited. Of the 84 journals that contained articles with 2 or more citations, the top 10 journals contained 66.99% of those articles, while the top 5 journals contained 58.01% of those articles. **(252)**

■ A survey reported in 1978 of a stratified random sample of 811 sociologists from 183 graduate departments (response rate: 526 or 64.86%) reporting which social science journals they regularly read *showed that*, of the top 20 journals, 40.00% are interdisciplinary journals or journals from other social science disciplines. **(261)**

Ibid. . . . *showed that* the top 7 journals read regularly by respondents were (multiple responses allowed):

American Sociological Review	83.84%	respondents
American Sociologist	78.89%	respondents
American Journal of Sociology	65.01%	respondents
Social Forces	40.49%	respondents
Society/Trans-Action	30.93%	respondents
Social Problems	29.46%	respondents
Psychology Today	24.14%	respondents **(261)**

Ibid. . . . *showed that* comparing the rank order list of regularly read journals with the rank order of sociology journals by citation indicated that 55% of the 20 most reported regularly read journals were found on the list of the 20 most cited journals. However, the citation list tended to focus on interdisciplinary and nonsociological journals, whereas the regularly read list had a "distinctive, disciplinary focus." **(261)**

Selection Tools—General Issues

General

■ A 1967 study comparing *Cumulative Book Index* (CBI) with *Canadiana* in terms of its coverage of English-language books published in Canada (209 titles from the first 3 months of 1966 *Canadiana* searched in CBI for 1965-66-67) *showed that* 154 titles (74%) were located in CBI, while 55 (26%) were not found. Of the 55 titles not found in CBI, 26 (12.4% of the total) were the products of publishers not on CBI's list of publishers, while 29 (13.9% of the total) were on CBI's list of publishers. **(595)**

Ibid. . . . *showed that*, of the 154 titles located in CBI, 17 (11%) of the titles appeared in CBI before they appeared in *Canadiana*, 22 (14%) titles appeared in CBI within a month or 2 of their appearance in *Canadiana*, and 115 (75%) appeared in CBI at least 2 months after appearing in *Canadiana*. Further, 93 (60.4%) of the titles found in CBI appeared 4-5 months after appearing in *Canadiana*. **(595)**

■ A study reported in 1979 of the English-language literature of library administration (2,877 citations to materials cited in 364 refereed articles indexed in *Library Literature* between 1961-70) *showed that* the distribution of cited works by type was as follows:

monographs	1,247 (43.3%)	cited works
journals	1,149 (39.9%)	cited works
governmental publications	338 (11.7%)	cited works
miscellaneous	143 (4.9%)	cited works **(566)**

Academic

■ A study reported in 1969 of the bibliographic coverage of a stratified sample of 1,527 agricultural economics publications (20%), taken from a population of 7,624 publications reported published by U.S. agricultural economists during the 3-year period 1961-63, *showed that* the *Bibliography of Agriculture* referenced 39.40% of the sample publications; *Agricultural*

Index (now *Biological and Agricultural Index*) referenced 17.83%; *World Agricultural Economics and Rural Sociology Abstracts* referenced 8.71%; *Public Affairs Information Service* referenced 3.58%; *International Bibliography of Economics* referenced 2.6%; *Dairy Science Abstracts* referenced 0.44%; *Journal of Economics Abstracts* referenced 0.16%; and *Business Periodicals Index* referenced 0.13%. **(245)**

Ibid. . . . *showed that*, if a publication appeared as a part of a series or in a periodical, it had a statistically significantly better chance (significant at the .01 level) of being indexed than if it appeared as a separate publication. For example, while 72% of the research monographs in a series were indexed, only 13% of the separate research reports were indexed. **(245)**

Ibid. . . . *showed that* national-level publications were more likely to be indexed than state- or regional-level publications. For example, 65.29% of the U.S. federal publications and 54.13% of the national or regional organization or society publications were indexed, compared to 21.58% of the state government agency publications and 10.94% of the local or state organization publications. **(245)**

■ A study reported in 1972 of the 1967 *RILM Abstracts (Repertoire International de la Litterature Musicale)*, involving every tenth entry from the subject index (158 items), *showed that* the 3 most popular languages were English (72.5 or 46% articles), German (20 or 12.5% articles), and French (15 or 9.5% articles). Articles published in 2 languages were counted as .5 in each language. **(401)**

Ibid. . . . *showed that* an examination of every twelfth entry in the 1967 cumulative index (1125 entries) indicated that the 4 most common publication forms were articles from periodicals (612 or 54.4%), monographs (145 or 13.7%), articles from Festschriften (75 or 6.7%), and book reviews (72 or 6.4%). **(401)**

Ibid. . . . *showed that* a comparison of potential descriptors for the 158 sample items with the actual index terms used by RILM revealed that overall 13.5% of important terms were overlooked. This was considered a low number. **(401)**

■ A study reported in 1972 of the bibliographic control of doctoral dissertations in the areas of sociology, psychology, biology, and education, involving 3,012 dissertations selected from *American Doctoral Disserta-*

Selection Tools

tions, showed that 1,665 (55.3%) dissertations were abstracted in either *Microfilm Abstracts* or the following *Dissertation Abstracts* during the period 1934-69. **(400)**

Ibid. . . . *showed that*, of those dissertations abstracted in *Dissertation Abstracts* and available on microfilm, 1,604 (90.5%) were abstracted within 2 years of the date of degree issuance. However, this comprised only 53.4% of the total number of dissertations issued. **(400)**

■ A study reported in 1975 of index control and overlap in the area of geochemistry, involving 879 citations of materials published between 1960 and 1966 taken from selected bibliographies and searched in *Chemical Abstracts, Bibliography of North American Geology, Bibliography and Index of Geology Exclusive of North America*, and *Geoscience Abstracts, showed that* 135 (15%) were not found in any of the 4 indexing and abstracting tools, while 560 (64%) were found in *Chemical Abstracts*, 258 (29%) were found in *Bibliography and Index of Geology Exclusive of North America*, 250 (28%) were found in *Geoscience Abstracts*, and 220 (25%) were found in *Bibliograhpy of North American Geology*. **(408)**

■ A survey reported in 1976 of 179 journals cited by political science books and journals *showed that* only 29.05% of the cited journals were classified by *Ulrich's International Periodical Directory* as political science. **(053)**

■ A survey reported in 1982 of library/media specialists in institutions with student enrollments of 1,000 or more in technical programs to investigate the tools used to select vocational-technical library materials (survey size: 422 institutions; responding: 232 or 55%) *showed that*, based on a numerical ranking of usefulness (1 to 5 where 5 was most useful), the 5 most highly rated selection sources (out of 15) were (in descending order of importance):

faculty recommendations	4.2 average rank	
publisher's catalogs	3.7 average rank	
New Technical Books	3.6 average rank	
Materials for Occupational Education	3.5 average rank	
Vocational Technical Core Collection	3.5 average rank	**(778)**

Public

■ A study reported in 1978 of 19 bibliographic tools listing materials for young adults, involving a total of 19,405 titles in conjunction with a purposeful sample of 270 papers collected from college-bound high school students (grades 10 through 12) in a large metropolitan area from a wide variety of schools, *showed that* only 22% of the titles appeared in more than 1 of the 19 bibliographic tools. **(523)**

Ibid. . . . *showed that*, of the 100 most frequently cited titles in the 19 bibliographic tools, 58 (58%) were fiction with only 2 (2%) titles that could be classified as science. Further, there was a "lack of materials covering economics, anthropology, sociology and psychology." **(523)**

Ibid. . . . .*showed that* the proportion of materials referenced in the bibliographies of the 270 papers was monographic references (67%), journal references (20%), and other, including encyclopedias, documents, primary materials, etc. (13%). Further, only 14% of the 270 papers had half or more of their total references to materials that were 5 years old or less at the time the paper was written. **(523)**

Ibid. . . . *showed that*, of the 1,862 monographs cited in these papers that it was possible to check, 578 (31%) appeared in 1 or more of the 19 selection tools. Further, 3 tools accounted for 79% of the 578 citations:
   Senior High School Catalog
   Junior High School Catalog
   Books for Secondary School Libraries
with *Senior High School Catalog* and *Books for Secondary School Libraries* accounting for 69% of the 578 citations. **(523)**

Ibid. . . . *showed that*, of the 578 citations made in student papers to materials listed in 1 of the 19 bibliographic tools, "lists of recommended titles" accounted for 13.3% of the total; titles recommended by "textbooks on adolescent literature and information services" accounted for 4.8% of the total; and "annual listing" accounted for 2.8% of the total. **(523)**

Ibid. . . . *showed that*, of the 602 journal citations made in the 270 student papers, 6 journal titles supplied 32% of the citations; 16 titles supplied 50%

Selection Tools

of the citations; 52 titles supplied 75% of the citations; and 170 titles were required to supply 100% of the citations. **(523)**

School

■ A study reported in 1978 of 19 bibliographic tools listing materials for young adults, involving a total of 19,405 titles in conjunction with a purposeful sample of 270 papers collected from college-bound high school students (grades 10 through 12) in a large metropolitan area from a wide variety of schools, *showed that* only 22% of the titles appeared in more than 1 of the 19 bibliographic tools. **(523)**

Ibid. . . . *showed that*, of the 100 most frequently cited titles in the 19 bibliographic tools, 58 (58%) were fiction with only 2 (2%) titles that could be classified as science. Further, there was a "lack of materials covering economics, anthropology, sociology and psychology." **(523)**

Ibid. . . . *showed that* the proportion of materials referenced in the bibliographies of the 270 papers was monographic references (67%), journal references (20%), and other, including encyclopedias, documents, primary materials, etc. (13%). Further, only 14% of the 270 papers had half or more of their total references to materials that were 5 years old or less at the time the paper was written. **(523)**

Ibid. . . . *showed that*, of the 1,862 monographs cited in these papers that it was possible to check, 578 (31%) appeared in 1 or more of the 19 selection tools. Further, 3 tools accounted for 79% of the 578 citations:
Senior High School Catalog
Junior High School Catalog
Books for Secondary School Libraries
with *Senior High School Catalog* and *Books for Secondary School Libraries* accounting for 69% of the 578 citations. **(523)**

Ibid. . . . *showed that*, of the 578 citations made in student papers to materials listed in 1 of the 19 bibliographic tools, "lists of recommended titles" accounted for 13.3% of the total; titles recommended by "textbooks on adolescent literature and information services" accounted for 4.8% of the total; and "annual listing" accounted for 2.8% of the total. **(523)**

Ibid. . . . *showed that*, of the 602 journal citations made in the 270 student papers, 6 journal titles supplied 32% of the citations; 16 titles supplied 50% of the citations; 52 titles supplied 75% of the citations; and 170 titles were required to supply 100% of the citations. **(523)**

Special

■ A study reported in 1972 of the 1967 *RILM Abstracts (Repertoire International de la Litterature Musicale)*, involving every tenth entry from the subject index (158 items), *showed that* the 3 most popular languages were English (72.5 or 46% articles), German (20 or 12.5% articles), and French (15 or 9.5% articles). Articles published in 2 languages were counted as .5 in each language. **(401)**

Ibid. . . . *showed that* an examination of every twelfth entry in the 1967 cumulative index (1125 entries) indicated that the 4 most common publication forms were articles from periodicals (612 or 54.4%), monographs (145 or 13.7%), articles from Festschriften (75 or 6.7%), and book reviews (72 or 6.4%). **(401)**

Ibid. . . . *showed that* a comparison of potential descriptors for the 158 sample items with the actual index terms used by RILM revealed that overall 13.5% of important terms were overlooked. This was considered a low number. **(401)**

■ A study reported in 1975 of index control and overlap in the area of geochemistry, involving 879 citations of materials published between 1960 and 1966 taken from selected bibliographies and searched in *Chemical Abstracts, Bibliography of North American Geology, Bibliography and Index of Geology Exclusive of North America*, and *Geoscience Abstracts*, *showed that* 135 (15%) were not found in any of the 4 indexing and abstracting tools, while 560 (64%) were found in *Chemical Abstracts*, 258 (29%) were found in *Bibliography and Index of Geology Exclusive of North America*, 250 (28%) were found in *Geoscience Abstracts*, and 220 (25%) were found in *Bibliography of North American Geology*. **(408)**

Selection Tools—Book Reviews

General

■ A study of 4 major book review journals *showed that* the time lag betweeen publishing date and appearance of the review for 11 Notable

Selection Tools 231

Books during the period 1973-75 was 1.5 days for *New Times Book Review*, 16.6 days for *Library Journal*, 57.6 days for *Booklist*, and 127.7 days for *Choice*. **(157)**

■ A study in 1978 comparing 2,600 book reviews in *Library Journal* and *Choice showed that* 55% of the *Choice* reviews and 70% of the *Library Journal* reviews compared the book neither to another book nor to the literature in general. **(039)**

Ibid. . . . *showed that* there was little evidence that *Choice* reviews were more substantive or critical than those in *Library Journal*, nor was there much evidence of a qualitative difference between reviews by college teachers and those by librarians. The latter point held true whether comparing *Library Journal* reviews as a group with *Choice* reviews as a group or *Library Journal* reviews by college teachers with *Library Journal* reviews by librarians. **(039)**

Ibid. . . . *showed that* the judgment used by editors of these 2 journals in selecting which books to review was substantially sound in that 90% of the books given negative reviews in either of the journals were not reviewed by the other journal. **(039)**

Ibid. . . . *showed that* the main issue for a new book was not the quality of the review but getting reviewed at all—a decision made by the editors of reviewing journals. For example, *Library Journal* reviews approximately 6,000 books a year from a pool of 25-30,000 submitted books and manuscripts, whereas, of the reviewed books, only 9% of the *Library Journal* books and 6% of the *Choice* books were given negative recommendations. **(039)**

■ A study reported in 1980 comparing the *Book Review Digest, Book Review Index*, and *Current Book Review Citations showed that* the number of journals covered by each tool was as follows:

Current Book Review Citations	1,261 journals
Book Review Index	270 journals
Book Review Digest	69 journals **(790)**

Ibid. . . . *showed that Book Review Digest* reviewed no journals that CBRC and BRI did not together review. Of the total journals reviewed by all 3 tools, *Current Book Review Citations* was the sole reviewer of 1,022 (78.9%) journals, while *Book Review Index* was the sole reviewer for 34 (2.6%) journals. The amount of overlap between BRI and CBRC was 170 (13.1%) journals, while the number of journals reviewed in all 3 tools was 66 (5.1%) journals. **(790)**

Ibid. . . . *showed that* the time lag in publishing the reviews [presumably the time between the publication date of the book and the publication of the reviewing issue of the tool] was as follows:

Current Book Review Citations: 50% of the reviews were 6 months old or less, 33% of the reviews were between 6-9 months old, and 17% of the reviews were more than 9 months old;

Book Review Index: 100% of the reviews were 6 months old or less;

Book Review Digest: 46% of the reviews were 6 months old or older, 34% of the reviews were 6-9 months old and 20% of the reviews were more than 9 months old. **(790)**

Ibid. . . . *showed that*, based on a sample check of 30 reviews in each of the tools, there were no errors due to faulty citations in any of the 3 tools. **(790)**

Academic

■ A study reported in 1969 comparing 1,336 (adult) nonfiction reviews in *Kirkus* for the year 1962 with books listed in *Books For College Libraries* (1967 edition) *showed that Kirkus* was a good reviewing medium for college libraries. Specifically, 450 (33.7%) of the *Kirkus* reviews were found in *Books For College Libraries*. **(589)**

■ A study reported in 1976 of the bibliographic coverage of 1,972 social science (psychology, sociology, political science, and economics) books and government publications (primarily 1971 and 1972 imprints searched in the bibliographic sources for the subsequent 3-4 years) *showed that* books reviewed in a discipline's journals are more likely than nonreviewed books to be cited in the bibliographic services. For example:

in psychology, 115 of 170 books (68%) were reviewed overall, while 57 of 77 (74%) cited books were reviewed;

Selection Tools

in sociology, 108 of 270 books (40%) were reviewed overall, while 72 of 136 (53%) cited books were reviewed;

in political science, 44 of 105 (42%) books were reviewed overall, while 42 of 86 (49%) cited books were reviewed;

in economics, 44 of 149 (30%) books were reviewed overall, while 43 of 116 (37%) cited books were reviewed. **(410)**

■ A 1976 study at the Health Sciences Library of the University of Iowa involving 1,288 books received during a 6-month period *showed that*, of 730 (57%) books received on the approval plan, 330 (25%) were received due to orders placed on the basis of book reviews or publishers fliers; 131 (10%) were received due to orders generated as a result of patron request; and 97 (8%) were received due to standing order. **(467)**

■ A study reported in 1983 of the scholarly materials supporting research on 3 creative authors (John Milton, Henry James, and W. H. Auden), taken from the 1976-80 volumes of the *Arts and Humanities Citation Index* and involving 327 source articles and 2,876 citations found in the source articles, *showed that*:

of 174 source items on John Milton, 56.3% were book reviews and 43.7% were articles;

of 106 source items on Henry James, 58.5% were book reviews and 41.5% were articles;

and of 47 source items on W. H. Auden, 34% were book reviews and 66% were articles. **(520)**

■ A study reported in 1983 of the scholarly materials supporting research on 3 literary topics (symbolism, existentialism, and structuralism), involving 352 source articles and 4,144 citations taken from those source articles, *showed that* 45.5% of the source materials were book reviews and 54.5% were articles. Of the 4,144 citations, 78.8% were to books, 16.5% were to articles, and 4.6% were to other types of material. **(520)**

Public

■ A comparison reported in 1980 of the number of U.S. juvenile books published in the period 1972-74 (7,160 titles) with the number of reviews published in 5 major reviewing media for the same period *showed that School Library Journal* reviews 97% of the new titles; *Booklist* reviews

40% of the new titles; *Bulletin of the Center for Children's Books* reviews 32% of the new titles; *Horn Book* reviews 17% of the new titles; and the *New York Times Book Review* reviews 13% of the new titles. **(218)**

■ A study reported in 1980 of a sample of 30 titles selected at random from the 1972-73-74 lists of Notable Children's Books and checked in *Book Review Index* to locate reviews *showed that* the *Bulletin of the Center for Children's Books* had reviewed 29 of the books (97%); *Booklist* and *School Library Journal* had each reviewed 28 of the books (93%); *Horn Book* had reviewed 23 of the books (77%); and the *New York Times Book Review* had reviewed 17 (57%). **(218)**

Ibid. . . . *showed that* 11 of the sample titles were reviewed by all 5 periodicals; 14 of the titles were reviewed by 4 periodicals; 4 of the titles were reviewed by 3 periodicals; and 1 title was reviewed by 2 periodicals. **(218)**

Ibid. . . . *showed that* the time lag between publication date and review averaged 54.6 days for the *New York Times Book Review*, 64.2 days for *Booklist*, 80.7 days for *School Library Journal*, 118.6 days for *Horn Book*, and 136 days for the *Bulletin of the Center for Children's Books*. **(218)**

Ibid. . . . *showed that* the number of critical themes (evaluative, subjective comments such as "well-written") per title reviewed in *Booklist* averaged 4.89; for the *Bulletin of the Center for Children's Books* averaged 5.24; for the *School Library Journal* averaged 5.64; for *Horn Book* averaged 6.3; and for the *New York Times Book Review* averaged 6.64. **(218)**

■ A study reported in 1981 investigating the degree to which book reviews affect library purchase of books and the degree to which (sexually) controversial books were purchased by libraries based on book selection in 30 medium-sized (total annual expenditures for 1972-74 between $200,000-750,000) public libraries in New Jersey, Illinois, and Michigan and involving 250 controversial books and 360 noncontroversial books (adult nonfiction published between 1972-74 in the U.S.) *showed that* there was a statistically significant relationship between the number of reviews a book received and the number of libraries owning it, with more frequently reviewed books owned by more libraries. The strength of the correlation was $r = .71$ and was significant at the .001 level. **(782)**

Selection Tools

Ibid. . . . *showed that* a test of the hypothesis that there was no statistically significant relationship between the nature of the reviews (favorable, unfavorable, or neutral) of a book and the number of libraries owning the book gave ambigious results. For books receiving 1, 2, 5, or 6 reviews there was no statistically significant difference in their likelihood of being included in the library's collection, while for books receiving 3 or 4 reviews there was a statistically significant difference, with favorably reviewed books owned by more libraries (significant at the .05 level). (It was suggested that books with 1 or 2 reviews were routinely seldom purchased and books with 5 or 6 reviews were routinely always purchased, while only with books with 3 or 4 reviews did the nature of the review come into play.) **(782)**

Ibid. . . . *showed that* potentially sexually controversial books appeared as often in library collections as noncontroversial books. Specifically, there was no statistically significant difference in the number of potentially controversial books found in the libraries' collections versus the number of noncontroversial randomly selected books found in the libraries' collections when the number and nature of the reviews of the books were controlled for. In fact, 16 of the libraries owned more of the potentially controversial books than of the randomly selected books. **(782)**

■ A study reported in 1982 to investigate the reviewing of the 81 books on the 1980 list of the Outstanding Science Trade Books for Children in 7 periodicals (*Appraisal, Booklist, Bulletin of the Center for Children's Books, Horn Book, Kirkus Reviews, School Library Journal*, and *Science Books and Films*) *showed that* the 81 titles received 378 reveiws in these journals, for an average of 4.66 reviews per title. The number of titles reviewed in each journal was as follows:

School Library Journal	69 (85%)	titles
Booklist	68 (84%)	titles
Science Books and Films	61 (75%)	titles
Kirkus Reviews	53 (65%)	titles
Appraisal	50 (62%)	titles
Bulletin of the Center for Children's Books	34 (42%)	titles
Horn Book	32 (40%)	titles

(779)

Ibid. . . . *showed that* the average time lag between publication date of the book and appearance of the review for each of the 7 journals was as follows:

Booklist	9 days time lag
Kirkus Reviews	52 days time lag

continued

Bulletin of the Center for
   Children's Books   121 days time lag
School Library Journal   128 days time lag
Horn Book   140 days time lag
Science Books and Films   231 days time lag
Appraisal   238 days time lag   **(779)**

Ibid. . . . *showed that* the number of reviews in each of the 7 reviewing journals that referred to the accuracy of the book was as follows:

Appraisal   54% of the reviews
Science Books and Films   46% of the reviews
Horn Book   22% of the reviews
Bulletin of the Center for
   Children's Books   21% of the reviews
School Library Journal   19% of the reviews
Kirkus Reviews   13% of the reviews
Booklist   12% of the reviews   **(779)**

Ibid. . . . *showed that* the number of reviews in each of the 7 reviewing journals that referred to the readability (e.g., such issues as clarity, simplicity, appeal, or style) of the book was as follows:

Appraisal   98% of the reviews
Bulletin of the Center for
   Children's Books   88% of the reviews
Science Books and Films   84% of the reviews
Kirkus Reviews   77% of the reviews
Booklist   76% of the reviews
School Library Journal   75% of the reviews
Horn Book   63% of the reviews   **(779)**

Ibid. . . . *showed that* the number of reviews in each of the 7 reviewing journals that referred to the format (e.g., mention of illustrations, print style or size, paper quality, or page layout) of the book was as follows:

Appraisal   94% of the reviews
School Library Journal   87% of the reviews
Booklist   84% of the reviews
Science Books and Films   82% of the reviews
Horn Book   69% of the reviews

continued

Selection Tools

    Bulletin of the Center for
      Children's Books   65% of the reviews
    Kirkus Reviews   62% of the reviews   **(779)**

Ibid. . . . *showed that* the number of reviews in each of the 7 reviewing journals that contained 3 or 4 of the 4 central reviewing elements (description, evaluation of accuracy, evaluation of readability, and evaluation of format) was as follows:

    Appraisal   49 (98%) of the reviews
    Science Books and Films   50 (82%) of the reviews
    School Library Journal   50 (72%) of the reviews
    Bulletin of the Center for
      Children's Books   22 (65%) of the reviews
    Booklist   43 (63%) of the reviews
    Kirkus Reviews   31 (59%) of the reviews
    Horn Book   18 (56%) of the reviews   **(779)**

School

■ A comparison reported in 1980 of the number of U.S. juvenile books published in the period 1972-74 (7,160 titles) with the number of reviews published in 5 major reviewing media for the same period *showed that School Library Journal* reviews 97% of the new titles; *Booklist* reviews 40% of the new titles; *Bulletin of the Center for Children's Books* reviews 32% of the new titles; *Horn Book* reviews 17% of the new titles; and the *New York Times Book Review* reviews 13% of the new titles. **(218)**

■ A study reported in 1980 of a sample of 30 titles selected at random from the 1972-73-74 lists of Notable Children's Books and checked in *Book Review Index* to locate reviews *showed that* the *Bulletin of the Center for Children's Books* had reviewed 29 of the books (97%); *Booklist* and *School Library Journal* had each reviewed 28 of the books (93%); *Horn Book* had reviewed 23 of the books (77%); and the *New York Times Book Review* had reviewed 17 (57%). **(218)**

Ibid. . . . *showed that* 11 of the sample titles were reviewed by all 5 periodicals; 14 of the titles were reviewed by 4 periodicals; 4 of the titles were reviewed by 3 periodicals; and 1 title was reviewed by 2 periodicals.
(218)

238 COLLECTION DEVELOPMENT

Ibid. . . . *showed that* the time lag between publication date and review averaged 54.6 days for the *New York Times Book Review*, 64.2 days for *Booklist*, 80.7 days for *School Library Journal*, 118.6 days for *Horn Book*, and 136 days for the *Bulletin of the Center for Children's Books*.
(218)

Ibid. . . . *showed that* the number of critical themes (evaluative, subjective comments such as "well-written") per title reviewed in *Booklist* averaged 4.89; for the *Bulletin of the Center for Children's Books* averaged 5.24; for the *School Library Journal* averaged 5.64; for *Horn Book* averaged 6.3; and for the *New York Times Book Review* averaged 6.64. **(218)**

■ A study reported in 1981 of 197 undergraduate and graduate students enrolled in children's literature classes at the University of Iowa and Michigan State University *showed that* a warning indicator signaling possible objectionable content arbitrarily assigned an otherwise favorable book review statistically significantly (significant at the .05 level) reduced the chances for that book to be chosen for a school library collection.
(220)

Ibid. . . . *showed that* a warning indicator signaling possible objectionable content arbitrarily assigned an otherwise favorable book review did not affect books chosen for grades none through second, third through fifth, and sixth through eighth in a statistically significant differential manner. The warning indicator reduced selection probability equally across the 3 groups. **(220)**

■ A study reported in 1982 to investigate the reviewing of the 81 books on the 1980 list of the Outstanding Science Trade Books for Children in 7 periodicals (*Appraisal, Booklist, Bulletin of the Center for Children's Books, Horn Book, Kirkus Reviews, School Library Journal*, and *Science Books and Films*) *showed that* the 81 titles received 378 reveiws in these journals, for an average of 4.66 reviews per title. The number of titles reviewed in each journal was as follows:

School Library Journal	69 (85%)	titles
Booklist	68 (84%)	titles
Science Books and Film	61 (75%)	titles
Kirkus Reviews	53 (65%)	titles
Appraisal	50 (62%)	titles
Bulletin of the Center for Children's Books	34 (42%)	titles
Horn Book	32 (40%)	titles **(779)**

Selection Tools

Ibid. . . . *showed that* the average time lag between publication date of the book and appearance of the review for each of the 7 journals was as follows:

Booklist	9 days time lag
Kirkus Reviews	52 days time lag
Bulletin of the Center for Children's Books	121 days time lag
School Library Journal	128 days time lag
Horn Book	140 days time lag
Science Books and Films	231 days time lag
Appraisal	238 days time lag **(779)**

Ibid. . . . *showed that* the number of reviews in each of the 7 reviewing journals that referred to the accuracy of the book was as follows:

Appraisal	54% of the reviews
Science Books and Films	46% of the reviews
Horn Book	22% of the reviews
Bulletin of the Center for Children's Books	21% of the reviews
School Library Journal	19% of the reviews
Kirkus Reviews	13% of the reviews
Booklist	12% of the reviews **(779)**

Ibid. . . . *showed that* the number of reviews in each of the 7 reviewing journals that referred to the readability (e.g., such issues as clarity, simplicity, appeal, or style) of the book was as follows:

Appraisal	98% of the reviews
Bulletin of the Center for Children's Books	88% of the reviews
Science Books and Films	84% of the reviews
Kirkus Reviews	77% of the reviews
Booklist	76% of the reviews
School Library Journal	75% of the reviews
Horn Book	63% of the reviews **(779)**

Ibid. . . . *showed that* the number of reviews in each of the 7 reviewing journals that referred to the format (e.g., mention of illustrations, print style or size, paper quality, or page layout) of the book was as follows:

Appraisal	94% of the reviews
School Library Journal	87% of the reviews
Booklist	84% of the reviews
Science Books and Films	82% of the reviews
Horn Book	69% of the reviews
Bulletin of the Center for Children's Books	65% of the reviews
Kirkus Reviews	62% of the reviews **(779)**

Ibid. . . . *showed that* the number of reviews in each of the 7 reviewing journals that contained 3 or 4 of the 4 central reviewing elements (description, evaluation of accuracy, evaluation of readability, and evaluation of format) was as follows:

Appraisal	49 (98%) of the reviews
Science Books and Films	50 (82%) of the reviews
School Library Journal	50 (72%) of the reviews
Bulletin of the Center for Children's Books	22 (65%) of the reviews
Booklist	43 (63%) of the reviews
Kirkus Reviews	31 (59%) of the reviews
Horn Book	18 (56%) of the reviews **(779)**

Special

■ A study reported in 1974 of 3,347 biomedical book reviews (2,067 titles) taken from the 1970 issues of 54 English-language biomedical journals (excluding *Science* and *Nature*) that contained "bona fide" book reviews *showed that* the 7 journals with the most reviews accounted for 52.8% of the reviews, while the 31 journals with the most reviews accounted for 90% of the reviews. Since "about one-third" of the books were reviewed more than once, the author suggested that these 31 titles covered the review literature adequately. A list of the 54 titles was given.
(699)

Ibid. . . . *showed that* the 10 journals with the highest numbers of reviews were as follows (together accounting for 2,100 or 63.03% of the total reviews):

British Medical Journal	375 (11.20%) reviews
Lancet	317 (9.47%) reviews
Annals of Internal Medicine	277 (8.28%) reviews

continued

Selection Tools

Journal of the American
Medical Association   260 (7.76%) reviews
Archives of Internal Medicine   211 (6.30%) reviews
New England Journal of Medicine   174 (5.19%) reviews
Quarterly Review of Biology   155 (4.63%) reviews
Bioscience   123 (3.68%) reviews
Canadian Medical Association
Journal   116 (3.47%) reviews
American Journal of the Medical
Sciences   102 (3.05%) reviews   **(699)**

■ A study reported in 1974 of 3,347 biomedical book reviews (2,067 titles) taken from the 1970 issues of 54 English-language biomedical journals (excluding *Science* and *Nature*) that contained "bona fide" book reviews *showed that* the average time lags (difference between publication date of a book and the date of the journal issue containing the review of the book) for the 54 journals varied widely, ranging from 5.8 months for *Lancet* to 42 months for *Acta Radiologica: Therapy, Physics, Biology.* 29.7% of the 3,347 reviews appeared in the same year as the book was published. **(700)**

Ibid. . . . *showed that* the length of the reviews ranged from 50 words to 1,650 words with "most . . . over 265 words." Further, reviews in all but 3 of the 54 journals were signed. **(700)**

Ibid. . . . *showed that* the lag time for individual reviews ranged from 0 months to 108 months (9 years). The modal lag for individual reviews was 8 months, while the average lag was 10.43 months. **(700)**

■ A study reported in 1974 of 3,347 biomedical book reviews (2,067 titles) taken from the 1970 issues of 54 English-language biomedical journals (excluding *Science* and *Nature*) that contained "bona fide" book reviews *showed that* 727 (35.17%) titles were reviewed more than once. 420 (57.77%) of the 727 titles were reviewed twice; 162 (22.28%) were reviewed 3 times; and 145 (19.95%) were reviewed from 4 to 11 times.
(703)

Ibid. . . . *showed that* 5 journals covered 680 (93.53%) of the books reviewed more than once and 1,131 titles (54.71%) of the total titles reviewed. These journals were:

British Medical Journal 375 (18.1%) total titles
Annals of Internal Medicine 243 (11.8%) total titles
Lancet 212 (10.3%) total titles
Journal of the American Medical Association 184 (8.9%) total titles
New England Journal of Medicine 117 (5.7%) total titles **(703)**

■ A study reported in 1974 of 3,347 biomedical book reviews (2,067 titles) taken from the 1970 issues of 54 English-language biomedical journals (excluding *Science* and *Nature*) that contained "bona fide" book reviews *showed that*, of the 1,674 titles available in the U.S., 1,479 (88.35%) were published by trade publishers, while 147 (8.78%) were published by university presses. **(704)**

■ A 1976 study at the Health Sciences Library of the University of Iowa involving 1,288 books received during a 6-month period *showed that*, of 730 (57%) books received on the approval plan, 330 (25%) were received due to orders placed on the basis of book reviews or publishers fliers; 131 (10%) were received due to orders generated as a result of patron request; and 97 (8%) were received due to standing order. **(467)**

Selection Tools—Media

Academic

■ A study reported in 1977 of audiovisual catalogs in the Learning Resources Center of the University of Connecticut Health Center Library (64 catalogs selected randomly from a total collection of 640 domestic and foreign catalogs) *showed that*:

> the catalogs provided a title 100% of the time and a summary and physical description at least 75% of the time;

> the catalogs provided information about intended audience 44-47% of the time, date of production 31-53% of the time, and producer 47-53% of the time;

> the catalogs provided a title index 25% of the time and a subject index 16-22% of the time. **(713)**

Selection Tools

Special

■ A study reported in 1977 of audiovisual catalogs in the Learning Resources Center of the University of Connecticut Health Center Library (64 catalogs selected randomly from a total collection of 640 domestic and foreign catalogs) *showed that*:

> the catalogs provided a title 100% of the time and a summary and physical description at least 75% of the time;
>
> the catalogs provided information about intended audience 44-47% of the time, date of production 31-53% of the time, and producer 47-53% of the time;
>
> the catalogs provided a title index 25% of the time and a subject index 16-22% of the time. **(713)**

Selection Tools—Monographs

General

■ An analysis reported in 1970 of listings in the 1969 edition of *Books in Print*, which serves as an index to *Publisher's Trade List Annual* (sample size: 2,000 listings from PTLA checked both in BIP author and title volumes for a total of 4,000 entries) *showed that* there were 351 discrepancies, for an error rate of 8.8% or a range of expected errors 8.3 to 9.3% with a 95% confidence interval. If only author and title discrepancies that make it difficult to locate items in BIP are considered, the error range drops to 2.1%-3.1%. Other discrepancies involved prices and dates.
(087)

■ A study reported in 1971 to evaluate the success of the National Program for Acquisitions and Cataloging (also known as the Shared Cataloging Program) by comparing Australian, British, and French publications entered in the *National Union Catalog* before (1962) and after (1967) the program began (180 titles from *British National Bibliography*, *Australian National Bibliography*, and *Bibliographie de la France* for 1962; 200 titles from the same 3 works for 1967) *showed that* the number of titles from these 3 countries appearing in the NUC had substantially increased. Specifically, searching each of the 380 titles in the 14 monthly issues of NUC after the title appeared in the foreign bibliography revealed that 118

(66%) of the 1962 sample titles were found in NUC, compared to 173 (87%) of the 1967 sample titles. This was an increase of 21% after the program began. **(594)**

Ibid. . . . *showed that* foreign titles appear to show up more quickly in the NUC since the shared cataloging program began. Specifically, of the 118 book titles from the 3 countries found in NUC before the shared cataloging program began, 13 (11.0%) titles appeared in NUC within 4 months of appearing in their national bibliography. Of the 173 titles from the 3 countries found in the NUC after the shared cataloging program began, 102 (59.0%) appeared in the NUC within 4 months of appearing in their national bibliography. **(594)**

■ A study in 1978 comparing 2,600 book reviews in *Library Journal* and *Choice showed that* the judgment used by editors of these 2 journals in selecting which books to review was substantially sound in that 90% of the books given negative reviews in either of the journals were not reviewed by the other journal. **(039)**

Ibid. . . . *showed that* the main issue for a new book was not the quality of the review but getting reviewed at all—a decision made by the editors of reviewing journals. For example, *Library Journal* reviews approximately 6,000 books a year from a pool of 25-30,000 submitted books and manuscripts, whereas of the reviewed books, only 9% of the LJ books and 6% of the *Choice* books were given negative recommendations. **(039)**

Ibid. . . . *showed that* 55% of the *Choice* reviews and 70% of the LJ reviews compared the book neither to another book nor to the literature in general. **(039)**

Ibid. . . . *showed that* there was little evidence that *Choice* reviews were more substantive or critical than those in LJ, nor was there much evidence of a qualitative difference between reviews by college teachers and those by librarians. The latter point held true whether comparing LJ reviews as a group with *Choice* reviews as a group or LJ reviews by college teachers with LJ reviews by librarians. **(039)**

■ A study reported in 1979 of the English-language literature of library administration (2,877 citations to materials cited in 364 refereed articles indexed in *Library Literature* between 1961-70) *showed that* the distribution of cited works by type was as follows:

monographs	1,247 (43.3%) cited works	
journals	1,149 (39.9%) cited works	
governmental publications	338 (11.7%) cited works	
miscellaneous	143 (4.9%) cited works	**(566)**

Academic

■ A study during the 1981-82 academic year in the main library at Purdue concerning books undergraduates selected to read (involving interviews with 240 undergraduate borrowers and analysis of 598 of the mongraphic titles borrowed by both students and nonstudents) *showed that* the "best and most critically acclaimed" books did not make up the majority of undergraduate reading. For example, of 252 books checked out by undergraduates that had been published before 1973, only 61 (24.2%) were listed in *Books for College Libraries*, while of 246 books published after 1963, only 74 (30.1%) were reviewed in *Choice*, and of these, only 35% were given top recommendations. **(530)**

School

■ A 1960 survey of 298 high school participants in the Annual Central New Jersey Science Fair (265 responding) *showed that*, of 123 books (out of 190) that could be verified in *Books in Print* that students reported they had used for their project, only 40 titles could be found on 1 or more of 4 lists of standard school library titles, including *Standard Catalog for High School Libraries, The AAAS Science Book List* (1959), *An Inexpensive Science Library* (1959), and the Bingham list "Science Fair Bibliography" in *Junior Libraries*. **(276)**

Selection Tools—Periodicals

General

■ A study reported in 1972 of the 1967 *RILM Abstracts (Repertoire International de la Litterature Musicale)*, involving every tenth entry from the subject index (158 items), *showed that* the 3 most popular languages were English (72.5 or 46% articles), German (20 or 12.5% articles), and

French (15 or 9.5% articles). Articles published in 2 languages were counted as .5 in each language. **(401)**

Ibid. . . . *showed that* an examination of every twelfth entry in the 1967 cumulative index (1,125 entries) indicated that the 4 most common publication forms were articles from periodicals (612 or 54.4%), monographs (145 or 13.7%), articles from Festschriften (75 or 6.7%), and book reviews (72 or 6.4%). **(401)**

■ A comparison reported in 1978 of 3 guides (*Ulrich's International Periodicals Directory*, Katz's *Magazines for Libraries*, and *Chicorel Index to Abstracting and Indexing Services*) that identify where periodicals are indexed or abstracted, based on a study of 46 periodical titles written in or translated into English and 6 indexing/abstracting tools (*Sociological Abstracts, Social Sciences and Humanities Index, Abstracts for Social Workers, Public Affairs Information Service, Social Sciences Citation Index,* and *Psychological Abstracts*), *showed that*, of 46 titles, Katz gave correct information on where the journals were indexed or abstracted in 13 instances (28%); of the 43 titles covered by *Ulrich's*, the correct information was provided in 7 instances (16%); and of the 44 titles covered by *Chicorel*, the correct information was given in 3 cases (6%). **(153)**

Ibid. . . . *showed that* the number of times 1 of the 6 indexing/abstracting tools indicated coverage of 1 of the 46 titles when this fact was not reported by 1 of the 3 guides was 63 times in *Chicorel*, 41 times in *Ulrich's*, and 39 times in Katz. **(153)**

Ibid. . . . *showed that* the number of times 1 of the 3 guides reported a title as indexed or abstracted in 1 of the 6 indexing/abstracting tools when in fact it was not was 16 times in *Ulrich's*, 13 times in Katz, and 5 times in *Chicorel*. **(153)**

Ibid. . . . *showed that* indexing in *Sociological Abstracts* was most frequently omitted by the 3 guides (55 times) compared to an average of 18 omissions each for the other 5 indexing/abstracting tools; while *Public Affairs Information Service* was the indexing/abstracting tool which was most often credited with indexing or abstracting 1 of the 46 titles when in fact it did not (20 instances compared to a mode of 2 for the other 5 indexing/abstracting tools). **(153)**

Selection Tools 247

Ibid. . . . *showed that* a check of the front matter of half of the 46 periodical titles indicated that only 8 of the 23 included indexing and abstracting information and that none of these 8 gave completely accurate information on where they were indexed and abstracted, judging from the coverage reported by the 6 indexing/abstracting tools. **(153)**

■ A study reported in 1979 of the English-language literature of library administration (2,877 citations to materials cited in 364 refereed articles indexed in *Library Literature* between 1961-70) *showed that* the distribution of cited works by type was as follows:

monographs	1,247 (43.3%)	cited works
journals	1,149 (39.9%)	cited works
governmental publications	338 (11.7%)	cited works
miscellaneous	143 (4.9%)	cited works **(566)**

■ An evaluation reported in 1980 of the degree to which the 17th edition of *Ulrich's* correctly reported journal indexing and abstracting, based on a study of 31 frequently cited journals in health and related fields, *showed that Ulrich's* reported correctly only 28% of the indexes and abstracts that covered 31 journals. *Ulrich's* reported a total of 177 references to indexes/abstracts for the 31 journals. 8 of these references were incorrect, and *Ulrich's* missed a total of 224 references to indexes/abstracts that it reportedly covers. A further 191 references were missed by *Ulrich's* in indexes and abstracts that it does not cover. **(159)**

■ A study reported in 1980 comparing the *Book Review Digest, Book Review Index*, and *Current Book Review Citations* showed that the number of journals covered by each tool was as follows:

Current Book Review Citations	1,261 journals	
Book Review Index	270 journals	
Book Review Digest	69 journals	**(790)**

Ibid. . . . *showed that Book Review Digest* reviewed no journals that CBRC and BRI did not together review. Of the total journals reviewed by all 3 tools, *Current Book Review Citations* was the sole reviewer of 1,022 (78.9%) journals, while *Book Review Index* was the sole reviewer for 34 (2.6%) journals. The amount of overlap between BRI and CBRC was 170 (13.1%) journals, while the number of journals reviewed in all 3 tools was 66 (5.1%) journals. **(790)**

Ibid. . . . *showed that* the time lag in publishing the reviews [presumably the time between the publication date of the book and the publication of the reviewing issue of the tool] was as follows:

Current Book Review Citations: 50% of the reviews were 6 months old or less, 33% of the reviews were between 6-9 months old, and 17% of the reviews were more than 9 months old;

Book Review Index: 100% of the reviews were 6 months old or less;

Book Review Digest: 46% of the reviews were 6 months old or older, 34% of the reviews were 6-9 months old, and 20% of the reviews were more than 9 months old. **(790)**

Ibid. . . . *showed that*, based on a sample check of 30 reviews in each of the tools, there were no errors due to faulty citations in any of the 3 tools.
(790)

■ A 1982 investigation to identify a core group of business journals by selecting those periodicals that were listed in at least 3 of 4 business reference tools (*ABI/Inform, Business Index, Business Periodicals Index*, and *F and S Index United States*) or which were cited more than the median number of times business and business-related journals were cited in the 1981 *Social Sciences Citation Index Journal Reports showed that* the percentage of the 283 business periodicals indexed in each of the 4 tools was as follows:

Business Index	91% of the core periodicals
Business Periodicals Index	84% of the core periodicals
ABI/Inform	81% of the core periodicals
F and S Index United States	43% of the core periodicals **(561)**

Ibid. . . . *showed that* the number of the core periodicals as a percentage of the total periodicals indexed in each of the 4 tools was as follows:

Business Periodicals Index	78% of total periodicals indexed
Business Index	46% of total periodicals indexed
ABI/Inform	42% of total periodicals indexed
F and S Index United States	22% of total periodicals indexed

(561)

■ A study reported in 1983 comparing the OCLC data base and *New Serial Titles* as an information resource for serials, based on searching 200 titles randomly selected from OCLC in *New Serial Titles* and 200 titles randomly selected from *New Serial Titles* in OCLC, *showed that* there

Selection Tools

was only a moderate amount of overlap between the 2 tools. Specifically, a total of 217 (54.3%) titles were found in both. Further, 96 (48%) of the OCLC titles were found in *New Serial Titles*, while 121 (60.5%) of the *New Serial Titles* were found in OCLC. **(776)**

Ibid. . . . *showed that* different information appeared to be contributed by OCLC and NST for the 217 serial titles they reported in common. For example, bibliographic information present in the NST record but absent in the OCLC record was as follows:

ISSN	21 (9.7%) records
Dewey number	127 (58.5%) records
beginning date/number	21 (9.7%) records
place of publication	4 (1.8%) records
publisher's address	24 (11.1%) records
price	10 (4.6%) records
frequency	9 (4.1%) records **(776)**

Ibid. . . . *showed that* information absent from both the OCLC and NST for the 217 records held in common was as follows:

ISSN	absent from 108 (49.8%) records
beginning date/number	absent from 76 (35.0%) records
publisher's address	absent from 119 (54.8%) records
price	absent from 161 (74.2%) records
frequency	absent from 89 (41.0%) records **(776)**

Ibid. . . . *showed that*, of the 217 titles held in common, OCLC records contained 273 notes, while NST records held 220 notes. 102 (37.4%) of the OCLC notes supplied information not contained in the NST notes, while 15.9% [no raw number given] of the NST notes provided information not contained in the OCLC notes. **(776)**

Academic

■ A study reported in 1970 of the cardiovascular literature involving 78 journals "solely concerned with publishing papers dealing with some aspect of the heart and/or blood vessels, i.e. c-v speciality journals" plus 789 journals that published the findings of National Heart Institute grantees in fiscal 1967 (5,860 papers) *showed that* the coverage given to the

78 cardiovascular speciality journals by the major indexing and abstracting services was as follows:

Index Medicus	48 (62%) journals	
Excerpta Medica	47 (60%) journals	
Biological Abstracts	35 (45%) journals	
Chemical Abstracts	33 (42%) journals	
Science Citation Index	15 (19%) journals	**(607)**

Special

■ A study reported in 1970 of the cardiovascular literature involving 78 journals "solely concerned with publishing papers dealing with some aspect of the heart and/or blood vessels, i.e. c-v speciality journals" plus 789 journals that published the findings of National Heart Institute grantees in fiscal 1967 (5,860 papers) *showed that* the coverage given to the 78 cardiovascular speciality journals by the major indexing and abstracting services was as follows:

Index Medicus	48 (62%) journals	
Excerpta Medica	47 (60%) journals	
Biological Abstracts	35 (45%) journals	
Chemical Abstracts	33 (42%) journals	
Science Citation Index	15 (19%) journals	**(607)**

Sources of Materials

Academic

■ A study reported in 1974 of 3,347 biomedical book reviews (2,067 titles) taken from the 1970 issues of 54 English-language biomedical journals (excluding *Science* and *Nature*) that contained "bona fide" book reviews *showed that* the 3 presses that had published the most books in the present sample (together accounting for 26.46% of the 1,674 titles available in the U.S.) were Williams and Wilkins of Baltimore (177 books or 10.57% of the U.S. books), Charles C. Thomas of Springfield, Illinois (159 or 9.50% of the U.S. books), and Academic Press of New York (107 or 6.39% of the U.S. books). Further, the 18 most active presses published

Sources of Materials

75.70% of the 1,674 titles available in the U.S. The full 1,674 titles were published by 161 publishers. **(704)**

Ibid. . . . *showed that*, of the 2,067 books, 1,370 (66.3%) titles were originally published in the U.S.; 354 (17.1%) titles were published in Great Britain (of which 274 titles were reprinted or distributed by American publishers and/or distributors); and 343 (16.6%) titles were published elsewhere. **(704)**

■ A study reported in 1974 investigating the materials used by master's and doctoral candidates completing theses after 1966 in public health at 5 universities (Yale; Harvard; University of California, Los Angeles; University of California, Berkeley; and California State University, Northridge), involving 3,456 citations taken from 44 theses *showed that*, of 3,304 citations to materials for which the type of publisher was known, 1,508 (46%) citations were to materials published by professional societies; 1,219 (37%) citations were to materials published by trade publishers; and 577 (17%) were to materials published by "others." **(698)**

■ A survey reported in 1978 of 31 Ph.D. dissertations in the field of business/management (13 from the State University of New York at Buffalo and 18 from SUNYAB incoming faculty but completed at other schools) *showed that* the overall distribution of 2,805 citations indicated that the 2 most frequently cited types of publishers for periodicals were association publications (717 or 52.1% of periodical citations) and university publications (435 or 31.6% of periodical citations), while the 2 most frequently cited types of publishers for monographs were commercial (663 or 74.1% of monographic citations) and university (163 or 18.2% of monographic citations). **(461)**

Special

■ A study reported in 1974 of 3,347 biomedical book reviews (2,067 titles) taken from the 1970 issues of 54 English-language biomedical journals (excluding *Science* and *Nature*) that contained "bona fide" book reviews *showed that* the 3 presses that had published the most books in the present sample (together accounting for 26.46% of the 1,674 titles available in the U.S.) were Williams and Wilkins of Baltimore (177 books or 10.57% of the U.S. books), Charles C. Thomas of Springfield, Illinois (159 or 9.50% of the U.S. books), and Academic Press of New York (107 or 6.39% of the U.S. books). Further, the 18 most active presses published 75.70% of the 1,674 titles available in the U.S. The full 1,674 titles were published by 161 publishers. **(704)**

Ibid. . . . *showed that,* of the 2,067 books, 1,370 (66.3%) titles were originally published in the U.S.; 354 (17.1%) titles were published in Great Britain (of which 274 titles were reprinted or distributed by American publishers and/or distributors); and 343 (16.6%) titles were published elsewhere. **(704)**

Special Collections—Faculty Libraries (Law)

Academic

■ A 1978 survey of academic law libraries concerning the issue of faculty libraries (a separate collection or library set aside for the use of the law faculty) (survey size: 169 libraries; responding: 115 or 68.0%) *showed that* 70 (60.9%) respondents had faculty libraries, while 45 (39.1%) did not. Further, 10 (22.2%) of the 45 respondents without faculty libraries reported that they had previously had such libraries. **(795)**

Ibid. . . . *showed that,* of the 70 faculty libraries, 41 (58.6%) had been established within 7 years of the survey date. However, 14 libraries had been in existence from 20 to 40 years. **(795)**

Ibid. . . . *showed that,* of the 70 respondents with faculty libraries, 35 were located in private institutions, while 35 were located in publicly supported institutions. **(795)**

Ibid. . . . *showed that,* of the 70 respondents with faculty libraries, the collections included "for the most part . . . primary materials related to the individual states in which the libraries [were located] plus Federal materials." Further:

    95% of the faculty libraries included periodicals, with an average subscription rate of 75 titles per library;
    6 (8.6%) of the faculty libraries included microfilms. **(795)**

Ibid. . . . *showed that* 16 (22.9%) respondents allowed student access to the faculty library, while 54 (77.1%) did not. Further, 41 (58.6%) respondents reported that the faculty library was not set up as a reading room only. "Many of these facilities have kitchens within the faculty library," while 12 (17.1%) respondents reported carrels located in the faculty library. **(795)**

Ibid. . . . *showed that*, of the 70 respondents with faculty libraries, 41 (58.6%) allowed checkout privileges from the main collection to the faculty library. **(795)**

Special Collections—Labor

Public

■ A 1976 survey of 723 public libraries in communities of more than 10,000 and having a central labor council, by the Joint Committee on Library Services to Labor Groups, RASD, ALA, (385 or 53.2% responding), *showed that* 18 libraries reported that they have special collections of materials for use by labor unions and/or organizations. This compares to 46 libraries reporting such collections (out of 384) in an unpublished 1967 survey. A further 317 libraries (in the 1976 survey) reported labor materials as a part of their regular collections, with size ranging from 4 to 5,250 items and averaging 498 items. **(152)**

Ibid. . . . *showed that* 45 or 11.6% had approached the central labor body or local unions to offer library services to them or secure suggestions for needed library services. This compares to 156 or 41% of the libraries (out of 384) in an unpublished 1967 survey. **(152)**

Ibid. . . . *showed that* 14 or 4% of the responding libraries reported that a staff member was assigned to work with labor organizations and/or labor-related materials. This compares to 22 or 6% of responding libraries (out of 384) in an unpublished 1967 survey. **(152)**

Special Collections—Maps

Academic

■ A 1972 study of Map Room use at Southern Illinois University during summer and fall quarters, involving the circulation of 2,721 maps and aerial photos to 223 borrowers, *showed that* borrowers were undergraduates (44%), graduate students (32%), and faculty (19%). However, graduate students accounted for 72% of the loans, undergraduates for 16%, and faculty for 10%. **(403)**

Ibid. . . . *showed that* the stated purpose of 60% of the loans was research. **(403)**

Ibid. . . . *showed that* borrowers were "widely scattered in approximately 40 departments." The largest number of borrowers came from the Forestry Department and included 23 individuals or 10% of the borrowing population. **(403)**

Ibid. . . . *showed that*, in terms of broad areas, 58 (26%) borrowers came from the social sciences, 52 (23%) from the sciences, 37 (17%) from the applied sciences, 24 (11%) from education, and 22 (10%) from humanities. **(403)**

Ibid. . . . *showed that*, of the items borrowed, 1,869 (68%) were maps and aerial photos of Illinois areas; 253 (9%) were maps and aerial photos of nearby states; 430 (16%) were U.S. areas except for Illinois and nearby states; 77 (3%) were Canadian and Latin American areas; and 70 (3%) were areas in the Eastern Hemisphere. **(403)**

Ibid. . . . *showed that* the 2 most common types of maps borrowed were aerial photos (1,641 items or 60% of the total) and topographic maps (639 maps or 23% of the total). **(403)**

■ A survey reported in 1981 of 85 North American academic map libraries that have medium or large research collections (usable responses: 49 or 58%) *showed that* the average map collection of respondents was 158,000 sheets with approximately 65% of the collection consisting of topographic maps. **(216)**

Ibid. . . . *showed that* in conjunction with data from the 2nd and 3rd editions of *Map Collections in the United States and Canada*, the average size of map collections had grown from 83,650 sheets in 1968 to 113,816 in 1975 (an increase of 36.0%) to 157,696 in 1980 (a further increase of 38.6%). The average annual accession rate for 1968 was 4,654 sheets; for

Special Collections 255

1975 it was 5,565 (an increase of 19.6%); and for 1980 it was 5,734 (a further increase of 3.0%). **(216)**

Ibid. . . . *showed that* in conjunction with data from the 2nd and 3rd editions of *Map Collections in the United States and Canada*, 77% of the respondents reported depository membership in the United States Geological Survey in 1968, 94% in 1975, and 96% in 1980. 84% reported depository membership in the Defense Mapping Agency in 1968, 86% in 1975, and 88% in 1980. 13% reported depository membership in the National Ocean Survey in 1968, 27% in 1975, and 49% in 1980.
(216)

Special Collections—Newspapers

Academic

■ A 1976-77 study of undergraduate use of newspapers on microfilm at the University of Illinois during 2 peak months of the 1976-77 academic year involving 279 requests for newspaper microfilm (excluding use of *New York Times, Wall Street Journal*, and *Chicago Tribune*) *showed that* the 5 most frequently requested titles were:

Daily Illini	31 (11.1%) requests
Washington Post	31 (11.1%) requests
Morning Courier (Champaign, Ill.)	30 (10.8%) requests
Los Angeles Times	22 (7.9%) requests
News-Gazette (Champaign, Ill.)	19 (6.8%) requests

(471)

Ibid. . . . *showed that* 5 newspaper titles satisfied 47.7% of the requests; 10 titles satisfied 65.6% of the requests; 15 titles satisfied 77.1% of the requests; and 20 titles satsified 84.6% of the requests. **(471)**

Ibid. . . . *showed that* indexed newspapers received more use than nonindexed newspapers by almost a 2 to 1 ratio. Specifically, during the period 1972-76 indexed newspapers accounted for 68.7% of the requests. **(471)**

Special Collections—Recreational Reading

Academic

■ A 1980 survey of 110 academic libraries (83 or 75.5% responding) of all types and sizes concerning their provision of a collection or services for the recreational reading interests of the campus community *showed that* 51 (61.4%) of the respondents reported that they provided some form of recreational reading services. However, 7 (13.7%) libraries reported anticipated cutbacks in this service. **(315)**

Ibid. . . . *showed that* the distance from campus to the nearest public library reported by respondents with recreational reading services (90.2% of the libraries with programs responding) averaged 1.87 miles with a median of 1 mile. **(315)**

Ibid. . . . *showed that* 64.2% of the average recreational reading services (RRS) collection was fiction (79% of those with RRS responding); that 32.4% of the average RRS collection consisted of paperbacks (99% responding); that 42 (82.4%) of the respondents with RRS collections reported crafts and hobbies books in the collection; that the average size of the RRS collection was 1,636 titles with a median size of 700 titles; and that 18 (35.3%) libraries reported periodicals as part of their RRS collection (averaging 47 titles). 39% of these 18 libraries circulate their RRS periodicals. **(315)**

Ibid. . . . *showed that* the average age of the recreational reading services programs was 16.5 years with a median of 8 years. While 9 respondents reported their RRS program over 25 years old, 15 libraries (29.4%) reported that their program was 5 years old or less. **(315)**

Special Collections—Teacher Collections

School

■ A survey reported in 1963 of principals of elementary schools in 50 states (sample size: 730; responding: 424 or 58%) *showed that* 326 (76.9%) of the respondents reported that their schools had a collection of professional periodicals and books. An additional 23 principals reported a professional collection of books but no periodicals, and 36 reported a professional collection of periodicals but no books. **(277)**

Ibid. . . . *showed that* the book collections ranged from 5 to 500 with the median between 46-50, with the range of new books added each year 0 to 32 with a median of 5. **(277)**

Special Collections—University Collections

Academic

■ A 1981 survey of academic libraries selected randomly from OCLC academic library participants concerning the issue of university collections, i.e., collections of publications by the university's own faculty and affiliates (sample size: 184; responding: 103 or 56%) *showed that* 43 (42%) had a university collection within their library. 64% of the respondents reported using no selection criteria other than the author's association with the institution. **(647)**

Ibid. . . . *showed that* 61% of the respondents reported their university collections were housed in closed-access areas, with 79% reporting that the material was noncirculating. However, 86 (83%) did report purchasing duplicates of the university collection for circulation. **(647)**

Ibid. . . . *showed that*, of 60 respondents, 10% (all with budgets in excess of $250,001) had discontinued university collections. **(647)**

Standards

Academic

■ A study of 1977 survey information gathered by the National Center for Educational Statistics (U.S. Office of Education) concerning the degree to which 1,146 college and university libraries (Liberal Arts Colleges I and II; Comprehensive Universitites and Colleges I and II) met the 1975 Standards for College Libraries (ACRL) *showed that* the majority did not meet the minimum collection size for monographs. Although the standard for each library must be computed for each institutional situation, a collection size of at least 100,000 volumes is almost always required. Specifically, 43% had monograph collections under 100,000 volumes; 34% had collections 100,000-199,999 volumes; 13% had collections 200,000-299,999 volumes; and 10% had collections of 300,000 volumes or more. The average number of volumes was 151,700 volumes; and the median was 112,800 volumes. **(486)**

Ibid. . . . *showed that* 63% of the libraries did not meet the minimum standards for annual new monographic acquisitions in that the number of new books added annually to the collection was less than 5% of the collection. However, the average number of new annual acquisitions based on collection size was 5.3%, while the median number of new annual acquisitions based on collection size was 4.3%. Further, the average number of actual volumes added was 7,490, while the median was 4,770 volumes. **(486)**

■ A study reported in 1981 of data on 1,146 2-year colleges, as reported in the 1977 Higher Education General Information Surveys and compared to the 1979 Association of College and Research Libraries standards, *showed that* in terms of periodical subscriptions the number of schools meeting minimum standards (by enrollment ranges of FTE students) was as follows:

less than 1,000 students (200 titles minimum)	49% met standards
1,000 to 2,999 students (300 titles minimum)	48% met standards
3,000 to 4,999 students (500 titles minimum)	29% met standards
5,000 to 6,999 students (700 titles minimum)	13% met standards
7,000 to 8,999 students (710 titles minimum)	25% met standards
9,000 to 10,999 students (720 titles minimum)	53% met standards

The overall average number of periodicals held per school was 350 titles. **(500)**

Ibid. . . . *showed that* in terms of book collection the number of schools meeting minimum standards (by enrollment ranges of FTE students) was as follows:

less than 1,000 students (20,000 volumes minimum)	61% met standards
1,000 to 2,999 students (30,000 volumes minimum)	39% met standards
3,000 to 4,999 students (50,000 volumes minimum)	24% met standards
5,000 to 6,999 students (70,000 volumes minimum)	12% met standards
7,000 to 8,999 students (82,000 volumes minimum)	14% met standards
9,000 to 10,999 students (94,000 volumes minimum)	32% met standards

The overall average number of volumes held per school was 33,900 volumes. **(500)**

Ibid. . . . *showed that*, overall, 37% of the respondents, including 60% of the privately supported schools and 31% of the publicly supported schools, did not increase their book stock by 5% per year as specified in the standards. However, the overall average increase was 8.8%, with the overall median increase 6.1%. **(500)**

Translations—Periodicals

General

■ A study reported in 1978 comparing foreign-language scientific and technical articles that received *ad hoc* or selective translations to those that did not receive such translations (articles in journals receiving regular cover-to-cover translations were excluded from the study), involving 2 groups of 266 articles each selected from *Science Citation Index* and *Translations Register-Index, showed that* there was a statistically significant difference between the 2 groups on the basis of subject content. For example, 100% (14 articles) of the photography articles, 96% (25 articles) of the metallurgy articles, and 82% (18 articles) of the physics articles received *ad hoc* or selective translations, compared to 17% (4 articles) in general science, 26% (5 articles) in biology, and 32% (18 articles) in medicine (differences significant at beyond the .001 level; measure of association, eta = .50). **(621)**

Ibid. . . . *showed that* there was a statistically significant difference between the 2 groups on the basis of original language of the article. For example, 94% (16 articles) of the Russian, 67% (2 articles) of the Polish, and 58% (84 articles) of the German articles received *ad hoc* or selective translations, compared to no translations of the Swedish/Norwegian (total of 2 articles) or Hungarian (total of 2 articles) and translations for only 18% (2 articles) of the Italian articles (differences significant at beyond the .001 level; measure of assocation, eta = .37). **(621)**

Ibid. . . . *showed that* there was a statistically significant difference between the 2 groups on the basis of number of references cited by the article, with the articles with more references more likely to receive *ad hoc* or selective translations. For example, only 28% (12 articles) of the articles with no references received *ad hoc* or selective translations, compared to

69% (22 articles) of the articles with more than 29 references (differences significant at beyond the .001 level; measure of association, eta = .31).
(621)

Whole Collections

General

■ A review reported in 1975 of the acquisition of whole collections to libraries during the period 1940-70 as reported in *College and Research Libraries* and *College and Research Libraries News*, involving 1,454 collections and 301 libraries, *showed that* the acquisition of the collections was not equally distributed among libraries. In the total sample, 148 (49%) of the libraries reported adding only 1 collection, while 45 (15%) reported adding 10 or more. **(104)**

Academic

■ A review reported in 1975 of the acquisition of whole collections to libraries during the period 1940-70 as reported in *College and Research Libraries* and *College and Research Libraries News*, involving 1,454 collections and 301 libraries, *showed that* among academic libraries reporting acquisition of collections the receipt of collections was distributed unevenly. 15% of the academic libraries accounted for 66% of the collection acquired by academic libraries. In more detail, 21.5% of the public academic libraries accounted for 66% of the collections acquired by that type of library, while 10.5% of the private academic libraries accounted for 62% of the collections acquired by that type of library. **(104)**

Public

■ A review reported in 1975 of the acquisition of whole collections to libraries during the period 1940-70 as reported in *College and Research Libraries* and *College and Research Libraries News*, involving 1,454 collections and 301 libraries, *showed that* among public libraries the Library of Congress accounted for 77 (75%) of the collections acquired by public libraries. A similar situation holds for state libraries, with one state library (Virginia) receiving 10 (71.5%) of the collections received by this type of library. **(104)**

3. Collection Use

Age of Material—General Issues

General

■ A 1977 study of 9,605 volumes retrieved for patrons at the Library of Congress during a 3-day period in November 1977 (almost 100% of volumes retrieved) *showed that* 41.7% of the retrieved volumes had been published in the 1970s; 23% in the 1960s; 8.7% in the 1950s; 6.2% in the 1940s; 5.0% in the 1930s; and 3.4% in the 1920s. **(262)**

Ibid. . . . *showed that* the decline in use over time was not a function of size of holdings. Circulation during the study period divided by holdings size showed the following probability of use: 1970s, .0015753; 1960s, 0011797; 1950s, .0006134; 1940s, .0005414; 1930s, .0004071; 1920s, .0003865. **(262)**

Ibid. . . . *showed that*, although use declined in all subject areas over time, the rate of decline was different for different subject areas. Use in the natural sciences declined most quickly, followed by social sciences, humanities, and history, in that order. Circulation during the study period divided by holding size and then standardized so that 1.00 represented the overall average use rate for all imprints 1940-77 revealed the following use rates for the 4 decades beginning with the 1970s: natural sciences: 1.31, .60, .28, .19; social sciences: 1.91, 1.28, .48, .31; humanities: 1.10, 1.13, .62, .59; history: 1.57, 1.53, .98, .90. **(262)**

Ibid. . . . *showed that*, although serials represent 39.8% of the holdings, they accounted for only 24% of the sample use. However, their use declined over time at essentially the same rate as monographs. Percentage of serials used during the study period versus monographs used broken down by imprint for the 6 decades beginning with the 1970s and concluding with the 1920s was as follows: 43.2 vs. 41.2, 23.5 vs. 22.8, 9.5 vs. 8.5, 5.4 vs. 6.4, 4.0 vs. 5.3, and 2.5 vs. 3.6. **(262)**

Ibid. . . . *showed that*, while 62% of the holdings were in English, they accounted for 89% of the sample use. Inspection revealed no systematic changes in language use over time in the sample, with 90% of the 1970s imprints in English, 86% of the 1950s imprints in English, and 87% of the 1930s imprints in English. **(262)**

■ A study reported in 1981 of citations in English-language research papers dealing with library science research appearing in 39 North American, British, or international journals for selected years during the period 1950-75 (716 papers; 5,334 citations) *showed that* 25% of the citations were 7 years old or older at the time the citing article was published. **(571)**

Academic

■ A 1968-69 study over a period of 9 months of the use of materials at the Midwest Regional Medical Library (John Crerar Library), involving a random sample of 1,071 requests for material, *showed that*, of 1,061 requests, the age of the materials requested was as follows: under 1 year old (18.0%), 5 years old or less (53.8%), 10 years old or less (66.2%), and more than 10 years old (33.7%). **(688)**

■ A study reported in 1974 investigating the materials used by master's and doctoral candidates completing theses after 1966 in public health at 5 universities (Yale; Harvard; University of California, Los Angeles; University of California, Berkeley; and California State University, Northridge), involving 3,456 citations taken from 44 theses, *showed that*, of 3,360 citations to materials for which the date of publication was known, 2,020 (61%) citations were to materials published after 1960, while 1,340 (39%) citations were to materials published before 1960. **(698)**

Ibid. . . . *showed that* the median age of materials cited was 7 years. The median age of materials in various other scientific disciplines as reported in 8 other studies and summarized in this study was 5 years. **(698)**

■ A 1977 study of book circulation in Columbia-Greene Community College (sample size: 1,317 items or 6% of holdings) *showed that* as a group older materials tended to circulate less than newer materials. During a 15-month period 29% of a sample of 107 items purchased in 1969 circulated, compared to 55% circulation in a sample of 162 items purchased in 1977, with a definite overall movement in the intervening years toward higher circulation rates for newer materials. **(229)**

■ A 1978 study in the Biology Library of Temple University involving a citation analysis of publications by full-time Temple biology faculty, doctoral dissertations of Temple biology Ph.D.'s, and preliminary doctoral qualifying briefs written by second-year graduate biology students at

Age of Material

Temple during the 3-year period 1975-77 (153 source items with 4,155 citations) *showed that* in 51 of the 60 most frequently cited periodical titles "over 80%" of the citations were to articles published within 18 years.
(650)

■ A 1982 study at the University of Wisconsin, Milwaukee concerning the use of gift books in 2 separate parts of the collection, both the PS 3537-PS 3545 section (American literature, 1,039 nongift books and 104 gift books) and the QC 6-QC 75 section (physics, 1,023 nongifts and 16 gift books) *showed that* gift books tended to be older than nongift books. For example, in the PS section 375 (36.1%) of the nongift books had been published after 1970 compared to 11 (10.6%) of the gift books; in the QC section 380 (37.1%) of the nongift books had been published after 1970 compared to 2 (12.5%) of the gift books.
(807)

Ibid. . . . *showed that* gift books tended to be old when given to the library. For example, in the PS section 68 (65.4%) of the gift books were over 20 years old when given to the library, while of the PS and QC sections combined, 105 (87.5%) of the gifts were over 10 years old when given to the library.
(807)

School

■ A study reported in 1979 of term paper bibliographies of high school students (270 students/papers from 6 high schools, involving 3,165 identifiable references) *showed that* the students did not use particularly recent sources for their papers. Only 14% of the papers had more than half of their citations referring to sources published within 5 years of the study, while only 30% of the papers had more than half of the citations referring to sources published within 10 years of the study.
(564)

Special

■ A 1968-69 study over a period of 9 months of the use of materials at the Midwest Regional Medical Library (John Crerar Library), involving a random sample of 1,071 requests for material, *showed that*, of 1,061 requests, the age of the materials requested was as follows: under 1 year old (18.0%), 5 years old or less (53.8%), 10 years old or less (66.2%), and more than 10 years old (33.7%).
(688)

Age of Material—Books

Academic

■ A 1964 study at the Yale Medical Library involving patron use of books (survey size: 831 borrowers; responding: 430) during a 5-month period *showed that* the frequency of books used by year of publication was as follows:

1 year old	15 (3.5%) books
2 years old or less	92 (21.4%) books
5 years old or less	243 (56.6%) books
9 years old or less	324 (75.5%) books

(672)

■ A 1-year study during 1964-65 at the Yale Medical Library concerning book and journal circulation (34,825 circulations) *showed that* currency was more important for journals than for books. For example, 71% of the journals circulated had been published within the last 9 years, while only 66% of the books that circulated had been published within 9 years. Further, 90% of the journal circulations involved materials no more than 22 years old, while 90% of the book circulations required materials up to 28 years old. **(674)**

Ibid. . . . *showed that* the importance of book currency varied considerably by subject area. For example, in the areas of biochemistry, neurology, and neoplasms, 90% of the circulations were accounted for by imprints going back 12 years, 17 years, and 17 years, respectively, while in the areas of surgery, biology, and infectious diseases, 90% of the circulations were accounted for by imprints going back 42 years, 39 years, and 37 years, respectively. **(674)**

■ A 1970 study at Sir George Williams University (Canada) of monographic circulation in the social sciences and humanities (sample size: 444 volumes) *showed that* 53% of the collection had circulated within the last 2 years; 43% had circulated within the last year; and 15% had circulated within the last 3 months. **(538)**

■ A review in 1974-75 of faculty book requests in the economics and political science library of Indiana University *showed that* book availability is related to the age of the book. 76% of the books not immediately available were published in 1970 or later, while only 61% of the books

Age of Material

immediately available were so recently published. (012)

■ A study reported in 1977 at the University of Pittsburgh, based on the complete circulation history during the period October 1968-June 1976, *showed that*, if a book did not circulate within the first 2 years of ownership, "the chances of its ever being borrowed were reduced to less than 1 in 5." Further, if the book did not circulate within the first 6 years of ownership, its chances of "ever being borrowed were reduced to less than 1 chance in 50." (666)

■ A survey reported in 1978 of 31 Ph.D. dissertations in the field of business/management (13 from the State University of New York at Buffalo and 18 from SUNYAB incoming faculty but completed at other schools) *showed that*:

42.7% of the periodical citations and 36.0% of the monographic citations were to materials 5 years old or less;

72.8% of the periodical citations and 66.2% of the monographic citations were to materials 10 years old or less;

87.0% of the periodical citations and 80.7% of the monographic citations were to materials 15 years old or less;

and 93.0% of the periodical citations and 89.5% of the monographic citations were to materials 20 years old or less. (461)

■ A study reported in 1978 at the University of Pittsburgh of 98%+ of its circulation records for the book/monograph collection during the period October 1968-December 1975 (1,500,000 total circulations) *showed that* 16% of newly acquired items were used in the first year; 24% were used in the second year; and 8% in the third year. (667)

■ A study reported in 1979 at the Polk Library of the University of Wisconsin, Oshkosh, of a random sample of 1,098 books in the collection *showed that* 129 (11.8%) had been in the collection for at least 7.5 years and had not circulated, compared to 351 (32%) that had circulated and 618 (56.3%) that had not been in the collection that long. (473)

Ibid. . . . *showed that* of the 129 books that had been in the collection for at least 7.5 years and had not circulated, the reasons for their nonuse appeared to be:

   specialized (historical sources, 64 (49.6%) books
   technical/scholarly, foreign
   language)

continued

obsolete (superceded, outdated controversy)   35 (27.1%) books
out-of-fashion literature and art   23 (17.8%) books
irrelevant/no obvious reason   7 (5.4%) books   **(473)**

■ A study reported in 1981 at DePauw University of circulation patterns over a 5-year period (1973-77) for a group of newly acquired monographs (sample size: 1,904 books) *showed that* in 5 years the following circulation pattern obtained:

no circulation	702 (36.9%) books	
1-5 circulations	951 (49.9%) books	
6-10 circulations	166 (8.7%) books	
11+ circulations	85 (4.5%) books	**(573)**

Ibid. . . . *showed that*, generally, circulation decreased with the books' length of time in the library. Comparing the circulation rate of the 1,904 books during the first 3 years with their circulation rate during the fourth and fifth years revealed that, while 356 (18.6%) increased their circulation rate, 719 (37.7%) had no change in circulation rate, and 829 (43.5%) had a decrease in circulation rate. Further, 83.3% of the books uncirculated in years 1-3 remained uncirculated in years 4-5.   **(573)**

Special

■ A 1964 study at the Yale Medical Library involving patron use of books (survey size: 831 borrowers; responding: 430) during a 5-month period *showed that* the frequency of books used by year of publication was as follows:

1 year old	15 (3.5%) books	
2 years old or less	92 (21.4%) books	
5 years old or less	243 (56.6%) books	
9 years old or less	324 (75.5%) books	**(672)**

■ A 1-year study during 1964-65 at the Yale Medical Library concerning book and journal circulation (34,825 circulations) *showed that* currency was more important for journals than for books. For example, 71% of the journals circulated had been published within the last 9 years, while only

Age of Material

66% of the books that circulated had been published within 9 years. Further, 90% of the journal circulations involved materials no more than 22 years old, while 90% of the book circulations required materials up to 28 years old. **(674)**

Ibid. . . . *showed that* the importance of book currency varied considerably by subject area. For example, in the areas of biochemistry, neurology, and neoplasms, 90% of the circulations were accounted for by imprints going back 12 years, 17 years, and 17 years, respectively, while in the areas of surgery, biology, and infectious diseases, 90% of the circulations were accounted for by imprints going back 42 years, 39 years, and 37 years, respectively. **(674)**

Age of Material—Gifts

Academic

■ A 1982 study at the University of Wisconsin, Milwaukee, concerning the use of gift books in 2 separate parts of the collection, both the PS 3537-PS 3545 section (American literature, 1,039 nongift books and 104 gift books) and the QC 6-QC 75 section (physics, 1,023 nongifts and 16 gift books) *showed that* gift books tended to be older than nongift books. For example, in the PS section 375 (36.1%) of the nongift books had been published after 1970 compared to 11 (10.6%) of the gift books; in the QC section 380 (37.1%) of the nongift books had been published after 1970 compared to 2 (12.5%) of the gift books. **(807)**

Ibid. . . . *showed that* gift books tended to be old when given to the library. For example, in the PS section 68 (65.4%) of the gift books were over 20 years old when given to the library, while of the PS and QC sections combined, 105 (87.5%) of the gifts were over 10 years old when given to the library. **(807)**

Age of Material—Newspapers

Academic

■ A 1976-77 study of undergraduate use of newspapers on microfilm at the University of Illinois during 2 peak months of the 1976-77 academic year, involving 279 requests for newspaper microfilm (excluding use of

New York Times, Wall Street Journal, and *Chicago Tribune*), *showed that* a 5-year backfile satisfied 47.9% of the user requests; a 10-year backfile satisfied 67.2% of the requests; a 15-year backfile satisfied 77.1% of the requests; and a 20-year backfile satisfied 84.5% of the requests. **(471)**

■ A study reported in 1978 at Indiana University, Bloomington, of materials requested through a delivery service to faculty in the political science and economics departments during a 32-month period (October 1972-June 1975), involving 39 political scientists and 14 economists (40-50% of the faculty in the departments) and 5,478 articles from 620 different journals and newspapers, *showed that* articles published after 1950 (the study concluded June 1975) accounted for 97.6% of the requests.
(421)

Age of Material—Periodicals

Academic

■ A 1-year study during 1964-65 at the Yale Medical Library concerning book and journal circulation (34,825 circulations) *showed that* currency was more important for journals than for books. For example, 71% of the journals circulated had been published within the last 9 years, while only 66% of the books that circulated had been published within 9 years. Further, 90% of the journal circulations involved materials no more than 22 years old, while 90% of the book circulations required materials up to 28 years old. **(674)**

Ibid. . . . *showed that* the importance of journal currency varied considerably by subject area. For example, in the areas of nursing, science, and the cardiovascular system, 90% of the circulations were accounted for by 12 years, 13 years, and 15 years of backfiles of journal materials, respectively, while in the areas of anatomy, pathology, and psychology, 90% of the circulations required 30 years of backfiles of journal materials each.
(674)

Ibid. . . . *showed that* the importance of book currency varied considerably by subject area. For example, in the areas of biochemistry, neurology, and neoplasms, 90% of the circulations were accounted for by imprints going back 12 years, 17 years, and 17 years, respectively, while in the areas of surgery, biology, and infectious diseases, 90% of the circulations were

Age of Material

accounted for by imprints going back 42 years, 39 years, and 37 years, respectively. **(674)**

■ A 6-month study during 1967-68 in the Medical Library of the Children's Hospital of Michigan concerning periodical use through circulation, room use, and interlibrary loan (1,898 uses) *showed that* current-year journal issues accounted for 753 (39.67%) uses; journal issues 5 years old or less accounted for 1,408 (74.18%) uses; and journal issues 15 years old or less accounted for 1,813 (95.51%) uses. **(686)**

■ A 1968-69 study over a period of 9 months of the use of materials at the Midwest Regional Medical Library (John Crerar Library), involving a random sample of 1,071 requests for material, *showed that*, of 1,061 requests, the age of the materials requested was as follows: under 1 year old (18.0%), 5 years old or less (53.8%), 10 years old or less (66.2%), and more than 10 years old (33.7%). **(688)**

■ A 1971 study at the MIT Science Library of in-room use (journals do not circulate) of 220 physics journals over a 3.5-month period *showed that* journal use by age of journal was as follows:

1 year old or less	288 (6.7%) of total uses
3 years old or less	1,250 (29.1%) of total uses
6 years old or less	2,239 (52.2%) of total uses
10 years old or less	3,174 (74.0%) of total uses
17 years old or less	4,039 (94.1%) of total uses

Only 253 (5.9%) uses were made of journals more than 17 years old, i.e., 18 years old or older. **(608)**

Ibid. . . . *showed that* journals receiving heavy use have a later "point of obsolescence" than journals receiving light use. For example, for *Physical Review* (a heavy use item), volumes more than 10 years old accounted for 33.2% of its total use, compared to the overall group of 220 journals, whose volumes more than 10 years old accounted for only 26% of their use. **(608)**

■ A 1972 study at the University of Minnesota Bio-Medical Library concerning in-house use of periodicals during 2 1-week periods (1st period: 727 uses involving 269 different titles; 2nd period: 533 uses involving 209 different titles) *showed that* combined data from both periods indicated that 58% of total use came from periodicals 5 years old or less. Further, for every 3.4 years of material age (for materials in the 1st period) and every 3.2 years of material age (for materials in the 2nd period) the materials use decreased by half. **(697)**

■ A 1972-73 study of periodical usage in the Education-Psychology Library at Ohio State University *showed that*, based on 7,623 periodical circulation transactions generated in just over a month, 5 years of holdings provided 75.6% of the materials circulated, and 8 years of holdings provided 90.6% of the materials circulated. **(455)**

■ A 1975-76 study of journal title usage through the extension services of the University of Oklahoma Health Sciences Center Library (Oklahoma City) to hospital clients (4,216 articles from 1,055 journal titles requested) *showed that* health professionals in hospitals without libraries needed more recent information than their counterparts in hospitals with libraries. 82.3% of the journal articles requested by individuals had been published within the last 5 years, and 91.8% of the journal articles requested by individuals had been published within the last 10 years, while 74.6% of the articles requested by libraries had been published within the last 5 years, and 86.7% had been published within the last 10 years. **(429)**

■ A 1977 study of biomedical journal use in the Lane Medical Library at Stanford University Medical Center during the month of November, involving the bound volumes of 334 journal titles for a 10-year period (1967-76), *showed that* the higher use of newer volumes was not due to their containing more articles. For example, for the 10-year period of holdings there was an exponential decrease in use but only a linear decrease in shelf space occupied. Specifically, 24.35% of the journal use involved bound volumes 1 year old, while volumes 10 years old received only 3.12% of the total use; bound volumes 1 year old occupied 10.63% of the shelf space, while volumes 10 years old occupied 9.26% of the shelf space. **(567)**

■ A survey reported in 1978 of 31 Ph.D. dissertations in the field of business/management (13 from the State University of New York at Buffalo and 18 from SUNYAB incoming faculty but completed at other schools) *showed that*:

42.7% of the periodical citations and 36.0% of the monographic citations were to materials 5 years old or less;

72.8% of the periodical citations and 66.2% of the monographic citations were to materials 10 years old or less;

87.0% of the periodical citations and 80.7% of the monographic citations were to materials 15 years old or less;

and 93.0% of the periodical citations and 89.5% of the monographic citations were to materials 20 years old or less. **(461)**

Age of Material

■ A study reported in 1978 at Indiana University, Bloomington of materials requested through a delivery service to faculty in the political science and economics departments during a 32-month period (October 1972-June 1975), involving 39 political scientists and 14 economists (40-50% of the faculty in the departments) and 5,478 articles from 620 different journals and newspapers, *showed that* articles published after 1950 (the study concluded June 1975) accounted for 97.6% of the requests.

(421)

Special

■ A 1-year study during 1964-65 at the Yale Medical Library concerning book and journal circulation (34,825 circulations) *showed that* currency was more important for journals than for books. For example, 71% of the journals circulated had been published within the last 9 years, while only 66% of the books that circulated had been published within 9 years. Further, 90% of the journal circulations involved materials no more than 22 years old, while 90% of the book circulations required materials up to 28 years old. **(674)**

Ibid. . . . *showed that* the importance of journal currency varied considerably by subject area. For example, in the areas of nursing, science, and the cardiovascular system, 90% of the circulations were accounted for by 12 years, 13 years, and 15 years of backfiles of journal materials, respectively, while in the areas of anatomy, pathology, and psychology, 90% of the circulations required 30 years of backfiles of journal materials each.

(674)

■ A study reported in 1966 at the library of the Electronics Systems Center of the International Business Machines Corporation (Owego, New York) concerning periodical usage during a 2-year period (1963-64), involving 4,221 separate uses during this time, *showed that*:

current-year requests totaled 1,470 (34.8% of the total);

requests for materials between 1 and 2 years old totaled 812 (19% of the total);

requests for materials between 2 and 3 years old totaled 480 (11% of the total);

requests for materials 5 years old or less totaled 3,379 (80.1% of the total);

requests for materials 10 years old or less totaled 3,874 (91.8% of the total). **(587)**

274 COLLECTION USE

■ A 6-month study during 1967-68 in the Medical Library of the Children's Hospital of Michigan concerning periodical use through circulation, room use, and interlibrary loan (1,898 uses) *showed that* current-year journal issues accounted for 753 (39.67%) uses; journal issues 5 years old or less accounted for 1,408 (74.18%) uses; and journal issues 15 years old or less accounted for 1,813 (95.51%) uses. **(686)**

■ A 1968-69 study over a period of 9 months of the use of materials at the Midwest Regional Medical Library (John Crerar Library), involving a random sample of 1,071 requests for material, *showed that*, of 1,061 requests, the age of the materials requested was as follows: under 1 year old (18.0%), 5 years old or less (53.8%), 10 years old or less (66.2%), and more than 10 years old (33.7%). **(688)**

■ A 1972 study at the University of Minnesota Bio-Medical Library concerning in-house use of periodicals during 2 1-week periods (1st period: 727 uses involving 269 different titles; 2nd period: 533 uses involving 209 different titles), *showed that* combined data from both periods indicated that 58% of total use came from periodicals 5 years old or less. Further, for every 3.4 years of material age (for materials in the 1st period) and every 3.2 years of material age (for materials in the 2nd period) the materials use decreased by half. **(697)**

■ A 1975-76 study of journal title usage through the extension services of the University of Oklahoma Health Sciences Center Library (Oklahoma City) to hospital clients (4,216 articles from 1,055 journal titles requested) *showed that* health professionals in hospitals without libraries needed more recent information than their counterparts in hospitals with libraries. 82.3% of the journal articles requested by individuals had been published within the last 5 years, and 91.8% of the journal articles requested by individuals had been published within the last 10 years, while 74.6% of the articles requested by libraries had been published within the last 5 years, and 86.7% had been published within the last 10 years. **(429)**

■ A 1977 study of biomedical journal use in the Lane Medical Library at Stanford University Medical Center during the month of November, involving the bound volumes of 334 journal titles for a 10-year period (1967-76), *showed that* the higher use of newer volumes was not due to their containing more articles. For example, for the 10-year period of holdings there was an exponential decrease in use but only a linear decrease in shelf space occupied. Specifically, 24.35% of the journal use involved bound volumes 1 year old, while volumes 10 years old received only 3.12% of the total use; bound volumes 1 year old occupied 10.63% of the shelf space, while volumes 10 years old occupied 9.26% of the shelf space. **(567)**

Books—General Issues

Academic

■ A study reported in 1974 investigating the materials used by master's and doctoral candidates completing theses after 1966 in public health at 5 universities (Yale; Harvard; University of California, Los Angeles; University of California, Berkeley; and California State University, Northridge), involving 3,456 citations taken from 44 theses, *showed that* the distribution of materials by format was as follows:

journals	1,785 (52%) citations
books	961 (28%) citations
documents	293 (8%) citations
unpublished	242 (7%) citations
serials	131 (4%) citations
theses	44 (1%) citations

(698)

■ A 1977 study of book circulation in Columbia-Greene Community College (sample size 1,317 items or 6% of holdings) *showed that* 35% of the titles circulated during a 15-month period. **(229)**

■ A study reported in 1977 at the University of Pittsburgh, based on the complete circulation history of monographs during the period October 1968-June 1976, *showed that* approximately 40% of the new acquisitions did not circulate. Specifically, of 36,892 books/monographs acquired in 1969, 14,697 (39.8%) had never circulated in a 7-year period. Further, of the 22,172 items that did circulate 1 or more times during the first 7 years, 72.76% were circulated 1 or more times during their first or second year in the library. "The six-year circulation history of all books and monographs acquired in the calendar year 1970 exhibited a strikingly similar pattern." **(666)**

Ibid. . . . *showed that* over a 1-year period the circulation pattern showed a "log normal distribution." Further, during a 1-year period the number of items that circulated 2 times was roughly half the number of items that circulated once; the number of items that circulated 3 times was roughly half the number of items that circulated twice; and so on. For example, for 1974:

circulating 1 time	63,526 items
circulating 2 times	25,653 items
circulating 3 times	11,855 items
circulating 4 times	6,055 items
circulating 5 times	3,264 items

(666)

Ibid. . . . *showed that* external circulation was a good indicator of total book/monograph use. For example, based on 30-day samples of in-house use taken over a period of 2 academic terms and involving 29,098 items, 75% of the items used in-house had also circulated externally by the end of the sample period, with an additional 4% of the in-house items circulating the following year. Further, of 4,250 books/monographs loaned on interlibrary loan during the period January 1969-December 1975, 3,246 (76.4%) had external circulations, with the remaining 1,004 items accounting for only .34% of the total circulation during the period of the study. Finally, of 33,277 books/monographs selected for reserve during the period January 1969-December 1975, 27,854 (83.7%) had external circulations, with the remaining 5,423 items accounting for only 1.84% of the total circulation during the period of this study. **(666)**

Ibid. . . . *showed that*, if a book did not circulate within the first 2 years of ownership, "the chances of its ever being borrowed were reduced to less than 1 in 5." Further, if the book did not circulate within the first 6 years of ownership, its chances of "ever being borrowed were reduced to less than 1 chance in 50." **(666)**

■ A survey reported in 1978 of 31 Ph.D. dissertations in the field of business/management (13 from the State University of New York at Buffalo and 18 from SUNYAB incoming faculty but completed at other schools) *showed that* the 7 most frequently cited subject areas (based on 1,161 citations to monographs and serials) were:

business (HF 5001-6351)	14.7% citations
economics: labor (HD 4801-8942)	11.5% citations
economics: production (HD 1-100)	10.8% citations
psychology (BF)	8.2% citations
sociology (HM-HX)	7.3% citations

continued

Books

      finance (HG)   6.4% citations
      economic theory   6.0% citations   **(461)**

■ A study reported in 1978 at the University of Pittsburgh of 98%+ of its circulation records for the book/monograph collection during the period October 1968-December 1975 (1,500,000 total circulations) *showed that* 16% of newly acquired items were used in the first year; 24% were used in the second year; and 8% in the third year.   **(667)**

■ A study reported in 1979 at the Polk Library of the University of Wisconsin, Oshkosh, of books circulated to faculty and students during 6 sample days (1,371 titles circulated) *showed that* 157 (11%) books circulated every 30 days or more frequently; 392 (29%) books circulated every 90 days or more frequently; 879 (64%) books circulated once a year or more frequently; and 1,360 (99.1%) circulated at least once every 8 years or more frequently.   **(473)**

■ A study reported in 1979 at the Polk Library of the University of Wisconsin, Oshkosh, of a random sample of 1,098 books in the collection *showed that* 129 (11.8%) had been in the collection for at least 7.5 years and had not circulated compared to 351 (32%) that had circulated and 618 (56.3%) that had not been in the collection that long.   **(473)**

Ibid. . . . *showed that*, of the 129 books that had been in the collection for at least 7.5 years and not circulated, the reasons for their nonuse appeared to be:

    specialized (historical sources, technical/scholarly, foreign language)   64 (49.6%) books
    obsolete (superceded, outdated controversy)   35 (27.1%) books
    out-of-fashion literature and art   23 (17.8%) books
    irrelevant/no obvious reason   7 (5.4%) books   **(473)**

■ A 1980 survey of law school libraries with collections in excess of 175,000 volumes (sample size: 50; responding: 37 or 70%) *showed that* the demand for old case books was:

for faculty, frequent (1 library), occasional (18 libraries), almost none (17 libraries), and no answer (1 library);

for students, frequent (2 libraries), occasional (8 libraries), almost none (24 libraries), and no answer (3 libraries);

for other patrons, frequent (1 library), occasional (6 libraries), almost none (27 libraries), and no answer (3 libraries). (369)

School

■ A study reported in 1979 of term paper bibliographies of high school students (270 students/papers from 6 high schools, involving 3,165 identifiable references) *showed that* the number of references in individual papers ranged from 2 to 47, with the average 11.7 and the median and mode both 10. The median number of monographs cited per paper was 7.1, while the median number of journal articles cited was 2.9. (564)

■ A 1981 study of 53 ninth-grade honors students in science in a suburban Philadelphia public high school *showed that* out of 47 bibliographies 83% had magazine citations; 66% had book citations; 45% had encyclopedia citations; 44% had government document/pamphlet citations; 24% had newspaper citations; and 4% had nonprint citations. Out of a total of 409 citations, magazine citations constituted 46% of the total, books 25%, encyclopedias 10%, government documents/pamphlets 10%, newspapers 7%, and nonprint 1%. (222)

Special

■ A 1973 survey of all county law libraries listed in the 1972 American Association of Law Libraries *Directory of Law Libraries* (population: 260; responding: 86 or 33.1%) *showed that* 75 (85%) respondents reported that the library book collection was adequate to meet the needs of those who use the library. Further, of 62 respondents, 38 (61.3%) reported that 1% or less of their material is unused or unneeded; 8 (12.9%) reported that unused and unneeded material ran 2 to 10% of the collection; and 6 (9.7%) reported that unused and unneeded material exceeded 11% of the collection. [No data was given for the remaining respondents.] (392)

■ A 1980 survey of law school libraries with collections in excess of 175,000 volumes (sample size: 50; responding: 37 or 70%) *showed that* the demand for old case books was:

for faculty, frequent (1 library), occasional (18 libraries), almost none (17 libraries), and no answer (1 library);

for students, frequent (2 libraries), occasional (8 libraries), almost none (24 libraries), and no answer (3 libraries);

for other patrons, frequent (1 library), occasional (6 libraries), almost none (27 libraries), and no answer (3 libraries). **(369)**

Books—Bradford Distribution, Implicit

Academic

■ A 1970 study at Sir George Williams University (Canada) of monographic circulation in the social sciences and humanities (sample size: 444 volumes) *showed that* 60% of the collection had circulated once in the last 3 years; 25% had circulated more than 3 times in the last 3 years; and 10% had circulated more than 8 times in the last 3 years. **(538)**

■ A study reported in 1979 at the Washington State Library, based on 5 days' circulation information (1,878 items) and a shelflist sample of 159 titles, *showed that*:

90% of the user needs for monographs could be satisfied with monographs that had circulated within the past 35 months (these constituted 50% of the collection);

95% of the user needs for monographs could be satisfied with monographs that had circulated within the past 58 months (these constituted 60% of the collection);

and 99% of the user needs for monographs could be satisfied with monographs that had circulated within the past 131 months (these constituted 85% of the collection).

Data accurate to ±1.55 months at the .99 confidence level. **(527)**

■ A 1982 study at the University of Wisconsin, Milwaukee, concerning the use of gift books in 2 separate parts of the collection, both the PS 3537-PS 3545 section (American literature, 1,039 nongift books and 104 gift books) and the QC 6-QC 75 section (physics, 1,023 nongifts and 16 gift books), *showed that* the use of gift books followed a Bradford-like distribution. For example, in the PS section, the 14 (13.5%) most frequently used books accounted for 80 (62.5%) of the uses. **(807)**

School

■ A study reported in 1979 of term paper bibliographies of high school students (270 students/papers from 6 high schools, involving 3,165 identifiable references) *showed that*, of 1,862 complete references to monographs published since 1900, title overlap was minimal. Only 25 titles were cited by 3 or more papers, while only 9 titles were cited 4 or more times. **(564)**

Books—Hardbound versus Paperback

Public

■ A study reported in 1979 at the Oklahoma City/County Metropolitan Library System *showed that* during FY 1978-79, for an uncataloged paperback collection of 76,862 items, each item circulated an average of 4.75 times during the year. This compares to an average circulation of 2.31 times per item during the same period for a collection of 465,326 cataloged hardback books. **(231)**

Ibid. . . . *showed that*, during the month of July 1979, the average number of circulations per volume for 15,784 cataloged adult hardback volumes purchased in FY 1976-77 was .25, for 18,163 volumes purchased in FY 1977-78 was .33, and for 18,569 volumes purchased in FY 1978-79 was .64. This compares to the average number of circulations per volume for adult uncataloged paperbacks of .32 for a group of 6,743 volumes purchased in FY 1976-77, .54 for a group of 11,760 volumes purchased in FY 1977-78, and .87 for 19,138 volumes purchased in FY 1978-79. **(231)**

Ibid. . . . *showed that*, during the month of July 1979, the average number of circulations per volume for 4,723 juvenile cataloged hardback volumes purchased in FY 1976-77 was 1.20, for 4,777 volumes purchased in FY 1977-78 was 1.18, and for 4,771 volumes purchased in 1978-79 was 1.28. This compares to the average number of circulations per volumes for juvenile uncataloged paperbacks of .79 for 2,973 volumes purchased in FY 1976-77, 1.06 for 3,349 volumes purchased in FY 1977-78, and 1.09 for 3,037 volumes purchased in FY 1978-79. **(231)**

Books—Type of Patron

Academic

■ A 1-year study during 1964-65 at the Yale Medical School Library concerning patron use patterns of library materials (based on 34,825 book/journal circulations) *showed that* 14,262 book circulations were distributed among members of the medical school as follows (accounting for 51.7% of the book use):

students	24.6% book uses
full-time faculty	17.6% book uses
house officers	6.5% book uses
part-time faculty	3.0% book uses

(675)

■ A study reported in 1978 at the University of Pittsburgh of 98%+ of its circulation records for the book/monograph collection during the period October 1968-December 1975 (1,500,000 total circulations) *showed that* book/monograph usage by academic status was as follows:

undergraduates	40% total usage
graduate students	33% total usage
faculty	4 to 5% total usage
all others	15% total usage

(667)

■ A study during the 1981-82 academic year in the main library at Purdue concerning books undergraduates selected to read (involving interviews with 240 undergraduate borrowers and analysis of 598 of the monographic titles borrowed by both students and nonstudents) *showed that* undergraduates (and surprisingly) graduate students tended to use a core of heavily used titles, while faculty tended to use materials that had never before circulated. For example, of 67 items circulated to faculty, 18 (26.9%) had circulated 6 or more times, while of 131 items circulated to graduate students, 77 (58.8%) had been circulated 6 or more times, and of 364 items circulated to undergraduates, 253 (69.5%) had been circulated 6 or more times. (There were 36 missing cases.)

(530)

Ibid. . . . *showed that*, based on 364 items circulated to undergraduates, only 15.9% of the titles selected by undergraduates were based on instructor recommendation (direct recommendation or reading lists), while the remaining titles were selected without instructor direction.

86.6% were selected for subject matter relating to a specific course; 11.6% were selected for leisure reading; and 1.8% were selected for research in the student's major with no specific course in mind. **(530)**

Ibid. . . . *showed that* titles recommended by instructors and checked out by undergraduates were no more likely to fall within the core of highly circulating materials than outside it. For example, of 111 titles that circulated less than 6 times, 16 or 14.4% had been recommended by faculty, while of 253 titles that had circulated 6 times or more, 42 (16.6%) had been recommended by faculty. **(530)**

Ibid. . . . *showed that* the "best and most critically acclaimed" books did not make up the majority of undergraduate reading. For example, of 252 books checked out by undergraduates that had been published before 1973, only 61 (24.2%) were listed in *Books for College Libraries*, while of 246 books published after 1963, only 74 (30.1%) were reviewed in *Choice*, and of these, only 35% were given top recommendations. **(530)**

Public

■ A 1968 study of the summer reading of 23 seventh-graders from the Joyce Kilmer School in Chicago during a 5-week period *showed that*, of the 191 books reported read, the 3 most frequent reasons given for selecting a particular book were reputation of the book (63.5 or 33.2% of the books); subject of the book (34 or 17.8% of the books); and title of the book (34 or 17.8% of the books). (When 2 reasons were given for selecting a book, each was counted as .5.) **(247)**

Ibid. . . . *showed that* the basis of a book's reputation was largely personal recommendation. Of the 63.5 books so selected, the source of the recommendation was friend (21.5 books), classmate (10 books), parent (9 books), sibling (8 books), librarian (7 books), and advertisements/book reviews (8 books). **(247)**

Special

■ A 1-year study during 1964-65 at the Yale Medical School Library concerning patron use patterns of library materials (based on 34,825 book/journal circulations) *showed that* 14,262 book circulations were distributed among members of the medical school as follows (accounting for 51.7% of the book use):

students	24.6%	book uses
full-time faculty	17.6%	book uses
house officers	6.5%	book uses
part-time faculty	3.0%	book uses

(675)

Books versus Periodicals

General

■ A 1977 study of 9,605 volumes retrieved for patrons at the Library of Congress during a 3-day period in November 1977 (almost 100% of volumes retrieved) *showed that*, although serials represent 39.8% of the holdings, they accounted for only 24% of the sample use. However, their use declined over time at essentially the same rate as monographs. Percentage of serials used during the study period versus monographs used broken down by imprint for the 6 decades beginning with the 1970s and concluding with the 1920s was as follows: 43.2 vs. 41.2, 23.5 vs. 22.8, 9.5 vs. 8.5, 5.4 vs. 6.4, 4.0 vs. 5.3, and 2.5 vs. 3.6. **(262)**

Academic

■ A 1964 study at the Yale Medical Library involving patron use of books (survey size: 831 borrowers; responding: 430) during a 5-month period *showed that*, of 13,704 items circulated, 7,718 (56.3%) were serials, and 5,986 (43.7%) were books. **(672)**

■ A 1-year study during 1964-65 at the Yale Medical Library concerning book and journal circulation (34,825 circulations) *showed that* journals accounted for 59.1% of the circulations, while books accounted for 40.9% of the circulations. **(674)**

Ibid. . . . *showed that* the ratio of book to journal circulations varied considerably by subject. For example, of 1,171 circulations in the area of experimental medicine, journals accounted for 98.8% of the circulations, while in the area of zoology, journals accounted for 14.3% of the circulations. **(674)**

■ A 1968-69 study over a period of 9 months of the use of materials at the Midwest Regional Medical Library (John Crerar Library), involving a random sample of 1,071 requests for material, *showed that*, of 1,069 requests, 141 (13.2%) were for books, while 928 (86.8%) were for journals. **(688)**

■ A study reported in 1974 investigating the materials used by master's and doctoral candidates completing theses after 1966 in public health at 5 universities (Yale; Harvard; University of California, Los Angeles; University of California, Berkeley; and California State University, Northridge), involving 3,456 citations taken from 44 theses, *showed that* the distribution of materials by format was as follows:

journals	1,785 (52%) citations
books	961 (28%) citations
documents	293 (8%) citations
unpublished	242 (7%) citations
serials	131 (4%) citations
theses	44 (1%) citations **(698)**

■ A survey reported in 1978 of 31 Ph.D. dissertations in the field of business/management (13 from the State University of New York at Buffalo and 18 from SUNYAB incoming faculty but completed at other schools) *showed that* the overall distribution of 2,805 citations by form was:

periodicals	1,377 (49.1%) citations
monographs	895 (31.9%) citations
serials	266 (9.5%) citations
miscellaneous	267 (9.5%) citations **(461)**

■ A study reported in 1978 at the West Virginia University College of Engineering of the citations found in the master's theses accepted over a 4-year period (126 theses between 1971-74), *showed that* nonjournal (i.e., book) literature was more important in the engineering sciences than previously thought, by showing that, of 3,002 references overall, only 1,000 (33.3%) were journal citations, with the proportion of journal citations by department ranging from 11.4% of the references in aerospace theses to 49.4% of the references in chemical theses. **(460)**

•

School

■ A study reported in 1978 of 19 bibliographic tools listing materials for young adults, involving a total of 19,405 titles in conjunction with a purposeful sample of 270 papers collected from college-bound high school students (grades 10 through 12) in a large metropolitan area from a wide variety of schools, *showed that* the proportion of materials referenced in the bibliographies of the 270 papers was monographic references (67%); journal references (20%); and other, including encyclopedias, documents, primary materials, etc. (13%). Further, only 14% of the 270 papers had half or more of their total references to materials that were 5 years old or less at the time the paper was written. **(523)**

■ A study reported in 1979 of term paper bibliographies of high school students (270 students/papers from 6 high schools, involving 3,165 identifiable references) *showed that* 2,117 (67%) of the references were to monographs; 624 (20%) were to journals; and 424 (13%) were to miscellaneous sources. **(564)**

■ A 1981 study of 53 ninth-grade honors students in science in a suburban Philadelphia public high school *showed that* out of 47 bibliographies 83% had magazine citations, 66% had book citations, 45% had encyclopedia citations, 44% had government document/pamphlet citations, 24% had newspaper citations, and 4% had nonprint citations. Out of a total of 409 citations, magazine citations constituted 46% of the total, books 25%, encyclopedias 10%, government documents/pamphlets 10%, newspapers 7%, and nonprint 1%. **(222)**

Special

■ A 1964 study at the Yale Medical Library involving patron use of books (survey size: 831 borrowers; responding: 430) during a 5-month period *showed that*, of 13,704 items circulated, 7,718 (56.3%) were serials, and 5,986 (43.7%) were books. **(672)**

■ A 1-year study during 1964-65 at the Yale Medical Library concerning book and journal circulation (34,825 circulations) *showed that* journals accounted for 59.1% of the circulations, while books accounted for 40.9% of the circulations. **(674)**

■ A 1968-69 study over a period of 9 months of the use of materials at the Midwest Regional Medical Library (John Crerar Library), involving a random sample of 1,071 requests for material, *showed that*, of 1,069 requests, 141 (13.2%) were for books, while 928 (86.8%) were for journals. **(688)**

Browsing

General

■ A pilot study at the Library of Congress in 1960 of patron stack use, based on a random sample (sample size 200; 181 responding) of patrons in the book stacks, *showed that* 55% were in the stacks to obtain specific books for which they already knew the call numbers, while 38% were browsers. (The remainder were there for both or other reasons.) The majority of patrons in the stacks for work-related reasons were looking for specific books; the majority (57%) in the stacks for recreational or other non-work related reasons were browsers. 123 (68%) of the sample were LC employees. **(068)**

■ A 1970 survey of psychiatrists randomly selected from the 1968 membership of the American Psychiatric Association (survey size: 394; responding: 290 or 74%) *showed that* the 4 most frequently mentioned prime methods of searching the literature (out of 11) were:

library reference services	23% respondents
abstracts and indexes	17% respondents
bibliographies	17% respondents
review articles	16% respondents

Use of the card catalog as a prime method of searching the literature was reported by 5% of the respondents, while browsing as a prime method was reported by 4% of the respondents. **(690)**

Academic

■ A 1973 survey of physicists in 6 universities of the greater Boston area (Boston University, Brandeis, Brown, Harvard, MIT, and Northeastern) to determine how they meet their information needs (sample size: 339; responding: 179 or 52.8%) *showed that* the reasons for library use (Harvard chemistry faculty respondents included) were (multiple re-

Browsing

sponses allowed): specific information (160 respondents), keeping up (122 respondents), browsing (88 respondents), and other (6 respondents). No number of respondents given. **(404)**

■ A survey reported in 1975 of 50 faculty patrons who had not used a new system of departmental microfiche catalogs of the total collection or an accompanying twice daily book delivery system at Georgia Tech, *showed that* the following were the reasons for not using the new system (multiple responses allowed):

REASON	NUMBER
inertia	13 (26.0%)
I like to go to the library	14 (28.0%)
I have not had occasion to use the new system	9 (18.0%)
It is more convenient for me to go to the library	15 (30.0%)
I like to browse or look at the books I select	8 (16.0%)
I do not fully understand the (new system)	6 (12.0%)

(106)

■ A survey reported in 1981 of historians listed in the 1978 *Directory of American Scholars* concerning their use of and attitudes toward periodicals (survey size: 767 historians, although not all questionnaires could be delivered; responding: 360 or 46.9%, with respondents tending to be younger and with a higher scholarly productivity record than nonrespondents) *showed that* the invisible college was not important in making accidental discoveries. For example, the 3 most frequently reported ways of making frequent accidental discoveries (out of 6) were:

scanning current periodicals	173 (48.1%) respondents
looking up a given reference and spotting something else	151 (41.9%) respondents
wandering along library shelves	108 (30.0%) respondents

"In conversation with colleagues" ranked fourth with 78 (21.7%) respondents. **(780)**

Public

■ A 1966 survey of 21,385 adult (12 years old or older) public library users in the Baltimore-Washington metropolitan region of Maryland, conducted during a 6-week period, entering the library (79.1% of patrons approached filled out the survey instrument) *showed that* the use made of the library was as follows (multiple responses allowed): browsing (43.1%), reference books (22.1%), library catalogs (19.0%), help from a librarian (16.0%), consulting books or magazines (12.4%), read new magazines or newspapers (8.7%), periodical indexes (5.7%), recordings (2.7%), films (0.7%), other (2.0%), and no response (11.1%). **(301)**

Special

■ A 1970 survey of psychiatrists randomly selected from the 1968 membership of the American Psychiatric Association (survey size: 394; responding: 290 or 74%) *showed that* the 4 most frequently mentioned prime methods of searching the literature (out of 11) were:

library reference services	23% respondents
abstracts and indexes	17% respondents
bibliographies	17% respondents
review articles	16% respondents

Use of the card catalog as a prime method of searching the literature was reported by 5% of the respondents, while browsing as a prime method was reported by 4% of the respondents. **(690)**

Copyright—Reserves

Academic

■ A review of reserve photocopy requests at Southern Illinois University, Carbondale, in academic 1978-79 *showed that* gratis copying permission was granted in 311 of 358 cases. Furthermore, 18 responses indicated that permission was not needed for reserve/classroom use, and 3 blanket permissions were granted for reserve purposes. **(031)**

Ibid. . . . *showed that* during academic 1978-79, 135 hours of staff time were required to request copyright permission for 361 articles requested for reserve. **(031)**

Ibid. . . . *showed that* the degree to which articles cluster in a few journals was limited. Out of 361 requested articles, 91 were found in 4 periodical titles, while 103 were in 1 periodical title each. **(031)**

■ A 1981 survey of reserve room copyright policies in institutions of higher education in Virginia (survey size: 44; responding: 37 or 84.1%) *showed that* 33 (89.2%) used either fair use (section 107) or the associated

Costs

"Guidelines for Classroom Copying" as the basis for reserve room photocopying policies. **(512)**

Ibid. . . . *showed that* 28 (75.7%) libraries accepted 1 fair use copy for reserve without author permission, including 13 (35.1% of the total) that allowed further additional copies with permission of the author, 7 (18.9% of the total) that permitted additional copies without author permission, and 8 (21.6% of the total) that permitted only the 1 fair use copy. Of the remaining 9, 4 (10.8%) reported that the instructor assumed responsibility for copyright compliance and accepted all copies placed on reserve by the instructor with little or no restriction; 3 (8.1%) followed the "Guidelines of Classroom Copying" permitting a set number of copies depending on the number of students in the class; and 1 (2.7%) allowed 1 copy only regardless of circumstances. 1 library did not respond to the question. **(512)**

Ibid. . . . *showed that* 28 (75.7%) respondents reported no restrictions concerning the number of terms copyrighted material could be placed on reserve, while 9 (24.3%) restricted copyright materials to 1 term on reserve only. **(512)**

Ibid. . . . *showed that* 28 (75.7%) respondents reported that the instructor was the party required to seek permission for making multiple copies of copyrighted material, while 8 (21.6%) respondents reported that the library staff was the party required to request copyright releases. **(512)**

Ibid. . . . *showed that* 35 (94.6%) respondents accepted material for reserve that was not necessarily from the library collection, while 2 (5.4%) restricted reserve collections to materials from their own library. **(512)**

Costs

Academic

■ A comparison of periodical costs (1975 cost data, including subscription costs [actual], ordering [estimated], receiving [estimated], processing [estimated], accounting and shelving costs [estimated], binding preparation [estimated], and binding costs [estimated]) and use rates (based on use during the period 1972-75) in an academic library (unspecified) *showed that*, for the 25 most requested journals out of 528 political science journals (use determined by an earlier study: Robert Goehlert, "Periodical Use in an Academic Library," *Special Libraries*, 69 (Februrary 1978), 51-60), the cost for each use of the periodical ranged from $.17 to $4.98 with a median of $.53 per use. **(307)**

Ibid. . . . *showed that* the cost per individual user (many users made multiple requests) of the 25 most requested journals out of 528 political science journals (use determined by an earlier study: Robert Goehlert, "Periodical Use in an Academic Library," *Special Libraries*, 69 (February 1978), 51-60) ranged from $.78 to $4.64 per user, with a median of $2.27 per user. **(307)**

Dissertations and Theses

Academic

■ A study reported in 1964 of the number of citations to medical dissertations in the period 1821-1960, based on the citations found in a sample of 10 American and European medical journals for that period, *showed that* there was a steady growth in the percentage of citations of dissertations from 0.8% of all citations in 1821-30 to a high of 4% in the 1881-1910 period, followed by a marked and generally steady decline in dissertation citations up to 1951-60 with a new low of 0.7% for that period. **(168)**

■ A study reported in 1974 investigating the materials used by master's and doctoral candidates completing theses after 1966 in public health at 5 universities (Yale; Harvard; University of California, Los Angeles; University of California, Berkeley; and California State University, Northridge), involving 3,456 citations taken from 44 theses, *showed that* doctoral theses had a higher proportion of journal citations than masters' theses to a statistically significant degree (significant at the .02 level). However, in terms of overall number of citations per thesis, there was no statistically significant difference between doctoral and masters' theses when method of investigation was considered. **(698)**

Special

■ A study reported in 1964 of the number of citations to medical dissertations in the period 1821-1960, based on the citations found in a sample of 10 American and European medical journals for that period,

showed that there was a steady growth in the percentage of citations of dissertations from 0.8% of all citations in 1821-30 to a high of 4% in the 1881-1910 period, followed by a marked and generally steady decline in dissertation citations up to 1951-60 with a new low of 0.7% for that period.
(168)

Foreign Languages

General

■ A 1977 study of 9,605 volumes retrieved for patrons at the Library of Congress during a 3-day period in November 1977 (almost 100% of volumes retrieved) *showed that*, while 62% of the holdings were in English, they accounted for 89% of the sample use. Inspection revealed no systematic changes in language use over time in the sample, with 90% of the 1970s imprints in English, 86% of the 1950s imprints in English, and 87% of the 1930s imprints in English. **(262)**

Academic

■ A 1968-69 study over a period of 9 months of the use of materials at the Midwest Regional Medical Library (John Crerar Library), involving a random sample of 1,071 requests for material, *showed that*, of 1,069 requests, the breakdown by language was as follows:

English	909 (85.0%)	requests
German	57 (5.3%)	requests
French	45 (4.2%)	requests
Other	58 (5.4%)	requests

(688)

■ A 1971 study at the MIT Science Library of in-room use (journals do not circulate) of 220 physics journals over a 3.5-month period *showed that*, of the 138 journals that were used in the 3.5-month period, English-language journals or journals in which English-language articles predominate accounted for 111 (50.5%) journals and 4,090 (95.3%) of the uses, while German-language journals or journals in which German-language articles predominate accounted for 11 (5%) journals and 157 (3.7%) of the uses. The remaining journals that received use in the 3.5-month period were published in Russian (9 journals), French (6 journals), and Czech (1 journal). **(608)**

■ A 1977 study at the Music Library of the University of California, Berkeley, to investigate weeding criteria (based on a sample of 116 circulated volumes and a sample of 515 volumes from the shelf) *showed that* weeding on the basis of language alone was not a feasible idea. For example, during the period 1950-77, while 84.8% of the English-language books in the sample circulated, 79.3% of the French-language books and 71.8% of the German language books circulated as well. Overall, during the 1950-77 period, 45.6% of the materials circulated were non-English language materials. **(756)**

■ A survey reported in 1978 of 31 Ph.D. dissertations in the field of business/management (13 from the State University of New York at Buffalo and 18 from SUNYAB incoming faculty but completed at other schools) *showed that*, of the 2,805 citations, only 4 (0.1%) were to non-English titles. These included 2 citations to French-language materials and 1 citation each to Spanish- and German-language materials. **(461)**

■ A survey reported in 1981 of historians listed in the 1978 *Directory of American Scholars* concerning their use of and attitudes toward periodicals (survey size: 767 historians, although not all questionnaires could be delivered; responding: 360 or 46.9%, with respondents tending to be younger and with a higher scholarly productivity record than nonrespondents) *showed that* 58% of the respondents "do not attempt to keep up with research published in foreign languages." Further, when asked if they felt their research was restricted in any way because of a language problem, 334 respondents reported as follows:

no restriction	138 (41.3%) respondents
slight restriction	136 (40.7%) respondents
moderate restriction	42 (12.6%) respondents
substantial restriction	18 (5.4%) respondents

Finally, when encountering a reference in a foreign language they did not read, respondents reported the following responses:

try to get article translated	30.3% respondents
search for summary or abstract	21.7% respondents
try to get gist on own	34.7% respondents
ignore	13.3% respondents **(780)**

Public

■ A 1969 survey of Canadian public libraries serving populations of more than 10,000 people as well as all county and regional libraries belonging to the Canadian Library Association concerning holdings and use of non-

English collections (survey size: 203; responding: 83 or 41%) *showed that* the demand for non-English material did not come from predominately French-speaking Canadians. Specifically, 37 (44%) of the libraries reported that their non-English material was primarily used by new Canadians, while only 19 (23%) libraries reported that their non-English material was used primarily by native Canadians. **(534)**

Special

■ A 1968-69 study over a period of 9 months of the use of materials at the Midwest Regional Medical Library (John Crerar Library), involving a random sample of 1,071 requests for material, *showed that*, of 1,069 requests, the breakdown by language was as follows:

English	909 (85.0%) requests
German	57 (5.3%) requests
French	45 (4.2%) requests
Other	58 (5.4%) requests

(688)

■ A 1977 study at the Music Library of the University of California, Berkeley, to investigate weeding criteria (based on a sample of 116 circulated volumes and a sample of 515 volumes from the shelf) *showed that* weeding on the basis of language alone was not a feasible idea. For example, during the period 1950-77, while 84.8% of the English-language books in the sample circulated, 79.3% of the French-language books and 71.8% of the German-language books circulated as well. Overall, during the 1950-77 period, 45.6% of the materials circulated were non-English language materials. **(756)**

Gifts

Academic

■ A study reported in 1981 at DePauw University of circulation patterns over a 5-year period (1973-77) for a group of newly acquired monographs (sample size: 1,904 books) *showed that* there was a statistically significant difference in the circulation rates of gift books and those books purchased on the recommendation of classroom instructors or librarians, with the gift books circulating less than the purchased books (significant at the .01 level). For example, of 189 gift books, 121 (64.0%) did not circulate at all [during the 5-year period], while of 1,715 purchased books, 581 (33.8%) did not circulate at all [during the 5-year period]. **(573)**

■ A 1982 study at the University of Wisconsin, Milwaukee concerning the use of gift books in 2 separate parts of the collection, both the PS 3537-PS 3545 section (American literature, 1,039 nongift books and 104 gift books) and the QC 6-QC 75 section (physics, 1,023 nongifts and 16 gift books) *showed that* the average use of gift books was considerably lower than the use of nongift books. Specifically, nongift books in the PS section averaged 5.30 uses since added to the collection, while gift books averaged 1.23 uses; nongift books in the QC section averaged 5.31 uses since added to the collection, while gift books averaged 2.25 uses. **(807)**

Ibid. . . . *showed that* a higher percentage of gift books than nongift books did not circulate at all and that of the books that circulated at least once gift books circulated much less on the average than nongift books. Specifically, in the PS section 343 (33.0%) of the nongift books did not circulate, compared to 59 (56.7%) of the gift books, while in the QC section 272 (26.6%) of the nongift books did not circulate, compared to 6 (60.0%) of the gift books. Further, of the books that did circulate, the average number of uses for PS nongifts was 7.92 since added to the collection, compared to 2.84 uses for gifts, while the average number of uses for QC nongifts was 7.23 since added to the collection, compared to 3.60 uses for gifts. **(807)**

Ibid. . . . *showed that* the use of gift books followed a Bradford-like distribution. For example, in the PS section, the 14 (13.5%) most frequently used books accounted for 80 (62.5%) of the uses. **(807)**

Ibid. . . . *showed that* gift books tended to be older than nongift books. For example, in the PS section 375 (36.1%) of the nongift books had been published after 1970, compared to 11 (10.6%) of the gift books; in the QC section 380 (37.1%) of the nongift books had been published after 1970, compared to 2 (12.5%) of the gift books. **(807)**

Ibid. . . . *showed that* gift books tended to be old when given to the library. For example, in the PS section 68 (65.4%) of the gift books were over 20 years old when given to the library, while of the PS and QC sections combined, 105 (87.5%) of the gifts were over 10 years old when given to the library. **(807)**

Government Documents

Academic

■ A survey reported in 1972 of 1/3 of the social science and humanities faculty at Case Western Reserve University (sample size: 116; responding: 103 or 89%) concerning government document use *showed that* 62% (64) never used documents; 23% (24) used documents 1-2 times a year; 14% (14) used documents 1-2 times a semester; and 1% (1) used documents 2-3 times a month. **(209)**

Ibid. . . . *showed that*, of 87 faculty respondents, the 2 main reasons for nonuse of the document department reported by faculty respondents was lack of need of government documents (46%) and obtaining their own copies (32%). **(209)**

■ A 1982 survey of economics and political science faculty members in 9 colleges and universities serving as academic depository institutions in Massachusetts for the Government Printing Office (sample size: 216, including 105 economists and 111 political scientists; responding: 155 or 71.8%, including 86 economists and 69 political scientists) *showed that* 125 (80.6%) had made some use of federal government documents during the past year, while 53 (42.2%) reported citing a federal government publication in 1 or more of their scholarly writings in the past 3 years. **(316)**

Ibid. . . . *showed that* the 125 faculty respondents who used documents reported using U.S. govenment publications as follows (multiple responses allowed): for research or scholarly writing (117 respondents), for teaching (95 respondents), for consulting activities (33 respondents), and for recreational reading or statistical data necessary for presentations before community groups (6 respondents). **(316)**

Ibid. . . . *showed that* the top 3 kinds of federal documents sought by the 125 respondents who used documents were statistical data (82 respondents), research and technical reports (77 respondents), and resources that may be of value to students (74 respondents). The difference between the responses given by economists and political scientists was not great, with a Spearman rank correlation coefficient showing a strong relationship between the responses of the 2 groups (rho = .87). **(316)**

Ibid. . . . *showed that* the top 6 methods used by the 125 respondents who used documents to locate federal documents were (multiple responses allowed): finding citations in the general literature of the subject discipline (97 respondents); receiving assistance from librarians (84 respondents); being on the mailing lists of federal agencies (70 respondents); finding citations in indexes, abstracts, and subject bibliographies (68); receiving citations from colleagues (53 respondents); and contacting federal agencies (46 respondents). The differnce between the responses given by economists and political scientists was not great, with a Spearman rank correlation coefficient showing a strong relationship between the responses of the 2 groups (rho = .97). **(316)**

Ibid. . . . *showed that*, of the 125 respondents who used federal documents, in addition to use of federal documents in paper copy format; 24 (19.2%) respondents also used federal documents in microformat; 21 (16.8%) used machine-readable federal government information; and 13 (10.4%) used audiovisual federal government information. Of these responses, economists accounted for 70.8% of the reported use of microform and 90.5% of the use of machine-readable formats. **(316)**

Ibid. . . . *showed that*, for the 125 respondents who used federal documents, the top 3 kinds of federal documents used frequently by economists were (multiple responses allowed): statistical reports (47 respondents), annual reports (21 respondents), and reports of investigation and research (19 respondents), while the top 3 kinds of federal documents used frequently by political scientists were (multiple responses allowed): statistical reports (13 respondents), decisions and opinions, e.g., from the Supreme Court (12 respondents), and journals and proceedings, e.g., from the *Congressional Record* (11 respondents). **(316)**

Ibid. . . . *showed that*, for the 125 respondents who used federal documents if the kinds of federal documents faculty respondents used frequently were only available on microform, 41 (32.8%) reported they would adapt (albeit "grudgingly") to the format change; 40 (32%) reported they would no longer consult the documents but instead look for the information elsewhere or do without; and 18 (14.4%) reported they would use the documents less frequently. **(316)**

Ibid. . . . *showed that*, when informed that microfiche was now the primary format for the distribution of federal govenment publications to depository libraries, 75 (60%) of the 125 faculty respondents who used federal documents felt that their information-gathering patterns would be affected; 45 (36%) thought that their information-gathering patterns would not be affected; and 5 (4%) could not speculate on the effect. **(316)**

Government Documents

Ibid. . . . *showed that*, if a promising document were in microformat, 66 (52.8%) of the 125 respondents who reported using documents reported that they would look at the document to determine its value to them; 38.4% reported that they would not bother checking the library's microform copy and instead contact their congressional representative or the issuing agency (to get hard copy); 6 (4.8%) suggested they would not use the document at all; and 5 (4%) reported an interest in having their own personal copy of microtext. (316)

Ibid. . . . *showed that* 120 (6%) of the 125 respondents who reported using federal government documents reported that they did not have ready access to microform readers in their office, department, or home. Only 5 reported immediate access to viewing equipment outside the central library. (316)

Ibid. . . . *showed that* 87 (69.6%) of the 125 respondents who reported using federal government documents reported they felt that even with the increased number of federal documents the microform program made available, this use of microform format would decrease their use of documents; 14 (11.2%) thought that with more material available their use of documents might increase; 18 (14.4%) would not speculate on how their frequency of use of federal documents might change; and 6 (4.8%) thought their use of documents would not change. (316)

School

- A study reported in 1979 of term paper bibliographies of high school students (270 students/papers from 6 high schools, involving 3,165 identifiable references) *showed that*, of 424 miscellaneous citations, the following distribution obtained:

newspapers	141 (33.3%) misc. citations
encyclopedias	120 (28.3%) misc. citations
government documents and/or pamphlet references	80 (18.9%) misc. citations
nonprint sources, including interviews	23 (05.4%) misc. citations
other special materials	44 (10.4%) misc. citations **(564)**

- A 1981 study of 53 ninth-grade honors students in science in a suburban Philadelphia public high school *showed that* out of 47 bibliographies 83% had magazine citations, 66% had book citations, 45% had encyclopedia citations, 44% had government document/pamphlet citations, 24% had newspaper citations, and 4% had nonprint citations. Out of a total of 409 citations, magazine citations constituted 46% of the total, books 25%, encyclopedias 10%, government documents/pamphlets 10%, newspapers 7%, and nonprint 1%. **(222)**

In-house

Academic

■ 2 studies reported in 1971 undertaken at the University of Southwestern Louisiana, comparing circulation by subject area with in-house use by subject area, *showed that* there was a strong positive correlation. In the first study 8,954 circulated books were compared with 4,532 books used in-house using finely delineated LC and Dewey class spans relating to academic departments. The overall Pearson correlation was $r = .86$, with a significance level no greater than .05. In the second study 2,386 circulated books were compared to 1,102 books used in-house using broader subject areas based on LC first and second letters and Dewey tens. The overall Pearson correlation was $r = .84$, with a significance level no greater than .01. **(207)**

■ A 1972 study at the University of Minnesota Bio-Medical Library concerning in-house use of periodicals during 2 1-week periods (1st period: 727 uses involving 269 different titles; 2nd period: 533 uses involving 209 different titles) *showed that* the numbers of titles accounting for different levels of use were as follows (2nd period figures reported in parentheses):

4% (5%) of the titles	27% (26%) of total use
8% (9%) of the titles	38% (37%) of total use
28% (29%) of the titles	68% (64%) of total use **(697)**

■ A study reported in 1972 at the University of Southeastern Louisiana of 8,953 circulated books, 4,507 books left on tables, and 158,569 books left on the shelves *showed that* books whose class numbers matched profiles of class numbers associated with courses taught were more likely to be charged out after being taken from the shelves than left on the tables. The study was statistically significant at the .005 level. **(211)**

Ibid. . . . *showed that*, of 13,460 books taken off the shelves vs. 158,569 books left on the shelves, books whose class numbers matched profiles of

In-house

class numbers associated with courses taught were more likely to be taken off the shelves than left on the shelves. The study was statistically significant at the .005 level. **(211)**

■ A study reported in 1977 at the University of Pittsburgh, based on the complete circulation history during the period October 1968-June 1976, *showed that* external circulation was a good indicator of total book/monograph use. For example, based on 30-day samples of in-house use taken over a period of 2 academic terms and involving 29,098 items, 75% of the items used in-house had also circulated externally by the end of the sample period, with an additional 4% of the in-house items circulating the following year. Further, of 4,250 books/monographs loaned on interlibrary loan during the period January 1969-December 1975, 3,246 (76.4%) had external circulations, with the remaining 1,004 items accounting for only .34% of the total circulation during the period of the study. Finally, of 33,277 books/monographs selected for reserve during the period January 1969-December 1975, 27,854 (83.7%) had external circulations, with the remaining 5,423 items accounting for only 1.84% of the total circulation during the period of this study. **(666)**

Public

■ An attempt reported in 1982 to establish 4 input measures and 4 output measures for public libraries, based on published statistical reports for 301 New Jersey public libraries over a 6-year period (1974-79) and survey data for 96 public libraries in New Jersey, *showed that* ("per capita" based on the population of the library's service area):

INPUT MEASURES

The proportion of budget spent on materials averaged 19.9%, with a standard deviation of .081 (based on 301 libraries).

The new volumes per capita averaged .181 with a standard deviation of .097 (based on 301 libraries).

The periodical titles per capita averaged .0094, with a standard deviation of .0054 (based on 301 libraries).

The circulation per volume averaged 1.79, with a standard deviation of .77 (based on 301 libraries).

OUTPUT MEASURES

The circulation per capita averaged 5.04, with a standard deviation of 3.07 (based on 301 libraries).

The patron visits per capita averaged 2.82, with a standard deviation of 1.82 (based on 96 libraries).

The reference questions per capita averaged 1.12, with a standard deviation of .79 (based on 96 libraries).

The in-library uses of materials per capita averaged 2.29, with a standard deviation of 2.02 (based on 96 libraries). **(576)**

Special

■ A 1972 study at the University of Minnesota Bio-Medical Library concerning in-house use of periodicals during 2 1-week periods (1st period: 727 uses involving 269 different titles; 2nd period: 533 uses involving 209 different titles) *showed that* the numbers of titles accounting for different levels of use were as follows (2nd period figures reported in parentheses):

        4% (5%) of the titles   27% (26%) of total use
        8% (9%) of the titles   38% (37%) of total use
       28% (29%) of the titles   68% (64%) of total use   **(697)**

Maps

Academic

■ A 1972 study of Map Room use at Southern Illinois University during summer and fall quarters, involving the circulation of 2,721 maps and aerial photos to 223 borrowers, *showed that* borrowers were undergraduates (44%), graduate students (32%), and faculty (19%). However, graduate students accounted for 72% of the loans, undergraduates for 16%, and faculty for 10%. **(403)**

Ibid. . . . *showed that* the stated purpose of 60% of the loans was research. **(403)**

Ibid. . . . *showed that*, of the items borrowed, 1,869 (68%) were maps and aerial photos of Illinois areas; 253 (9%) were maps and aerial photos of nearby states; 430 (16%) were U.S. areas except for Illinois and nearby states; 77 (3%) were Canadian and Latin American areas; and 70 (3%) were areas in the Eastern Hemisphere. **(403)**

Maps

Ibid. . . . *showed that* the 2 most common types of maps borrowed were aerial photos (1,641 items or 60% of the total) and topographic maps (639 maps or 23% of the total). **(403)**

■ A 1972-75 study at Southern Illinois University (Carbondale) of map and aerial photograph circulation from the Map Room showed that, for all three years (1972-73, 1973-74, and 1974-75), undergraduate circulation consistently increased with academic status. Freshmen borrowed less than sophomores, sophomores less than juniors, and juniors less than seniors. **(420)**

Ibid. . . . *showed that* over the 3-year period undergraduates made up 49-52% of the borrowers in any given year; graduate students made up of 25-28% of the borrowers; faculty made up 12-15% of the borrowers; and "other" made up 8-11% of the borrowers. **(420)**

Ibid. . . . *showed that* over the 3-year period undergraduates accounted for 34-38% of the borrowing in any given year; graduates accounted for 30-38% of the borrowing; faculty accounted for 14-22% of the borrowing; and "other" accounted for 8-14% of the borrowing. **(420)**

Ibid. . . . *showed that* over the 3-year period 5 departments accounted for 33-37% of the borrowers and 45-50% of the borrowing. These were forestry, geology, geography, zoology, and botany. The other borrowers were scattered throughout 80 other departments. **(420)**

Ibid. . . . *showed that* the main general trend over the 3-year period was a decrease in social science use (from 26% of the borrowers and 22% of the borrowing in 1972-73 to 16% of the borrowers and 8% of the borrowing in 1974-75) and an increase in science use (from 22% of the borrowers and 39% of the borrowing in 1972-73 to 25% of the borrowers and 46% of the borrowing in 1974-75). **(420)**

Ibid. . . . *showed that* for 2,699 loans in 1972-73 the purpose of borrowing the material was as follows:

class use	741 (27%) items
research	544 (20%) items
recreation	512 (19%) items
travel	460 (17%) items
theses and dissertations	271 (10%) items
other	170 (06%) items

(420)

Ibid. . . . *showed that* over the 3-year period the region covered by the maps and photos borrowed was Southern Illinois (37-53% of the borrowing), northern and central Illinois (3-5% of the borrowing), nearby states (10-20% of the borrowing), U.S. (24-31% of the borrowing), and other including space maps (6-13% of the borrowing). **(420)**

Ibid. . . . *showed that* each year the proportion of male to female borrowers was "about 80% male, 20% female, although university enrollment was 36-38% female during this period." **(420)**

Media

Academic

■ A 1972 study of audiovisual use in U.S. law schools undertaken by the American Association of Law Libraries Audio-Visual Committee (population: 149 law schools taken from the 1970 edition of the *Directory of Law Libraries*; responding: 142 or 95.3%) *showed that* the 4 types of AV media most commonly reported as heavily used (i.e., more than several times a year) were a standard TV reciever (20.59% respondents), a television camera (16.28% respondents), a videotape recorder (14.00% respondents), and a cassette tape recorder (12.93% respondents). **(387)**

School

■ A survey reported in 1978 of factors influencing selection of school media materials, involving 107 wholesaler/distributors (25 responses or 27%), 106 publishers/producers (46 responses or 49%), and 516 media program personnel (222 responses or 44%), *showed that* 16% of the school media personnel reported the importance of the teacher's guide packaged with school media center materials as essential; 65% reported them helpful; 13% reported them as of little use; and 6% reported them never used. **(217)**

■ A study reported in 1979 of term paper bibliographies of high school students (270 students/papers from 6 high schools, involving 3,165 identifiable references) *showed that*, of 424 miscellaneous citations, the following distribution obtained:

    newspapers   141 (33.3%) misc. citations
    encyclopedias   120 (28.3%) misc. citations

continued

Method of Selection

government documents and/or pamphlet references	80 (18.9%) misc. citations
nonprint sources, including interviews	23 (05.4%) misc. citations
other special materials	44 (10.4%) misc. citations **(564)**

■ A 1981 study of 53 ninth-grade honors students in science in a suburban Philadelphia public high school *showed that* out of 47 bibliographies 83% had magazine citations, 66% had book citations, 45% had encyclopedia citations, 44% had government document/pamphlet citations, 24% had newspaper citations, and 4% had nonprint citations. Out of a total of 409 citations, magazine citations constituted 46% of the total, books 25%, encyclopedias 10%, government documents/pamphlets 10%, newspapers 7%, and nonprint 1%. **(222)**

Special

■ A 1972 study of audiovisual use in U.S. law schools undertaken by the American Association of Law Libraries Audio-Visual Committee (population: 149 law schools taken from the 1970 edition of the *Directory of Law Libraries*; responding: 142 or 95.3%) *showed that* the 4 types of AV media most commonly reported as heavily used (i.e., more than several times a year) were a standard TV reciever (20.59% respondents), a television camera (16.28% respondents), a videotape recorder (14.00% respondents), and a cassette tape recorder (12.93% respondents). **(387)**

Method of Selection

Academic

■ A study reported in 1974 comparing the effectiveness of collection development of librarians, teaching faculty, and approval plans in 5 academic libraries (3 college, 2 university) by comparing books bought by each of these groups with the books' subsequent circulation records (7,213 books studied in total) *showed that* the circulation rates of the materials selected by each of the 3 groups were different to a statistically significant degree, with materials selected by librarians circulating most, materials selected by teaching faculty circulating next most often, and approval plan materials circulating the least (significance level not given). **(628)**

■ A study reported in 1981 at DePauw University of circulation patterns over a 5-year period (1973-77) for a group of newly acquired monographs (sample size: 1,904 books) *showed that* there was a statistically significant difference in the circulation rates of books selected by the classroom instructors (1,542 books) and those books selected by librarians (173 books), with the books selected by the librarians circulating more (significant at the .01 level). For example, 74% of the librarian-selected books were either lightly circulated or not circulated at all, compared to 87.3% of the books selected by classroom instructors, while 26% of the librarian-selected books were either moderately or heavily circulated, compared to 12.7% of the books selected by classroom instructors. **(573)**

Ibid. . . . *showed that* there was a statistically significant difference in the circulation rates of gift books and those books purchased on the recommendation of classroom instructors or librarians, with the gift books circulating less than the purchased books (significant at the .01 level). For example, of 189 gift books, 121 (64.0%) did not circulate at all [during the 5-year period], while of 1,715 purchased books 581 (33.8%) did not circulate at all [during the 5-year period]. **(573)**

■ A study during the 1981-82 academic year in the main library at Purdue concerning books undergraduates selected to read (involving interviews with 240 undergraduate borrowers and analysis of 598 of the mongraphic titles borrowed by both students and nonstudents) *showed that*, based on 364 items circulated to undergraduates, only 15.9% of the titles selected by undergraduates were based on instructor recommendation (direct recommendation or reading lists), while the remaining titles were selected without instructor direction. 86.6% were selected for subject matter relating to a specific course; 11.6% were selected for leisure reading; and 1.8% were selected for research in the student's major with no specific course in mind. **(530)**

Ibid. . . . *showed that* titles recommended by instructors and checked out by undergraduates were no more likely to fall within the core of highly circulating materials than outside it. For example, of 111 titles that circulated less than 6 times, 16 or 14.4% had been recommended by faculty, while of 253 titles that had circulated 6 times or more, 42 (16.6%) had been recommended by faculty. **(530)**

Ibid. . . . *showed that* the "best and most critically acclaimed" books do not make up the majority of undergraduate reading. For example, of 252 books checked out by undergraduates that had been published before 1973, only 61 (24.2%) were listed in *Books for College Libraries*, while of

Microforms

246 books published after 1963, only 74 (30.1%) were reviewed in *Choice*, and of these, only 35% were given top recommendations. **(530)**

Microforms

Academic

■ A survey reported in 1976 of 120 randomly selected patrons of the Bobst Library Microform Center of New York University *showed that* this was a user population of 4 faculty, 9 visitors, 63 graduates, and 44 undergraduates. **(224)**

Ibid. ... *showed that* 55 (46%) used the center either seldom or occasionally while 65 (54%) used it often (at least once a month) or frequently (at least once a week). 15 (35%) reported spending 30 minutes or less per session; 24 (20%) spent 30 minutes to 1 hour; 39 (33%) spent 1-2 hours; 28 (23%) spent 2-4 hours; and 14 (12%) spent more than 4 hours. **(224)**

■ A 1976-77 study of undergraduate use of newspapers on microfilm at the University of Illinois during 2 peak months of the 1976-77 academic year, involving 279 requests for newspaper microfilm (excluding use of *New York Times, Wall Street Journal* and *Chicago Tribune*), *showed that* the 5 most frequently requested titles were:

Daily Illini	31 (11.1%) requests	
Washington Post	31 (11.1%) requests	
Morning Courier (Champaign, Ill.)	30 (10.8%) requests	
Los Angeles Times	22 (7.9%) requests	
News-Gazette (Champaign, Ill.)	19 (6.8%) requests	**(471)**

Ibid. ... *showed that* 5 newspaper titles satisfied 47.7% of the requests; 10 titles satisfied 65.6% of the requests; 15 titles satisfied 77.1% of the requests; and 20 titles satsified 84.6% of the requests. **(471)**

Ibid. ... *showed that* a 5-year backfile satisfied 47.9% of the user requests; a 10-year backfile satisfied 67.2% of the requests; a 15-year backfile satisfied 77.1% of the requests; and a 20-year backfile satisfied 84.5% of the requests. **(471)**

Ibid. . . . *showed that* indexed newspapers received more use than nonindexed newspapers by almost a 2 to 1 ratio. Specifically, during the period 1972-76 indexed newspapers accounted for 68.7% of the requests. **(471)**

■ A 1982 survey of economics and political science faculty members in 9 colleges and universities serving as academic depository institutions in Massachusetts for the Government Printing Office (sample size: 216, including 105 economists and 111 political scientists; responding: 155 or 71.8%, including 86 economists and 69 political scientists) *showed that*, of the 125 respondents who used federal documents, in addition to use of federal documents in paper copy format, 24 (19.2%) respondents also used federal documents in microformat; 21 (16.8%) used machine-readable federal government information; and 13 (10.4%) used audiovisual federal government information. Of these responses, economists accounted for 70.8% of the reported use of microform and 90.5% of the use of machine-readable formats. **(316)**

Ibid. . . . *showed that*, for the 125 respondents who used federal documents if the kinds of federal documents faculty respondents used frequently were only available on microform, 41 (32.8%) reported they would adapt (albeit "grudgingly") to the format change; 40 (32%) reported they would no longer consult the documents but instead look for the information elsewhere or do without; and 18 (14.4%) reported they would use the documents less frequently. **(316)**

Ibid. . . . *showed that*, when informed that microfiche was now the primary format for the distribution of federal govenment publications to depository libraries, 75 (60%) of the 125 faculty respondents who used federal documents felt that their information-gathering patterns would be affected; 45 (36%) thought that their information-gathering patterns would not be affected; and 5 (4%) could not speculate on the effect. **(316)**

Ibid. . . . *showed that*, if a promising document were in microformat, 66 (52.8%) of the 125 respondents who reported using documents reported that they would look at the document to determine its value to them; 38.4% reported that they would not bother checking the library's microform copy and instead contact their congressional representative or the issuing agency (to get hard copy); 6 (4.8%) suggested they would not use the document at all; and 5 (4%) reported an interest in having their own personal copy of microtext. **(316)**

Ibid. . . . *showed that* 120 (6%) of the 125 respondents who reported using federal government documents reported that they did not have ready access to microform readers in their office, department, or home. Only 5 reported immediate access to viewing equipment outside the central library. **(316)**

Ibid. . . . *showed that* 87 (69.6%) of the 125 respondents who reported using federal government documents reported they felt that even with the increased number of federal documents the microform program made available, this use of microform format would decrease their use of documents; 14 (11.2%) thought that with more material available their use of documents might increase; 18 (14.4%) would not speculate on how their frequency of use of federal documents might change; and 6 (4.8%) thought their use of documents would not change. **(316)**

Special

■ A study reported in 1978 in an industrial R and D laboratory evaluating the shift from use of a hard copy of *Chemical Abstracts* to use of a microfilm copy, involving 33 laboratory professionals who had used both formats, *showed that* the microfilm was considered less accessible than hard copy to a statistically significant degree. Specifically, on a scale of 1 to 10 where 1 was "very accessible" and 10 was "not very accessible," the average rating for the hard copy version was 2.55, while the average rating for the microfilm copy was 4.12. This difference was statistically significant at the .001 level. **(524)**

Ibid. . . . *showed that* the microfilm was considered less easy to use than hard copy to a statistically significant degree. Specifically, on a scale of 1 to 10 where 1 was "very easy to use" and 10 was "not very easy to use," the average rating for the hard copy version was 3.36, while the average rating for the microfilm copy was 4.97. This difference was statistically significant at the .01 level. **(524)**

Newspapers

Academic

■ A 1976-77 study of undergraduate use of newspapers on microfilm at the University of Illinois during 2 peak months of the 1976-77 academic year, involving 279 requests for newspaper microfilm (excluding use of

New York Times, Wall Street Journal *and* Chicago Tribune), *showed that* the 5 most frequently requested titles were:

<table>
<tr><td>Daily Illini</td><td>31 (11.1%) requests</td></tr>
<tr><td>Washington Post</td><td>31 (11.1%) requests</td></tr>
<tr><td>Morning Courier
(Champaign, Ill.)</td><td>30 (10.8%) requests</td></tr>
<tr><td>Los Angeles Times</td><td>22 (7.9%) requests</td></tr>
<tr><td>News-Gazette
(Champaign, Ill.)</td><td>19 (6.8%) requests   **(471)**</td></tr>
</table>

Ibid. . . . *showed that* 5 newspaper titles satisfied 47.7% of the requests; 10 titles satisfied 65.6% of the requests; 15 titles satisfied 77.1% of the requests; and 20 titles satsified 84.6% of the requests. **(471)**

Ibid. . . . *showed that* a 5-year backfile satisfied 47.9% of the user requests; a 10-year backfile satisfied 67.2% of the requests; a 15-year backfile satisfied 77.1% of the requests; and a 20-year backfile satisfied 84.5% of the requests. **(471)**

Ibid. . . . *showed that* indexed newspapers received more use than nonindexed newspapers by almost a 2 to 1 ratio. Specifically, during the period 1972-76 indexed newspapers accounted for 68.7% of the requests. **(471)**

School

■ A study reported in 1979 of term paper bibliographies of high school students (270 students/papers from 6 high schools, involving 3,165 identifiable references) *showed that*, of 424 miscellaneous citations, the following distribution obtained:

<table>
<tr><td>newspapers</td><td>141 (33.3%) misc. citations</td></tr>
<tr><td>encyclopedias</td><td>120 (28.3%) misc. citations</td></tr>
<tr><td>government documents and/or
   pamphlet references</td><td>80 (18.9%) misc. citations</td></tr>
<tr><td>nonprint sources, including
   interviews</td><td>23 (05.4%) misc. citations</td></tr>
<tr><td>other special materials</td><td>44 (10.4%) misc. citations **(564)**</td></tr>
</table>

■ A 1981 study of 53 ninth-grade honors students in science in a suburban Philadelphia public high school *showed that* out of 47 bibliographies 83%

Outreach and Extension

had magazine citations, 66% had book citations, 45% had encyclopedia citations, 44% had government document/pamphlet citations, 24% had newspaper citations, and 4% had nonprint citations. Out of a total of 409 citations, magazine citations constituted 46% of the total, books 25%, encyclopedias 10%, government documents/pamphlets 10%, newspapers 7%, and nonprint 1%. **(222)**

Outreach and Extension

Academic

■ A 1971-72 study of the articles supplied by the University of Oklahoma Health Sciences Center Library to state health professionals and institutions during a 4-month period, involving 1,756 articles (from 373 journals) sent to individual health professionals and 1,620 articles (from 527 journals) sent to health institutions, *showed that*, in terms of the publication dates of the articles sent to individuals, 28% of the information requests could have been filled with a journal backfile of 1 year; 57% could have been filled with a backfile of 2 years; 72% with a backfile of 3 years; 80% with a backfile of 4 years; 85% with a backfile of 5 years. **(409)**

Ibid. . . . *showed that*, of the 1,620 articles sent to institutions, 24.5% [no raw number given] of the articles were supplied by 26 titles, each contributing 10 or more articles, while 53% [no raw number given] of the articles were supplied by 100 titles, each contributing 5 or more articles. **(409)**

Ibid. . . . *showed that*, in terms of publication dates of the articles, 69.3% of the information requests could have been filled with a journal backfile of 5 years, while 85.5% of the information requests could have been filled with a journal backlog of 10 years. **(409)**

■ A 1975-76 study of journal title usage through the extension services of the University of Oklahoma Health Sciences Center Library (Oklahoma City) to hospital clients (4,216 articles from 1,055 journal titles requested) *showed that* ranking journal use by number of requesters was not the same as ranking journal use by number of requests. Although the 4 titles with the most requests were also the 4 titles with the most requesters (though the ranked order differs slightly), the 20 titles with the most requests included 6 titles that were not among the 20 titles with the most requesters. **(429)**

Ibid. . . . *showed that* the journal titles requested by individuals in hospitals without libraries were different from the journal titles requested by hospitals with libraries. Of 27 journal titles requested 15 times or more by individuals and 7 journal titles requested 15 times or more by libraries, only 1 title appeared in common—the *British Medical Journal*. **(429)**

■ A survey reported in 1983 of U.S. dental school libraries concerning their service to dental practitioners (population: 60 dental school libraries; responding: 53 or 88%) *showed that*, of 51 respondents, 22 (43%) libraries reported using at least 1 method (e.g., articles in local or state association journals, alumni bulletin, information given to graduating students, etc.) to promote library services to dental practitioners, while 29 (57%) reported they do not advertise such service at all. **(752)**

Special

■ A 1971-72 study of the articles supplied by the University of Oklahoma Health Sciences Center Library to state health professionals and institutions during a 4-month period, involving 1,756 articles (from 373 journals) sent to individual health professionals and 1,620 articles (from 527 journals) sent to health institutions, *showed that*, in terms of the publication dates of the articles sent to individuals, 28% of the information requests could have been filled with a journal backfile of 1 year; 57% could have been filled with a backfile of 2 years; 72% with a backfile of 3 years; 80% with a backfile of 4 years; 85% with a backfile of 5 years. **(409)**

Ibid. . . . *showed that*, of the 1,620 articles sent to institutions, 24.5% [no raw number given] of the articles were supplied by 26 titles, each contributing 10 or more articles, while 53% [no raw number given] of the articles were supplied by 100 titles, each contributing 5 or more articles. **(409)**

Ibid. . . . *showed that*, in terms of publication dates of the articles, 69.3% of the information requests could have been filled with a journal backfile of 5 years, while 85.5% of the information requests could have been filled with a journal backlog of 10 years. **(409)**

■ A 1975-76 study of journal title usage through the extension services of the University of Oklahoma Health Sciences Center Library (Oklahoma City) to hospital clients (4,216 articles from 1,055 journal titles requested) *showed that* ranking journal use by number of requesters was not the same as ranking journal use by number of requests. Although the 4 titles with

Periodicals

the most requests were also the 4 titles with the most requesters (though the ranked order differs slightly), the 20 titles with the most requests included 6 titles that were not among the 20 titles with the most requesters. **(429)**

Ibid. . . . *showed that* the journal titles requested by individuals in hospitals without libraries were different from the journal titles requested by hospitals with libraries. Of 27 journal titles requested 15 times or more by individuals and 7 journal titles requested 15 times or more by libraries, only 1 title appeared in common—the *British Medical Journal*. **(429)**

■ A survey reported in 1983 of U.S. dental school libraries concerning their service to dental practitioners (population: 60 dental school libraries; responding: 53 or 88%) *showed that*, of 51 respondents, 22 (43%) libraries reported using at least 1 method (e.g., articles in local or state association journals, alumni bulletin, information given to graduating students, etc.) to promote library services to dental practitioners, while 29 (57%) reported they do not advertise such service at all. **(752)**

Periodicals—General Issues

Academic

■ A 1971 study of journal availability at the Woodward Biomedical Library (University of British Columbia, Canada) during a 12-day period *showed that*, out of 4,326 journal items, 370 (8.6%) were not found immediately. The reasons for unavailability were as follows:

title not held or issue not received	100 (27%)	items
in use or awaiting reshelving	98 (26%)	items
being bound	66 (18%)	items
user errors	41 (11%)	items
administrative reasons (on "hold" shelf, misshelved, etc.)	40 (11%)	items
unspecified reasons	25 (7%)	items **(692)**

■ A 1971 study at the MIT Science Library of in-room use (journals do not circulate) of 220 physics journals over a 3.5-month period *showed that*, of the 138 journals that were used in the 3.5-month period, English-language journals or journals in which English-language articles predominate accounted for 111 (50.5%) journals and 4,090 (95.3%) of the uses, while German-language journals or journals in which German-language articles predominate accounted for 11 (5%) journals and 157 (3.7%) of the uses. The remaining journals that received use in the 3.5-month period were published in Russian (9 journals), French (6 journals), and Czech (1 journal). **(608)**

■ A 1972-73 study of periodical usage in the Education-Psychology Library at Ohio State University *showed that*, of the 360 periodical titles that circulated 11 or more times, 337 (93.6%) were indexed by at least one of the following services: *Readers' Guide, Education Index, Current Index to Journals in Education* and *Psychological Abstracts*. Further, all of the 50 most used titles were indexed in one of the 4 services mentioned, while only 34 (17.7%) of the 192 journals that did not circulate at all were indexed in one of the 4 services. **(455)**

■ A 1973 survey of physicists in 6 universities of the greater Boston area (Boston University, Brandeis, Brown, Harvard, MIT, and Northeastern) to determine how they meet their information needs (sample size: 339; responding: 179 or 52.8%) *showed that* of 185 respondents (Harvard chemistry respondents included) the numbers of journals scanned per week by physicists were:

0 journals	4 (2.16%) respondents
1-3 journals	105 (56.76%) respondents
4-6 journals	62 (33.51%) respondents
7-9 journals	10 (5.41%) respondents
10+ journals	4 (2.16%) respondents **(404)**

■ A study reported in 1974 investigating the materials used by master's and doctoral candidates completing theses after 1966 in public health at 5 universities (Yale; Harvard; University of California, Los Angeles; University of California, Berkeley; and California State University, Northridge), involving 3,456 citations taken from 44 theses, *showed that* the distribution of materials by format was as follows:

journals	1,785 (52%) citations
books	961 (28%) citations
documents	293 (8%) citations
unpublished	242 (7%) citations
serials	131 (4%) citations
theses	44 (1%) citations **(698)**

Periodicals 313

Ibid. . . . *showed that* doctoral theses had a higher proportion of journal citations than masters' theses to a statistically significant degree (significant at the .02 level). However, in terms of overall number of citations per thesis, there was no statistically significant difference between doctoral and masters' theses when method of investigation was considered. **(698)**

■ A comparison of periodical costs (1975 cost data including subscription costs [actual], ordering [estimated], receiving [estimated], processing [estimated], accounting and shelving costs [estimated], binding preparation [estimated], and binding costs [estimated]) and use rates (based on use in an academic library [institution not specified] during the period 1972-75) *showed that*, for the 25 most requested journals out of 528 political science journals (use determined by an earlier study: citation 361), the cost for each use of the periodical ranged from $.17 to $4.98 with a median of $.53 per use. **(307)**

Ibid. . . . *showed that* the cost per individual user (many users made multiple requests) of the 25 most requested jourals out of 528 political science journals (use determined by an earlier study: citation 361) ranged from $.78 to $4.64 per user, with a median of $2.27 per user. **(307)**

■ A 1977 study at the University of Illinois Law Library of periodical usage over a 3-month period (275 periodicals, all indexed in 1977 *Index to Legal Periodicals*; 90% of the data came from in-house use, although reserve, ILL, and faculty charges were also counted) *showed that* a comparison of the 25 most used journals from this study had 15 (60%) titles in common with the 25 most cited journals from an earlier citation study (Olavi Maru, "Measuring the Impact of Legal Periodicals," *American Bar Foundation Research Journal* 1976, 227-249); however, a comparison of the 50 most used journals from this study with the 50 most cited journals from the citation study showed only 23 titles (46%) in common. **(360)**

■ A study reported in 1978 at Indiana University, Bloomington of materials requested through a delivery service to faculty in the political science and economics departments during a 32-month period (October 1972-June 1975), involving 39 political scientists and 14 economists (40-50% of the faculty in the departments) and 5,478 articles from 620 different journals and newspapers, *showed that* the chief reason for a journal's being unavailable was reshelving, which accounted for 56% of the unavailable journals. **(421)**

■ A 1978 study in the Biology Library of Temple University, involving a citation analysis of publications by full-time Temple biology faculty, doctoral dissertations of Temple biology Ph.D.'s, and preliminary doctoral qualifying briefs written by second-year graduate biology students at Temple during the 3-year period 1975-77 (153 source items with 4,155 citations), *showed that* 3,739 (90.0% [91% reported]) citations were to journal articles in 336 journals. **(650)**

■ A survey reported in 1978 of 31 Ph.D. dissertations in the field of business/management (13 from the State University of New York at Buffalo and 18 from SUNYAB incoming faculty but completed at other schools), *showed that* the 7 most frequently cited subject areas (based on 1,161 citations to monographs and serials) were:

business (HF 5001-6351)	14.7% citations
economics: Labor (HD 4801-8942)	11.5% citations
economics: production (HD 1-100)	10.8% citations
psychology (BF)	8.2% citations
sociology (HM-HX)	7.3% citations
finance (HG)	6.4% citations
economic theory	6.0% citations **(461)**

Public

■ A 1966 survey of 21,385 adult (12 years old or older) public library users in the Baltimore-Washington metropolitan region of Maryland, conducted during a 6-week period, entering the library (79.1% of patrons approached filled out the survey instrument) *showed that* the use made of the library was as follows (multiple responses allowed): browsing (43.1%), reference books (22.1%), library catalogs (19.0%), help from a librarian (16.0%), consulting books or magazines (12.4%), read new magazines or newspapers (8.7%), periodical indexes (5.7%), recordings (2.7%), films (0.7%), other (2.0%), and no response (11.1%). **(301)**

■ A survey reported in 1968 of Michigan public libraries (559 libraries or branches queried; 462 or 82% responding) receiving periodicals from the state *showed that*, while most libraries (252) reported that their periodicals are used about equally for current reading and for reference, a substantial number revealed a trend for increasingly larger libraries to report their periodicals used more for reference, starting with libraries serving populations in excess of 5,000. **(133)**

Periodicals

School

■ A study reported in 1979 of term paper bibliographies of high school students (270 students/papers from 6 high schools, involving 3,165 identifiable references) *showed that* 426 (68%) of 624 journal citations were indexed in *Readers' Guide*. Nevertheless, 43% of the students citing journals selected journals not covered by *Readers' Guide*. **(564)**

Ibid. . . . *showed that* the number of references in individual papers ranged from 2 to 47, with the average 11.7 and the median and mode both 10. The median number of monographs cited per paper was 7.1, while the median number of journal articles cited was 2.9. **(564)**

■ A survey reported in 1980 of 1,178 high school students (representing a sample from 73 classes, 15 schools, and 5 school districts), including a study of their bibliographic citations to periodical articles, *showed that* only 460 students (39%) cited at least 1 periodical article. Overall, 62% of the total citations were to books, 19% to periodicals, and the rest to newspapers, encyclopedias, etc. **(219)**

Ibid. . . . *showed that* of the 460 students citing periodical articles; 138 (30.0%) cited 1 article; 300 (65.2%) cited 3 or less articles; and 416 (90.4%) cited 7 or less articles. Only 12 students (2.6%) cited more than 10 articles. **(219)**

Ibid. . . . *showed that* holdings of back issues up through 5 years would have supplied 60% of all cited articles; 10 years of back issues would have supplied 74% of all cited articles; and 20 years of back holdings would have supplied 85% of all cited articles. **(219)**

Ibid. . . . *showed that*, of the 1,490 articles cited, 1,224 (82%) were from titles covered by *Readers Guide*. Only 12 titles involving a total of 24 citations were indexed in *Periodicals for School Media Programs* but not indexed in *Readers Guide*. **(219)**

■ A 1981 study of 53 ninth-grade honors students in science in a surburban Philadelphia public high school *showed that* out of 47 bibliographies 83% had magazine citations, 66% had book citations, 45% had encyclopedia citations, 44% had government document/pamphlet citations, 24% had newspaper citations, and 4% had nonprint citations. Out of a total of 409 citations, magazine citations constituted 46% of the total, books 25%, encyclopedias 10%, government documents/pamphlets 10%, newspapers 7%, and nonprint 1%. **(222)**

Special

■ A 1971 study of journal availability at the Woodward Biomedical Library (University of British Columbia, Canada) during a 12-day period *showed that*, out of 4,326 journal items, 370 (8.6%) were not found immediately. The reasons for unavailability were as follows:

title not held or issue not received	100 (27%) items
in use or awaiting reshelving	98 (26%) items
being bound	66 (18%) items
user errors	41 (11%) items
administrative reasons (on "hold" shelf, misshelved, etc.)	40 (11%) items
unspecified reasons	25 (7%) items **(692)**

■ A 1977 study at the University of Illinois Law Library of periodical usage over a 3-month period (275 periodicals all indexed in 1977 *Index to Legal Periodicals*; 90% of the data came from in-house use, although reserve, ILL, and faculty charges were also counted) *showed that* a comparison of the 25 most used journals from this study had 15 (60%) titles in common with the 25 most cited journals from an earlier citation study (Olavi Maru, "Measuring the Impact of Legal Periodicals," *American Bar Foundation Research Journal* 1976, 227-249); however, a comparison of the 50 most used journals from this study with the 50 most cited journals from the citation study showed only 23 titles (46%) in common. **(360)**

Periodicals—Bradford Distribution, Implicit

Academic

■ A study reported in 1964 of journal circulation in the Columbia and Yale Medical libraries during a 6-month period for Columbia and a 1-year period for Yale [total circulation not given] *showed that* the number of journals needed to supply various use levels was as follows:

Periodicals

4 journal titles	10% of total journal use
10 journal titles	20% of total journal use
63 journal titles	50% of total journal use
262 journal titles	80% of total journal use
920 journal titles	100% of total journal use

(670)

■ A 1971 study at the MIT Science Library of in-room use (journals do not circulate) of 220 physics journals over a 3.5-month period *showed that*, of 4,292 uses the number of titles involved was as follows:

3 (1.4%) of the titles accounted for 1,384 (32.2%) of the uses;
14 (6.4%) of the titles accounted for 2,502 (58.3%) of the uses;
55 (25.0%) of the titles accounted for 3,949 (91.2%) of the uses;
138 (62.7%) of the titles accounted for 4,292 (100%) of the uses. **(608)**

■ A 1972 study at the University of Minnesota Bio-Medical Library concerning in-house use of periodicals during 2 1-week periods (1st period: 727 uses involving 269 different titles; 2nd period: 533 uses involving 209 different titles) *showed that* the number of titles accounting for different levels of use were as follows (2nd period figures reported in parentheses):

4% (5%) of the titles	27% (26%) of total use
8% (9%) of the titles	38% (37%) of total use
28% (29%) of the titles	68% (64%) of total use

(697)

■ A 1972-73 study of periodical usage in the Education-Psychology Library at Ohio State University *showed that*, based on 57,332 periodical circulation transactions generated over an almost complete academic year, 100 titles (out of 804) provided 72.4% of the materials circulated, and 150 titles provided 83.8% of the materials circulated. Further, 23.9% of the 804 titles were not used at all, and 48% were used no more than 5 times.
(455)

■ A study reported in 1974 investigating the materials used by master's and doctoral candidates completing theses after 1966 in public health at 5 universities (Yale; Harvard; University of California, Los Angeles; University of California, Berkeley; and California State University, Northridge), involving 3,456 citations taken from 44 theses, *showed that* 50% of the citations were accounted for by 40 different journal titles, while

63% of the citations were accounted for by 115 different journal titles.
(698)

■ A 1978 study in the Biology Library of Temple University involving a citation analysis of publications by full-time Temple biology faculty, doctoral dissertations of Temple biology Ph.D.'s, and preliminary doctoral qualifying briefs written by second-year graduate biology students at Temple during the 3-year period 1975-77 (153 source items with 4,155 citations) *showed that*, of 3,739 citations in 336 journals, the cumulative number of citations by journal rank was as follows:

top 5 journals	1,033 (28%)	citations
top 10 journals	1,585 (42%)	citations
top 60 journals	3,013 (81%)	citations
top 100 journals	3,228 (89%)	citations
top 300 journals	3,703 (99%)	citations **(650)**

School

■ A study reported in 1979 of term paper bibliographies of high school students (270 students/papers from 6 high schools, involving 3,165 identifiable references) *showed that*, of 602 periodical citations, 6 journal titles accounted for 193 (32%) periodical citations; 16 titles accounted for 301 (50%) periodical citations; 52 titles accounted for 457 (75.9%) citations; and 170 titles accounted for 602 (100%) citations. **(564)**

■ A survey reported in 1980 of 1,178 high school students (representing a sample from 73 classes, 15 schools, and 5 school districts), including a study of their bibliographic citations to periodical articles, *showed that*, of 1,490 citations, 6 primary periodicals accounted for 30.2% of the citations. 9.1% of the citations referred to *Newsweek*, 7.5% to *Time*, 5.1% to *U.S. News*, 3.7% to *Sports Illustrated*, 2.5% to *New Republic*, 2.3 to *Saturday Review*. (Taken from a ranked list of the 20 most heavily cited periodicals.)
(219)

■ A 1981 study of 53 ninth-grade honors students in science in a surburban Philadelphia public high school *showed that*, of the 189 magazine citations in the 47 bibliographies 50% of all citations were from 8 magazines. These were: *Newsweek* (9%), *Time* (8%), *National Geographic* (7%), *U.S. News* (6%), *Business Week* (6%), *Forbes* (5%), *Science* (5%), *Fortune* (4%). (Taken from a list of 13 magazines in rank order.)
(222)

Periodicals

Special

■ A study reported in 1964 of journal circulation in the Columbia and Yale Medical libraries during a 6-month period for Columbia and a 1-year period for Yale [total circulation not given] *showed that* the number of journals needed to supply various use levels was as follows:

4 journal titles	10% of total journal use
10 journal titles	20% of total journal use
63 journal titles	50% of total journal use
262 journal titles	80% of total journal use
920 journal titles	100% of total journal use

(670)

■ A 1972 study at the University of Minnesota Bio-Medical Library concerning in-house use of periodicals during 2 1-week periods (1st period: 727 uses involving 269 different titles; 2nd period: 533 uses involving 209 different titles) *showed that* the numbers of titles accounting for different levels of use were as follows (2nd period figures reported in parentheses):

4% (5%) of the titles	27% (26%) of total use
8% (9%) of the titles	38% (37%) of total use
28% (29%) of the titles	68% (64%) of total use

(697)

Periodicals—Core

General

■ 2 surveys, 1 conducted in 1973 (sample size: 300; responding: 259 or 86.3%) and then repeated in 1978 (sample size: 429; responding: 357 or 83.2%) of ACRL (Association of College and Research Libraries) academic librarians concerning professional reading *showed that* the 4 most frequently read journals in each of the 2 surveys were as follows:

IN 1973	READ BY
American Libraries	90.0% of sample
College and Research Libraries	86.1% of sample
Library Journal	69.9% of sample
Library Resources and Technical Services	57.9% of sample

continued

IN 1978	READ BY	
American Libraries	92.2% of sample	
College and Research Libraries	88.6% of sample	
Library Journal	69.3% of sample	
Journal of Academic Librarianship	44.0% of sample	**(508)**

Academic

■ A study reported in 1964 of journal circulation in the Columbia and Yale Medical libraries during a 6-month period for Columbia and a 1-year period for Yale [total circulation not given] *showed that* the 6 most frequently used journal titles were:

Biochimica et Biophysica Acta	238 uses
Journal of Biological Chemistry	206 uses
American Journal of Medicine	169 uses
Nature	167 uses
Lancet	157 uses
New England Journal of Medicine	145 uses

(670)

■ A 1973 survey of physicists in 6 universities of the greater Boston area (Boston University, Brandeis, Brown, Harvard, MIT, and Northeastern) to determine how they meet their information needs (sample size: 339; responding: 179 or 52.8%) *showed that* the 3 most frequently reported journals scanned weekly by 179 responding physicists were *Physics Review Letters* (73 or 40.8% respondents), *Physics Reviews* (66 or 36.9% respondents), and *Physics Letters* (30 or 16.8% respondents). Although in a different order, these were also the 3 journals which physicists ranked most important. **(404)**

■ 2 surveys, 1 conducted in 1973 (sample size: 300; responding: 259 or 86.3%) and then repeated in 1978 (sample size: 429; responding: 357 or 83.2%) of ACRL (Association of College and Research Libraries) academic librarians concerning professional reading *showed that* the 4 most frequently read journals in each of the 2 surveys were as follows:

IN 1973	READ BY
American Libraries	90.0% of sample
College and Research Libraries	86.1% of sample
Library Journal	69.9% of sample
Library Resources and Technical Services	57.9% of sample

continued

Periodicals

IN 1978	READ BY	
American Libraries	92.2% of sample	
College and Research Libraries	88.6% of sample	
Library Journal	69.3% of sample	
Journal of Academic Librarianship	44.0% of sample	**(508)**

■ A 1977 study at the University of Illinois Law Library of periodical usage over a 3-month period (275 periodicals, all indexed in 1977 *Index to Legal Periodicals*; 90% of the data came from in-house use, although reserve, ILL, and faculty charges were also counted) *showed that* the 6 most used periodicals (out of 195 listed) were:

Harvard Law Review	145 uses	
University of Illinois Law Forum	135 uses	
Yale Law Journal	92 uses	
Illinois Bar Journal	84 uses	
Northwestern University Law Review	76 uses	
University of Chicago Law Review	70 uses	**(360)**

■ A survey reported in 1978 of a stratified random sample of 811 sociologists from 183 graduate departments (response rate: 526 or 64.86%) reporting which social science journals they regularly read *showed that* the top 7 journals read regularly by respondents were *American Sociological Review* (83.84%), *American Sociologist* (78.89%), *American Journal of Sociology* (65.01%), *Social Forces* (40.49%), *Society/Trans-action* (30.93%), *Social Problems* (29.46%), and *Psychology Today* (24.14%).
(261)

■ A 1978 study in the Biology Library of Temple University, involving a citation analysis of publications by full-time Temple biology faculty, doctoral dissertations of Temple biology Ph.D.'s, and preliminary doctoral qualifying briefs written by second-year graduate biology students at Temple during the 3-year period 1975-77 (153 source items with 4,155 citations), *showed that* the 5 most frequently cited journals (out of 60 listed) were:

Proceedings of the National Academy of Science (USA)	307 (8.2%) citations
Journal of Cellular Biology	198 (5.3%) citations
Nature	185 (4.9%) citations

continued

Science	177 (4.7%) citations	
Journal of Molecular Biology	166 (4.4%) citations	**(650)**

School

■ A study reported in 1978 of 19 bibliographic tools listing materials for young adults, involving a total of 19,405 titles in conjunction with a purposeful sample of 270 papers collected from college-bound high school students (grades 10 through 12) in a large metropolitan area from a wide variety of schools, *showed that* the 3 most frequently cited journal titles in the 270 student papers were:

Newsweek	54 (8.9%) citations	
Time	48 (8.0%) citations	
Scientific American	29 (4.8%) citations	**(523)**

■ A study reported in 1979 of term paper bibliographies of high school students (270 students/papers from 6 high schools, involving 3,165 identifiable references) *showed that* the 6 most frequently cited journals were as follows:

Newsweek	54 (8.9%) total citations	
Time	48 (7.9%) total citations	
Scientific American	29 (4.8%) total citations	
American Heritage	23 (3.8%) total citations	
New Republic	20 (3.3%) total citations	
US News and World Report	19 (3.1%) total citations	**(564)**

■ A survey reported in 1980 of 1,178 high school students (representing a sample from 73 classes, 15 schools, and 5 school districts), including a study of their bibliographic citations to periodical articles, *showed that*, of 1,490 citations, 6 primary periodicals accounted for 30.2% of the citations. 9.1% of the citations referred to *Newsweek*, 7.5% to *Time*, 5.1% to *U.S. News*, 3.7% to *Sports Illustrated*, 2.5% to *New Republic*, 2.3 to *Saturday Review*. (Taken from a ranked list of the 20 most heavily cited periodicals.) **(219)**

■ A 1981 study of 53 ninth-grade honors students in science in a suburban Philadelphia public high school *showed that*, of the 189 magazine citations in the 47 bibliographies 50% of all citations were from 8 magazines. These were *Newsweek* (9%), *Time* (8%), *National Geographic* (7%), *U.S. News*

Periodicals

(6%), *Business Week* (6%), *Forbes* (5%), *Science* (5%), and *Fortune* (4%). (Taken from a list of 13 magazines in rank order.)　　　　　　　　**(222)**

Special

■ A study reported in 1964 of journal circulation in the Columbia and Yale Medical libraries during a 6-month period for Columbia and a 1-year period for Yale [total circulation not given] *showed that* the 6 most frequently used journal titles were:

Biochimica et Biophysica Acta	238 uses
Journal of Biological Chemistry	206 uses
American Journal of Medicine	169 uses
Nature	167 uses
Lancet	157 uses
New England Journal of Medicine	145 uses

(670)

■ A 1977 study at the University of Illinois Law Library of periodical usage over a 3-month period (275 periodicals, all indexed in 1977 *Index to Legal Periodicals*; 90% of the data came from in-house use, although reserve, ILL, and faculty charges were also counted) *showed that* the 6 most used periodicals (out of 195 listed) were:

Harvard Law Review	145 uses
University of Illinois Law Forum	135 uses
Yale Law Journal	92 uses
Illinois Bar Journal	84 uses
Northwestern University Law Review	76 uses
University of Chicago Law Review	70 uses

(360)

Periodicals—Type of Patron

Academic

■ A 1-year study during 1964-65 at the Yale Medical School Library concerning patron use patterns of library materials (based on 34,825 book/journal circulations) *showed that* 20,563 journal circulations were distributed among members of the medical school as follows (accounting for 74.6% of the journal use):

full-time faculty   32.0% journal uses
students   27.2% journal uses
house officers   11.6% journal uses
part-time faculty   3.8% journal uses   **(675)**

■ A 1968 study of graduate students at the University of Michigan concerning their use of periodical literature (sample size: 399; responding: 338 or 85%) *showed that* approximately 78% of the students use the library about once a week, while 61% reported using the periodical literature about once a week. **(195)**

Ibid. . . . *showed that*, of those reporting use of the periodical literature during the term (284), 20% were interested in general/professional reading; 65% were interested in research reading; 7% were interested in both; and 8% did not respond. **(195)**

Ibid. . . . *showed that*, of those reporting use of the periodical literature during the term (284), 49.3% had the precise reference to the article before coming to the library, while 50% did not. **(195)**

Ibid. . . . *showed that*, of those reporting use of the periodical literature during the term (284), 80.3% found the article for which they were looking, while 16.9% did not, and 2.8% did not respond. **(195)**

Ibid. . . . *showed that* respondents who indicated they used the periodical literature at least once a week were 79% of all users of the science libraries and 68% of all users of nonscience libraries. **(195)**

■ A 1977 study of social science faculty use of periodicals at the University of Illinois (population: 320 faculty; responding: 226; usable: 69% [no raw number given]) *showed that* 204 (93%) respondents reported using the "serial literature" in the previous academic year. **(474)**

Ibid. . . . *showed that*, of the 204 respondents who had used the serial collection in the previous year, 7% reported "almost never" having used the serial collection in the previous year, while 25% reported using the serial collection at least once a week. The average use of the serial collection was "once every two to three weeks." **(474)**

Periodicals

Ibid. . . . *showed that*, of the 204 respondents who had used the serial collection in the previous year, the most recent time respondents used the serial collection they were:

> looking for a specific article (47%)
> looking for information in their subject (24%)
> keeping up with the literature (19%)
> browsing (3%)
> other (7%) **(474)**

Ibid. . . . *showed that*, of the 204 respondents who had used the serial collection in the previous year, 97% reported reading journals regularly, with the number of journals regularly read ranging from 1 to 20 with a median of 8. 88% of the respondents subscribed to 1 or more of the journals they reguarly read, with the median number of subscriptions 4. 67% of the respondents read at least 1 journal in the library, with the median number read in the library 2. **(474)**

Ibid. . . . *showed that*, of the 204 respondents who had used the serial collection in the previous year, the following had "usually" served as sources of the article desired (multiple responses allowed):

bibliographies/footnotes in journals	69.4%	respondents
bibliographies/footnotes in books	51.3%	respondents
subject bibliographies	17.0%	respondents
abstracting journals	12.6%	respondents
colleagues	13.6%	respondents
librarians or library staff	2.4%	respondents
other	14.8%	respondents **(474)**

Ibid. . . . *showed that*, of the 204 respondents who had used the serial collection in the previous year, the following action was "usually" taken when a desired item was not in the collection:

borrow from colleagues	27.7%	respondents
initiate interlibrary loan	17.6%	respondents
secure reprint from author	14.6%	respondents
abandon search	9.3%	respondents
request that it be purchased	8.3%	respondents
purchase	7.6%	respondents
consult library collections other than those at the University of Illinois	3.3%	respondents

(474)

■ A survey reported in 1978 of a stratified random sample of 811 sociologists from 183 graduate departments (response rate: 526 or 64.86%) reporting which social science journals they regularly read *showed that*, of the top 20 journals, 40.00% are interdisciplinary journals or journals from other social science disciplines. **(261)**

Special

■ A 1-year study during 1964-65 at the Yale Medical School Library concerning patron use patterns of library materials (based on 34,825 book/journal circulations) *showed that* 20,563 journal circulations were distributed among members of the medical school as follows (accounting for 74.6% of the journal use):

full-time faculty	32.0% journal uses
students	27.2% journal uses
house officers	11.6% journal uses
part-time faculty	3.8% journal uses

(675)

Reference Materials and Tools

Academic

■ A 1968 survey concerning purchase and use of loose leaf business services of 92 public libraries specializing in business reference service and 47 graduate business school libraries (139 total; 67 or 73% of public libraries responding and 39 or 83% of business school libraries responding) *showed that* over half of the responding business school libraries took and reported frequent use of the following services:

SERVICE	% TAKING
U.S. Dept. of Commerce Overseas Business Reports	69
Funk & Scott Financial Index	69
Moody's Investors Service	97
Standard & Poor's Corporation Records	67
Standard & Poor's Industry Surveys	95
Standard & Poor's Trade and Securities Stats.	87
Value Line Service	71
Wiesenberger Investment Report	62
BNA Labor Relations Reporter	67
BNA Collective Bargaining Negotiations & Contr.	62
BNA Labor Relations Expediter	51

continued

Reference Materials and Tools 327

SERVICE	% TAKING
CCH Standard Federal Tax Reporter	69
CCH State Tax Guide	51
Prentice-Hall Federal Tax Service (complete)	71

(138)

■ A survey reported in 1981 of historians listed in the 1978 *Directory of American Scholars* concerning their use of and attitudes toward periodicals (survey size: 767 historians, although not all questionnaires could be delivered; responding: 360 or 46.9%, with respondents tending to be younger and with a higher scholarly productivity record than nonrespondents) *showed that* the 5 most frequently reported indexing and abstracting services (out of 8) used for current research were (multiple responses allowed):

Readers' Guide	132 (36.7%) respondents	
Historical Abstracts	113 (31.4%) respondents	
America: History and Life	86 (23.9%) respondents	
Social Sciences Index	73 (20.3%) respondents	
Humanities Index	66 (18.3%) respondents	**(780)**

Ibid. . . . *showed that* respondents clearly preferred bibliographic tools providing abstracts over those providing simple author and title entries. Specifically, when asked to compare the value of bibliographic tools providing abstracts in contrast to simple author and title entries, 23.7% reported the abstracts "about the same"; 46.4% reported the abstracts "somewhat more satisfactory"; and 29.9% reported the abstracts "much more satisfactory." **(780)**

Public

■ A 1966 survey of 21,385 adult (12 years old or older) public library users in the Baltimore-Washington metropolitan region of Maryland, conducted during a 6-week period, entering the library (79.1% of patrons approached filled out the survey instrument) *showed that* the use made of the library was as follows (multiple responses allowed): browsing (43.1%), reference books (22.1%), library catalogs (19.0%), help from a librarian (16.0%), consulting books or magazines (12.4%), read new magazines or newspapers (8.7%), periodical indexes (5.7%), re-

cordings (2.7%), films (0.7%), other (2.0%), and no response (11.1%).
(301)

■ A 1968 survey concerning purchase and use of loose leaf business services of 92 public libraries specializing in business reference service and 47 graduate business school libraries (139 total; 67 or 73% of public libraries responding and 39 or 83% of business school libraries responding) *showed that* over half of the responding public libraries took and reported frequent use of the following services:

SERVICE	% TAKING
U.S. Dept. of Commerce Overseas Business Reports	70
Moody's Investors Service	96
Standard and Poor's Corporation Records	51
Standard and Poor's Industry Surveys	63
Standard and Poor's Stock Reports OTC	52
Value Line Service	61
Wiesenberger Investment Report	56
CCH State Tax Guide	57

(138)

School

■ A study reported in 1978 of 19 bibliographic tools listing materials for young adults, involving a total of 19,405 titles in conjunction with a purposeful sample of 270 papers collected from college-bound high school students (grades 10 through 12) in a large metropolitan area from a wide variety of schools, *showed that* the proportion of materials referenced in the bibliographies of the 270 papers was monographic references (67%); journal references (20%); and other, including encyclopedias, documents, primary materials, etc. (13%). Further, only 14% of the 270 papers had half or more of their total references to materials that were 5 years old or less at the time the paper was written. **(523)**

■ A study reported in 1979 of term paper bibliographies of high school students (270 students/papers from 6 high schools, involving 3,165 identifiable references) *showed that*, of 424 miscellaneous citations, the following distribution obtained:

newspapers	141 (33.3%) misc. citations
encyclopedias	120 (28.3%) misc. citations
government documents and/or pamphlet references	80 (18.9%) misc. citations
nonprint sources, including interviews	23 (05.4%) misc. citations
other special materials	44 (10.4%) misc. citations **(564)**

Relation to Personal Collection

Academic

■ A 1971 survey of owners (primarily academics) of personal library collections (sample selected from authors of 300 single-author articles published during 1969-70 in one of 3 broad areas: humanities, social science, and science; 178 authors responding of which 175 owned personal collections) *showed that*, of the 5,175 citations made in the 178 articles, 3,055 (59%) came from materials in the authors' personal libraries; 1,320 (25.5%) came from materials in either the departmental or main library; 530 (10.2%) came from materials in libraries in other cities or countries; and 270 (5.2%) came from other sources. **(258)**

Ibid. . . . *showed that* a physical check of the libraries reported used by 45 (25%) of the respondents indicated that the 244 (21%) of the cited materials that they reported as in the library were in fact in the library, as well as 592 (88%) of the personal collection works cited by this group.
(258)

Ibid. . . . *showed that* the location of cited materials was statistically significantly different for science and social science materials as compared to humanities materials (significant at the .001 level). Personal collections accounted for 983 (73.9%) of the science materials, 1,366 (73.3%) of the social science materials, and 3,055 (59.0% of the humanities materials; departmental/main libraries accounted for 278 (20.6%) of the science, 366 (19.6%) of the social science, and 676 (34.2%) of the humanities materials; libraries in other cities and countries accounted for 17 (1.3%) of the science, 33 (1.8%) of the social science, and 480 (24.3%) of the humanities materials; while "other" accounted for 57 (4.2%) of the science, 100 (5.2%) of the social science, and 113 (5.6%) of the humanities materials.
(258)

Restrictions

Academic

■ A 1971 survey of law school libraries (population: 147 ABA-approved libraries; responding: 108 or 73.5%) *showed that* 51 (47.2%) respondents attempted to exclude at least 1 group from library use. **(388)**

Ibid. . . . *showed that* the 4 most commonly given reasons for excluding certain classes of patrons were:

inadequate staff to administer extra services	51 (47.2% respondents)
insufficient seating capacity	50 (46.3% respondents)
security of collection	48 (44.4% respondents)
insufficient library materials for other than primary patrons	35 (32.4% respondents)

(388)

■ A survey reported in 1983 of U.S. dental school libraries concerning their service to dental practitioners (population: 60 dental school libraries; responding: 53 or 88%) *showed that*, of 51 respondents, 36 (70.6%) libraries reported it important to offer library services to dental practitioners; 12 (23.5%) reported that offering such service was important but could not provide such service due to limited resources; and 3 (5.9%) reported that only faculty and students are served by the dental library.
(752)

Special

■ A 1971 survey of law school libraries (population: 147 ABA-approved libraries; responding: 108 or 73.5%) *showed that* 51 (47.2%) respondents attempted to exclude at least 1 group from library use. **(388)**

Ibid. . . . *showed that* the 4 most commonly given reasons for excluding certain classes of patrons were:

inadequate staff to administer extra services	51 (47.2% respondents)
insufficient seating capacity	50 (46.3% respondents)
security of collection	48 (44.4% respondents)
insufficient library materials for other than primary patrons	35 (32.4% respondents)

(388)

■ A survey reported in 1983 of U.S. dental school libraries concerning their service to dental practitioners (population: 60 dental school libraries; responding: 53 or 88%) *showed that*, of 51 respondents, 36 (70.6%) libraries reported it important to offer library services to dental practitioners; 12 (23.5%) reported that offering such service was important but

could not provide such service due to limited resources; and 3 (5.9%) reported that only faculty and students are served by the dental library.
(752)

Stack Policy

General

■ A pilot study at the Library of Congress in 1960 of patron stack use based on a random sample (sample size 200; 181 responding) of patrons in the book stacks *showed that* 55% were in the stacks to obtain specific books for which they already knew the call numbers, while 38% were browsers. (The remainder were there for both or other reasons.) The majority of patrons in the stacks for work-related reasons were looking for specific books; the majority (57%) in the stacks for recreational or other non-work related reasons were browsers. 123 (68%) of the sample were LC employees. **(068)**

Academic

■ A survey reported in 1977 of moderate-sized (120,000-500,000 volumes) U.S. academic libraries listed in the 1972-73 *American Library Directory* (survey size: 200; responding: 147 or 74%) *showed that*, for current-issue stack areas, 118 libraries (80%) reported open stacks; 16 (11%) reported closed stacks; and 13 (9%) reported some "other" arrangement. For bound volume stack areas, 139 (95%) libraries reported open stacks; 5 (3%) libraries reported closed stacks; and 1 (0.7%) library reported "other" arrangement. **(454)**

■ A study reported in 1978 at Indiana University, Bloomington, of materials requested through a delivery service to faculty in the political science and economics departments during a 32-month period (October 1972-June 1975), involving 39 political scientists and 14 economists (40-50% of the faculty in the departments) and 5,478 articles from 620 different journals and newspapers, *showed that* availability of the materials requested on the delivery service, based on 2,544 requests and a library policy that does not allow periodicals to circulate outside of the library, was as follows:

90% of the material was immediately available;

98% of the material was ultimately available from the library's holdings;

and an additional 1% was available through interlibrary loan. **(421)**

■ A study reported in 1980 over a 6-year period (1973-1978) at West Virginia University main library concerning the effect of switching from closed to open stacks in 1976 with a collection of just under 1 million volumes of primarily humanities and social science materials *showed that* annual nonreserve circulation decreased from 194,899 in 1973 to 146,949 in 1978. During this period a substantial growth in enrollment took place. **(484)**

Ibid. . . . *showed that* loss rate and disorder did not appear to increase under the open stack system. Specifically, for books requested on the delivery system the number that could not be accounted for during the closed stacks system (1974, no number of requests given) was 15.0%, while 2 studies of books requested on the delivery system after the stacks were opened showed 11.2% unavailable in 1977 and 12.2% unavailable in 1978 (no number of requests given). **(484)**

Ibid. . . . *showed that* building use increased after the switch to open stacks. Specifically, in 1973 the annual building use was 431,285 patrons, while in 1978 the annual building use was 500,178 patrons, even though circulation decreased during this period. **(484)**

■ A 1981 survey of academic libraries selected randomly from OCLC academic library participants concerning the issue of university collections, i.e., collections of publications by the university's own faculty and affiliates (sample size: 184; responding: 103 or 56%) *showed that* 61% of the respondents reported their university collections were housed in closed access areas, with 79% reporting that the material was noncirculating. However, 86 (83%) did report purchasing duplicates of the university collection for circulation. **(647)**

Special

■ A 1974 survey of a random sample of U.S. museum libraries (including history, art, and science museums) listed in the 1973 *Official Museum Directory* (population: 2,556; sample size: 856; responding: 374 or 43.7%) *showed that* 46% reported open stacks; 49% reported closed stacks; and 5% reported open stacks with restrictions. Further, 76% of the libraries did not lend books. **(412)**

Subject Areas

Academic

■ A 1-year study during 1964-65 at the Yale Medical Library concerning book and journal circulation (34,825 circulations) *showed that* not all subject areas covered in the library are equally used. Specifically, of 67 subject fields covered in the library, "over half" of the book and journal circulations fell into 7 subject fields, while 82% of the circulations fell into 21 of the subject fields. **(674)**

■ A 1968-69 study over a period of 9 months of the use of materials at the Midwest Regional Medical Library (John Crerar Library), involving a random sample of 1,071 requests for material, *showed that*, of 1,071 requests, the 2 subject areas in which the most materials were requested were "Pathology, Disease and Treatment" (315 or 29.4%) and "Materia Medica" (268 or 25.0%). **(688)**

■ Studies at the University of Southwestern Louisiana and the South Dakota School of Mines and Technology on circulation data gathered during academic 1969-70 and 1967-68, respectively, *showed that* books whose class numbers matched profiles of class numbers associated with courses taught were more likely to circulate than books whose class numbers did not match the profiles. The Louisiana study was based on 56,828 items circulated vs. 115,201 items not circulated and was statistically signifcant at the .005 level. The South Dakota study was based on 7,696 items circulated vs. 40,433 items not circulated and was statistically significant at the .005 level. **(211)**

■ A survey reported in 1978 of 31 Ph.D. dissertations in the field of business/management (13 from the State University of New York at Buffalo and 18 from SUNYAB incoming faculty but completed at other schools) *showed that* the 7 most frequently cited subject areas (based on 1,161 citations to monographs and serials) were:

business (HF 5001-6351)	14.7% citations
economics: labor (HD 4801-8942)	11.5% citations
economics: production (HD 1-100)	10.8% citations
psychology (BF)	8.2% citations
sociology (HM-HX)	7.3% citations
finance (HG)	6.4% citations
economic theory	6.0% citations

(461)

■ A survey reported in 1978 of a stratified random sample of 811 sociologists from 183 graduate departments (response rate: 526 or 64.86%) reporting which social science journals they regularly read *showed that*, of the top 20 journals, 40.00% were interdisciplinary journals or journals from other social science disciplines. **(261)**

Ibid. . . . *showed that* comparing the rank order list of regularly read journals with the rank order of sociology journals by citation indicated that 55% of the 20 most reported regularly read journals were found on the list of the 20 most cited journals. However, the citation list tended to focus on interdisciplinary and nonsociological journals, whereas the regularly read list had a "distinctive, disciplinary focus." **(261)**

■ A study reported in 1979 of the degree to which students in 43 undergraduate and 19 graduate academic areas used books classed in the same academic area as their major, based on undergraduate and graduate book circulation during academic years 1974-75 and 1975-76 at the University of Southwestern Louisiana, *showed that* for undergraduates the number of books used in their major academic area ranged from 71.7% for music majors to 0% for majors in vocational education. The median fell between 18.3% (applied arts majors) and 17.9% (French majors). **(476)**

Ibid. . . . *showed that* for graduate students the number of books used in their major area of study ranged from 87.4% for graduate music students to 2.2% for graduate management students, with a median of 45.7% for graduate computer science students. **(476)**

Ibid. . . . *showed that* for undergraduates the number of books in each discipline charged to nonmajors ranged from 100% in vocational education to 24.7% in nursing, with the median falling between 81.9% (home economics) and 81.6% (applied arts). **(476)**

Ibid. . . . *showed that* for graduate students the number of books in each discipline charged to graduate students not in that discipline ranged from 98.5% in management to 13.1% in computer science, with the median 55.2% in biology. **(476)**

Ibid. . . . *showed that* for the 19 academic areas common to both undergraduates and graduates the degree to which undergraduate majors used materials classed in their major area of study was 23.8% overall, while the degree to which graduate students used materials in their discipline was

Subject Areas

47.0% overall. Further, for undergraduates 80.2% of the materials in each subject area were circulated to nonmajors, while for graduates 57.2% of the material in each subject area was circulated to graduate students not in that discipline. **(476)**

Public

■ A 1966 survey of 21,385 adult (12 years old or older) public library users in the Baltimore-Washington metropolitan region of Maryland, conducted during a 6-week period, entering the library (79.1% of patrons approached filled out the survey instrument) *showed that*, of the 6,212 respondents who were seeking materials or information on a subject and who named a subject, 45.2% reported a social science subject; 30.6% reported a humanities subject; and 24.2% reported a science/technology subject. The 2 main social science subjects were history (40.7%) and business/economics (14.8%); the 2 main humanities subjects were literature (53.8%) and art (24.8%); and the two main science and technology subjects were engineering (17.5%) and medicine (12.2%). **(301)**

■ A 1973 experimental project with SDI service in the Mideastern Michigan Library Cooperative (a random sample of 2,498 were invited to participate; 96 responded) *showed that* the most popular SDI topics were fiction with the following headings: fiction with a twentieth-century setting (50%), mystery-suspense (43%), historical fiction (38%). The 3 most popular nonfiction categories were drawing and decorative arts (35%), recreation (30%), and psychology (30%). **(144)**

Special

■ A 1-year study during 1964-65 at the Yale Medical Library concerning book and journal circulation (34,825 circulations) *showed that* not all subject areas covered in the library are equally used. Specifically, of 67 subject fields covered in the library, "over half" of the book and journal circulations fell into 7 subject fields, while 82% of the circulations fell into 21 of the subject fields. **(674)**

■ A 1968-69 study over a period of 9 months of the use of materials at the Midwest Regional Medical Library (John Crerar Library), involving a random sample of 1,071 requests for material, *showed that*, of 1,071 requests, the 2 subject areas in which the most materials were requested were "Pathology, Disease and Treatment" (315 or 29.4%) and "Materia Medica" (268 or 25.0%). **(688)**

Success Rate and Problems—General Issues

Academic

■ A 1964 study at the Yale Medical Library involving patron use of books (survey size: 831 borrowers; responding: 430) during a 5-month period *showed that* 338 (78.6%) borrowers reported they had obtained what they wanted from the book. **(672)**

■ A 1968-69 study over a period of 9 months of the use of materials at the Midwest Regional Medical Library (John Crerar Library), involving a random sample of 1,071 requests for material, *showed that*, of 1,058 requests, 701 (66.3%) were filled, while 357 (33.7%) were not filled. Of those requests filled, the time required was as follows:

same day or 1 day	265 (37.8%)	requests
2 days	127 (18.1%)	requests
3-7 days	262 (37.4%)	requests
8-14 days	42 (6.0%)	requests
15 days and over	5 (0.7%)	requests

(688)

■ A 1971 study of journal availability at the Woodward Biomedical Library (University of British Columbia, Canada) during a 12-day period *showed that*, out of 4,326 journal items, 370 (8.6%) were not found immediately. The reasons for unavailability were as follows:

title not held or issue not received	100 (27%)	items
in use or awaiting reshelving	98 (26%)	items
being bound	66 (18%)	items
user errors	41 (11%)	items
administrative reasons (on "hold" shelf, misshelved, etc.)	40 (11%)	items
unspecified reasons	25 (7%)	items

(692)

■ A 1973 survey of physicists in 6 universities of the greater Boston area (Boston University, Brandeis, Brown, Harvard, MIT, and Northeastern) to determine how they meet their information needs (sample size: 339; responding: 179 or 52.8%) *showed that* 83.2% reported always or usually finding what they want when assisted by a librarian, compared to 76.6%

Success Rate and Problems

who reported always or usually finding what they want without assistance from a librarian. **(404)**

■ A review in 1974-75 of faculty book requests in the Economics and Political Science Library of Indiana University *showed that* 24% of the books immediately available had multiple copies, while only 15.8% of those not immediately available had more than one copy. **(012)**

Ibid. . . . *showed that* book availability was unrelated to subject of book.
(012)

Ibid. . . . *showed that* document availability over time was as follows:

immediately available	48%
after 1 week	59%
after 2 weeks	73%
after 3 weeks	84%

(012)

■ A survey in 1976 of 999 library users at San Jose State University *showed that* 29% of the items patrons could not find in the book stacks were in fact in their proper places. **(010)**

■ A study reported in 1977 at the University of Minnesota Twin Cities campus concerning attitudes held by heads of academic units toward departmental libraries independent of the university library system (sample size: 167; responding: 108 or 64.7%, including 67 respondents with independent departmental libraries and 41 respondents without such libraries) *showed that* 67% [no raw number given] of the respondents with independent departmental libraries reported finding materials sought after in the official [main] library more than 50% of the time, while 83% [no raw number given] of the respondents without independent departmental libraries reported finding desired materials more than 50% of the time.
(451)

■ A 1977 survey of faculty at Clark University, the College of the Holy Cross, and the Worcester Polytechnic Institute (population: 474; sample size: 121; responding: 87 or 72%) concerning faculty perception of academic libraries *showed that* broad subject area correlated with expectation of success in a known-item search. Specifically, 30 (85.7%) of the science faculty members, 15 (68.2%) of the humanities, and 12 (52.1%) of the social science faculty "always" or "frequently" expected success with a known-item search. These were statistically significant differences at the .02 significance level. **(478)**

Ibid. . . . *showed that* faculty rank and length of time at an institution correlated with expectation of success in a known-item search. Specifically, 28 (90.3%) of the full professors, 19 (70.4%) of the associate professors, and 15 (53.6%) of the assistant professors, lecturers, and instructors "always" or "frequently" expected success with a known-item search. These were statistically significant differences at the .003 significance level. Further, 42 (85.7%) of the faculty who had been at the institution for 7 or more years "always" or "frequently" expected success with a known-item search, compared to 20 (55.5%) of the faculty whose stay had been less than 7 years. This was a statistically significant difference at the .004 significance level. **(478)**

■ A study reported in 1978 at the undergraduate library of the University of Tennessee, Knoxville, of patron success rate in finding books over a 5-week period (sample size: 1,010 patrons; responding: 503 or 49.5%), involving 2,375 titles *showed that* patrons found 1,278 of the titles immediately available in the library for a hit rate of 53.8%. **(466)**

Ibid. . . . *showed that*, of the 1,097 titles not immediately found, 117 (10.7%) titles were on reserve; 152 (13.9%) were actually on the shelf; and 828 (75.5%) were actually not available in the library. Of the 2,375 titles patrons searched for, 34.9% were actually not available in the library. **(466)**

Ibid. . . . *showed that* the 828 titles not available involved 1,025 volumes. The 2 main reasons for unavailability were volumes checked out (729 or 71.1%) and volumes unaccounted for (208 or 20.3%). Binding accounted for 22 (2.1%) volumes, while interlibrary loan accounted for 2 (0.2%) volumes. **(466)**

■ A study reported in 1978 at Indiana University, Bloomington, of materials requested through a delivery service to faculty in the political science and economics departments during a 32-month period (October 1972-June 1975), involving 39 political scientists and 14 economists (40-50% of the faculty in the departments) and 5,478 articles from 620 different journals and newspapers, *showed that* availability of the materials

Success Rate and Problems

requested on the delivery service, based on 2,544 requests and a library policy that did not allow periodicals to circulate outside of the library was as follows:

90% of the material was immediately available;

98% of the material was ultimately available from the library's holdings;

and an additional 1% was available through interlibrary loan. **(421)**

Ibid. . . . *showed that* the chief reason for a journal's being unavailable was reshelving, which accounted for 56% of the unavailable journals.
(421)

■ A study reported in 1980 of periodical accessibility conducted in a large academic library (involving 31 students searching for a total of 115 citations) *showed that* the 30% inaccessibility due to library operations failure broke down as follows:

torn out articles	9%
missing volumes	8%
binding	5%
circulation	5%
issues never received or successfully claimed	3%

(029)

Ibid. . . . *showed that* students were able to find 55% of the titles; 15% were not found due to user error; 5% were not found due to in-house circulation; and 25% not found due to library operations problems (e.g., at bindery, lost, etc.). **(029)**

Ibid. . . . *showed that* 61% of the students failed to find 1 or more of their 5 citations. The greatest cause of error was the separation of the microform and bound collection, which accounted for 83% of the user error. **(029)**

■ A 1980 survey of book stacks patrons in the Main Library at the University of Illinois, Urbana, involving success in locating both paged and self-sought monographs (379 patrons and 509 books) *showed that* 366 (71.9%) items were located immediately. Of those not located immediately (143 items), the following reasons obtained:

not owned by the Library	10 (2.0%) of total
bibliographic/location errors	48 (9.4%) of total

continued

circulating	29 (5.7%) of total	
library failures	25 (4.9%) of total	
patron/page mistakes	31 (6.1%) of total	**(518)**

■ A study reported in 1983 at a medium-sized academic library, involving 504 volumes chosen at random from the card catalog, *showed that* 437 (86.7%) were available on the shelf; 25 (5.0%) were in circulation; and 42 (8.3%) were not available for other reasons. **(521)**

■ A survey reported in 1983 of circulation professionals in public and academic libraries with more than 50,000 volumes concerning their interest in and use of management data (e.g., loss rates, effectiveness of fines) and the formal methods by which management data was generated (e.g., sampling, statistical tests) (survey size: 200 professionals; responding: 132 or 66%) *showed that* 20 (20.4%) respondents did not identify their periodical citations correctly (i.e., did not identify a major element correctly, such as periodical name, volume, or date), including 26% of the undergraduates and 12% of the graduate students. **(804)**

Public

■ A 1966 survey of 21,385 adult (12 years old or older) public library users in the Baltimore-Washington metropolitan region of Maryland, conducted during a 6-week period, entering the library (79.1% of patrons approached filled out the survey instrument) *showed that*, of those unsatisified respondents giving reasons for their dissatisfaction, 47.0% wanted a book (or books) that was in circulation; 35.9% wanted a book not in [owned by] the library; 14.4% could not locate material on the necessary subject; 6.4% found the material outdated; 6.1% felt the material they found was too elementary; 2.0% felt the material found was too advanced; and 12.9% reported other reasons. **(301)**

Ibid. . . . *showed that*, of the unsatisfied respondents, 5,104 (66%) planned to continue their quest. Of these, 59.3% planned to go to another library; 19.9% put a reserve on the book; 7.7% made arrangements for the library to get the material from another library; and 13.1% planned to use other alternatives (e.g., buying the book or borrowing it from friends). **(301)**

Success Rate and Problems

■ A 1981 study of 53 ninth-grade honors students in science in a suburban Philadelphia public high school *showed that* 98% of the students used school libraries (92% of these found information); 87% used public libraries (83% of these found information); 74% used home libraries (74% of these found information); 11% used college or university libraries (100% of these found information); 8% used private or special libraries (99% of these found information); and 6% used other institutions (67% of these found information). **(222)**

Special

■ A 1964 study at the Yale Medical Library involving patron use of books (survey size: 831 borrowers; responding: 430) during a 5-month period *showed that* 338 (78.6%) borrowers reported they had obtained what they wanted from the book. **(672)**

■ A 1968-69 study over a period of 9 months of the use of materials at the Midwest Regional Medical Library (John Crerar Library), involving a random sample of 1,071 requests for material, *showed that*, of 1,058 requests, 701 (66.3%) were filled, while 357 (33.7%) were not filled. Of those requests filled, the time required was as follows:

same day or 1 day	265 (37.8%)	requests
2 days	127 (18.1%)	requests
3-7 days	262 (37.4%)	requests
8-14 days	42 (6.0%)	requests
15 days and over	5 (0.7%)	requests

(688)

■ A 1971 study of journal availability at the Woodward Biomedical Library (University of British Columbia, Canada) during a 12-day period *showed that*, out of 4,326 journal items, 370 (8.6%) were not found immediately. The reasons for unavailability were as follows:

title not held or issue not received	100 (27%)	items
in use or awaiting reshelving	98 (26%)	items
being bound	66 (18%)	items
user errors	41 (11%)	items
administrative reasons (on "hold" shelf, misshelved, etc.)	40 (11%)	items
unspecified reasons	25 (7%)	items

(692)

Success Rate and Problems—Age of Material

Academic

■ A review reported in 1978 of faculty book requests in the economics and political science library of Indiana University in 1974-75 *showed that* book availability was related to the age of the book. 76% of the books not immediately available were published in 1970 or later, while only 61% of the books immediately available were so recently published. **(012)**

Success Rate and Problems—Loan Period

Academic

■ A study reported in 1977 at Case Western Reserve concerning the impact of shortening the loan period at the Sears Library, containing 200,000 volumes in science, technology, and management, from a semester loan (in 1972) to a 4-week loan (in 1974) *showed that* 203 of 423 book requests (48%) were immediately satisfied under the semester loan system, while 245 of 437 book requests (56%) were immediately satisfied under the 4-week loan system. **(447)**

Ibid. . . . *showed that*, of the 423 requests studied during the semester loan system, 70 (16.5%) were unavailable because circulating, while of 437 requests studied during the 4-week loan system, 43 (9.8%) were unavailable because circulating. **(447)**

Ibid. . . . *showed that*, of the 220 book requests not immediately satisfied under the semester loan system and the 192 book requsts not immediately satisfied under the 4-week loan system, reasons for failure were as follows:

REASON	SEMESTER LOAN	4-WEEK LOAN
not owned by library	52 (23.6%)	38 (19.8%)
on loan or in-house use	81 (36.8%)	48 (25.0%)
library malfunctions	29 (13.2%)	45 (23.4%)
user errors	49 (22.3%)	50 (26.0%)
other	9 (4.1%)	11 (5.7%)

(447)

BIBLIOGRAPHY OF ARTICLES

Note: This Bibliography cites all articles summarized in the six-volume set of *Handbooks*. Entries in the Bibliography are sequentially arranged by the citation reference numbers that correspond to the numbers appearing at the end of each research summary throughout the six volumes. The numbers in boldface located at the end of some citations refer only to those research summaries contained in this volume. Alphabetic access to the Bibliography is provided through the Author Index.

1 Pamela Kobelski and Jean Trumbore. "Student Use of On-line Bibliographic Services," *Journal of Academic Librarianship* 4:1 (March 1978), 14-18.

2 John V. Richardson, Jr. "Readability and Readership of Journals in Library Science," *Journal of Academic Librarianship* 3:1 (March 1977), 20-22.

3 Elizabeth Gates Kesler. "A Campaign against Mutilation," *Journal of Academic Librarianship* 3:1 (March 1977), 29-30.

4 Bruce Miller and Marilyn Sorum. "A Two Stage Sampling Procedure for Estimating the Proportion of Lost Books in a Library," *Journal of Academic Librarianship* 3:2 (May 1977), 74-80.

5 Jeffrey St. Clair and Rao Aluri. "Staffing the Reference Desk: Professionals or Nonprofessionals," *Journal of Academic Librarianship* 3:3 (July 1977), 149-153.

6 Valentine DeBruin. "Sometimes Dirty Things Are Seen on the Screen," *Journal of Academic Librarianship* 3:5 (November 1977), 256-266.

7 Herbert S. White. "The View from the Library School," *Journal of Academic Librarianship* 3:6 (January 1970), 321.

8 Stella Bentley. "Collective Bargaining and Faculty Status," *Journal of Academic Librarianship* 4:2 (May 1978), 75-81.

9 Steven Seokho Chwe. "A Comparative Study of Job Satisfaction: Catalogers and Reference Librarians in University Libraries," *Journal of Academic Librarianship* 4:3 (July 1978), 139-143.

10 Jo Bell Whitlatch and Karen Kieffer. "Service at San Jose State University: Survey of Document Availability," *Journal of Academic Librarianship* 4:4 (September 1978), 196-199. **(337)**

11 Joan Grant and Susan Perelmuter. "Vendor Performance Evaluation," *Journal of Academic Librarianship* 4:5 (November 1978), 366-367. **(40)**

BIBLIOGRAPHY OF ARTICLES

12 Robert Goehlert. "Book Availability and Delivery Service," *Journal of Academic Librarianship* 4:5 (November 1978), 368-371. **(111, 267, 337, 342)**

13 Linda L. Phillips and Ann E. Raup. "Comparing Methods for Teaching Use of Periodical Indexes," *Journal of Academic Librarianship* 4:6 (January 1979), 420-423.

14 Margaret Johnson Bennett, David T. Buxton and Ella Capriotti. "Shelf Reading in a Large, Open Stack Library," *Journal of Academic Librarianship* 5:1 (March 1979), 4-8.

15 Sarah D. Knapp and C. James Schmidt. "Budgeting To Provide Computer-Based Reference Services: A Case Study," *Journal of Academic Librarianship* 5:1 (March 1979), 9-13.

16 Herbert S. White. "Library Materials Prices and Academic Library Practices: Between Scylla and Charybdis," *Journal of Academic Librarianship* 5:1 (March 1979), 20-23. **(7, 10, 11, 17, 65, 95, 105, 145, 149)**

17 Dorothy P. Wells. "Coping with Schedules for Extended Hours: A Survey of Attitudes and Practices," *Journal of Academic Librarianship* 5:1 (March 1979), 24-27.

18 Johanna E. Tallman. "One Year's Experience with CONTU Guidelines for Interlibrary Loan Photocopies," *Journal of Academic Librarianship* 5:2 (May 1979), 71-74.

19 Robert Goehlert. "The Effect of Loan Policies on Circulation Recalls," *Journal of Academic Librarianship* 5:2 (May 1979), 79-82.

20 James R. Dwyer. "Public Response to an Academic Library Microcatalog," *Journal of Academic Librarianship* 5:3 (July 1979), 132-141.

21 Paul Metz. "The Role of the Academic Library Director," *Journal of Academic Librarianship* 5:3 (July 1979), 148-152.

22 Anne B. Piternick. "Problems of Resource Sharing with the Community: A Case Study," *Journal of Academic Librarianship* 5:3 (July 1979), 153-158.

23 Shelley Phipps and Ruth Dickstein. "The Library Skills Program at the University of Arizona: Testing, Evaluation and Critique," *Journal of Academic Librarianship* 5:4 (September 1979), 205-214.

24 Michael Stuart Freeman. "Published Study Guides: What They Say about Libraries," *Journal of Academic Librarianship* 5:5 (November 1979), 252-255.

25 James H. Richards, Jr. "Missing Inaction," *Journal of Academic Librarianship* 5:5 (November 1979), 266-269.

26 Philip H. Kitchens. "Engineers Meet the Library," *Journal of Academic Librarianship* 5:5 (November 1979), 277-282.

Bibliography of Articles

27 Michael Rouchton. "OCLC Serials Records: Errors, Omissions, and Dependability," *Journal of Academic Librarianship* 5:6 (January 1980), 316-321.

28 Charles R. McClure. "Academic Librarians, Information Sources, and Shared Decision Making," *Journal of Academic Librarianship* 6:1 (March 1980), 9-15.

29 Marjorie E. Murfin. "The Myth of Accessibility: Frustration and Failure in Retrieving Periodicals," *Journal of Academic Librarianship* 6:1 (March 1980), 16-19. **(339)**

30 Anthony W. Ferguson and John R. Taylor. "What Are You Doing? An Analysis of Activities of Public Service Librarians at a Medium-sized Research Library," *Journal of Academic Librarianship* 6:1 (March 1980), 24-29.

31 Regina Shelton. "Adaption: A One-Year Survey of Reserve Photocopying," *Journal of Academic Librarianship* 6:2 (May 1980), 74-76. **(288)**

32 Dorothea M. Thompson. "The Correct Uses of Library Data Bases Can Improve Interlibrary Loan Efficiency," *Journal of Academic Librarianship* 6:2 (May 1980), 83-86.

33 Joan Repp and Julia A. Woods. "Student Appraisal Study and Allocation Formula: Priorities and Equitable Funding in a University Setting," *Journal of Academic Librarianship* 6:2 (May 1980), 87-90.

34 Elaine S. Friedman. "Patron Access to Online Cataloging Systems: OCLC in the Public Service Environment," *Journal of Academic Librarianship* 6:3 (July 1980), 132-139.

35 Edward C. Jestes. "Manual vs. Automated Circulation: A Comparison of Operating Costs in a University Library," *Journal of Academic Librarianship* 6:3 (July 1980), 144-150.

36 Kathleen A. Johnson and Barbara S. Plake. "Evaluation of PLATO Library Instructional Lessons: Another View," *Journal of Academic Librarianship* 6:3 (July 1980), 154-158.

37 Priscilla C. Yu. "International Gift and Exchange: The Asian Experience," *Journal of Academic Librarianship* 6:6 (January 1981), 333-338. **(116, 164)**

38 George W. Black, Jr. "Estimating Collection Size Using the Shelf List in a Science Library," *Journal of Academic Librarianship* (January 1981), 339-341.

39 Beth Macleod. "*Library Journal* and *Choice*: A Review of Reviews," *Journal of Academic Librarianship* 7:1 (March 1981), 23-28. **(231, 244)**

40 Frank Wm. Goudy. "HEA, Title II-C Grant Awards: A Financial Overview from FY 1978-79 through FY 1981-82," *Journal of Academic Librarianship* 8:5 (November 1982), 264-269.

41 Larry Hardesty and John Wright. "Student Library Skills and Attitudes and Their Change: Relationships to Other Selected Variables," *Journal of Academic Librarianship* 8:4 (September 1982), 216-220.

42 Penelope Pearson and Virginia Teufel. "Evaluating Undergraduate Library Instruction at the Ohio State University," *Journal of Academic Librarianship* 7:6 (January 1982), 351-357.

43 David S. Ferriero. "ARL Directors as Proteges and Mentors," *Journal of Academic Librarianship* 7:6 (January 1982), 358-365.

44 Albert F. Maag. "So You Want to be a Director...," *Journal of Academic Librarianship* 7:4 (September 1981), 213-217.

45 Mary Noel Gouke and Sue Pease. "Title Searches in an Online Catalog and a Card Catalog: A Comparative Study of Patron Success in Two Libraries," *Journal of Academic Librarianship* 8:3 (July 1982), 137-143.

46 John K. Mayeski and Marilyn T. Sharrow. "Recruitment of Academic Library Managers: A Survey," *Journal of Academic Librarianship* 8:3 (July 1982), 151-154.

47 Linda K. Rambler. "Syllabus Study: Key to a Responsive Academic Library," *Journal of Academic Librarianship* 8:3 (July 1982), 155-159.

48 Marion T. Reid. "Effectiveness of the OCLC Data Base for Acquisitions Verification," *Journal of Academic Librarianship* 2:6 (January 1977), 303-326. **(43, 46)**

49 James D. Culley, Denis F. Healy and Kermit G. Cudd. "Business Students and the University Library: An Overlooked Element in the Business Curriculum," *Journal of Academic Librarianship* 2:6 (January 1977), 293-296.

50 Edward Kazlauskas. "An Exploratory Study: A Kenesic Analysis of Academic Library Service Points," *Journal of Academic Librarianship* 2:3 (July 1976), 130-134.

51 Helen Gothberg. "Immediacy: A Study of Communication Effect on the Reference Process," *Journal of Academic Librarianship* 2:3 (July 1976), 126-129.

52 John Vasi. "Building Libraries for the Handicapped: A Second Look," *Journal of Academic Librarianship* 2:2 (May 1976), 82-83.

53 Elliot S. Palais. "The Significance of Subject Dispersion for the Indexing of Political Science Journals," *Journal of Academic Librarianship* 2:2 (May 1976), 72-76. **(77, 162, 227)**

54 Ruth Carol Cushman. "Lease Plans—A New Lease on Life for Libraries," *Journal of Academic Librarianship* 2:1 (March 1976), 15-19. **(134)**

Bibliography of Articles

55 Charles R. McClure. "Subject and Added Entries as Access to Information," *Journal of Academic Librarianship* 2:1 (March 1976), 9-14.

56 Marilyn L. Miller and Barbara B. Moran. "Expenditures for Resources in School Library Media Centers FY '82-'83," *School Library Journal* 30:2 (October 1983), 105-114. **(68, 92, 93, 94, 101, 125, 126, 131, 132, 133)**

57 Karen Lee Shelley. "The Future of Conservation in Research Libraries," *Journal of Academic Librarianship* 1:6 (January 1976), 15-18.

58 Maryan E. Reynolds. "Challenges of Modern Network Development," *Journal of Academic Librarianship* 1:2 (May 1975), 19-22.

59 Marjorie E. Martin and Clyde Hendrick. "Ripoffs Tell Their Story: Interviews with Mutilators in a University Library," *Journal of Academic Librarianship* 1:2 (May 1975), 8-12.

60 Audrey Tobias. "The Yule Curve Describing Periodical Citations by Freshmen: Essential Tool or Abstract Frill?" *Journal of Academic Librarianship* 1:1 (March 1975), 14-16. **(190, 197)**

61 Allan J. Dyson. "Organizing Undergraduate Library Instruction," *Journal of Academic Librarianship* 1:1 (March 1975), 9-13.

62 David F. Kohl. "High Efficiency Inventorying through Predictive Data," *Journal of Academic Librarianship* 8:2 (May 1982), 82-84.

63 Eleanor Phinney. "Trends in Public Library Adult Services," *ALA Bulletin* 57:3 (March 1963), 262-266.

64 Zelia J. French. "Library-Community Self-studies in Kansas," *ALA Bulletin* 56:1 (January 1962), 37-41.

65 Guy Garrison. "Nonresident Library Fees in Suburban Chicago," *ALA Bulletin* 55:6 (June 1961), 1013-1017.

66 James E. Bryan. "The Christmas Holiday Jam," *ALA Bulletin* 55:6 (June 1961), 526-530.

67 Joint Libraries Committee on Fair Use in Photocopying, American Library Association. "Fair Use in Photocopying: Report on Single Copies," *ALA Bulletin* 55:6 (June 1961), 571-573.

68 Henry J. Dubester. "Stack Use of a Research Library," *ALA Bulletin* 55:10 (November 1961), 891-893. **(286, 331)**

69 Mary Virginia Gaver. "Teacher Education and School Libraries," *ALA Bulletin* 60:1 (January 1966), 63-72.

70 Richard Waters. "Free Space: Can Public Libraries Receive It?" *ALA Bulletin* 58:3 (March 1964), 232-234.

71 Frank L. Schick. "Professional Library Manpower," *ALA Bulletin* 58:4 (April 1964), 315-317.

72 Milbrey Jones. "Socio-Economic Factors in Library Service to Students," *ALA Bulletin* 58:11 (December 1964), 1003-1006.

73 Elizabeth W. Stone. "Administrators Fiddle while Employees Burn or Flee," *ALA Bulletin* 63:2 (February 1969), 181-187.

74 Staff Organizations Round Table, American Library Association. "Opinions on Collective Bargaining," *ALA Bulletin* 63:6 (June 1969), 803-808.

75 Library Administration Division, American Library Association. "Library Employment of Minority Group Personnel," *ALA Bulletin* 63:7 (July-August 1969), 985-987.

76 Eli M. Oboler. "The Case for ALA Regional Annual Conferences," *ALA Bulletin* 63:8 (September 1969), 1099-1101.

77 Edward N. Howard. "Breaking the Fine Barrier," *ALA Bulletin* 63:11 (December 1969), 1541-1545.

78 Elin B. Christianson. "Variation of Editorial Material in Periodicals Indexed in *Reader's Guide*," *ALA Bulletin* 62:2 (February 1968), 173-182. **(175)**

79 Insurance for Libraries Committee, American Library Association. "The Makings of a Nationwide Scandal," *ALA Bulletin* 62:4 (April 1968), 384-386.

80 George L. Gardiner. "Collective Bargaining: Some Questions Asked," *ALA Bulletin* 62:8 (September 1968), 973-976.

81 Barbara M. Conant. "Trials and Tribulations of Textbook Price Indexing," *ALA Bulletin* 61:2 (February 1967), 197-199. **(12, 97)**

82 Henry T. Drennan and Sarah R. Reed. "Library Manpower," *ALA Bulletin* 61:8 (September 1967), 957-965.

83 Jerry L. Walker. "Changing Attitudes toward the Library and the Librarian," *ALA Bulletin* 61:8 (September 1967), 977-981.

84 William R. Monat. "The Community Library: Its Search for a Vital Purpose," *ALA Bulletin* 61:11 (December 1967), 1301-1310.

85 Irene A. Braden. "Pilot Inventory of Library Holdings," *ALA Bulletin* 62:9 (October 1968), 1129-1131.

86 Genevieve Casey. "Library Manpower in the Detroit Metropolitan Region," *American Libraries* 1:8 (September 1970), 787-789.

Bibliography of Articles

87 Nora Cambier, Barton Clark, Robert Daugherty and Mike Gabriel. "Books in Print 1969: An Analysis of Errors," *American Libraries* 1:9 (October 1970), 901-902. **(243)**

88 Tom Childers and Beth Krevitt. "Municipal Funding of Library Services," *American Libraries* 3:1 (January 1972), 53-57.

89 Albert H. Rubenstein, David J. Werner, Gustave Rath, John A. Kernaghan, and Robert D. O'Keefe. "Search versus Experiment—the Role of the Research Librarian," *College and Research Libraries* 34:4 (July 1973), 280-286.

90 Frank F. Kuo. "A Comparison of Six Versions of Science Library Instruction," *College and Research Libraries* 34:4 (July 1973), 287-290.

91 Laurence Miller. "The role of Circulation Services in the Major University Library," *College and Research Libraries* 34:6 (November 1973), 463-471.

92 Ruth Hyman and Gail Schlachter. "Academic Status: Who Wants It?" *College and Research Libraries* 34:6 (November 1973), 472-478.

93 Larry E. Harrelson. "Large Libraries and Information Desks," *College and Research Libraries* 35:1 (January 1974), 21-27.

94 Robert B. Downs. "Library Resources in the United States," *College and Research Libraries* 35:2 (March 1974), 97-108. **(118)**

95 Richard J. Beeler. "Late-Study Areas: A Means of Extending Library Hours," *College and Research Libraries* 35:3 (May 1974), 200-203.

96 Rolland E. Stevens. "A Study of Interlibrary Loan," *College and Research Libraries* 35:5 (September 1974), 336-343.

97 Jay B. Clark. "An Approach to Collection Inventory," *College and Research Libraries* 35:5 (September 1974), 354-359.

98 Jan Baaske, Don Tolliver and Judy Westerberg. "Overdue Policies: A Comparison of Alternatives," *College and Research Libraries* 35:5 (September 1974), 354-359.

99 Clyde Hendrick and Marjorie E. Murfin. "Project Library Ripoff: A Study of Periodical Mutilation in a University Library," *College and Research Libraries* 35:6 (November 1974), 402-411.

100 Peter Marshall. "How Much, How Often?" *College and Research Libraries* 35:6 (November 1974), 453-456.

101 Robert Balay and Christine Andres. "Use of the Reference Service in a Large Academic Library," *College and Research Libraries* 36:1 (January 1975), 9-26.

BIBLIOGRAPHY OF ARTICLES

102 Guy Walker. "Preservation Efforts in Larger U.S. Academic Libraries," *College and Research Libraries* 36:1 (January 1975), 39-44.

103 Susanne Patterson Wahba. "Job Satisfaction of Librarians: A Comparison between Men and Women," *College and Research Libraries* 36:1 (January 1975), 45-51.

104 Grant T. Skelley. "Characteristics of Collections Added to American Research Libraries 1940-1970: A Preliminary Investigation," *College and Reseach Libraries* 36:1 (January 1975), 52-60. **(47, 48, 260)**

105 Laura M. Boyer and William C. Theimer, Jr. "The Use and Training of Nonprofessional Personnel at Reference Desks in Selected College and University Libraries," *College and Research Libraries* 36:3 (May 1975), 193-200.

106 Robert J. Greene. "LENDS: An Approach to the Centralization/Decentralization Dilemma," *College and Research Libraries* 36:3 (May 1975), 201-207. **(287)**

107 Frances L. Meals and Walter T. Johnson. "We Chose Microfilm," *College and Research Libraries* 21:3 (May 1960), 223-228.

108 George Caldwell. "University Libraries and Government Publications: A Survey," *College and Research Libraries* 22:1 (January 1961), 30-34.

109 Allen Story. "Leo in Libraryland," *American Libraries* 7:9 (October 1976), 569-571.

110 Leslie R. Morris. "The Rise and Fall of the Library Job Market," *American Libraries* 12:9 (October 1981), 557-558.

111 Richard De Gennaro. "Escalating Journal Prices: Time To Fight Back," *American Libraries* 8:1 (January 1977), 69-74. **(149)**

112 Joe A. Hewitt. "The Impact of OCLC," *American Libaries* 7:5 (May 1976), 268-275. **(43)**

113 Fritz Veit. "Book Order Procedures in the Publicly Controlled Colleges and Universities of the Midwest," *College and Research Libraries* 23:1 (January 1962), 33-40. **(31)**

114 Keyes D. Metcalf. "Compact Shelving," *College and Research Libraries* 23:2 (March 1962), 103-111.

115 Natalie N. Nicholson and Eleanor Bartlett. "Who Uses University Libraries," *College and Research Libraries* 23:3 (May 1962), 217-259.

116 H. William Axford. "Rider Revisited," *College and Research Libraries* 23:4 (July 1962), 345-347. **(4, 88)**

Bibliography of Articles

117 E.J. Josey. "The Role of the College Library Staff in Instruction in the Use of the Library," *College and Research Libraries* 23:6 (November 1962), 492-498.

118 Edwin E. Williams. "Magnitude of the Paper-Deterioration Problems as Measured by a National Union Catalog Sample," *College and Research Libraries* 23:6 (November 1962), 499.

119 Stella Frank Mosborg. "Measuring Circulation Desk Activities Using a Random Alarm Mechanism," *College and Research Libraries* 41:5 (September 1980), 437-444.

120 Jean E. Koch and Judith M. Pask. "Working Papers in Academic Business Libraries," *College and Research Libraries* 41:6 (November 1980), 517-523. **(116, 117, 145, 163, 174, 175)**

121 Paul Metz. "Administrative Succession in the Academic Library," *College and Research Libraries* 39:5 (September 1978), 358-364.

122 Libby Trudell and James Wolper. "Interlibrary Loan in New England," *College and Research Libraries* 39:5 (September 1978), 365-371.

123 Richard M. Dougherty. "The Evaluation of Campus Library Document Delivery Service," *College and Research Libraries* 34:1 (January 1973), 29-39.

124 Ung Chon Kim. "A Comparison of Two Out-of-Print Book Buying Methods," *College and Research Libraries* 34:5 (September 1973), 258-264. **(13, 29, 99)**

125 Ann Gwyn, Anne McArthur and Karen Furlow. "Friends of the Library," *College and Research Libraries* 36:4 (July 1975), 272-282.

126 John J. Knightly. "Library Collections and Academic Curricula: Quantitative Relationships," *College and Research Libraries* 36:4 (July 1975), 295-301. **(140, 141)**

127 Alice S. Clark and Rita Hirschman. "Using the 'Guidelines': A Study of the State-Supported Two-Year College Libraries in Ohio," *College and Research Libraries* 36:5 (September 1975), 364-370.

128 Virginia E. Yagello and Gerry Gutherie. "The Effect of Reduced Loan Periods on High Use Items," *College and Research Libraries* 36:5 (September 1975), 411-414.

129 George Piternick. "Library Growth and Academic Quality," *College and Research Libraries* 24:3 (May 1963), 223-229. **(4, 5, 88)**

130 Robert N. Broadus. "An Analysis of Faculty Circulation in a University Library," *College and Research Libraries* 24:4 (July 1963), 323-325.

131 Perry D. Morrison. "The Personality of the Academic Librarian," *College and Research Libraries* 24:5 (September 1963), 365-368.

132 W.J. Bonk. "What is Basic Reference?" *College and Research Libraries* 25:3 (May 1964), 5-8.

133 Jean Legg "The Periodical Scene," *RQ* 7:3 (Spring 1968), 129-132.**(181, 314)**

134 Richard H. Perrine. "Catalog Use Difficulties," *RQ* 7:4 (Summer 1968), 169-174.

135 Thelma E. Larson. "A Survey of User Orientation Methods," *RQ* 8:3 (Spring 1969), 182-187.

136 Phil Hoehn and Jean Hudson. "Academic Library Staffing Patterns," *RQ* 8:4 (Summer 1969), 242-244.

137 T.H. Milby. "Two Approaches to Biology," *RQ* 11:3 (Spring 1972), 231-235.

138 James B. Way. "Loose Leaf Business Services," *RQ* 9:2 (Winter 1969), 128-133. **(327, 328)**

139 Mary Jane Swope and Jeffrey Katzer. "Why Don't They Ask Questions?" *RQ* 12:2 (Winter 1972), 161-165.

140 Robert M. Simmons. "Finding That Government Document," *RQ* 12:2 (Winter 1972), 167-171.

141 Lee Regan. "Status of Reader's Advisory Service," *RQ* 12:3 (Spring 1973), 227-233.

142 Bruce Cossar. "Interlibrary Loan Costs," *RQ* 12:3 (Spring 1973), 243-246.

143 Mary R. Turtle and William C. Robinson. "The Relationship between Time Lag and Place of Publication in *Library and Information Science Abstracts* and *Library Literature*," *RQ* 14:1 (Fall 1974), 28-31.

144 Rosemary Magrill and Charles H. Davis. "Public Library SDI; A Pilot Study," *RQ* 14:2 (Winter 1974), 131-137. **(335)**

145 Steve Parker and Kathy Essary. "A Manual SDI System for Academic Libraries," *RQ* 15:1 (Fall 1975), 47-54.

146 Carl F. Orgren and Barbara J. Olson. "Statewide Teletype Reference Service," *RQ* 15:3 (Spring 1976), 203-209.

147 Anne S. Mavor, Jose Orlando Toro and Ernest R. Deprospo. "An Overview of the National Adult Independent Learning Project," *RQ* 15:4 (Summer 1976), 293-308.

148 Danuta A. Nitecki. "Attitudes toward Automated Information Retrieval Services among RASD Members," *RQ* 16:2 (Winter 1976), 133-141.

149 Rhoda Garoogian. "Library Use of the New York Times Information Bank: A Preliminary Survey," *RQ* 16:1 (Fall 1976), 59-64.

Bibliography of Articles 353

150 Marcella Ciucki. "Recording of Reference/Information Service Activities: A Study of Forms Currently Used," *RQ* 16:4 (Summer 1977), 273-283.

151 Mollie Sandock. "A Study of University Students' Awareness of Reference Services," *RQ* 16:4 (Summer 1977), 284-296.

152 Kathleen Imhoff and Larry Brandwein. "Labor Collections and Services in Public Libraries throughout the United States, 1976," *RQ* 17:2 (Winter 1977), 149-158. **(253)**

153 Cynthia Swenk and Wendy Robinson. "A Comparison of the Guides to Abstracting and Indexing Services Provided by Katz, Chicorel and Ulrich," *RQ* (Summer 1978), 317-319. **(246, 247)**

154 John P. Wilkinson and William Miller. "The Step Approach to Reference Service," *RQ* (Summer 1978), 293-299.

155 Gerald Johoda, Alan Bayer and William L. Needham. "A Comparison of On-Line Bibliographic Searches in One Academic and One Industrial Organization," *RQ* 18:1 (Fall 1978), 42-49.

156 Stephen P. Harter and Mary Alice S. Fields. "Circulation, Reference and the Evaluation of Public Library Service," *RQ* 18:2 (Winter 1978), 147-152.

157 Daniel Ream. "An Evaluation of Four Book Review Journals," *RQ* 19:2 (Winter 1979), 149-153. **(231)**

158 Joseph W. Palmer. "Review Citations for Best-Selling Books," *RQ* 19:2 (Winter 1979), 154-158.

159 "An Evaluation of References to Indexes and Abstracts in Ulrich's 17th Edition," *RQ* 20:2 (Winter 1980), 155-159. **(247)**

160 Victoria T. Kok and Anton R. Pierce. "The Reference Desk Survey: A Management Tool in an Academic Research Library," *RQ* 22:2 (Winter 1982), 181-187.

161 Sheila S. Intner. "Equality of Cataloging in the Age of AACR2," *American Libraries* 14:2 (February 1983), 102-103.

162 Joseph W. Palmer. "The Future of Public Library Film Service," *American Libraries* 13:2 (February 1982), 140-142.

163 Robert Grover and Mary Kevin Moore. "Print Dominates Library Service to Children," *American Libraries* 13:4 (April 1982), 268-269. **(125, 131)**

164 Richard H. Evensen and Mary Berghaus Levering. "Services Are 500% Better," *American Libraries* 10:6 (June 1979), 373.

165 Judith Schick. "Job Mobility of Men and Women Librarians and How It Affects Career Advancement," *American Libraries* 10:11 (December 1979), 643-647.

BIBLIOGRAPHY OF ARTICLES

166 Elizabeth Rountree. "Users and Nonusers Disclose Their Needs," *American Libraries* 10:8 (September 1979), 486-487.

167 George Bobinski. "A Survey of Faculty Loan Policies," *College and Research Libraries* 24:6 (November 1963), 483-486.

168 L. Miles Raisig and Frederick G. Kilgour. "The Use of Medical Theses as Demonstrated by Journal Citations, 1850-1960," *College and Research Libraries* 25:2 (March 1964), 93-102. **(76, 81, 291)**

169 George H. Fadenrecht. "Library Facilities and Practices in Colleges of Veterinary Medicine," *College and Research Libraries* 25:4 (July 1964), 308-335.

170 Donald Thompson. "Working Conditions in Selected Private College Libraries," *College and Research Libraries* 25:4 (July 1964), 261-294.

171 Benedict Brooks and Frederick G. Kilgour. "Catalog Subject Searches in the Yale Medical Library," *College and Research Libraries* 25:6 (November 1964), 483-487.

172 Patrick Barkey. "Patterns of Student Use of a College Library," *College and Research Libraries* 26:2 (March 1965), 115-118.

173 Genevieve Porterfield. "Staffing of Interlibrary Loan Service," *College and Research Libraries* 26:4 (July 1965), 318-320.

174 Harold Mathis. "Professional or Clerical: A Cross-Validation Study," *College and Research Libraries* 26:6 (November 1965), 525-531.

175 David H. Doerrer. 'Overtime' and the Academic Librarian," *College and Research Libraries* 27:3 (May 1966), 194-239.

176 Lois L. Luesing. "Church Historical Collections in Liberal Arts Colleges," *College and Research Libraries* 27:5 (July 1966), 291-317. **(150)**

177 W.C. Blankenship. "Head Librarians: How Many Men? How Many Women?" *College and Research Libraries* 28:1 (January 1967), 41-48.

178 Morrison C. Haviland. "Loans to Faculty Members in University Libraries," *College and Research Libraries* 28:3 (May 1967), 171-174.

179 R. Vernon Ritter. "An Investigation of Classroom-Library Relationships on a College Campus as Seen in Recorded Circulation and GPA's," *College and Research Libraries* 29:1 (January 1968), 3-4.

180 Peter Spyers-Duran. "Faculty Studies: A Survey of Their Use in Selected Libraries," *College and Research Libraries* 29:1 (January 1968), 55-61.

181 Raymond Kilpela. "The University Library Committee," *College and Research Libraries* 29:2 (March 1968), 141-143.

Bibliography of Articles

182 W. Porter Kellam and Dale L. Barker. "Activities and Opportunities of University Librarians for Full Participation in the Educational Enterprise," *College and Research Libraries* 29:5 (May 1968), 195-199.

183 Lloyd A. Kramer and Martha B. Kramer. "The College Library and the Drop-Out," *College and Research Libraries* 29:4 (July 1968), 310-312.

184 Carl Hintz. "Criteria for Appointment to and Promotion in Academic Rank," *College and Research Libraries* 29:5 (September 1968), 341-346.

185 Desmond Taylor. "Classification Trends in Junior College Libraries," *College and Research Libraries* 29:6 (September 1968), 351-356.

186 Raj Madan, Eliese Hetler and Marilyn Strong. "The Status of Librarians in Four-Year State Colleges and Universities," *College and Research Libraries* 29:5 (September 1968), 381-386.

187 Victor Novak. "The Librarian in Catholic Institutions," *College and Research Libraries* 29:5 (September 1968), 403-410.

188 Barbara H. Phipps. "Library Instruction for the Undergraduate," *College and Research Libraries* 29:5 (September 1968), 411-423.

189 Ashby J. Fristoe. "Paperbound Books: Many Problems, No Solutions," *College and Research Libraries* 29:5 (September 1968), 437-442. **(29, 36, 154)**

190 Sidney Forman. "Innovative Practices in College Libraries," *College and Research Libraries* 29:6 (November 1968), 486-492. **(29, 154)**

191 Richard W. Trueswell. "Some Circulation Data from a Research Library," *College and Research Libraries* 29:6 (November 1968), 493-495.

192 Jane P. Kleiner. "The Information Desk: The Library's Gateway to Service," *College and Research Libraries* 29:6 (November 1968), 496-501.

193 J.E.G. Craig, Jr. "Characteristics of Use of Geology Literature," *College and Research Libraries* 3:3 (May 1969), 230-236. **(57, 71, 84, 189, 198)**

194 Ronald A. Hoppe and Edward C. Simmel. "Book Tearing: The Bystander in the University Library," *College and Research Libraries* 3:3 (May 1969), 247-251.

195 Stephen L. Peterson. "Patterns of Use of Periodical Literature," *College and Research Libraries* 30:5 (September 1969), 422-430. **(324)**

196 Mary B. Cassata. "Teach-in: The Academic Librarian's Key to Status," *College and Research Libraries* 31:1 (January 1970), 22-27.

197 E.J. Josey. "Community Use of Junior College Libraries—A Symposium," *College and Research Libraries* 31:3 (May 1970), 185-198.

198 Virgil F. Massman. "Academic Library Salaries in a Seven-State Area," *College and Research Libraries* 3:6 (November 1969), 477-482.

BIBLIOGRAPHY OF ARTICLES

199 James Krikelas. "Subject Searches Using Two Catalogs: A Comparative Evaluation," *College and Research Libraries* 30:6 (November 1969), 506-517.

200 James Wright. "Fringe Benefits for Academic Library Personnel," *College and Research Libraries* 31:1 (January 1970), 18-21.

201 Howard Clayton. "Femininity and Job Satisfaction among Male Library Students at One Midwestern University," *College and Research Libraries* 31:6 (November 1970), 388-398.

202 Philip V. Rzasa and John H. Moriarty. "The Types and Needs of Academic Library Users: A Case Study of 6,568 Responses," *College and Research Libraries* 31:6 (November 1970), 403-409.

203 Bob Carmack and Trudi Loeber. "The Library Reserve System—Another Look," *College and Research Libraries* 32:2 (March 1971), 105-109.

204 C. James Schmidt and Kay Shaffer. "A Cooperative Interlibrary Loan Service for the State-Assisted University Libraries in Ohio," *College and Research Libraries* 32:3 (May 1971), 197-204.

205 Edward S. Warner. "A Tentative Analytical Approach to the Determination of Interlibrary Loan Network Effectiveness," *College and Research Libraries* 32:3 (May 1971), 217-221.

206 Irving Zelkind and Joseph Sprug. "Increased Control through Decreased Controls: A Motivational Approach to a Library Circulation Problem," *College and Research Libraries* 32:3 (May 1971), 222-226.

207 William E. McGrath. "Correlating the Subjects of Books Taken Out Of and Books Used Within an Open-Stack Library," *College and Research Libraries* 32:4 (July 1971), 280-285. **(298)**

208 Thomas Kirk. "A Comparison of Two Methods of Library Instruction for Students in Introductory Biology," *College and Research Libraries* 32:6 (November 1971), 465-474.

209 Dawn McCaghy and Gary Purcell. "Faculty Use of Government Publications," *College and Research Libraries* 33:1 (January 1972), 7-12. **(295)**

210 Joe A. Hewitt. "Sample Audit of Cards from a University Library Catalog," *College and Research Libraries* 33:1 (January 1972), 24-27.

211 William E. McGrath. "The Significance of Books Used According to a Classified Profile of Academic Departments," *College and Research Libraries* 33:3 (May 1972), 212-219. **(298, 299, 333)**

212 Carlos A. Cuadra and Ruth J. Patrick. "Survey of Academic Library Consortia in the U.S.," *College and Research Libraries* 33:4 (July 1972), 271-283.

213 Marjorie Johnson. "Performance Appraisal of Librarians—A Survey," *College and Research Libraries* 33:5 (September 1972), 359-367.

Bibliography of Articles 357

214 Marvin E. Wiggins. "The Development of Library Use Instruction Programs," *College and Research Libraries* 33:6 (November 1972), 473-479.

215 Margaret E. Monroe. "Community Development as a Mode of Community Analysis," *Library Trends* 24:3 (January 1976), 497-514.

216 Janet K. Rudd and Larry G. Carver. "Topographic Map Acquisition in U.S. Academic Libraries," *Library Trends* 29:3 Winter 1981), 375-390. **(6, 10, 25, 36, 91, 98, 254, 255)**

217 John Belland. "Factors Influencing Selection of Materials," *School Media Quarterly* 6:2 (Winter 1978), 112-119. **(33, 34, 37, 146, 147, 148, 170, 302)**

218 Virginia Witucke. "A Comparative Analysis of Juvenile Book Review Media," *School Media Quarterly* 8:3 (Spring 1980), 153-160. **(234, 237, 238)**

219 M. Carl Drott and Jacqueline C. Mancall. "Magazines as Information Sources: Patterns of Student Use," *School Media Quarterly* 8:4 (Summer 1980), 240-250. **(315, 318, 322)**

220 Jerry J. Watson and Bill C. Snider. "Book Selection Pressure on School Library Media Specialists and Teachers," *School Media Quarterly* 9:2 (Winter 1981), 95-101. **(70, 71, 238)**

221 Jerry J. Watson and Bill C. Snider. "Educating the Potential Self-Censor," *School Media Quarterly* 9:4 (Summer 1981), 272-276. **(70, 71)**

222 Lucy Anne Wozny. "Online Bibliographic Searching and Student Use of Information: An Innovative Teaching Approach," *School Library Media Quarterly* 11:1 (Fall 1982), 35-42. **(182, 192, 278, 285, 298, 303, 309, 316, 318, 323, 341)**

223 Carol A. Doll. "School and Public Library Collection Overlap and the Implications for Networking," *School Library Media Quarterly* 11:3 (Spring 1983), 193-199. **(142)**

224 Arthur Tannenbaum and Eva Sidhom. "User Environment and Attitudes in an Academic Microform Center," *Library Journal* 101:18 (October 15, 1976), 2139-2143. **(26, 305)**

225 Timothy Hays, Kenneth D. Shearer and Concepcion Wilson. "The Patron Is Not the Public," *Library Journal* 102:16 (September 15, 1977), 1813-1818. **(164)**

226 Wilma Lee Woolard. "The Combined School and Public Library: Can It Work?" *Library Journal* 103:4 (February 15, 1978), 435-438.

227 David C. Genaway. "Bar Coding and the Librarian Supermarket: An Analysis of Advertised Library Vacancies," *Library Journal* 103:3 (February 1, 1978), 322-325.

228 Hoyt Galvin. "Public Library Parking Needs," *Library Journal* 103:2 (November 15, 1978), 2310-2313.

229 Harold J. Ettelt. "Book Use at a Small (Very) Community College Library," *Library Journal* 103:2 (November 15, 1978), 2314-2315. **(264, 275)**

230 Frederick G. Kilgour. "Interlibrary Loans On-Line," *Library Journal* 104:4 (February 15, 1979), 460-463.

231 Paul Little. "The Effectiveness of Paperbacks," *Library Journal* 104:2 (November 15, 1979), 2411-2416. **(11, 30, 96, 154, 155, 280)**

232 Ken Kister. "Encyclopedias and the Public Library: A National Survey," *Library Journal* 104:8 (April 15, 1979), 890-893. **(166)**

233 Arlene T. Dowell. "Discrepancies in CIP: How Serious Is the Problem," *Library Journal* 104:19 (November 1, 1979), 2281-2287.

234 Gary D. Byrd, Mary Kay Smith and Norene McDonald. "MINET in K.C.," *Library Journal* 104:17 (October 1, 1979), 2044-2047.

235 Ray L. Carpenter. "The Public Library Patron," *Library Journal* 104:3 (February 1, 1979), 347-351.

236 Cathy Schell. "Preventive Medicine: The Library Prescription," *Library Journal* 105:8 (April 15, 1980), 929-931.

237 Michael Gonzalez, Bill Greeley and Stephen Whitney. "Assessing the Library Needs of the Spanish-speaking," *Library Journal* 105:7 (April 1, 1980), 786-789.

238 Thomas Childers. "The Test of Reference," *Library Journal* 105:8 (April 15, 1980), 924-928.

239 Mary Noel Gouke and Marjorie Murfin. "Periodical Mutilization: The Insidious Disease," *Library Journal* 105:16 (September 15, 1980), 1795-1797.

240 Sheila Creth and Faith Harders. "Requirements for the Entry Level Librarian," *Library Journal* 105:18 (October 15, 1980), 2168-2169.

241 Kathleen M. Heim and Leigh S. Estabrook. "Career Patterns of Librarians," *Drexel Library Quarterly* 17:3 (Summer 1981), 35-51.

242 Margaret Peil. "Library Use by Low-Income Chicago Families," *Library Quarterly* 33:4 (October 1963), 329-333.

243 Herbert Goldhor and John McCrossan. "An Exploratory Study of the Effect of a Public Library Summer Reading Club on Reading Skills," *Library Quarterly* 36:1 (June 1966), 14-24.

244 Robert Sommer. "Reading Areas in College Libraries," *Library Quarterly* 38:3 (July 1968), 249-260.

245 Isaac T. Littleton. "The Literature of Agricultural Economics: Its Bibliographic Organization and Use," *Library Quarterly* 39:2 (April 1969), 140-152. **(226)**

Bibliography of Articles 359

246 G. Edward Evans. "Book Selection and Book Collection Usage in Academic Libraries," *Library Quarterly* 40:3 (July 1970), 297-308. **(40, 143)**

247 Marilyn Werstein Greenberg. "A Study of Reading Motivation of Twenty-Three Seventh-Grade Students," *Library Quarterly* 40:3 (July 1970), 309-317. **(282)**

248 Ben-Ami Lipetz. "Catalog Use in a Large Research Library," *Library Quarterly* 42:1 (January 1972), 129-130.

249 John Aubry. "A Timing Study of the Manual Searching of Catalogs," *Library Quarterly* 42:4 (October 1972), 399-415.

250 Kenneth H. Plate and Elizabeth W. Stone. "Factors Affecting Librarians' Job Satisfaction: A Report of Two Studies," *Library Quarterly* 44:2 (April 1974), 97-109.

251 Elizabeth Warner McElroy. "Subject Variety in Adult Reading: I. Factors Related to Variety in Reading," *Library Quarterly* 38:1 (April 1968), 154-167.

252 James C. Baughman. "A Structural Analysis of the Literature of Sociology," *Library Quarterly* 44:4 (October 1974), 293-308. **(73, 190, 224)**

253 Edd E. Wheeler. "The Bottom Lines: Fifty Years of Legal Footnoting in Review," *Law Library Journal* 72:2 (Spring 1979), 245-259. **(77, 82, 83)**

254 Daniel O'Connor and Phyllis Van Orden. "Getting into Print," *College and Research Libraries* 39:5 (September 1978), 389-396.

255 Howard Fosdick. "Library Education in Information Science: Present Trends," *Special Libraries* 69:3 (March 1978), 100-108.

256 Paula de Simone Watson. "Publication Activity among Academic Librarians," *College and Research Libraries* 38:5 (September 1977), 375-384.

257 Susan Andriette Ariew. "The Failure of the Open Access Residence Hall Library," *College and Research Libraries* 39:5 (September 1978), 372-380.

258 Mary Ellen Soper. "Characteristics and Use of Personal Collections," *Library Quarterly* (October 1976), 397-415. **(140, 329)**

259 Ronald R. Powell. "An Investigation of the Relationships Between Quantifiable Reference Service Variables and Reference Performance in Public Libraries," *Library Quarterly* 48:1 (January 1978), 1-19.

260 Mary Jo Lynch. "Reference Interviews in Public Libraries," *Library Quarterly* 48:2 (April 1978), 119-142.

261 William A. Satariano. "Journal Use in Sociology: Citation Analysis versus Readership Patterns," *Library Quarterly* 48:3 (July 1978), 293-300. **(178, 224, 225, 321, 326, 334)**

262 Paul Metz. "The Use of the General Collection in the Library of Congress," *Library Quarterly* 49:4 (October 1979), 415-434. **(263, 283, 291)**

263 Michael Halperin and Maureen Strazdon. "Measuring Students' Preferences for Reference Service: A Conjoint Analysis," *Library Quarterly* 50:2 (April 1980), 208-224.

264 Herbert S. White. "Factors in the Decisions by Individuals and Libraries To Place or Cancel Subscriptions to Scholarly and Research Journals," *Library Quarterly* 50:3 (July 1980), 287-309. **(32, 144, 145, 149, 150, 178, 179)**

265 George D'Elia. "The Development and Testing of a Conceptual Model of Public Library User Behavior," *Library Quarterly* 50:4 (October 1980), 410-430.

266 Donald A. Hicks. "Diversifying Fiscal Support by Pricing Public Library Services: A Policy Impact Analysis," *Library Quarterly* 50:4 (October 1980), 453-474.

267 Theodora Hodges and Uri Block. "Fiche or Film for COM Catalogs: Two Use Tests," *Library Quarterly* 52:2 (April 1982), 131-144.

268 Terry L. Weech and Herbert Goldhor. "Obtrusive versus Unobtrusive Evaluation of Reference Service in Five Illinois Public Libraries: A Pilot Study," *Library Quarterly* 52:4 (October 1982), 305-324.

269 Stephen E. Wiberley, Jr. "Journal Rankings From Citation Studies: A Comparison of National and Local Data From Social Work," *Library Quarterly* 52:4 (October 1982), 348-359. **(223)**

270 George D'Elia and Sandra Walsh. "User Satisfaction with Library Service— A Measure of Public Library Performance?" *Library Quarterly* 53:2 (April 1983), 109-133.

271 Edward A. Dyl. "A Note on Price Discrimination by Academic Journals," *Library Quarterly* 53:2 (April 1983), 161-168. **(15, 102, 103)**

272 Michael R. Kronenfeld and James A. Thompson. "The Impact of Inflation on Journal Costs," *Library Journal* 106:7 (April 1, 1981), 714-717. **(17, 18, 106)**

273 George D'Elia and Mary K. Chelton. "Paperback Books," *Library Journal* 107:16 (September 15, 1982), 1718-1721. **(11, 30, 32, 42, 96, 155, 156)**

274 Patsy Hansel and Robert Burgin. "Hard Facts about Overdues," *Library Journal* 108:4 (February 15, 1983), 349-352.

275 Robert Dale Karr. "Becoming a Library Director," *Library Journal* 108:4 (February 15, 1983), 343-346.

276 Mary V. Gaver. "The Science Collection—New Evidence To Consider," *Junior Libraries* (later *School Library Journal*) 7:6 (February 1961), 4-7. **(245)**

277 Dorothy G. Petersen. "Teachers' Professional Reading," *School Library Journal* 9:8 (April 1963), 24-27. **(124, 256, 257)**

Bibliography of Articles 361

278 Linda Kraft. "Lost Herstory: The Treatment of Women in Children's Encyclopedias," *School Library Journal* 19:5 (January 1973), 26-35.

279 John Stewig and Margaret Higgs. "Girls Grow Up: A Study of Sexism in Children's Literature," *School Library Journal* 19:5 (January 1973), 44-49. **(151)**

280 W. Bernard Lukenbill. "Fathers in Adolescent Novels," *School Library Journal* 20:6 (February 1974), 26-30. **(79, 80)**

281 Jacqueline C. Mancall and M. Carl Drott. "Tomorrow's Scholars: Patterns of Facilities Use," *School Library Journal* 20:7 (March 1980), 99-103.

282 John McCrossan. "Education of Librarians Employed in Small Public Libraries," *Journal of Education for Librarianship* 7:4 (Spring 1967), 237-245.

283 Gail Schlachter and Dennis Thomison. "The Library Science Doctorate: A Quantitative Analysis of Dissertations and Recipients," *Journal of Education for Librarianship* 15:2 (Fall 1974), 95-111.

284 Constance Rinehart and Rose Mary Magrill. "Characteristics of Applicants for Library Science Teaching Positions," *Journal of Education for Librarianship* 16:3 (Winter 1976), 173-182.

285 George W. Whitbeck. "Grade Inflation in the Library School—Myth or Reality," *Journal of Education for Librarianship* 17:4 (Spring 1977), 214-237.

286 Charles H. Davis. "Computer Programming for Librarians," *Journal of Education for Librarianship* 18:1 (Summer 1977), 41-52.

287 Helen M. Gothberg. "A Study of the Audio-Tutorial Approach to Teaching Basic Reference," *Journal of Education for Librarianship* 18:3 (Winter 1978), 193-202.

288 J. Periam Danton. "British and American Library School Teaching Staffs: A Comparative Inquiry," *Journal of Education for Librarianship* 19:2 (Fall 1978), 97-129.

289 Lucille Whalen. "The Role of the Assistant Dean in Library Schools," *Journal of Education for Librarianship* 20:1 (Summer 1979), 44-54.

290 A. Neil Yerkey. "Values of Library School Students, Faculty and Librarians: Premises for Understanding," *Journal of Education for Librarianship* 21:2 (Fall 1980), 122-134.

291 Judith B. Katz. "Indicators of Success: Queens College Department of Library Science," *Journal of Education for Librarianship* 19:2 (Fall 1978), 130-139.

292 Lawrence Auld, Kathleen H. Heim and Jerome Miller. "Market Receptivity for an Extended M.L.S.," *Journal of Education for Librarianship* 21:3 (Winter 1981), 235-245.

293 John Richardson, Jr. and Peter Hernon. "Theory vs. Practice: Student Preferences," *Journal of Education for Librarianship* 21:4 (Spring 1981), 287-300,

294 Richard I. Blue and James L. Divilbiss. "Optimizing Selection of Library School Students," *Journal of Education for Librarianship* 21:4 (Spring 1981), 301-312.

295 David H. Jonassen and Gerald G. Hodges. "Student Cognitive Styles: Implications for Library Educators," *Journal of Education for Librarianship* 22:3 (Winter 1982), 143-153.

296 Mary Kingsbury. "How Library Schools Evaluate Faculty Performance," *Journal of Education for Librarianship* 22:4 (Spring 1982), 219-238.

297 John W. Lee and Raymond L. Read. "The Graduate Business Student and the Library," *College and Research Libraries* 33:5 (September 1972), 403-407.

298 Carol Steer. "Authors Are Studied," *Canadian Library Journal* 39:3 (June 1982), 151-155.

299 Rashid Tayyeb. "Implementing AACR 2—A National Survey," *Canadian Library Journal* 39:6 (December 1982), 373-376.

300 Dick Matzek and Scott Smith. "Online Searching in the Small College Library—The Economics and the Results," *Online* (March 1982), 21-29.

301 Mary Lee Bundy. "Metropolitan Public Library Use," *Wilson Library Bulletin* 41:9 (May 1967), 950-961.   **(288, 314, 328, 335, 340)**

302 John Shipman. "Signifying Renewal as Well as Change: One Library's Experience with the Center for Research Libraries," *Library Acquisitions: Practice and Theory* 2:5 (1978), 243-248.

303 Nathan R. Einhorn. "The Inclusion of the Products of Reprography in the International Exchange of Publications," *Library Acquisitions: Practice and Theory* 2:5 (1978), 227-236

304 Nancy J. Williamson. "Education for Acquisitions Librarians: A State of the Art Review," *Library Acquisitions: Practice and Theory* 2:3-4 (1978), 199-208.

305 Janet L. Flowers. "Time Logs for Searchers: How Useful?" *Library Acquisitions: Practice and Theory* 2:2 (1978), 77-83.   **(46)**

306 D.N. Wood. "Current Exchange of Serials at the British Library Lending Division," *Library Acquisitions: Practice and Theory* 3:2 (1979), 107-113.   **(176)**

307 Robert Goehlert. "Journal Use Per Monetary Unit: A Reanalysis of Use Data," *Library Acquisitions: Practice and Theory* 3:2 (1979), 91-98.   **(290, 313)**

Bibliography of Articles

308 Margaret Landesman and Christopher Gates. "Performance of American Inprint Vendors: A Comparison at the University of Utah," *Library Acquisitions: Practice and Theory* 4:3-4 (1980), 187-192. **(39, 41)**

309 Kenton Pattie and Mary Ernst. "Chapter II Grants: Libraries Gain," *School Library Journal* 29:5 (January 1983), 17-19.

310 John Erlandson and Yvonne Boyer. "Acquistions of State Documents," *Library Acquisitions: Practice and Theory* 4:2 (1980), 117-127. **(10, 23, 35, 38, 47, 97, 98)**

311 George V. Hodowanec. "Analysis of Variables Which Help To Predict Book and Periodical Use," *Library Acquisitions: Practice and Theory* 4:1 (1980), 75-85.

312 Darrell L. Jenkins. "Acquiring Acquisitions Librarians," *Library Acquisitions: Practice and Theory* 5:2 (1981), 81-87.

313 Steven E. Maffeo. "Invoice Payment by Library Acquisitions: A Controlled Time Study," *Library Acquisitions: Practice and Theory* 5:2 (1981), 67-71. **(32, 41)**

314 Joyce G. McDonough, Carol Alf O'Connor and Thomas A. O'Connor. "Moving the Backlog: An Optimum Cycle for Searching OCLC," *Library Acquisitions: Practice and Theory* 6:3 (1982), 265-270.

315 Paul B. Wiener. "Recreational Reading Services in Academic Libraries: An Overview," *Library Acquisitions: Practice and Theory* 6:1 (1982), 59-70. **(256)**

316 Peter Hernon. "Use of Microformatted Government Publications," *Microform Review* 11:4 (Fall 1982), 237-252. **(295, 296, 297, 306, 307)**

317 Charles R. McClure. "Online Government Documents Data Base Searching and the Use of Microfiche Documents Online by Academic and Public Depository Librarians," *Microfilm Review* 10:4 (Fall 1981), 245-259. **(24, 27, 168, 169, 173)**

318 Peter Hernon and George W. Whitbeck. "Government Publications and Commercial Microform Publishers: A Survey of Federal Depository Libraries," *Microform Review* 6:5 (September 1977), 272-284. **(9, 26, 34, 35, 46, 97, 167, 168, 171, 172)**

319 Robert F. Jennings and Hathia Hayes. "The Use of Microfiche Copies of Children's Trade Books in Selected Fourth-Grade Classrooms," *Microform Review* 3:3 (July 1974), 189-193. **(173)**

320 E.R. Norten. "New Books in Microform: A Survey," *Microform Review* 1:4 (October 1972), 284-288. **(110, 111, 168, 172)**

321 Renata Tagliacozzo, Manfred Kochen and Lawrence Rosenberg. "Orthographic Error Patterns of Author Names in Catalog Searches," *Journal of Library Automation* 3:2 (June 1970), 93-101.

BIBLIOGRAPHY OF ARTICLES

322 Lorne R. Buhr. "Selective Dissemination of MARC: A User Evaluation," *Journal of Library Automation* 5:1 (March 1972), 39-50.

323 Gerry D. Guthrie and Steven D. Slifko. "Analysis of Search Key Retrieval on a Large Bibliographic File," *Journal of Library Automation* 6:2 (June 1972), 96-100.

324 Alan L. Landgraf and Frederick G. Kilgour. "Catalog Records Retrieved by Personal Author Using Derived Search Keys," *Journal of Library Automation* 6:2 (June 1973), 103-108.

325 Martha E. Williams. "Data Element Statistics for the MARC II Data Base," *Journal of Library Automation* 6:2 (June 1976), 89-100.

326 Michael D. Cooper and Nancy A. DeWath. "The Cost of On-Line Bibliographic Searching," *Journal of Library Automation* 9:3 (September 1976), 195-209.

327 Edward John Kazlauskas. "The Application of the Instrumental Development Process to a Module on Flowcharting," *Journal of Library Automation* 9:3 (September 1976), 234-244.

328 Lawrence K. Legard and Charles P. Bourne. "An Improved Title Word Search Key for Large Catalog Files," *Journal of Library Automation* 9:4 (December 1976), 318-327.

329 Ryan E. Hoover. "Patron Appraisal of Computer-Aided On-Line Bibliographic Retrieval Services," *Journal of Library Automation* 9:4 (December 1976), 335-350.

330 T.D.C. Kuch. "Analysis of the Literature of Library Automation through Citations in the *Annual Review of Information Science and Technology*," *Journal of Library Automation* 10:1 (March 1977), 82-84. **(201)**

331 Isobel Jean Mosley. "Cost-Effectiveness Analysis of the Automation of a Circulation System," *Journal of Library Automation* 10:3 (September 1977), 240-254.

332 Michael D. Cooper and Nancy A. DeWath. "The Effect of User Fees on the Cost of On-Line Searching in Libraries," *Journal of Library Automation* 10:4 (December 1977), 304-319.

333 James W. Bourg, Douglas Lacy, James Llinas and Edward T. O'Neill. "Developing Corporate Author Search Keys," *Journal of Library Automation* 11:2 (June 1978), 106-125.

334 Cynthia C. Ryans. "A Study of Errors Found in Non-MARC Cataloging in a Machine-Assisted System," *Journal of Library Automation* 11:2 (June 1978), 125-132.

335 Joselyn Druschel. "Cost Analysis of an Automated and Manual Cataloging and Book Processing System," *Journal of Library Automation* 14:1 (March 1981), 24-49.

Bibliography of Articles

336 Kunj B. Bastogi and Ichiko T. Morita. "OCLC Search Key Usage Patterns in a Large Research Library," *Journal of Library Automation* 14:2 (June 1981), 90-99.

337 Georgia L. Brown. "AACR 2: OCLC's Implementation and Database Conversion," *Journal of Library Automation* 14:3 (September 1981), 161-173.

338 James R. Martin. "Automation and the Service Attitudes of ARL Circulation Managers," *Journal of Library Automation* 14:3 (September 1981), 190-194.

339 University of Oregon Library. "A Comparison of OCLC, RLG/RLIN and WLN," *Journal of Library Automation* 14:3 (September 1981), 215-217.

340 Terence Crowley. "Comparing Fiche and Film: A Test of Speed," *Journal of Library Automation* 14:4 (December 1981), 292-294.

341 Public Service Satellite Consortium. "Cable Library Survey Results," *Journal of Library Automation* 14:4 (December 1981), 304-313.

342 Dennis Reynolds. "Entry of Local Data on OCLC: The Options and Their Impact on the Processing of Archival Tapes," *Information Technology and Libraries* 1:1 (March 1982), 5-14.

343 Joseph Ford. "Network Service Centers and Their Expanding Role," *Information Technology and Libraries* 1:1 (March 1982), 28-35.

344 Carolyn A. Johnson. "Retrospective Conversion of Three Library Collections," *Information Technology and Libraries* 1:2 (June 1982), 133-139.

345 Lynn L. Magrath. "Computers in the Library: The Human Element," *Information Technology and Libraries* 1:3 (September 1982), 266-270.

346 Izabella Taler. "Automated and Manual ILL: Time Effectiveness and Success Rate," *Information Technology and Libraries* 1:3 (September 1982), 277-280.

347 Martha E. Williams, Stephen W. Barth and Scott E. Preece. "Summary of Statistics for Five Years of the MARC Data Base," *Journal of Library Automation* 12:4 (December 1979), 314-337.

348 Susan U. Golden and Gary A. Golden. "Access to Periodicals: Search Key versus Keyword," *Information Technology and Libraries* 2:1 (March 1983), 26-32.

349 Ray R. Larson and Vicki Graham. "Monitoring and Evaluating MELVYL," *Information Technology and Libraries* 2:1 (March 1983), 93-104.

350 Barbara E. Carr. "Improving the Periodicals Collection through an Index Correlation Study," *Reference Services Review* 9:4 (October/December 1981), 27-31.

351 I.N. Sengupta. "Impact of Scientific Serials on the Advancement of Medical Knowledge: An Objective Method of Analysis," *International Library Review* 4:2 (April 1972), 169-195. **(72, 74, 203, 206)**

352 June L. Stewart. "The Literature of Politics: A Citation Analysis," *International Library Review* 2:3 (July 1970), 329-353. **(57, 84, 221, 222)**

353 I.N. Sengupta. "The Literature of Microbiology," *International Library Review* 6:3 (July 1974), 353-369. **(72, 74, 215, 216, 217)**

354 I.N. Sengupta. "The Literature of Pharmacology," *International Library Review* 6:4 (October 1974), 483-504. **(72, 74, 85, 87, 218, 219, 220)**

355 A.W. Hafner. "Citation Characteristics of Physiology Literature, 1970-72," *International Library Review* 8:1 (January 1976), 85-115. **(55, 56, 58, 61, 73, 75, 85, 88, 210, 211, 212, 213)**

356 Hans Hanan Wellisch. "Script Conversion Practices in the World's Libraries," *International Library Review* 8:1 (January 1976), 55-84.

357 Christine Anderson Brock and Gayle Smith Edelman. "Teaching Practices of Academic Law Librarians," *Law Library Journal* 71:1 (February 1978), 96-107. **(5, 94)**

358 Charles B. Wolfe. "Current Problems Facing State Law Libraries," *Law Library Journal* 71:1 (February 1978), 108-114). **(180)**

359 Mindy J. Myers. "The Impact of Lexis on the Law Firm Library: A Survey," *Law Library Journal* 71:1 (February 1978), 158-169.

360 Nancy P. Johnson. "Legal Periodical Usage Survey: Method and Application," *Law Library Journal* 71:1 (February 1978), 177-186. **(313, 316, 321, 323)**

361 Ann M. Carter. "Budgeting in Private Law Firm Libraries," *Law Library Journal* 71:1 (February 1978), 187-194.

362 James F. Bailey, III and Oscar M. Trelles, II. "Autonomy, Librarian Status, and Librarian Tenure in Law School Libraries: The State of the Art, 1978," *Law Library Journal* 71:3 (August 1978), 425-462. **(31, 34, 144, 148)**

363 Frank Wm. Goudy. "Funding Local Public Libraries: FY 1966 to FY 1980," *Public Libraries* 21:2 (Summer 1982), 52-54.

364 Guy Garrison. "A Look At Research on Public Library Problems in the 1970's," *Public Libraries* 19:1 (Spring 1980), 4-8.

365 Terry L. Weech. "School and Public Library Cooperation—What We Would Like To Do, What We Do," *Public Libraries* 18:2 (Summer 1979), 33-34.

Bibliography of Articles

366   Patricia L. Piper and Cecilia Hing Ling Kwan. "Cataloging and Classification Practices in Law Libraries: Results of a Questionnaire," *Law Library Journal* 71:3 (August 1978), 481-483.

367   Christian M. Boissonnas. "The Quality of OCLC Bibliographic Records: The Cornell Law Library Experience," *Law Library Journal* 72:1 (Winter 1979), 80-85.

368   Kent Schrieffer and Linnea Christiani. "Ballots at Boalt," *Law Library Journal* 72:3 (Summer 1979), 497-512.

369   Ermina Hahn. "Survey of Technical Services Practices at Fifty Large Law School Libraries," *Law Library Journal* 73:3 (Summer 1980), 715-725. **(111, 112, 113, 121, 128, 164, 165, 185, 186, 278, 279)**

370   Lana Caswell Garcia. "Legal Services Law Librarianship—An Investigation of Salary and Benefits in a Pioneer Field," *Law Library Journal* 73:3 (Summer 1980), 731-733.

371   Reynold J. Kosek. "Faculty Status and Tenure for Nondirector, Academic Law Librarians" a section within "Status of Academic Law Librarians," *Law Library Journal* 73:4 (Fall 1980), 892-905.

372   Martha C. Adamson and Gloria J. Zamora. "Authorship Characteristics in *Law Library Journal*: A Comparative Study," *Law Library Journal* 74:3 (Summer 1981), 527-533.

373   David G. Badertscher. "An Examination of the Dynamics of Change in Information Technology as Viewed from Law Libraries and Information Centers," *Law Library Journal* 75:2 (Spring 1982), 198-211. **(76)**

374   Donald J. Dunn. "The Law Librarian's Obligation To Publish," *Law Library Journal* 75:2 (Spring 1982), 225-231.

375   Audio-Visual Committee, American Association of Law Libraries. "Summary of Audio-Visual Materials Used in Legal Education: Audio-Visual Committee Report—June 1967," *Law Library Journal* 60:3 (August 1967), 272-276.

376   Cameron Allen. "Duplicate Holding Practices of Approved American Law School Libraries." *Law Library Journal* 62:2 (May 1969), 191-200. **(110, 112)**

377   Margaret Shediac. "Private Law Libraries Special Interest Section 1980 Salary Survey," *Law Library Journal* 74:2 (Spring 1981), 444-457. **(34)**

378   Bettie H. Scott. "Price Index for Legal Publications," *Law Library Journal* 75:1 (Winter 1982), 171-174. **(12, 20, 95, 103, 104)**

379   Silvia A. Gonzalez. "County Law Library Survey," *Law Library Journal* 74:3 (Summer 1981), 654-691.

380   Silvia A. Gonzalez. "Survey of State Law Libraries," *Law Library Journal* 74:1 (Winter 1981), 160-201.

381 Silvia A. Gonzalez. "Survey of Court Law Libraries," *Law Library Journal* 74:2 (Spring 1981), 458-494.

382 David A. Thomas. "1980 Statistical Survey of Law School Libraries and Librarians," *Law Library Journal* 74:2 (Spring 1981), 359-443. **(14, 99, 101)**

383 Marija Hughes. "Sex-Based Discrimination in Law Libraries," *Law Library Journal* 64:1 (February 1971), 13-22.

384 Oscar M. Trelles. "Law Libraries and Unions," *Law Library Journal* 65:2 (May 1972), 158-180.

385 Claudia Sumler, Kristine Barone and Art Goetz. "Getting Books Faster and Cheaper: A Jobber Acquisitions Study," *Public Libraries* 19:4 (Winter 1980), 103-105. **(22, 39, 42, 110)**

386 Vernon A. Rayford. "A Black Librarian Takes a Look at Discrimination: by a Law School Library Survey," *Law Library Journal* 65:2 (May 1972), 183-189.

387 Audio-Visual Committee, American Association of Law Libraries. "The Use of Audio-Visual Teaching Aids and Library Microforms in American Legal Education," *Law Library Journal* 66:1 (February 1973), 84-87. **(223) (169, 170, 302, 303)**

388 Cameron Allen. "Whom We Shall Serve: Secondary Patrons of the University Law School Library," *Law Library Journal* 66:2 (May 1973), 160-171. **(329, 330)**

389 O. James Werner. "The Present Legal Status and Conditions of Prison Law Libraries," *Law Library Journal* 66:3 (August 1973), 259-269. **(127)**

390 George S. Grossman. "Clinical Legal Education and the Law Library," *Law Library Journal* 67:1 (February 1974), 60-78.

391 Kurt Schwerin and Igor I. Kavass. "Foreign Legal Periodicals in American Law Libraries 1973 Union List," *Law Library Journal* 67:1 (February 1974), 120-126. **(112, 142)**

392 Bethany J. Ochal. "County Law Libraries," *Law Library Journal* 67:2 (May 1974), 177-234. **(127, 278)**

393 Peter Enyingi. "Subject Cataloging Practices in American Law Libraries: A Survey," *Law Library Journal* 68:1 (February 1975), 11-17.

394 Sandra Sadow and Benjamin R. Beede. "Library Instruction in American Law Schools," *Law Library Journal* 68:1 (February 1975), 27-32.

395 Michael L. Richmond. "Attitudes of Law Librarians to Theft and Mutilation Control Methods," *Law Library Journal* 68:1 (February 1975), 60-81.

Bibliography of Articles

396 Ellin B. Christianson. "Mergers in the Publishing Industry, 1958-1970," *Journal of Library History, Philosophy and Comparative Librarianship* 7:1 (January 1972), 5-32. **(36)**

397 Eugene E. Graziano. "Interlibrary Loan Analysis: Diagnostic for Scientific Serials Backfile Acquisitions," *Special Libraries* 53:5 (May/June 1962), 251-257.

398 John E. James. "Library Technician Program: The Library Technician Graduates' Point of View," *Special Libraries* 62:6 (July/August 1971), 268-278.

399 James M. Matarazzo. "Scientific Journals: Page or Price Explosion?" *Special Libraries* 63:2 (February 1972), 53-58. **(16, 17, 89, 90, 105)**

400 Julie L. Moore. "Bibliographic Control of American Doctoral Dissertations," *Special Libraries* 63:7 (July 1972), 285-291. **(165, 227)**

401 Robert T. Bottle and William W. Chase. "Some Characteristics of the Literature on Music and Musicology," *Special Libraries* 63:10 (October 1972), 469-476. **(84, 87, 161, 217, 226, 230, 246)**

402 William P. Koughan and John A. Timour. "Are Hospital Libraries Meeting Physicians' Information Needs?" *Special Libraries* 64:5/6 (May/June 1972), 222-227.

403 Jean M. Ray. "Who Borrows Maps from a University Library Map Collection —And Why?" *Special Libraries* 65:3 (March 1974), 104-109. **(254, 300, 301)**

404 Ching-Chih Chen. "How Do Scientists Meet Their Information Needs?" *Special Libraries* 65:7 (July 1974), 272-280. **(221, 287, 312, 320, 337)**

405 Katherine C. Owen. "Productive Journal Titles in the Pharmaceutical Industry," *Special Libraries* 65:10/11 (October/November 1974), 430-439. **(218)**

406 Stanley A. Elman. "Cost Comparison of Manual and On-Line Computerized Literature Searching," *Special Libraries* 66:1 (January 1975), 12-18.

407 Jerome P. Fatcheric. "Survey of Users of a Medium-Sized Technical Library," *Special Libraries* 66:5/6 (May/June 1975), 245-251.

408 Bahaa El-Hadidy. "Bibliographic Control among Geoscience Abstracting and Indexing Services," *Special Libraries* 66:5/6 (May/June 1975), 260-265. **(227, 230)**

409 Ruth W. Wender. "Hospital Journal Title Usage Study," *Special Libraries* 66:11 (November 1975), 532-537. **(58, 60, 138, 139, 183, 309, 310)**

410 Thelma Freides. "Bibliographic Gaps in the Social Science Literature," *Special Libraries* 67:2 (February 1976), 68-75. **(152, 233)**

411 Eileen E. Hitchingham. "MEDLINE Use in a University without a School of Medicine," *Special Libraries* 67:4 (April 1976), 188-194.

BIBLIOGRAPHY OF ARTICLES

412 David Hull and Henry D. Fearnley. "The Museum Library in the United States: A Sample," *Special Libraries* 67:7 (July 1976), 289-298. **(128, 332)**

413 Amelia Breiting, Marcia Dorey and Deirdre Sockbeson. "Staff Development in College and University Libraries," *Special Libraries* 67:7 (July 1976), 305-309.

414 Arley L. Ripin and Dorothy Kasman. "Education for Special Librarianship: A Survey of Courses Offered in Accredited Programs," *Special Libraries* 67:11 (November 1976), 504-509.

415 George W. Black, Jr. "Selected Annaul Bound Volume Production," *Special Libraries* 67:11 (November 1976), 534-536.

416 Howard Fosdick. "An SDC-Based On-Line Search Service: A Patron Evaluation Survey and Implications," *Special Libraries* 68:9 (September 1977), 305-312.

417 Diane M. Nelson. "Methods of Citation Analysis in the Fine Arts," *Special Libraries* 68:11 (November 1977), 390-395.

418 Annette Corth. "Coverage of Marine Biology Citations,"*Special Libraries* 68:12 (December 1977), 439-446.

419 Jean K. Martin. "Computer-Based Literature Searching: Impact on Interlibrary Loan Service," *Special Libaries* 69:1 (January 1978), 1-6.

420 Jean M. Ray. "Who Borrows Maps from a University Library Map Collection —and Why? Report II," *Special Libraries* 69:1 (January 1978), 13-20. **(301, 302)**

421 Robert Goehlert. "Periodical Use in an Academic Library: A Study of Economists and Political Scientists," *Special Libraries* 69:2 (February 1978), 51-60. **(197, 222, 270, 273, 313, 332, 339)**

422 Sandra J. Springer, Robert A. Yokel, Nancy M. Lorenzi, Leonard T. Sigell and E. Don Nelson. "Drug Information to Patient Care Areas via Television: Preliminary Evaluation of Two Years' Experience," *Special Libraries* 69:4 (April 1978), 155-163.

423 Martha J. Bailey. "Requirement for Middle Managerial Positions," *Special Libraries* 69:9 (September 1978), 323-331.

424 Carolyn L. Warden. "An Industrial Current Awareness Service: A User Evaluation Study," *Special Libraries* 69:12 (December 1978), 459-467.

425 Charles H. Davis. "Programming Aptitude as a Function of Undergraduate Major," *Special Libraries* 69:12 (December 1978), 482-485.

426 Jean Mace Schmidt. "Translation of Periodical Literature in Plant Pathology," *Special Libraries* 70:1 (January 1979), 12-17. **(114)**

Bibliography of Articles 371

427 Susan Dingle-Cliff and Charles H. Davis. "Collection Overlap in Canadian Addictions Libraries," *Special Libraries* 70:2 (February 1979), 76-81. **(143)**

428 John J. Knightly. "Overcoming the Cirterion Problem in the Evaluation of Library Performance," *Special Libraries* 70:4 (April 1979), 173-178.

429 Ruth W. Wender. "Counting Journal Title Usage in the Health Sciences," *Special Libraries* 70:5/6 (May/June 1975), 219-226. **(204, 207, 272, 274, 309, 310, 311)**

430 John Steuben. "Interlibrary Loan of Photocopies of Articles under the New Copyright Law," *Special Libraries* 70:5/6 (May/June 1979), 227-232.

431 John Kok and Edward G. Strable. "Moving Up: Librarians Who Have Become Officers of Their Organization," *Special Libraries* 71:1 (January 1980), 5-12.

432 Rebecca J. Jensen, Herbert D. Asbury and Radford G. King. "Costs and Benefits to Industry of Online Literature Searches," *Special Libraries* 71:7 (July 1980), 291-299.

433 C. Margaret Bell. "The Applicability of OCLC and Inforonics in Special Libraries," *Special Libraries* 71:9 (September 1980), 398-404.

434 A. Neil Yerkey. "The Psychological Climate of Librarianship: Values of Special Librarians," *Special Libraries* 72:3 (July 1981), 195-200.

435 Virgil P. Diodato. "Author Indexing," *Special Libraries* 72:4 (October 1981), 361-369.

436 Judith M. Pask. "Bibliographic Instruction in Business Libraries," *Special Libraries* 72:4 (October 1981), 370-378. **(121)**

437 Ann T. Dodson, Paul P. Philbin and Kunj B. Rastogi. "Electronic Interlibrary Loan in the OCLC Library: A Study of its Effectiveness," *Special Libraries* 73:1 (January 1982), 12-20.

438 Gloria J. Zamora and Martha C. Adamson. "Authorship Characteristics in *Special Libraries*: A Comparative Study," *Special Libraries* 73:2 (April 1982), 100-107.

439 Robert K. Poyer. "Time Lag in Four Indexing Services," *Special Libraries* 73:2 (April 1982), 142-146.

440 Pauline R. Hodges. "Keyword in Title Indexes: Effectiveness of Retrieval in Computer Searches," *Special Libraries* 74:1 (January 1983), 56-60.

441 D.K. Varma. "Increased Subscription Costs and Problems of Resource Allocation," *Special Libraries* 74:1 (January 1983), 61-66. **(16, 104)**

442 Michael Halperin and Ruth A. Pagell. "Searchers' Perceptions of Online Database Vendors," *Special Libraries* 74:2 (April 1973), 119-126.

443 Michael E.D. Koenig. "Education for Special Librarianship," *Special Libraries* 74:2 (April 1983), 182-196.

444 Powell Niland and William H. Kurth. "Estimating Lost Volumes in a University Library Collection," *College and Research Libraries* 37:2 (March 1976), 128-136.

445 Rush G. Miller. "The Influx of Ph.D.s into Librarianship: Intrusion or Transfusion?" *College and Research Libraries* 37:2 (March 1976), 158-165.

446 Steven Leach. "The Growth Rates of Major Academic Libraries: Rider and Purdue Reviewed," *College and Research Libraries* 37:6 (November 1976), 531-542. **(90, 91)**

447 T. Saracevic, W.M. Shaw, Jr. and P.B. Kantor. "Causes and Dynamics of User Frustration in an Academic Library," *College and Research Libraries* 38:1 (January 1977), 7-18. **(342)**

448 R.W. Meyer and Rebecca Panetta. "Two Shared Cataloging Data Bases: A Comparison," *College and Research Libraries* 38:1 (January 1977), 19-24.

449 Peter Hernon and Maureen Pastine. "Student Perceptions of Academic Librarians," *College and Research Libraries* 38:2 (March 1977), 129-139.

450 Catherine V. Von Schon. "Inventory 'By Computer'," *College and Research Libraries* 38:2 (March 1977), 147-152.

451 David C. Genaway and Edward B. Stanford. "Quasi-Departmental Libraries," *College and Research Libraries* 38:3 (May 1977), 187-194. **(337)**

452 Elizabeth W. Matthews. "Trends Affecting Community College Library Administrators," *College and Research Libraries* 38:3 (May 1977), 210-217. **(130)**

453 Lawrence J. Perk. "Secondary Publications in Education: A Study of Duplication," *College and Research Libraries* 38:3 (May 1977), 221-226.

454 Geraldine Murphy Wright. "Current Trends in Periodical Collections," *College and Research Libraries* 38:3 (May 1977), 234-240. **(4, 31, 119, 130,**

455 Lawrence J. Perk and Noelle Van Pulis. "Periodical Usage in an Education-Psychology Library," *College and Research Libraries* 38:4 (July 1977), 304-308. **(272, 312, 317)**

456 Egill A. Halldorsson and Marjorie E. Murfin. "The Performance of Professionals and Nonprofessionals in the Reference Interview," *College and Research Libraries* 38:5 (September 1977), 385-395.

457 Susan A. Lee. "Conflict and Ambiguity in the Role of the Academic Library Director," *College and Research Libraries* 38:5 (September 1977), 396-403.

Bibliography of Articles

458 Glenn R. Wittig. "Dual Pricing of Periodicals," *College and Research Libraries* 38:5 (September 1977), 412-418. **(14, 102)**

459 Miriam A. Drake. "Attribution of Library Costs," *College and Research Libraries* 38:6 (November 1977), 514-519.

460 Harry M. Kriz. "Subscriptions vs. Books in a Constant Dollar Budget," *College and Research Libraries* 39:2 (March 1978), 105-109. **(85, 152, 158, 178, 284)**

461 Charles J. Popovich. "The Characteristics of a Collection for Research in Business/Management," *College and Research Libraries* 39:2 (March 1978), 117. **(55, 59, 73, 86, 120, 152, 157, 158, 196, 251, 267, 272, 277, 284, 292, 314, 333)**

462 Jean A. Major. "The Visually Impaired Reader in the Academic Library," *College and Research Libraries* 39:3 (May 1978), 191-196.

463 Herbert S. White and Karen Momenee. "Impact of the Increase in Library Doctorates," *College and Research Libraries* 39:3 (May 1978), 207-214.

464 James Michalko and Toby Heidtmann. "Evaluating the Effectiveness of an Electronic Security System," *College and Research Libraries* 39:4 (July 1978), 263-267.

465 William M. McClellan. "Judging Music Libraries," *College and Research Libraries* 39:4 (July 1978), 281-286.

466 Rita Hoyt Smith and Warner Granade. "User and Library Failures in an Undergraduate Library," *College and Research Libraries* 39:6 (November 1978), 467-473. **(338)**

467 Linda Ann Hulbert and David Stewart Curry. "Evaluation of an Approval Plan," *College and Research Libraries* 39:6 (November 1978), 485-491. **(3, 65, 144, 148, 233, 242)**

468 Julia F. Baldwin and Robert S. Rudolph. "The Comparative Effectiveness of a Slide/Tape Show and a Library Tour," *College and Research Libraries* 40:1 (January 1979), 31-35.

469 Melissa D. Trevvett. "Characteristics of Interlibrary Loan Requests at the Library of Congress," *College and Research Libraries* 40:1 (January 1979), 36-43.

470 Elaine Zaremba Jennerich and Bessie Hess Smith. "A Bibliographic Instruction Program in Music," *College and Research Libraries* 40:3 (May 1979), 226-233.

471 William J. Maher and Benjamin F. Shearer. "Undergraduate Use Patterns of Newspapers on Microfilm," *College and Research Libraries* 40:3 (May 1979), 254-260. **(255, 270, 305, 306, 308)**

472 Larry Hardesty, Nicholas P. Lovrich, Jr. and James Mannon. "Evaluating Library-Use Instruction," *College and Research Libraries* 40:4 (July 1979), 309-317.

473 Seymour H. Sargent. "The Uses and Limitations of Trueswell," *College and Research Libraries* 40:5 (September 1979), 416-425. **(267, 268, 277)**

474 Patricia Stenstrom and Ruth B. McBride." Serial Use by Social Science Faculty: A Survey," *College and Research Libraries* 40:5 (September 1979), 426-431. **(324, 325)**

475 Elaine C. Clever. "Using Indexes as 'Memory Assists'," *College and Research Libraries* 40:5 (September 1979), 444-449.

476 William E. McGrath, Donald J. Simon and Evelyn Bullard. "Ethnocentricity and Cross-Disciplinary Circulation," *College and Research Libraries* 40:6 (November 1979), 511-518. **(334, 335)**

477 Michael Gorman and Jami Hotsinpiller. "ISBD: Aid or Barrier to Understanding," *College and Research Libraries* 40:6 (November 1979), 519-526.

478 Jinnie Y. Davis and Stella Bentley. "Factors Affecting Faculty Perceptions of Academic Libraries," *College and Research Libraries* 40:6 (November 1979), 527-532. **(338)**

479 Dennis J. Reynolds. "Regional Alternatives for Interlibrary Loan: Access to Unreported Holdings," *College and Research Libraries* 41:1 (January 1980), 33-42.

480 Ronald Rayman and Frank William Goudy. "Research and Publication Requirements in University Libraries," *College and Research Libraries* 41:1 (January 1980), 43-48.

481 John N. Olsgaard and Jane Kinch Olsgaard. "Authorship in Five Library Periodicals," *College and Research Libraries* 41:1 (January 1980), 49-53.

482 Albert F. Maag. "Design of the Library Director Interview: The Candidate's Perspective," *College and Research Libraries* 41:2 (March 1980), 112-121.

483 Thomas M. Gaughan. "Resume Essentials for the Academic Librarian," *College and Research Libraries* 41:2 (March 1980), 122-127.

484 Harold B. Shill. "Open Stacks and Library Performance," *College and Research Libraries* 41:3 (May 1980), 220-225. **(332)**

485 Robert L. Turner, Jr. "Femininity and the Librarian—Another Test," *College and Research Libraries* 41:3 (May 1980), 235-241.

486 Ray L. Carpenter. "College Libraries: A Comparative Analysis in Terms of the ACRL Standards," *College and Research Libraries* 42:1 (January 1981), 7-18. **(91, 119, 120, 178, 257, 258)**

487 George V. Hodowanec. "An Acquisition Rate Model for Academic Libraries," *College and Research Libraries* 39:6 (September 1978), 439-442.

Bibliography of Articles

488   Roland Person. "Long-Term Evaluation of Bibliographic Instruction: Lasting Encouragement," *College and Research Libraries* 42:1 (January 1981), 19-25.

489   Laslo A. Nagy and Martha Lou Thomas. "An Evaluation of the Teaching Effectiveness of Two Library Instructional Videotapes," *College and Research Libraries* 42:1 (January 1981), 26-30.

490   David N. King and John C. Ory. "Effects of Library Instruction on Student Research: A Case Study," *College and Research Libraries* 42:1 (January 1981), 31-41.

491   Herbert S. White. "Perceptions by Educators and Administrators of the Ranking of Library School Programs," *College and Research Libraries* 42:3 (May 1981), 191-202.

492   Russ Davidson, Connie Capers Thorson and Margo C. Trumpeter. "Faculty Status for Librarians in the Rocky Mountain Region: A Review and Analysis," *College and Research Libraries* 42:3 (May 1981), 203-213.

493   M. Kathy Cook. "Rank, Status, and Contribution of Academic Librarians as Perceived by the Teaching Faculty at Southern Illinois University, Carbondale," *College and Research Libraries* 42:3 (May 1981), 214-223.

494   John N. Olsgaard and Jane Kinch Olsgaard. "Post-MLS Educational Requirements for Academic Librarians," *College and Research Libraries* 42:3 (May 1981), 224-228.

495   Ronald Rayman. "Employment Opportunities for Academic Librarians in the 1970's: An Analysis of the Past Decade," *College and Research Libraries* 42:3 (May 1981), 229-234.

496   Martha C. Adamson and Gloria J. Zamora. "Publishing in Library Science Journals: A Test of the Olsgaard Profile," *College and Research Libraries* 42:3 (May 1981), 235-241.

497   Charles Sage, Janet Klass, Helen H. Spalding and Tracey Robinson. "A Queueing Study of Public Catalog Use," *College and Research Libraries* 42:4 (July 1981), 317-325.

498   Doris Cruger Dale. "Cataloging and Classsification Practices in Community College Libraries," *College and Research Libraries* 42:4 (July 1981), 333-339.

499   Dana Weiss. "Book Theft and Book Mutilation in a Large Urban University Library," *College and Research Libraries* 42:4 (July 1981), 341-347.

500   Raymond L. Carpenter. "Two-Year College Libraries: A Comparative Analysis in Terms of the ACRL Standards," *College and Research Libraries* 42:5 (September 1981), 407-415.   **(6, 66, 91, 122, 180, 258, 259)**

501   Paul D. Luyben, Leonard Cohen, Rebecca Conger and Selby U. Gration. "Reducing Noise in a College Library," *College and Research Libraries* 42:5 (September 1981), 470-481.

502 Prabha Sharma. "A Survey of Academic Librarians and Their Opinions Related to Nine-Month Contracts and Academic Status Configurations in Alabama, Georgia and Mississippi," *College and Research Libraries* 42:6 (November 1981), 561-570.

503 Priscilla Geahigan, Harriet Nelson, Stewart Saunders and Lawrence Woods. "Acceptability of Non-Library/Information Science Publications in the Promotion and Tenure of Academic Librarians," *College and Research Libraries* 42:6 (November 1981), 571-575.

504 Barbara Moore, Tamara J. Miller and Don L. Tolliver. "Title Overlap: A Study of Duplication in the University of Wisconsin System Libraries," *College and Research Libraries* 43:1 (January 1982), 14-21. **(141, 142)**

505 Gary A. Golden, Susan U. Golden and Rebecca T. Lenzini. "Patron Approaches to Serials: A User Study," *College and Research Libraries* 43:1 (January 1982), 22-30.

506 Thomas T. Surprenant. "Learning Theory, Lecture, and Programmed Instruction Text: An Experiment in Bibliographic Instruction," *College and Research Libraries* 43:1 (January 1982), 31-37.

507 Larry Hardesty, Nicholas P. Lovrich, Jr. and James Mannon. "Library-Use Instruction: Assessment of the Long-Term Effects," *College and Research Libraries* 43:1 (January 1982), 38-46.

508 Robert Swisher and Peggy C. Smith. "Journals Read by ACRL Academic Librarians, 1973 and 1978," *College and Research Libraries* 43:1 (January 1982), 51-58. **(200, 201, 320, 321)**

509 William Caynon. "Collective Bargaining and Professional Development of Academic Librarians," *College and Research Libraries* 43:2 (March 1982), 133-139.

510 Barbara J. Smith. "Background Characteristics and Education Needs of a Group of Instruction Librarians in Pennsylvania," *College and Research Libraries* 43:3 (May 1982), 199-207.

511 Gloria S. Cline. "*College and Research Libraries*: Its First Forty Years," *College and Research Libraries* 43:3 (May 1982), 208-232. **(84, 86, 180, 188, 191, 202)**

512 John B. Harer and C. Edward Huber. "Copyright Policies in Virginia Academic Library Reserve Rooms," *College and Research Libraries* 43:3 (May 1982), 233-241. **(289)**

513 Laurie S. Linsley. "Academic Libraries in an Interlibrary Loan Network," *College and Research Libraries* 43:4 (July 1982), 292-299.

514 Timothy D. Jewell. "Student Reactions to a Self-Paced Library Skills Workbook Program: Survey Evidence," *College and Research Libraries* 43:5 (September 1982), 371-378.

Bibliography of Articles

515 Mary Baier Wells. "Requirements and Benefits for Academic Librarians: 1959-1979," *College and Research Libraries* 43:6 (November 1982), 450-458.

516 Marjorie A. Benedict, Jacquelyn A. Gavryck and Hanan C. Selvin. "Status of Academic Librarians in New York State," *College and Research Libraries* 44:1 (January 1983), 12-19.

517 Carol Truett. "Services to Developmental Education Students in the Community College: Does the Library Have a Role?" *College and Research Libraries* 44:1 (January 1983), 20-28.

518 Gene K. Rinkel and Patricia McCandless. "Application of a Methodology Analyzing User Frustration," *College and Research Libraries* 44:1 (January 1983), 29-37. **(340)**

519 Jo Bell Whitlatch. "Library Use Patterns Among Full- and Part-Time Faculty and Students," *College and Research Libraries* 44:2 (March 1983), 141-152.

520 Madeleine Stern. "Characteristics of the Literature of Literary Scholarship," *College and Research Libraries* 44:4 (July 1983), 199-209. **(63, 87, 233)**

521 Philip Schwarz. "Demand-Adjusted Shelf Availability Parameters: A Second Look," *College and Research Libraries* 44:4 (July 1983), 210-219. **(340)**

522 Paul M. Anderson and Ellen G. Miller. "Participative Planning for Library Automation: The Role of the User Opinion Survey," *College and Research Libraries* 44:4 (July 1983), 245-254.

523 Raymond W. Barber and Jacqueline C. Mancall. "The Application of Bibliometric Techniques to the Analysis of Materials for Young Adults," *Collection Management* 2:3 (Fall 1978), 229-245. **(181, 182, 191, 228, 229, 230, 285, 322, 328)**

524 Kenneth C. Kirsch and Albert H. Rubenstein. "Converting from Hard Copy to Microfilm: An Administrative Experiment," *Collection Management* 2:4 (Winter 1978), 279-302. **(307)**

525 Herbert Goldhor. "U.S. Public Library Adult Non-Fiction Book Collections in the Humanities," *Collection Management* 3:1 (Spring 1979), 31-43.

526 Sally F. Williams. "Construction and Application of a Periodical Price Index," *Collection Management* 2:4 (Winter 1978), 329-344.

527 Mary Jane Pobst Reed. "Identification of Storage Candidates among Monographs," *Collection Management* 3:2/3 (Summer/Fall 1979), 203-214. **(279)**

528 Ung Chon Kim. "Participation of Teaching Faculty in Library Book Selection," *Collection Management* 3:4 (Winter 1979), 333-352. **(135)**

529 Glenn R. Lowry. "A Heuristic Collection Loss Rate Determination Methodology: An Alternative to Shelf-Reading," *Collection Management* 4:1/2 (Spring/Summer 1982), 73-83.

530 Stewart Saunders. "Student Reliance on Faculty Guidance in the Selection of Reading Materials: The Use of Core Collections," *Collection Management* 4:4 (Winter 1982), 9-23. **(135, 136, 153, 245, 281, 282, 304, 305)**

531 Ralph M. Daehn. "The Measurement and Projection of Shelf Space," *Collection Management* 4:4 (Winter 1982), 25-39. **(113)**

532 Igor I. Kavass. "Foreign and International Law Collections in Selected Law Libraries of the United States: Survey, 1972-73," *International Journal of Law Libraries* 1:3 (November 1973), 117-133.

533 Robert J. Garen. "Library Orientation on Television," *Canadian Library Journal* 24:2 (September 1967), 124-126.

534 D.W. Miller. "Non-English Books in Canadian Public Libraries," *Canadian Library Journal* 27:2 (March/April 1970), 123-129. **(113, 123, 293)**

535 Robert H. Blackburn. "Canadian Content in a Sample of Photocopying," *Canadian Library Journal* 27:5 (September/October 1970), 332-340.

536 Peter H. Wolters and Jack E. Brown. "CAN/SDI System: User Reaction to a Computer Information Retrieval System for Canadian Scientists and Technologists," *Canadian Library Journal* 28:1 (January/ February), 20-23.

537 M. Jamil Qureshi. "Academic Status, Salaries and Fringe Benefits in Community College Libraries of Canada," *Canadian Library Journal* 28:1 (January/February 1971), 41-45.

538 George J. Snowball. "Survey of Social Sciences and Humanities Monograph Circulation by Random Sampling of the Stack," *Canadian Library Journal* 28:5 (September/October 1971), 352-361. **(266, 279)**

539 Roop K. Sandhu and Harjit Sandhu. "Job Perception of University Librarians and Library Students," *Canadian Library Journal* 28:6 (November/December 1971), 438-445.

540 Brian Dale and Patricia Dewdney. "Canadian Public Libraries and the Physically Handicapped," *Canadian Library Journal* 29:3 (May/June 1972), 231-236.

541 R.G. Wilson. "Interlibrary Loan Experiments at the University of Calgary," *Canadian Library Journal* 30:1 (January/February 1973), 38-40.

542 Peter Simmons. "Studies in the Use of the Card Catalogue in a Public Library," *Canadian Library Journal* 31:4 (August 1974), 323-337.

543 L.J. Amey and R.J. Smith. "Combination School and Public Libraries: An Attitudinal Study," *Canadian Library Journal* 33:3 (June 1976), 251-261.

Bibliography of Articles 379

544 John Wilkinson. "The Library Market for Canadian Juvenile Fiction: A Further Analysis," *Canadian Library Journal* 34:1 (February 1977), 5-15. **(123, 124)**

545 Larry Orten and John Wiseman. "Library Service to Part-time Students," *Canadian Library Journal* 34:1 (February 1977), 23-27.

546 Esther L. Sleep. "Whither the ISSN? A Practical Experience," *Canadian Library Journal* 34:4 (August 1977), 265-270. **(24, 25, 194)**

547 Sarah Landy. "Why Johnny Can Read...but Doesn't," *Canadian Library Journal* 34:5 (October 1977), 379-387.

548 Sharon Mott. "An Edmonton High School Reduces Book Losses," *Canadian Library Journal* 35:1 (February 1978), 45-49.

549 Fotoula Pantazis. "Library Technicians in Ontario Academic Libraries," *Canadian Library Journal* 35:2 (April 1978), 77-91.

550 Dorothy Ryder. "Canadian Reference Sources—A 10 Year Overview," *Canadian Library Journal* 35:4 (August 1978), 289-293. **(119)**

551 Laurent-G. Denis. "Full-time Faculty Survey Describes Educators," *Canadian Library Journal* 36:3 (June 1979), 107-121.

552 Marie Foster. "Philosophy of Librarianship," *Canadian Library Journal* 36:3 (June 1979), 131-137.

553 Kenneth H. Plate and Jacob P. Seigel. "Career Patterns of Ontario Librarians," *Canadian Library Journal* 36:3 (June 1979), 143-148.

554 Mavis Cariou. "Liaison Where Field and Faculty Meet," *Canadian Library Journal* 36:3 (June 1979), 155-163.

555 Norman Horrocks. "Encyclopedias and Public Libraries: A Canadian Survey," *Canadian Library Journal* 38:2 (April 1981), 79-83.

556 Stephen B. Lawton. "Diffusion of Automation in Post-Secondary Institutions," *Canadian Library Journal* 38:2 (April 1980), 93-97.

557 Mary Ann Wasylycia-Coe. "Profile: Canadian Chief Librarians by Sex," *Canadian Library Journal* 38:3 (June 1981), 159-163.

558 Margaret Currie, Elaine Goettler and Sandra McCaskill. "Evaluating the Relationship between Library Skills and Library Instruction," *Canadian Library Journal* 39:1 (February 1982), 35-37.

559 Esther L. Sleep. "Periodical Vandalism: A Chronic Condition," *Canadian Library Journal* 39:1 (February 1982), 39-42.

560 Kenneth Setterington. "The Ph.D. in Library Administration: A Report of Research," *Library Research* (after Spring 1983 called *Library and Information Science Research*) 5:2 (Summer 1983), 177-194.

561 Robert F. Rose. "Identifying a Core Collection of Business Periodicals for Academic Libraries," *Collection Management* 5:1/2 (Spring/Summer 1983), 73-87. **(195, 196, 248)**

562 Raymond Kilpela. "A Profile of Library School Deans, 1960-81," *Journal of Education for Librarianship* 23:3 (Winter 1983), 173-191.

563 Charlene Renner and Barton M. Clark. "Professional and Nonprofessional Staffing Patterns in Departmental Libraries," *Library Research* 1 (1979), 153-170.

564 Jacqueline C. Mancall and M. Carl Drott. "Materials Used by High School Students in Preparing Independent Study Projects: A Bibliometric Approach," *Library Research* 1 (1979), 223-236. **(53, 182, 192, 265, 278, 280, 285, 297, 303, 308, 315, 318, 322, 328)**

565 Alan R. Samuels. "Assessing Organizational Climate in Public Libraries," *Library Research* 1 (1979), 237-254.

566 Diane Mittermeyer and Lloyd J. Houser. "The Knowledge Base for the Administration of Libraries," *Library Research* 1 (1979), 255-276. **(160, 175, 176, 187, 191, 201, 225, 245, 247)**

567 Michael V. Sullivan, Betty Vadeboncoeur, Nancy Shiotani and Peter Stangl. "Obsolescence in Biomedical Journals: Not an Artifact of Literature Growth," *Library Research* 2 (1980-81), 29-46. **(272, 275)**

568 Robert V. Williams. "Sources of the Variability in Level of Public Library Development in the United States: A Comparative Analysis," *Library Research* 2 (1980-81), 157-176.

569 Bluma C. Peritz. "The Methods of Library Science Research: Some Results from a Bibliometric Survey," *Library Research* 2 (1980-81), 251-268.

570 Nancy Van House DeWath. "Fees for Online Bibliographic Search Services in Publicly-Supported Libraries," *Library Research* 3 (1981), 29-45.

571 Bluma C. Peritz. "Citation Characteristics in Library Science: Some Further Results from a Bibliometric Survey," *Library Research* 3 (1981), 47-65. **(63, 86, 264)**

572 Gary Moore. "Library Long-Range Planning: A Survey of Current Practices," *Library Research* 3 (1981), 155-165.

573 Larry Hardesty. "Use of Library Materials at a Small Liberal Arts College," *Library Research* 3 (1981), 261-282. **(117, 135, 268, 294, 304)**

574 Stewart Saunders, Harriet Nelson and Priscilla Geahigan. "Alternatives to the Shelflist Measure for Determining the Size of a Subject Collection," *Library Research* 3 (1981), 383-391.

575 P. Robert Paustian. "Collection Size and Interlibrary Loan in Large Academic Libraries," *Library Research* 3 (1981), 393-400.

576 Daniel O. O'Connor. "Evaluating Public Libraries Using Standard Scores: The Library Quotient," *Library Research* 4 (1982), 51-70. **(8, 67, 100, 181, 300)**

Bibliography of Articles

577 Snunith Shoham. "A Cost-Preference Study of the Decentralization of Academic Library Services," *Library Research* 4 (1982), 175-194.

578 A.S. Pickett. "San Franscisco State College Library Technical Services Time Study," *Library Resources and Technical Services* 4:1 (Winter 1960), 45-46. **(37)**

579 Rosamond H. Danielson. "Cornell's Area Classification: A Space-Saving Device for Less-Used Books," *Library Resources and Technical Services* 5:2 (Spring 1961), 139-141.

580 Miriam C. Maloy. "Reclassification for the Divisional Plan," *Library Resources and Technical Services* 6:3 (Summer 1962), 239-242.

581 Andre Nitecki. "Costs of a Divided Catalog," *Library Resources and Technical Services* 6:4 (Fall 1962), 351-355.

582 Donald V. Black. "Automatic Classification and Indexing, for Libraries?" *Library Resources and Technical Services* 9:1 (Winter 1965), 35-52.

583 Perry D. Morrison. "Use of Library of Congress Classsification Decisions in Academic Libraries—An Empirical Study," *Library Resources and Technical Services* 9:2 (Spring 1965), 235-242.

584 Manuel D. Lopez. "Subject Catalogers Equal to the Future?" *Library Resources and Technical Services* 9:3 (Summer 1965), 371-375.

585 Ashby J. Fristoe. "The Bitter End," *Library Resources and Technical Services* 10:1 (Winter 1966), 91-95. **(46)**

586 Ole V. Groos. "Less-Used Titles and Volumes of Science Journals: Two Preliminary Notes," *Library Resources and Technical Services* 10:3 (Summer 1966), 289-290. **(183, 192)**

587 Paula M. Strain. "A Study of the Usage and Retention of Technical Periodicals," *Library Resources and Technical Services* 10:3 (Summer 1966), 295-304. **(53, 273)**

588 William R. Nugent. "Statistics of Collection Overlap at the Libraries of the Six New England State Universities," *Library Resources and Technical Services* 12:1 (Winter 1968), 31-36. **(140)**

589 Walter R. Stubbs and Robert N. Broadus. "The Value of the Kirkus Service for College Libraries," *Library Resources and Technical Services* 13:2 (Spring 1969), 203-205. **(232)**

590 Barton R. Burkhalter and LaVerne Hoag. "Another Look at Manual Sorting and Filing: Backwards and Forwards," *Library Resources and Technical Services* 14:3 (Summer 1970), 445-454.

591 "More on DC Numbers on LC Cards: Quantity and Quality," *Library Resources and Technical Services* 14:4 (Fall 1970), 517-527.

592 Carol A. Nemeyer. "Scholarly Reprint Publishing in the United States: Selected Findings from a Recent Survey of the Industry," *Library Resources and Technical Services* 15:1 (Winter 1971), 35-48. **(37, 174)**

593 Betty J. Mitchell and Carol Bedoian. "A Systematic Approach to Performance Evaluation of Out-of-Print Book Dealers: The San Fernando Valley State College Experience," *Library Resources and Technical Services* 15:2 (Spring 1971), 215-222. **(10, 13, 99, 137)**

594 Barbara Schrader and Elaine Orsini. "British, French and Australian Publications in the National Union Catalog: A Study of NPAC's Effectiveness," *Library Resources and Technical Services* 15:3 (Summer 1971), 345-353. **(244)**

595 Joel Levis. "Canadian Publications in the English Language: CBI vs. Canadiana," *Library Resources and Technical Services* 15:3 (Summer 1971), 354-358. **(42, 225)**

596 Zubaidah Isa. "The Entry-Word in Indonesian Names and Titles," *Library Resources and Technical Services* 15:3 (Summer 1971), 393-398.

597 Richard J. Hyman. "Access to Library Collections: Summary of a Documentary and Opinion Survey on the Direct Shelf Approach and Browsing," *Library Resources and Technical Services* 15:4 (Fall 1971), 479-491.

598 Robert L. Mowery. "The Cryptic Other," *Library Resources and Technical Services* 16:1 (Winter 1972), 74-78.

599 Ann Craig Turner. "Comparative Card Production Methods," *Library Resources and Technical Services* 16:3 (Summer 1972), pp. 347-358.

600 Edmund G. Hamann. "Expansion of the Public Card Catalog in a Large Library," *Library Resources and Technical Services* 16:4 (Fall 1972), 488-496.

601 Ernest R. Perez. "Acquisitions of Out-of-Print Materials," *Library Resources and Technical Services* 17:1 (Winter 1973), 42-59. **(12, 27, 28, 99, 136, 137)**

602 E. Dale Cluff and Karen Anderson. "LC Card Order Experiment Conducted at University of Utah Marriott Library," *Library Resources and Technical Services* 17:1 (Winter 1973), 70-72.

603 Betty J. Mitchell. "Methods Used in Out-of-Print Acquisition; A Survey of Out-of-Print Book Dealers," *Library Resources and Technical Services* 17:2 (Spring 1973), 211-215. **(28, 137)**

604 George Piternick. "University Library Arrearages," *Library Resources and Technical Services* 13:1 (Winter 1969), 102-114.

605 Nancy E. Brodie. "Evaluation of a KWIC Index for *Library Literature*," *Journal of the American Society for Information Science* 21:1 (January-February 1970), 22-28.

Bibliography of Articles

606 William S. Cooper. "The Potential Usefulness of Catalog Access Points Other than Author, Title and Subject," *Journal of the American Society for Information Science* 21:2 (March-April 1970), 112-127.

607 Barbara F. Frick and John M. Ginski. "Cardiovascular Serial Literature: Characteristics, Productive Journals, and Abstracting/Indexing Coverage," *Journal of the American Society for Information Science* 21:5 (September-October 1970), 338-344. **(189, 193, 208, 209, 210, 250)**

608 Ching-Chih Chen. "The Use Patterns of Physics Journals in a Large Academic Research Library," *Journal of the American Society for Information Science* 23:4 (July-August 1972), 254-265. **(57, 189, 220, 221, 271, 291, 312, 317)**

609 Janet Friedlander. "Clinician Search for Information," *Journal of the American Society for Information Science* 24:1 (January-February 1973), 65-69.

610 Tefko Saracevic and Lawrence J. Perk. "Ascertaining Activities in a Subject Area through Bibliometric Analysis," *Journal of the American Society for Information Science* 24:3 (March-April 1973), 120-134. **(187, 190, 200)**

611 Ruth Kay Maloney. "Title versus Title/Abstract Text Searching in SDI Systems," *Journal of the American Society for Information Science* 25:6 (November-December 1974), 370-373.

612 Gladys B. Dronberger and Gerald T. Kowitz. "Abstract Readability as a Factor in Information Systems," *Journal of the American Society for Information Science* 26:2 (March-April 1975), 108-111.

613 Jerry R. Byrne. "Relative Effectiveness of Titles, Abstracts and Subject Headings for Machine Retrieval from the COMPENDEX Services," *Journal of the American Society for Information Science* 26:4 (July-August 1975), 223-229.

614 Joseph D. Smith and James E. Rush. "The Relationship between Author Names and Author Entries in a Large On-Line Union Catalog as Retrieved Using Truncated Keys," *Journal of the American Society for Information Science* 28:2 (March 1977), 115-120.

615 Marcia J. Bates. "Factors Affecting Subject Catalog Search Success," *Journal of the American Society for Information Science* 28:3 (May 1977), 161-169.

616 Terry Noreault, Matthew Koll and Michael J. McGill. "Automatic Ranked Output from Boolean Searches in SIRE," *Journal of the American Society for Information Science* 28:6 (November 1977), 333-339.

617 Chai Kim and Eui Hang Shin. "Sociodemographic Correlates of Intercounty Variations in the Public Library Output," *Journal of the American Society for Information Science* 28:6 (November 1977), 359-365.

618 Harold E. Bamford, Jr. "Assessing the Effect of Computer Augmentation on Staff Productivity," *Journal of the American Society for Information Science* 30:3 (May 1979), 136-142.

619 Charles H. Davis and Deborah Shaw. "Collection Overlap as a Function of Library Size: A Comparison of American and Canadian Public Libraries," *Journal of the American Society for Information Science* 30:1 (January 1979), 19-24.

620 M. Carl Drott and Belver C. Griffith. "An Empirical Examination of Bradford's Law and the Scattering of Scientific Literature," *Journal of the American Society for Information Science* 29:5 (September 1978), 238-246. **(186, 187)**

621 James D. Anderson. "*Ad hoc* and Selective Translations of Scientific and Technical Journal Articles: Their Characteristicsand Possible Predictability," *Journal of the American Societyfor Information Science* 29:3 (May 1978), 130-135. **(259, 260)**

622 Richard C. Anderson, Francis Narin and Paul McAllister. "Publication Ratings versus Peer Ratings of Universities," *Journal of the American Society for Information Science* 29:2 (March 1978), 91-103.

623 Dennis R. Eichesen. "Cost-Effectiveness Comparison of Manual and On-line Retrospective Bibliographic Searching," *Journal of the American Society for Information Science* 29:2 (March 1978), 56-66.

624 Topsy N. Smalley. "Comparing *Psychological Abstracts* and *Index Medicus* for Coverage of the Journal Literature in a Subject Area in Psychology," *Journal of the American Society for Information Science* 31:3 (May 1980), 144-146.

625 Paul R. McAllister, Richard C. Anderson and Francis Narin. "Comparison of Peer and Citation Assessment of the Influence of Scientific Journals," *Journal of the American Society for Information Science* 31:3 (May 1980), 148-152.

626 Jerry Specht. "Patron Use of an Online Circulation System in Known-Item Searching," *Journal of the American Society for Information Science* 31:5 (September 1980), 335-346.

627 Guilbert C. Hentschke and Ellen Kehoe. "Serial Acquisition as a Capital Budgeting Problem," *Journal of the American Society for Information Science* 31:5 (September 1980), 357-362. **(7, 17, 32, 106, 146)**

628 G. Edward Evans and Claudia White Argyres. "Approval Plans and Collection Development in Academic Libraries," *Library Resources and Technical Services* 18:1 (Winter 1974), 35-50. **(134, 303)**

629 Doris E. New and Retha Zane Ott. "Interlibrary Loan Analysis as a Collection Development Tool," *Library Resources and Technical Services* 18:3 (Summer 1974), 275-283.

630 H. William Axford. "The Validity of Book Price Indexes for Budgetary Projections," *Library Resources and Technical Services* 19:1 (Winter 1975), 5-12. **(17, 40, 64, 105)**

Bibliography of Articles

631 Geza A. Kosa. "Book Selection Tools for Subject Specialists in a Large Research Library: An Analysis," *Library Resources and Technical Services* 19:1 (Winter 1975), 13-18. **(156, 157, 159, 162, 163)**

632 George P. D'Elia. "The Determinants of Job Satisfaction among Beginning Librarians," *Library Quarterly* 49:3 (July 1979), 283-302.

633 Tim LaBorie and Michael Halperin. "Citation Patterns in Library Science Dissertations," *Journal of Education for Librarianship* 16:4 (Spring 1976), 271-283. **(51, 72, 83, 85)**

634 Anne Woodsworth and Victor R. Neufeld. "A Survey of Physician Self-education Patterns in Toronto. Part 1: Use of Libraries," *Canadian Library Journal* 29:1 (January-February 1972), 38-44.

635 Richard Eggleton. "The ALA Duplicates Exchange Union—A Study and Evaluation," *Library Resources and Technical Services* 19:2 (Spring 1975), 148-163. **(22, 23, 115, 116)**

636 Katherine H. Packer and Dagobert Soergel. "The Importance of SDI for Current Awareness in Fields with Severe Scatter of Information," *Journal of the American Society for Information Science* 30:3 (May 1979), 125-135.

637 Doris M. Carson. "The Act of Cataloging," *Library Resources and Technical Services* 20:2 (Spring 1976), 149-153.

638 Robert L. Mowery. "The Cutter Classification: Still at Work," *Library Resources and Technical Services* 20:2 (Spring 1976), 154-156.

639 Kelly Patterson, Carol White and Martha Whittaker. "Thesis Handling in University Libraries," *Library Resources and Technical Services* 21:3 (Summer 1977), 274-285.

640 Sandra L. Stokley and Marion T. Reid. "A Study of Performance of Five Book Dealers Used by Louisiana State University Library," *Library Resources and Technical Services* 22:2 (Spring 1978), 117-125. **(38, 40)**

641 Hans H. Wellisch. "Multiscript and Multilingual Bibliographic Control: Alternatives to Romanization," *Library Resources and Technical Services* 22:2 (Spring 1978), 179-190.

642 Bert R. Boyce and Mark Funk. "Bradford's Law and the Selection of High Quality Papers," *Library Resources and Technical Services* 22:4 (Fall 1978), 390-401. **(186, 187)**

643 Susan Dingle-Cliff and Charles H. Davis. "Comparison of Recent Acquisitions and OCLC Find Rates for Three Canadian Special Libraries," *Journal of the American Society for Information Science* 32:1 (January 1981), 65-69.

644 Rose Mary Juliano Longo and Ubaldino Dantas Machado. "Characterization of Databases in the Agricultural Sciences," *Journal of the American Society for Information Science* 32:2 (March 1981), 83-91.

645 Edward S. Warner. "The Impact of Interlibrary Access to Periodicals on Subscription Continuation/Cancellation Decision Making," *Journal of the American Society for Information Science* 32:2 (March 1981), 93-95. **(150)**

646 Charles T. Payne and Robert S. McGee. "Comparisons of LC Proofslip and MARC Tape Arrival Dates at the University of Chicago Library," *Journal of Library Automation* 3:2 (June 1970), 115-121.

647 Wanda V. Dole and David Allerton. "University Collections: A Survey of Costs," *Library Acquistions: Practice and Theory* 6:2 (1982), 25-32. **(257, 332)**

648 Silvia A. Gonzalez. "1976 Statistical Survey of Law Libraries Serving a Local Bar," *Law Library Journal* 70:2 (May 1977), 222-237.

649 Carole J. Mankin and Jacqueline D. Bastille. "An Analysis of the Differences between Density-of-Use Ranking and Raw-Use Ranking of Library Journal Use," *Journal of the American Society for Information Science* 32:3 (May 1981), 224-228.

650 Katherine W. McCain and James E. Bobick. "Patterns of Journal Use in a Departmental Library: A Citation Analysis," *Journal of the American Society for Information Science* 32:4 (July 1981), 257-267. **(59, 190, 195, 265, 314, 318, 322)**

651 Manfred Kochen, Victoria Reich and Lee Cohen. "Influence on [sic] Online Bibliographic Services on Student Behavior," *Journal of the American Society for Information Science* 32:6 (November 1981), 412-420.

652 Mark P. Carpenter and Francis Narin. "The Adequacy of the *Science Citation Index* (SCI) as an Indicator of International Scientific Activity," *Journal of the American Society for Information Science* 32:6 (November 1981), 430-439.

653 Chai Kim. "Retrieval Languages of Social Sciences and Natural Sciences: A Statistical Investigation," *Journal of the American Society for Information Science* 33:1 (January 1982), 3-7.

654 Ann H. Schabas. "Postcoordinate Retrieval: A Comparison of Two Indexing Languages," *Journal of the American Society for Information Science* 33:1 (January 1982), 32-37.

655 Miranda Lee Pao. "Collaboration in Computational Musicology," *Journal of the American Society for Information Science* 33:1 (January 1982), 38-43. **(78, 83)**

656 Robert K. Poyer. "*Science Citation Index*'s Coverage of the Preclinical Science Literature," *Journal of the American Society for Information Science* 33:5 (September 1982), 333-337.

657 Stephen M. Lawani and Alan E. Bayer. "Validity of Citation Criteria for Assessing the Influence of Scientific Publications: New Evidence with Peer Assessment," *Journal of the American Society for Information Science* 34:1 (January 1983), 59-66. **(79)**

Bibliography of Articles

658 Edward G. Summers, Joyce Matheson and Robert Conry. "The Effect of Personal, Professional and Psychological Attributes, and Information Seeking Behavior on the Use of Information Sources by Educators," *Journal of the American Society for Information Science* 34:1 (January 1983), 75-85.

659 Bluma C. Peritz. "A Note on 'Scholarliness' and 'Impact,'" *Journal of the American Society for Information Science* 34:5 (September 1983), 360-362. **(78, 151)**

660 Michael D. Cooper. "Response Time Variations in an Online Search System," *Journal of the American Society for Information Science* 34:6 (November 1983), 374-380.

661 Richard S. Marcus. "An Experimental Comparison of the Effectiveness of Computers and Humans as Search Intermediaries," *Journal of the American Society for Information Science* 34:6 (November 1983), 381-404.

662 Michael J. Simonds, "Work Attitudes and Union Membership," *College and Research Libraries* 36:2 (March 1975), 136-142.

663 Jerold Nelson. "Faculty Awareness and Attitudes toward Academic Library Reference Services: A Measure of Communication," *College and Research Libraries* 34:5 (September 1973), 268-275.

664 Andre Nitecki, "Polish Books in America and the Farmington Plan," *College and Research Libraries* 27:6 (November 1966), 439-449. **(118, 140)**

665 Leslie R. Morris. "Projections of the Number of Library School Graduates," *Journal of Education for Librarianship* 22:4 (Spring 1982), 283-291.

666 Thomas J. Galvin and Allen Kent. "Use of a University Library Collection," *Library Journal* 102:20 (November 1977), 2317-2320. [For further and more complete information see Allen Kent, et al. *Use of Library Materials: The University of Pittsburgh Study*. New York: Marcel Dekker, 1979.] **(267, 275, 276, 299)**

667 Allen Kent. "Library Resource Sharing Networks: How To Make a Choice," *Library Acquisitions: Practice and Theory* 2 (1978), 69-76. [For further and more complete information see Allen Kent, et al. *Use of Library Materials: The University of Pittsburgh Study*. New York: Marcel Dekker, 1979.] **(267, 277, 281)**

668 Leigh S. Estabrook and Kathleen M. Heim. "A Profile of ALA Personal Members," *American Libraries* 11:11 (December 1980), 654-659. [For a fuller and more complete description of this study see Kathleen M. Heim and Leigh S. Estabrook. *Career Profiles and Sex Discrimination in the Library Profession*. Chicago: American Library Association, 1983.]

669 Mary Lee DeVilbiss. "The Approval-Built Collection in the Medium-Sized Academic Library," *College and Research Libraries* 36:6 (November 1975), 487-492. **(3, 64)**

670 Thomas P. Fleming and Frederick G. Kilgour. "Moderately and Heavily Used Biomedical Journals," *Bulletin of the Medical Library Association* 52:1 (January 1964), 234-241. **(202, 205, 317, 319, 320, 323)**

671 Richard J. Hyman. "Medical Interlibrary Loan Patterns," *Bulletin of the Medical Library Association* 53:2 (April 1965), 215-224.

672 L. Miles Raisig, Meredith Smith, Renata Cuff and Frederick G. Kilgour. "How Biomedical Investigators Use Library Books," *Bulletin of the Medical Library Association* 54:2 (April 1966), 104-107. **(54, 56, 266, 268, 283, 285, 336, 341)**

673 Helen Crawford. "Centralization vs. Decentralization in Medical School Libraries," *Bulletin of the Medical Library Association* 54:2 (April 1966), 199-205.

674 Peter Stangl and Frederick G. Kilgour. "Analysis of Recorded Biomedical Book and Journal Use in the Yale Medical Library," *Bulletin of the Medical Library Association* 55:3 (July 1967), 290-300. **(55, 56, 59, 60, 62, 63, 64, 266, 269, 270, 271, 273, 283, 284, 285, 333, 335)**

675 Peter Stangl and Frederick G. Kilgour. "Analysis of Recorded Biomedical Book and Journal Use in the Yale Medical Library," *Bulletin of the Medical Library Association* 55:3 (July 1967), 301-315. **(281, 283, 324, 326)**

676 Gwendolyn S. Cruzat. "Keeping Up with Biomedical Meetings," *Bulletin of the Medical Library Association* 56:2 (April 1968), 132-137.

677 Joan B. Woods, Sam Pieper and Shervert H. Frazier. "Basic Psychiatric Literature: I. Books," *Bulletin of the Medical Library Association* 56:3 (July 1968), 295-309. **(188, 192)**

678 Joan B. Woods, Sam Pieper and Shervert H. Frazier. "Basic Psychiatric Literature: II. Articles and Article Sources," *Bulletin of the Medical Library Association* 56:4 (October 1968), 404-427. **(188, 192)**

679 Reva Pachefsky. "Survey of the Card Catalog in Medical Libraries," *Bulletin of the Medical Library Association* 57:1 (January 1969), 10-20.

680 Janet Barlup. "Mechanization of Library Procedures in the Medium-sized Medical Library: VII. Relevancy of Cited Articles in Citation Indexing," *Bulletin of the Medical Library Association* 57:3 (July 1969), 260-263. **(176, 183)**

681 Wilhelm Moll. "Basic Journal List for Small Hospital Libraries," *Bulletin of the Medical Library Association* 57:3 (July 1969), 267-271. **(205)**

682 Lois Ann Colainni and Robert F. Lewis. "Reference Services in U.S. Medical School Libraries," *Bulletin of the Medical Library Association* 57:3 (July 1969), 272-274. **(143, 148)**

683 Vern M. Pings and Joyce E. Malin. "Access to the Scholarly Record of Medicine by the Osteopathic Physicians of Southeastern Michigan," *Bulletin of the Medical Library Association* 58:1 (January 1970), 18-22.

684 D.J. Goode, J.K. Penry and J.F. Caponio. "Comparative Analysis of *Epilepsy Abstracts* and a MEDLARS Bibliography," *Bulletin of the Medical Library Association* 58:1 (January 1970), 44-50.

Bibliography of Articles

685 Robert Oseasohn. "Borrower Use of a Modern Medical Library by Practicing Physicians," *Bulletin of the Medical Library Association* 59:1 (January 1970), 58-59.

686 Joan M.B. Smith. "A Periodical Use Study at Children's Hospital of Michigan," *Bulletin of the Medical Library Association* 58:1 (January 1970), 65-67. **(57, 60, 271, 274)**

687 Jean K. Miller. "Mechanization of Library Procedures in the Medium-sized Medical Library: XI. Two Methods of Providing Selective Dissemination of Information to Medical Scientists," *Bulletin of the Medical Library Association* 58:3 (July 1970), 378-397.

688 Stella S. Gomes. "The Nature and the Use and Users of the Midwest Regional Medical Library," *Bulletin of the Medical Library Association* 58:4 (October 1970), 559-577. **(51, 53, 264, 265, 271, 274, 284, 286, 291, 293, 333, 335, 336, 341)**

689 Donald A. Windsor. "Publications on a Drug before the First Report of Its Administration to Man," *Bulletin of the Medical Library Association* 59:3 (July 1971), 433-437. **(77, 81)**

690 Charles L. Bowden and Virginia M. Bowden. "A Survey of Information Sources Used by Psychiatrists," *Bulletin of the Medical Library Association* 59:4 (October 1971), 603-608. **(286, 288)**

691 Ruth E. Fenske. "Mechanization of Library Procedures in the Medium-sized Medical Library: XIV. Correlations between National Library of Medicine Classification Numbers and MeSH Headings," *Bulletin of the Medical Library Association* 60:2 (April 1972), 319-324.

692 Anne Brearley Piternick. "Measurement of Journal Availability in a Biomedical Library," *Bulletin of the Medical Library Association* 60:4 (October 1972), 534-542. **(311, 316, 336, 341)**

693 Isabel Spiegel and Janet Crager. "Comparison of SUNY and MEDLINE Searches," *Bulletin of the Medical Library Association* 61:2 (April 1973), 205-209.

694 Fred W. Roper. "Special Programs in Medical Library Education, 1957-1971: Part II: Analysis of the Programs," *Bulletin of the Medical Library Association* 61:4 (October 1973), 387-395.

695 Norma Jean Lodico. "Physician's Referral Letter Bibliographic Service: A New Method of Disseminating Medical Information," *Bulletin of the Medical Library Association* 61:4 (October 1973), 422-432.

696 Wilhelm Moll. "MEDLINE Evaluation Study," *Bulletin of the Medical Library Association* 62:1 (January 1974), 1-5.

697 Pamela Tibbetts. "A Method for Estimating the In-House Use of the Periodical Collection in the University of Minnesota Bio-Medical Library," *Bulletin of the Medical Library Association* 62:1 (January 1974), 37-48. **(58, 60, 189, 193, 271, 274, 298, 300, 317, 319)**

698 Joan Ash. "Library Use of Public Health Materials: Description and Analysis," *Bulletin of the Medical Library Association* 62:2 (April 1974), 95-104. **(52, 58, 60, 177, 190, 251, 264, 275, 284, 290, 312, 313, 318)**

699 Ching-Chih Chen. "Current Status of Biomedical Book Reviewing: Part I. Key Biomedical Reviewing Journals with Quantitative Significance," *Bulletin of the Medical Library Association* 62:2 (April 1974), 105-112. **(240, 241)**

700 Ching-Chih Chen. "Current Status of Biomedical Book Reviewing: Part II. Time Lag in Biomedical Book Reviewing," *Bulletin of the Medical Library Association* 62:2 (April 1974), 113-119. **(241)**

701 George Scheerer and Lois E. Hines. "Classification Systems Used in Medical Libraries," *Bulletin of the Medical Library Association* 62:3 (July 1974), 272-280.

702 Jo Ann Bell. "The Academic Health Sciences Library and Serial Selection," *Bulletin of the Medical Library Association* 62:3 (July 1974), 281-290. **(140, 143, 177, 184)**

703 Ching-Chih Chen. "Current Status of Biomedical Book Reviewing: Part III. Duplication Patterns in Biomedical Book Reviewing," *Bulletin of the Medical Library Association* 62:3 (July 1974), 296-301. **(241, 242)**

704 Ching-Chih Chen. "Current Status of Biomedical Book Reviewing: Part IV. Major American and British Biomedical Book Publishers," *Bulletin of the Medical Library Association* 62:3 (July 1974), 302-308. **(82, 95, 242, 251, 252)**

705 M. Sandra Wood and Robert S. Seeds. "Development of SDI Services from a Manual Current Awareness Service to SDILINE," *Bulletin of the Medical Library Association* 62:4 (October 1974), 374-384.

706 Margaret Butkovich and Robert M. Braude. "Cost-Performance of Cataloging and Card Production in a Medical Center Library," *Bulletin of the Medical Library Association* 63:1 (January 1975), 29-34.

707 Donald A. Windsor. "Science-Speciality Literatures: Their Legendary-Contemporary Parity, Based on the Transmission of Information between Generations," *Bulletin of the Medical Library Association* 63:2 (April 1975), 209-215. **(51, 52, 54, 76, 81, 176, 177, 183, 184)**

708 Helen J. Brown, Jean K. Miller and Diane M. Pinchoff. "Study of the Information Dissemination Service—Health Sciences Library, State University of New York at Buffalo," *Bulletin of the Medical Library Association* 63:3 (July 1975), 259-271. **(184)**

709 Rachel K. Goldstein and Dorothy R. Hill. "The Status of Women in the Administration of Health Science Libraries," *Bulletin of the Medical Library Association* 63:4 (October 1975), 386-395.

710 Janet G. Schnall and Joan W. Wilson. "Evaluation of a Clinical Medical

Bibliography of Articles 391

Librarianship Program at a University Health Sciences Library," *Bulletin of the Medical Library Association* (July 1976), 278-283.

711 Anne B. Piternick. "Effects of Binding Policy and Other Factors on the Availability of Journal Issues," *Bulletin of the Medical Library Association* 64:3 (July 1976), 284-292.

712 Richard B. Fredericksen and Helen N. Michael. "Subject Cataloging Practices in North American Medical School Libraries," *Bulletin of the Medical Library Association* 64:4 (October 1976), 356-366.

713 Paul M. McIlvaine and Malcolm H. Brantz. "Audiovisual Materials: A Survey of Bibliographic Controls in Distributors' Catalogs," *Bulletin of the Medical Library Association* 65:1 (January 1977), 17-21. **(170, 171, 242, 243)**

714 Bette Greenberg, Robert Breedlove and Wendy Berger. "MEDLINE Demand Profiles: An Analysis of Requests for Clinical and Research Information," *Bulletin of the Medical Library Association* 65:1 (January 1977), 22-28.

715 Renata Tagliacozzo. "Estimating the Satisfaction of Information Users," *Bulletin of the Medical Library Association* 65:2 (April 1977), 243-249.

716 Ruth W. Wender, Ester L. Fruehauf, Marilyn S. Vent and Constant D. Wilson. "Determination of Continuing Medical Education Needs of Clinicians from a Literature Search Study: Part I. The Study," *Bulletin of the Medical Library Association* 65:3 (July 1977), 330-337. **(138, 139)**

717 Ruth W. Wender, Ester L. Fruehauf, Marilyn S. Vent and Constant D. Wilson. "Determination of Continuing Medical Education Needs of Clinicians from a Literature Search Study: Part II. Questionnaire Results," *Bulletin of the Medical Library Association* 65:3 (July 1977), 338-341.

718 Donald J. Morton. "Analysis of Interlibrary Requests by Hospital Libraries for Photocopied Journal Articles," *Bulletin of the Medical Library Association* 65:4 (October 1977), 425-432. **(61, 184, 185, 193)**

719 Patrick W. Brennen and W. Patrick Davey. "Citation Analysis in the Literature of Tropical Medicine," *Bulletin of the Medical Library Association* 66:1 (January 1978), 24-30. **(73, 75, 191, 194, 213, 214)**

720 Theresa C. Strasser. "The Information Needs of Practicing Physicians in Northeastern New York State," *Bulletin of the Medical Library Association* 66:2 (April 1978), 200-209. **(204, 208)**

721 Inci A. Bowman, Elizabeth K. Eaton and J. Maurice Mahan. "Are Health Science Faculty Interested in Medical History? An Evaluative Case Study," *Bulletin of the Medical Library Association* 66:2 (April 1978), 228-231.

722 Maurice C. Leatherbury and Richard A. Lyders. "Friends of the Library Groups in Health Sciences Libraries," *Bulletin of the Medical Library Association* 66:3 (July 1978), 315-318.

723 Bette Greenberg, Sara Battison, Madeleine Kolisch and Martha Leredu. "Evaluation of a Clinical Medical Librarian Program at the Yale Medical Library," *Bulletin of the Medical Library Association* 66:3 (July 1978), 319-326.

724 Gloria Werner. "Use of On-Line Bibliographic Retrieval Services in Health Sciences Libraries in the United States and Canada," *Bulletin of the Medical Library Association* 67:1 (January 1979), 1-14.

725 B. Tommie Usdin. "Core Lists of Medical Journals: A Comparison," *Bulletin of the Medical Library Association* 67:2 (April 1979), 212-217. **(205, 208)**

726 John A. Timour. "Brief Communications: Use of Selected Abstracting and Indexing Journals in Biomedical Resource Libraries," *Bulletin of the Medical Library Association* 67:3 (July 1979), 330-335.

727 Rachel K. Goldstein and Dorothy R. Hill. "The Status of Women in the Administration of Health Sciences Libraries: A Five-Year Follow-Up Study, 1972-1977," *Bulletin of the Medical Library Association* 68:1 (January 1980), 6-15.

728 Richard T. West and Maureen J. Malone. "Communicating the Results of NLM Grant-supported Library Projects," *Bulletin of the Medical Library Association* 68:1 (January 1980), 33-39.

729 James A. Thompson and Michael R. Kronenfeld. "The Effect of Inflation on the Cost of Journals on the Brandon List," *Bulletin of the Medical Library Association* 68:1 (January 1980), 47-52. **(19, 107, 108)**

730 Carol C. Spencer. "Random Time Sampling with Self-observation for Library Cost Studies: Unit Costs of Reference Questions," *Bulletin of the Medical Library Association* 68:1 (January 1980), 53-57.

731 Justine Roberts. "Circulation versus Photocopy: Quid pro Quo?" *Bulletin of the Medical Library Association* 68:3 (July 1980), 274-277.

732 Dick R. Miller and Joseph E. Jensen. "Dual Pricing of Health Sciences Periodicals: A Survey," *Bulletin of the Medical Library Association* 68:4 (October 1980), 336-347. **(14, 15, 102, 103)**

733 Jacqueline D. Bastille. "A Simple Objective Method for Determining a Dynamic Journal Collection," *Bulletin of the Medical Library Association* 68:4 (October 1980), 357-366. **(185)**

734 Mary H. Mueller. "An Examination of Characteristics Related to Success of Friends Groups in Medical School Rare Book Libraries," *Bulletin of the Medical Library Association* 69:1 (January 1981), 9-13.

735 Scott Davis, Lincoln Polissar and Joan W. Wilson. "Continuing Education in Cancer for the Community Physician: Design and Evaluation of a Regional

Bibliography of Articles

Table of Contents Service," *Bulletin of the Medical Library Association* 69:1 (January 1981), 14-20.

736 Gary D. Byrd. "Copyright compliance in Health Sciences Libraries: A Status Report Two Years after the Implementation of PL 94-553," *Bulletin of the Medical Library Association* 69:2 (April 1981), 224-230.

737 Ester L. Baldinger, Jennifer P.S. Nakeff-Plaat and Margaret S. Cummings. "An Experimental Study of the Feasibility of Substituting Chemical Abstracts Online for the Printed Copy in a Medium-Sized Medical Library," *Bulletin of the Medical Library Association* 69:2 (April 1981), 247-251.

738 Doris R.F. Dunn. "Dissemination of the Published Results of an Important Clinical Trial: An Analysis of the Citing Literature," *Bulletin of the Medical Library Association* 69:3 (July 1981), 301-306.

739 Cynthia H. Goldstein. "A Study of Weeding Policies in Eleven TALON Resource Libraries," *Bulletin of the Medical Library Association* 69:3 (July 1981), 311-316.

740 K. Suzanne Johnson and E. Guy Coffee. "Veterinary Medical School Libraries in the United States and Canada, 1977-78," *Bulletin of the Medical Library Association* 70:1 (January 1982), 10-20. **(120, 121, 128, 130, 133, 179, 185)**

741 Suzanne F. Grefsheim, Robert H. Larson, Shelley A. Bader and Nina W. Matheson. "Automation of Internal Library Operations in Academic Health Sciences Libraries: A State of the Art Report," *Bulletin of the Medical Library Association* 70:2 (April 1982), 191-200.

742 Elizabeth R. Lenz and Carolyn F. Walz. "Nursing Educators' Satisfaction with Library Facilities," *Bulletin of the Medical Library Association* 70:2 (April l982), 20l-206.

743 Ruth Traister Morris, Edwin A. Holtum and David S. Curry. "Being There: The Effect of the User's Presence on MEDLINE Search Results," *Bulletin of the Medical Library Association* 70:3 (July 1982), 298-304.

744 James K. Cooper, Diane Cooper and Timothy P. Johnson. "Medical Library Support in Rural Areas," *Bulletin of the Medical Library Association* 71:1 (January 1983), 13-15.

745 Susan Crawford. "Health Science Libraries in the United States: I. Overview of the Post-World War II Years," *Bulletin of the Medical Library Association* 71:1 (January 1983), 16-20. **(92, 94)**

746 Susan Crawford and Alan M. Rees. "Health Sciences Libraries in the United States: II. Medical School Libraries, 1960-1980," *Bulletin of the Medical Library Association* 71:1 (January 1983), 21-29. **(7, 9, 66, 68, 69, 92, 94, 95, 96, 129)**

747 Susan Crawford. "Health Science Libraries in the United States: III. Hospital Health Science Libraries, 1969-1979," *Bulletin of the Medical Library Association* 71:1 (January 1983), 30-36. **(119, 123, 129)**

394 BIBLIOGRAPHY OF ARTICLES

748 Mark E. Funk and Carolyn Anne Reid. "Indexing Consistency in MEDLINE," *Bulletin of the Medical Library Association* 71:2 (April 1983), 176-183.

749 Michael R. Kronenfeld and Sarah H. Gable. "Real Inflation of Journal Prices: Medical Journals, U.S. Journals and Brandon List Journals," *Bulletin of the Medical Library Association* 71:4 (October 1983), 375-379.   **(20, 21, 108, 109, 129)**

750 Jane McCarthy. "Survey of Audiovisual Standards and Practices in Health Sciences Libraries," *Bulletin of the Medical Library Association* 71:4 (October 1983), 391-395.   **(131, 133, 146, 148, 170, 171)**

751 Rajia C. Tobia and David A. Kronick. "A Clinical Information Consultation Service at a Teaching Hospital," *Bulletin of the Medical Library Association* 71:4 (October 1983), 396-399.

752 Elizabeth R. Ashin. "Library Service to Dental Practitioners," *Bulletin of the Medical Library Association* 71:4 (October 1983), 400-402.   **(310, 311, 330, 331)**

753 Peter P. Olevnik. "Non-Formalized Point-of-Use Library Instruction: A Survey," *Catholic Library World* 50:5 (December 1978), 218-220.

754 Susan A. Stussy. "Automation in Catholic College Libraries," *Catholic Library World* 53:3 (October 1981), 109-111.

755 R.M. Longyear. "Article Citations and 'Obsolescence' in Musicological Journals," *Notes* 33:3 (March 1977), 563-571.   **(59, 61, 73, 75)**

756 Ann Basart. "Criteria for Weeding Books in a University Music Library," *Notes* 36:4 (June 1980), 819-836.   **(292, 293)**

757 Richard P. Smiraglia and Arsen R. Papakhian. "Music in the OCLC Online Union Catalog: A Review," *Notes* 38:2 (December 1981), 257-274.

758 William Gray Potter. "When Names Collide: Conflict in the Catalog and AACR 2," *Library Resources and Technical Services* 24:1 (Winter 1980), 3-16.

759 Rose Mary Magrill and Constance Rinehart. "Selection for Preservation: A Service Study," *Library Resources and Technical Services* 24:1 (Winter 1980), 44-57.

760 Sally Braden, John D. Hall and Helen H. Britton. "Utilization of Personnel and Bibliographic Resources for Cataloging by OCLC Participating Libraries," *Library Resources and Technical Services* 24:2 (Spring 1980), 135-154.

761 Cynthia C. Ryans. "Cataloging Administrators' Views on Cataloging Education," *Library Resources and Technical Services* 24:4 (Fall 1980), 343-351.

762 Thomas Schadlich. "Changing from Sears to LC Subject Headings," *Library Resources and Technical Services* 24:4 (Fall 1980), 361-363.

Bibliography of Articles

763 Elizabeth L. Tate. "For Our 25th Anniversary...," *Library Resources and Technical Services* 25:1 (January/March 1981), 3-7.

764 Barbara Moore. "Patterns in the Use of OCLC by Academic Library Cataloging Departments," *Library Resources and Technical Services* 25:1 (January/March 1981), 30-39.

765 Judith J. Johnson and Clair S. Josel. "Quality Control and the OCLC Data Base: A Report on Error Reporting," *Library Resources and Technical Services* 25:1 (January/March 1981), 40-47.

766 Edward T. O'Neill and Rao Aluri. "Library of Congress Subject Heading Patterns in OCLC Monographic Records," *Library Resources and Technical Services* 25:1 (January/March 1981), 63-80.

767 Elizabeth H. Groot. "A Comparison of Library Tools for Monograph Verification," *Library Resources and Technical Services* 25:2 (April/June 1981), 149-161. **(43, 44)**

768 Elizabeth G. Mikita. "Monographs in Microform: Issues in Cataloging and Bibliographic Control," *Library Resources and Technical Services* 25:4 (October/December 1981), 352-361.

769 Lee R. Nemchek. "Problems of Cataloging and Classification in Theater Librarianship," *Library Resources and Technical Services* 25:4 (October/December 1981), 374-385.

770 John Hostage. "AACR 2, OCLC, and the Card Catalog in the Medium-Sized Library," *Library Resources and Technical Services* 26:1 (January/March 1982), 12-20.

771 Robert H. Hassell. "Revising the Dewey Music Schedules: Tradition vs. Innovation," *Library Resources and Technical Services* 26:2 (April/June 1982), 192-203.

772 Patricia Dwyer Wanninger. "Is the OCLC Database Too Large? A Study of the Effect of Duplicate Records in the OCLC System," *Library Resources and Technical Services* 26:4 (October/December 1982), 353-361.

773 Stephen R. Salmon. "Characteristics of Online Public Catalogs," *Library Resources and Technical Services* 27:1 (January/March 1983), 36-67.

774 Thomas E. Nisonger. "A Test of Two Citation Checking Techniques for Evaluating Political Science Collections in University Libraries," *Library Resources and Technical Services* 27:2 (April/June 1983), 163-176. **(53, 74, 87, 89)**

775 John Rutledge and Willy Owen. "Changes in the Quality of Paper in French Books, 1860-1914: A Study of Selected Holdings of the Wilson Library, University of North Carolina," *Library Resources and Technical Services* (April/June 1983), 177-187. **(62)**

776 Jim Williams and Nancy Romero. "A Comparison of the OCLC Database and *New Serial Titles* as an Information Resource for Serials," *Library Resources and Technical Services* 27:2 (April/June 1983), 177-187. **(45, 249)**

777 Mary E. Clack and Sally F. Williams. "Using Locally and Nationally Produced Periodical Price Indexes in Budget Preparation," *Library Resources and Technical Services* 27:4 (October/December 1983), 345-356. **(18, 19, 107)**

778 Victoria Cheponis Lessard and Jack Hall. "Vocational Technical Collection Building: Does it Exist?" *Collection Building* 4:2 (1982), 6-18. **(227)**

779 Virginia Witucke. "The Reviewing of Children's Science Books," *Collection Building* 4:2 (1982) 19-30. **(235, 236, 237, 238, 239, 240)**

780 Margaret F. Stieg. "The Information Needs of Historians," *College and Research Libraries* 42:6 (November 1981), 549-560. **(114, 160, 180, 199, 287, 292, 327)**

781 Howard D. White. "Library Censorship and the Permissive Minority," *Library Quarterly* 51:2 (1981), 192-207. **(69, 70)**

782 Judith Serebnick. "Book Reviews and the Selection of Potentially Controversial Books in Public Libraries," *Library Quarterly* 51:4 (1981), 390-409. **(234, 235)**

783 Richard W. Scamell and Bette Ann Stead. "A Study of Age and Tenure as it Pertains to Job Satisfaction," *Journal of Library Administration* 1:1 (Spring 1980), 3-18.

784 Robert M. Hayes. "Citation Statistics as a Measure of Faculty Research Productivity," *Journal of Education for Librarianship* 23:3 (Winter 1983), 151-172.

785 William Skeh Wong and David S. Zubatsky. "The First-Time Appointed Academic Library Director 1970-1980: A Profile," *Journal of Library Administration* 4:1 (Spring 1983), 41-70.

786 James Rice, Jr. "An Assessment of Student Preferences for Method of Library Orientation," *Journal of Library Administration* 4:1 (Spring 1983), 87-93.

787 Frank William Goudy. "Affirmative Action and Library Science Degrees: A Statistical Overview, 1973-74 through 1980-81," *Journal of Library Administration* 4:3 (Fall 1983), 51-60.

788 Thomas G. English. "Librarian Status in the Eighty-Nine U.S. Academic Institutions of the Association of Research Libraries: 1982," *College and Research Libraries* 44:3 (May 1983), 199-211.

789 Nathan M. Smith and Veneese C. Nelson. "Burnout: A Survey of Academic Reference Librarians," *College and Research Libraries* 44:3 (May 1983), 245-250.

Bibliography of Articles

790 Floris W. Wood. "Reviewing Book Review Indexes," *Reference Services Review* (April/June 1980), 47-52. **(231, 232, 247, 248)**

791 Herbert Goldhor. "Public Library Circulation up 3%; Spending Jumps 11%," *American Libraries* 14:8 (September 1983), 534. **(8, 67)**

792 Laura N. Gasaway and Steve Margeton. "Continuing Education for Law Librarianship," *Law Library Journal* 70:1 (February 1977), 39-52.

793 Michael L. Renshawe. "The Condition of the Law Librarian in 1976," *Law Library Review* 69:4 (November 1976), 626-640.

794 Susanne Patterson Wahba. "Women in Libraries," *Law Library* Journal 69:2 (May 1976), 223-231.

795 Jean Finch and Lauri R. Flynn. "An Update on Faculty Libraries," *Law Library Journal* 73:1 (Winter 1980), 99-106. **(252, 253)**

796 Robert D. Swisher, Peggy C. Smith and Calvin J. Boyer. "Educational Change Among ACRL Academic Librarians," *Library Research* (*Library and Information Science Research* since Spring 1983) 5:2 (Summer 1983), 195-205.

797 Michael D. Cooper. "Economies of Scale in Academic Libraries," *Library Research* (*Library and Information Science Research* after Spring 1983) 5:2 (Summer 1983), 207-219.

798 Virgil Diodato. "Faculty Workload: A Case Study," *Journal of Education for Librarianship* 23:4 (Spring 1983), 286-295. **(9, 13)**

799 Jerry D. Saye. "Continuing Education and Library School Faculty," *Journal of Education for Librarianship* 24:1 (Summer 1983), 3-16.

800 Maurice P. Marchant and Carolyn F. Wilson. "Developing Joint Graduate Programs for Librarians," *Journal of Education for Librarianship* 24:1 (Summer 1983), 30-37. **(123)**

801 Barbara L. Stein and Herman L. Totten. "Cognitive Styles: Similarities Among Students," *Journal of Education for Librarianship* 24:1 (Summer 1983), 38-43.

802 Marilyn J. Markham, Keith H. Stirling and Nathan M. Smith. "Librarian Self-Disclosure and Patron Satisfaction in the Reference Interview," *RQ* 22:4 (Summer 1983), 369-374.

803 June L. Engle and Elizabeth Futas. "Sexism in Adult Encyclopedias," *RQ* 23:1 (Fall 1983), 29-39.

804 David F. Kohl. "Circulation Professionals: Management Information Needs and Attitudes," *RQ* 23:1 (Fall 1983), 81-86. **(340)**

805 Kevin Carey. "Problems and Patterns of Periodical Literature Searching at an Urban University Research Library," *RQ* 23:2 (Winter 1983), 211-218.

806 Beverly P. Lynch and Jo Ann Verdin. "Job Satisfaction in Libraries: Relationships of the Work Itself, Age, Sex, Occupational Group, Tenure, Supervisory Level, Career Commitment and Library Department," *Library Quarterly* 53:4 (October 1983), 434-447.

807 Louise W. Diodato and Virgil P. Diodato. "The Use of Gifts in a Medium Sized Academic Library," *Collection Management* 5:1/2 (Spring/Summer 1983), 53-71. **(52, 117, 118, 265, 269, 280, 294)**

AUTHOR INDEX TO BIBLIOGRAPHY OF ARTICLES

Note: The index is arranged alphabetically, word by word. All characters or groups of characters separated by spaces, dashes, hyphens, diagonal slashes or periods are treated as separate words. Acronyms not separated by spaces or punctuation are alphabetized as though they are single words, while initials separated by spaces or punctuation are treated as if each letter is a complete word. Personal names beginning with capital Mc, M' and Mac are all listed under Mac as though the full form were used, and St. is alphabetized as if spelled out.

Adamson, Martha C., **372, 438, 496**
Allen, Cameron, **376, 388**
Allerton, David, **647**
Aluri, Rao, **5, 766**
American Association of Law
   Libraries
   Audio-Visual Committee, **375, 387**
American Library Association
   Insurance for Libraries
     Committee, **79**
   Joint Libraries Committee on Fair
     Use in Photocopying, **67**
   Library Administration
     Division, **75**
   Staff Organizations Round
     Table, **74**
Amey, L.J., **543**
Anderson, James D., **621**
Anderson, Karen, **602**
Anderson, Paul M., **522**
Anderson, Richard C., **622, 625**
Andres, Christine, **101**
Argyes, Claudia White, **628**
Ariew, Susan Andriette, **257**
Asbury, Herbert D., **432**
Ash, Joan, **698**
Ashin, Elizabeth R., **752**
Aubry, John, **249**
Auld, Lawrence, **292**
Axford, H. William, **116, 630**

Baaske, Jan, **98**
Bader, Shelley A., **741**

Badertscher, David G., **373**
Bailey, James F., III, **362**
Bailey, Martha J., **423**
Balay, Robert, **101**
Baldinger, Ester L., **737**
Baldwin, Julia F., **468**
Bamford, Harold E., Jr., **618**
Barber, Raymond W., **523**
Barker, Dale L., **182**
Barkey, Patrick, **172**
Barlup, Janet, **680**
Barone, Kristine, **385**
Barth, Stephen W., **347**
Bartlett, Eleanor, **115**
Basart, Ann, **756**
Bastille, Jacqueline D., **733, 649**
Bastogi, Kunj B., **336**
Bates, Marcia J., **615**
Battison, Sara, **723**
Baughman, James C., **252**
Bayer, Alan, **155, 657**
Bedoian, Carol, **593**
Beede, Benjamin R., **394**
Beeler, Richard J., **95**
Bell, C. Margaret, **433**
Bell, Jo Ann, **702**
Belland, John, **217**
Benedict, Marjorie A., **516**
Bennett, Margaret Johnson, **14**
Bentley, Stella, **8, 478**
Berger, Wendy, **714**
Black, Donald V., **582**
Black, George W., Jr., **38, 415**
Blackburn, Robert H., **535**

AUTHOR INDEX

Blankenship, W.C., **177**
Block, Uri, **267**
Blue, Richard I., **294**
Bobick, James E., **650**
Bobinski, George, **167**
Boissonnas, Christian M., **367**
Bonk, W.J., **132**
Bottle, Robert T., **401**
Bourg, James W., **333**
Bourne, Charles P., **328**
Bowden, Charles L., **690**
Bowden, Virginia M., **690**
Bowman, Inci A., **721**
Boyce, Bert R., **642**
Boyer, Calvin J., **796**
Boyer, Laura M., **105**
Boyer, Yvonne, **310**
Braden, Irene A., **85**
Braden, Sally, **760**
Brandwein, Larry, **152**
Brantz, Malcolm H., **713**
Braude, Robert M., **706**
Breedlove, Robert, **714**
Breiting, Amelia, **413**
Brennen, Patrick W., **719**
Britton, Helen H., **760**
Broadus, Robert N., **130, 589**
Brock, Christine Anderson, **357**
Brodie, Nancy E., **605**
Brooks, Benedict, **171**
Brown, Georgia L., **337**
Brown, Helen J., **708**
Brown, Jack E., **536**
Bryan, James E., **66**
Buhr, Lorne R., **322**
Bullard, Evelyn, **476**
Bundy, Mary Lee, **301**
Burgin, Robert, **274**
Burkhalter, Barton R., **590**
Butkovich, Margaret, **706**
Buxton, David T., **14**
Byrd, Gary D., **234, 736**
Byrne, Jerry R., **613**

Caldwell, George, **108**
Cambier, Nora, **87**
Caponio, J.F., **684**
Capriotti, Ella, **14**
Carey, Kevin, **805**
Cariou, Mavis, **554**
Carmack, Bob, **203**
Carpenter, Mark P., **652**

Carpenter, Raymond L., **235, 486, 500**
Carr, Barbara E., **350**
Carson, Doris M., **637**
Carter, Ann M., **361**
Carver, Larry G., **216**
Casey, Genevieve, **86**
Cassata, Mary B., **196**
Caynon, William, **509**
Chase, William W., **401**
Chelton, Mary K., **273**
Chen, Ching-Chih, **404, 608, 699-700, 703-704**
Childers, Thomas, **88, 238**
Christiani, Linnea, **368**
Christianson, Elin B., **78, 396**
Chwe, Steven Seokho, **9**
Ciucki, Marcella, **150**
Clack, Mary E., **777**
Clark, Alice S., **127**
Clark, Barton, **87, 563**
Clark, Jay B., **97**
Clayton, Howard, **201**
Clever, Elaine C., **475**
Cline, Gloria S., **511**
Cluff, E. Dale, **602**
Coffee, E. Guy, **740**
Cohen, Lee, **651**
Cohen, Leonard, **501**
Colainni, Lois Ann, **682**
Conant, Barbara M., **81**
Conger, Rebecca, **501**
Conry, Robert, **658**
Cook, M. Kathy, **493**
Cooper, Diane, **744**
Cooper, James K., **744**
Cooper, Michael D., **326, 332, 660, 797**
Cooper, William S., **606**
Corth, Annette, **418**
Cossar, Bruce, **142**
Crager, Janet, **693**
Craig, J.E.G., Jr., **193**
Crawford, Helen, **673**
Crawford, Susan, **745-747**
Creth, Sheila, **240**
Crowley, Terence, **340**
Cruzat, Gwendolyn S., **676**
Cuadra, Carlos A., **212**
Cudd, Kermit G., **49**
Cuff, Renata, **672**
Culley, James D., **49**
Cummings, Margaret S., **737**

Author Index

Currie, Margaret, **558**
Curry, David S., **467, 743**
Cushman, Ruth Carol, **54**

Daehn, Ralph M., **531**
Dale, Brian, **540**
Dale, Doris Cruger, **498**
Danielson, Rosamond H., **579**
Danton, J. Periam, **288**
Daugherty, Robert, **87**
Davey, W. Patrick, **719**
Davidson, Russ, **492**
Davis, Charles H., **144, 286, 425, 427, 619, 643**
Davis, Jinnie Y., **478**
Davis, Scott, **735**
De Gennaro, Richard, **111**
DeBruin, Valentine, **6**
Deede, Benjamin R., **394**
D'Elia, George P., **265, 270, 273, 632**
Denis, Laurent-G., **551**
Deprospo, Ernest R., **147**
DeVilbiss, Mary Lee, **669**
DeWath, Nancy A., **326, 332**
DeWath, Nancy Van House, **570**
Dewdney, Patricia, **540**
Dickstein, Ruth, **23**
Dingle-Cliff, Susan, **427, 643**
Diodato, Louise W., **807**
Diodato, Virgil P., **435, 798, 807**
Divilbiss, James L., **294**
Dodson, Ann T., **437**
Doerrer, David H., **175**
Dole, Wanda V., **647**
Doll, Carol A., **223**
Dorey, Marcia, **413**
Dougherty, Richard M., **123**
Dowell, Arlene T., **233**
Downs, Robert B., **94**
Drake, Miriam A., **459**
Drennan, Henry T., **82**
Dronberger, Gladys B., **612**
Drott, M. Carl, **219, 281, 564, 620**
Druschel, Joselyn, **335**
Dubester, Henry J., **68**
Dunn, Donald J., **374**
Dunn, Doris R.F., **738**
Dwyer, James R., **20**
Dyl, Edward A., **271**
Dyson, Allan J., **61**

Eaton, Elizabeth K., **721**
Edelman, Gayle Smith, **357**
Eggleton, Richard, **635**
Eichesen, Dennis R., **623**
Einhorn, Nathan R., **303**
El-Hadidy, Bahaa, **408**
Elman, Stanley A., **406**
Engle, June L., **803**
English, Thomas G., **788**
Enyingi, Peter, **393**
Erlandson, John, **310**
Ernst, Mary, **309**
Essary, Kathy, **145**
Estabrook, Leigh S., **241, 668**
Ettelt, Harold J., **229**
Evans, G. Edward, **246, 628**
Evensen, Richard H., **164**

Fadenrecht, George H., **169**
Fatcheric, Jerome P., **407**
Fearnley, Henry D., **412**
Fenske, Ruth E., **691**
Ferguson, Anthony W., **30**
Ferrioro, David S., **43**
Fields, Mary Alice S., **156**
Finch, Jean, **560**
Fleming, Thomas P., **670**
Flowers, Janet L., **305**
Flynn, Lauri R., **560**
Ford, Joseph, **343**
Forman, Sidney, **190**
Fosdick, Howard, **255, 416**
Foster, Marie, **552**
Frazier, Shervert H., **677-678**
Fredericksen, Richard B., **712**
Freeman, Michael Stuart, **24**
Freides, Thelma, **410**
French, Zelia J., **64**
Frick, Barbara F., **607**
Friedlander, Janet, **609**
Friedman, Elaine S., **34**
Fristoe, Ashby J., **189, 585**
Fruehauf, Ester L., **716-717**
Funk, Mark, **642**
Funk, Mark E., **748**
Furlow, Karen, **125**
Futas, Elizabeth, **803**

Gable, Sarah H., **749**
Gabriel, Mike, **87**

AUTHOR INDEX

Galvin, Hoyt, **228**
Galvin, Thomas J., **666**
Garcia, Lana Caswell, **370**
Gardiner, George L., **80**
Garen, Robert J., **533**
Garoogian, Rhoda, **149**
Garrison, Guy, **65**, **364**
Gasaway, Laura N., **792**
Gates, Christopher, **308**
Gaughan, Thomas M., **483**
Gaver, Mary Virginia, **69**, **276**
Gavryck, Jacquelyn A., **516**
Geahigan, Priscilla, **503**, **574**
Genaway, David C., **227**, **451**
Ginski, John M., **607**
Goehlert, Robert, **12**, **19**, **307**, **421**
Goettler, Elaine, **558**
Goetz, Art, **385**
Golden, Gary A., **348**, **505**
Golden, Susan U., **348**, **505**
Goldhor, Herbert, **243**, **268**, **525**, **791**
Goldstein, Cynthia H., **739**
Goldstein, Rachel K., **709**, **727**
Gomes, Stella S., **688**
Gonzalez, Michael, **237**
Gonzalez, Silvia A., **379-381**, **648**
Goode, D.J., **684**
Gorman, Michael, **477**
Gothberg, Helen, **51**, **287**
Goudy, Frank William, **40**, **363**, **480**, **787**
Gouke, Mary Noel, **45**, **239**
Graham, Vicki, **349**
Granade, Warner, **466**
Grant, Joan, **11**
Gration, Selby U., **501**
Graziano, Eugene E., **397**
Greeley, Bill, **237**
Greenberg, Bette, **714**, **723**
Greenberg, Marilyn Werstein, **247**
Greene, Robert J., **106**
Grefsheim, Suzanne F., **741**
Griffith, Belver C., **620**
Groos, Ole V., **586**
Groot, Elizabeth H., **767**
Grossman, George S., **390**
Grover, Robert, **163**
Guthrie, Gerry, **128**, **323**
Gwyn, Ann, **125**

Hafner, A.W., **355**
Hahn, Ermina, **369**
Hall, Jack, **778**
Hall, John D., **760**
Halldorsson, Egill A., **456**
Halperin, Michael, **263**, **442**, **633**
Hamann, Edmund G., **600**
Hansel, Patsy, **274**
Harders, Faith, **240**
Hardesty, Larry, **41**, **472**, **507**, **573**
Harer, John B., **512**
Harrelson, Larry E., **93**
Harter, Stephen P., **156**
Hassell, Robert H., **771**
Haviland, Morrison C., **178**
Hayes, Hathia, **319**
Hayes, Robert M., **784**
Hays, Timothy, **225**
Healy, Denis F., **49**
Heidtmann, Toby, **464**
Heim, Kathleen M., **241**, **292**, **668**
Hendrick, Clyde, **59**, **99**
Hentschke, Guilbert C., **627**
Hernon, Peter, **293**, **316**, **318**, **449**
Hetler, Eliese, **186**
Hewitt, Joe A., **112**, **210**
Hicks, Donald A., **266**
Higgs, Margaret, **279**
Hill, Dorothy R., **709**, **727**
Hines, Lois E., **701**
Hintz, Carl, **184**
Hirschman, Rita, **127**
Hitchingham, Eileen E., **411**
Hoag, LaVerne, **590**
Hodges, Gerald G., **295**
Hodges, Pauline R., **440**
Hodges, Theodora, **267**
Hodowanec, George V., **311**, **487**
Hoehn, Phil, **136**
Holtum, Edwin A., **743**
Hoover, Ryan E., **329**
Hoppe, Ronald A., **194**
Horrocks, Norman, **555**
Hostage, John, **770**
Hotsinpiller, Jami, **477**
Houser, Lloyd J., **566**
Howard, Edward N., **77**
Huber, C. Edward, **512**
Hudson, Jean, **136**
Hughes, Marija, **383**
Hulbert, Linda Ann, **467**
Hull, David, **412**
Hyman, Richard J., **597**, **671**
Hyman, Ruth, **92**

Author Index

Imhoff, Kathleen, **152**
Intner, Sheila S., **161**
Isa, Zubaidah, **596**

James, John E., **398**
Jenkins, Darrell L., **312**
Jennerich, Elaine Zaremba, **470**
Jennings, Robert F., **319**
Jensen, Joseph E., **732**
Jensen, Rebecca J., **432**
Jestes, Edward C., **35**
Jewell, Timothy D., **514**
Johnson, Carolyn A., **344**
Johnson, Judith J., **765**
Johnson, K. Suzanne, **740**
Johnson, Kathleen A., **36**
Johnson, Marjorie, **213**
Johnson, Nancy P., **360**
Johnson, Timothy P., **744**
Johnson, Walter T., **107**
Johoda, Gerald, **155**
Jonassen, David H., **295**
Jones, Milbrey, **72**
Josel, Clair S., **765**
Josey, E.J., **117, 197**

Kantor, P.B., **447**
Karr, Robert Dale, **275**
Kasman, Dorothy, **414**
Katz, Judith B., **291**
Katzer, Jeffrey, **139**
Kavass, Igor I., **391, 532**
Kazlauskas, Edward, **50, 327**
Kehoe, Ellen, **627**
Kellam, W. Porter, **182**
Kent, Allen, **666-667**
Kernaghan, John A., **89**
Kesler, Elizabeth Gates, **3**
Kieffer, Karen, **10**
Kilgour, Frederick G., **168, 171, 230, 324, 670, 672, 674-675**
Kilpela, Raymond, **181, 562**
Kim, Chai, **617, 653**
Kim, Ung Chon, **124, 528**
King, David N., **490**
King, Radford G., **432**
Kingsbury, Mary, **296**
Kirk, Thomas, **208**
Kirsch, Kenneth C., **524**
Kister, Ken, **232**
Kitchens, Philip H., **26**
Klass, Janet, **497**

Kleiner, Jane P., **192**
Knapp, Sarah D., **15**
Knightly, John J., **126, 428**
Kobelski, Pamela, **1**
Koch, Jean E., **120**
Kochen, Manfred, **321, 651**
Koenig, Michael E.D., **443**
Kohl, David F., **62, 804**
Kok, John, **431**
Kok, Victoria T., **160**
Kolisch, Madeleine, **723**
Koll, Matthew, **616**
Kosa, Geza A., **631**
Kosek, Reynold J., **371**
Koughan, William P., **402**
Kowitz, Gerald T., **612**
Kraft, Linda, **278**
Kramer, Lloyd A., **183**
Kramer, Martha B., **183**
Krevitt, Beth, **88**
Krikelas, James, **199**
Kriz, Harry M., **460**
Kronenfeld, Michael R., **272, 729, 749**
Kronick, David A., **751**
Kuch, T.D.C., **330**
Kuo, Frank F., **90**
Kurth, William H., **444**
Kwan, Cecilia Hing Ling, **366**

LaBorie, Tim, **633**
Lacy, Douglas, **333**
Landesman, Margaret, **308**
Landgraf, Alan L., **324**
Landy, Sarah, **547**
Larson, Ray R., **349**
Larson, Robert H., **741**
Larson, Thelma E., **135**
Lawani, Stephen M., **657**
Lawton, Stephen B., **556**
Leach, Steven, **446**
Leatherbury, Maurice C., **722**
Lee, John W., **297**
Lee, Susan A., **457**
Legard, Lawrence K., **328**
Legg, Jean, **133**
Lenz, Elizabeth R., **742**
Lenzini, Rebecca T., **505**
Leredu, Martha, **723**
Lessard, Victoria Cheponis, **778**
Levering, Mary Berghaus, **164**
Levis, Joel, **595**

AUTHOR INDEX

Lewis, Robert F., **682**
Linsley, Laurie S., **513**
Lipetz, Ben-Ami, **248**
Little, Paul, **231**
Littleton, Isaac T., **245**
Llinas, James, **333**
Lodico, Norma Jean, **695**
Loeber, Trudi, **203**
Longo, Rose Mary Juliano, **644**
Longyear, R.M., **755**
Lopez, Manuel D., **584**
Lorenzi, Nancy M., **422**
Lovrich, Nicholas P., Jr., **472, 507**
Lowry, Glenn R., **529**
Luesing, Lois L., **176**
Lukenbill, W. Bernard, **280**
Luyben, Paul D., **501**
Lyders, Richard A., **722**
Lynch, Beverly P., **806**
Lynch, Mary Jo, **260**

Maag, Albert F., **44, 482**
McAllister, Paul R., **622, 625**
McArthur, Anne, **125**
McBride, Ruth B., **474**
McCaghy, Dawn, **209**
McCain, Katherine W., **650**
McCandless, Patricia, **518**
McCarthy, Jane, **750**
McCaskill, Sandra, **558**
McClellan, William M., **465**
McClure, Charles R., **28, 55, 317**
McCrossan, John, **243, 282**
McDonald, Norene, **234**
McDonough, Joyce G., **314**
McElroy, Elizabeth Warner, **251**
McGee, Robert S., **646**
McGill, Michael J., **616**
McGrath, William E., **207, 211, 476**
Machado, Ubaldino Dantas, **644**
McIlvaine, Paul M., **713**
Macleod, Beth, **39**
Madan, Raj, **186**
Maffeo, Steven E., **313**
Magrath, Lynn L., **345**
Magrill, Rose Mary, **284, 759**
Magrill, Rosemary, **144**
Mahan, J. Maurice, **721**
Maher, William J., **471**
Major, Jean A., **462**
Malin, Joyce E., **683**
Malone, Maureen J., **728**

Maloney, Ruth Kay, **611**
Maloy, Miriam C., **580**
Mancall, Jacqueline C., **219, 281, 523, 564**
Mankin, Carole J., **649**
Mannon, James, **472, 507**
Marchant, Maurice P., **800**
Marcus, Richard S., **661**
Margeton, Steve, **792**
Markham, Marilyn J., **802**
Marshall, Peter, **100**
Martin, James R., **338**
Martin, Jean K., **419**
Martin, Marjorie E., **59**
Massman, Virgil F., **198**
Matarazzo, James M., **399**
Matheson, Joyce, **658**
Matheson, Nina W., **741**
Mathis, Harold, **174**
Matthews, Elizabeth W., **452**
Matzek, Dick, **300**
Mavor, Anne S., **147**
Mayeski, John K., **46**
Meals, Frances L., **107**
Metcalf, Keyes D., **114**
Metz, Paul, **21, 121, 262**
Meyer, R.W., **448**
Michael, Helen N., **712**
Michalko, James, **464**
Mikita, Elizabeth G., **768**
Milby, T.H., **137**
Miller, Bruce, **4**
Miller, D.W., **534**
Miller, Dick R., **732**
Miller, Ellen G., **522**
Miller, Jean K., **687, 708**
Miller, Jerome, **292**
Miller, Laurence, **91**
Miller, Marilyn L., **56**
Miller, Rush G., **445**
Miller, Tamara J., **504**
Miller, William, **154**
Mitchell, Betty J., **593, 603**
Mittermeyer, Diane, **566**
Moll, Wilhelm, **681, 696**
Momenee, Karen, **463**
Monat, William R., **84**
Monroe, Margaret E., **215**
Moore, Barbara, **504, 764**
Moore, Gary, **572**
Moore, Julie L., **400**
Moore, Mary Kevin, **163**
Moran, Barbara B., **56**

Author Index

Moriarty, John H., 202
Morita, Ichiko T., 336
Morris, Leslie R., **110**, 665
Morris, Ruth Traister, 743
Morrison, Perry D., **131**, 583
Morton, Donald J., 718
Mosborg, Stella Frank, 119
Mosley, Isobel Jean, 331
Mott, Sharon, 548
Mowery, Robert L., **598**, 638
Mueller, Mary H., 734
Murfin, Marjorie E., **29**, **99**, **239**, 456
Myers, Mindy J., 359

Nagy, Laslo A., 489
Nakeff-Plaat, Jennifer P.S., 737
Narin, Francis, **622**, **625**, 652
Needham, William L., 155
Nelson, Diane M., 417
Nelson, E. Don, 422
Nelson, Harriet, **503**, 574
Nelson, Jerold, 663
Nelson, Veneese C., 789
Nemchek, Lee R., 769
Nemeyer, Carol A., 592
Neufeld, Victor R., 634
New, Doris E., 629
Nicholson, Natalie N., 115
Niland, Powell, 444
Nisonger, Thomas E., 774
Nitecki, Andre, **581**, 664
Nitecki, Danuta A., 148
Noreault, Terry, 616
Norten, E.R., 320
Novak, Victor, 187
Nugent, William R., 588

Oboler, Eli M., 76
Ochal, Bethany J., 392
O'Connor, Carol Alf, 314
O'Connor, Daniel O., **254**, 576
O'Connor, Thomas A., 314
O'Keefe, Robert, 89
Olevnik, Peter P., 753
Olsgaard, Jane Kinch, **481**, 494
Olsgaard, John N., **481**, 494
Olson, Barbara J., 146
O'Neill, Edward T., **333**, 766
Orgren, Carl F., 146
Orsini, Elaine, 594
Orten, Larry, 545
Ory, John C., 490

Oseasohn, Robert, 685
Ott, Retha Zane, 629
Owen, Katherine C., 405
Owen, Willy, 775

Pachefsky, Reva, 679
Packer, Katherine H., 636
Pagell, Ruth A., 442
Palais, Elliot S., 53
Palmer, Joseph W., **158**, 162
Panetta, Rebecca, 448
Pantazis, Fotoula, 549
Pao, Miranda Lee, 655
Papakhian, Richard P., 757
Parker, Steve, 145
Pask, Judith M., **120**, 436
Pastine, Maureen, 449
Patrick, Ruth J., 212
Patterson, Kelly, 639
Pattie, Kenton, 309
Paustian, P. Robert, 575
Payne, Charles T., 646
Pearson, Penelope, 42
Pease, Sue, 45
Peil, Margaret, 242
Penry, J.K., 684
Perelmuter, Susan, 11
Perez, Ernest R., 601
Peritz, Bluma C., **569**, **571**, 659
Perk, Lawrence J., **453**, **455**, 610
Perrine, Richard H., 134
Person, Roland, 488
Petersen, Dorothy G., 277
Peterson, Stephen L., 195
Philbin, Paul P., 437
Phillips, Linda L., 13
Phinney, Eleanor, 63
Phipps, Barbara H., 188
Phipps, Shelley, 23
Pickett, A.S., 578
Pieper, Sam, 677-678
Pierce, Anton R., 160
Pinchoff, Diane M., 708
Pings, Vern M., 683
Piper, Patricia L., 366
Piternick, Anne Brearley, **22**, **692**, 711
Piternick, George, **129**, 604
Plake, Barbara S., 36
Plate, Kenneth H., **250**, 553
Polissar, Lincoln, 735
Popovich, Charles J., 461
Porterfield, Genevieve, 173

Potter, William Gray, **758**
Powell, Ronald R., **259**
Poyer, Robert K., **439, 656**
Preece, Scott E., **347**
Public Service Satellite Consortium, **341**
Purcell, Gary, **209**

Qureshi, M. Jamil, **537**

Raisig, L. Miles, **168, 672**
Rambler, Linda K., **47**
Rastogi, Kunj B., **437**
Rath, Gustave, **89**
Raup, Ann E., **13**
Ray, Jean M., **403, 420**
Rayford, Vernon A., **386**
Rayman, Ronald, **480, 495**
Read, Raymond L., **297**
Ream, Daniel, **157**
Reed, Mary Jane Pobst, **527**
Reed, Sarah R., **82**
Rees, Alan M., **746**
Regan, Lee, **141**
Reich, Victoria, **651**
Reid, Carolyn Anne, **748**
Reid, Marion T., **48, 640**
Renner, Charlene, **563**
Renshawe, Michael L., **793**
Repp, Joan, **33**
Reynolds, Dennis, **342, 479**
Reynolds, Maryan E., **58**
Rice, James, Jr., **786**
Richards, James H., Jr., **25**
Richardson, John, Jr., **2, 293**
Richmond, Michael L., **395**
Rinehart, Constance, **284, 759**
Rinkel, Gene K., **518**
Ripin, Arley L., **414**
Ritter, R. Vernon, **179**
Roberts, Justine, **731**
Robinson, Tracey, **497**
Robinson, Wendy, **153**
Robinson, William C., **143**
Romero, Nancy, **776**
Roper, Fred W., **694**
Rose, Robert F., **561**
Rosenberg, Lawrence, **321**
Rouchton, Michael, **27**
Rountree, Elizabeth, **166**
Rubenstein, Albert H., **89, 524**
Rudd, Janet K., **216**

Rudolph, Robert S., **468**
Rush, James E., **614**
Rutledge, John, **775**
Ryans, Cynthia C., **334, 761**
Ryder, Dorothy, **550**
Rzasa, Philip V., **202**

Sadow, Sandra, **394**
Sage, Charles, **497**
St. Clair, Jeffrey, **5**
Salmon, Stephen R., **773**
Samuels, Alan R., **565**
Sandhu, Harjit, **539**
Sandhu, Roop K., **539**
Sandock, Mollie, **151**
Saracevic, Tefko, **447, 610**
Sargent, Seymour H., **473**
Satariano, William A., **261**
Saunders, Stewart, **503, 530, 574**
Saye, Jerry D., **799**
Scamell, Richard W., **783**
Schabas, Ann H., **654**
Schadlich, Thomas, **762**
Scheerer, George, **701**
Schell, Cathy, **236**
Schick, Frank L., **71**
Schick, Judith, **165**
Schlachter, Gail, **92, 283**
Schmidt, C. James, **15, 204**
Schmidt, Jean Mace, **426**
Schnall, Janet G., **710**
Schrader, Barbazra, **594**
Schrieffer, Kent, **368**
Schwarz, Philip, **521**
Schwerin, Kurt, **391**
Scott, Bettie H., **378**
Seeds, Robert S., **705**
Seigel, Jacob P., **553**
Selvin, Hanan C., **516**
Sengupta, I.N., **351, 353-354**
Serebnick, Judith, **782**
Setterington, Kenneth, **560**
Shaffer, Kay, **204**
Sharma, Prabha, **502**
Sharrow, Marilyn T., **46**
Shaw, Deborah, **619**
Shaw, W.M., Jr., **447**
Shearer, Benjamin F., **471**
Shearer, Kenneth D., **225**
Shediac, Margaret, **377**
Shelley, Karen Lee, **57**
Shelton, Regina, **31**

Author Index

Shill, Harold B., **484**
Shin, Eui Hang, **617**
Shiotani, Nancy, **567**
Shipman, John, **302**
Shoham, Snunith, **577**
Sidhom, Eva, **224**
Sigell, Leonard T., **422**
Simmel, Edward C., **194**
Simmons, Peter, **542**
Simmons, Robert M., **140**
Simon, Donald J., **476**
Simonds, Michael J., **662**
Skelley, Grant T., **104**
Sleep, Esther L., **546, 559**
Slifko, Steven D., **323**
Smalley, Topsy N., **624**
Smiraglia, Richard P., **757**
Smith, Barbara J., **510**
Smith, Bessie Hess, **470**
Smith, Joan M.B., **686**
Smith, Joseph D., **614**
Smith, Mary Kay, **234**
Smith, Meredith, **672**
Smith, Nathan M., **789, 802**
Smith, Peggy C., **508, 796**
Smith, R.J., **543**
Smith, Rita Hoyt, **466**
Smith, Scott, **300**
Snider, Bill C., **220-221**
Snowball, George J., **538**
Sockbeson, Deirdre, **413**
Soergel, Dagobert, **636**
Sommer, Robert, **244**
Soper, Mary Ellen, **258**
Sorum, Marilyn, **4**
Spalding, Helen H., **497**
Specht, Jerry, **626**
Spencer, Carol C., **730**
Spiegel, Isabel, **693**
Springer, Sandra J., **422**
Sprug, Joseph, **206**
Spyers-Duran, Peter, **180**
Stanford, Edward B., **451**
Stangl, Peter, **567, 674-675**
Stead, Bette Ann, **783**
Steer, Carol, **298**
Stein, Barbara L., **801**
Stenstrom, Patricia, **474**
Stern, Madeleine, **520**
Steuben, John, **430**
Stevens, Rolland E., **96**
Stewart, June L., **352**
Stewig, John, **279**

Stieg, Margaret F., **780**
Stirling, Keith H., **802**
Stokley, Sandra L., **640**
Stone, Elizabeth W., **73, 250**
Story, Allen, **109**
Strable, Edward G., **431**
Strain, Paula M., **587**
Strasser, Theresa C., **720**
Strazdon, Maureen, **263**
Strong, Marilyn, **186**
Stubbs, Walter R., **589**
Stussy, Susan A., **754**
Sullivan, Michael V., **567**
Sumler, Claudia, **385**
Summers, Edward G., **658**
Surprenant, Thomas T., **506**
Swenk, Cynthia, **153**
Swisher, Robert, **508, 796**
Swope, Mary Jane, **139**

Tagliacozzo, Renata, **321, 715**
Taler, Izabella, **346**
Tallman, Johanna E., **18**
Tannenbaum, Arthur, **224**
Tate, Elizabeth L., **763**
Taylor, Desmond, **185**
Taylor, John R., **30**
Tayyeb, Rashid, **299**
Teufel, Virginia, **42**
Theimer, William C., Jr., **105**
Thomas, David A., **382**
Thomas, Martha Lou, **489**
Thomison, Dennis, **283**
Thompson, Donald, **170**
Thompson, Dorothea M., **32**
Thompson, James A., **272, 729**
Thorson, Connie Capers, **492**
Tibbetts, Pamela, **697**
Timour, John A., **402, 726**
Tobia, Rajia C., **751**
Tobias, Audrey, **60**
Tolliver, Don, **98, 504**
Toro, Jose Orlando, **147**
Totten, Herman L., **801**
Trelles, Oscar M., II, **362, 384**
Trevvett, Melissa D., **469**
Trudell, Libby, **122**
Trueswell, Richard W., **191**
Truett, Carol, **517**
Trumbore, Jean, **1**
Trumpeter, Margo C., **492**
Turner, Ann Craig, **599**

AUTHOR INDEX

Turner, Robert L., Jr., **485**
Turtle, Mary R., **143**

University of Oregon Library, **339**
Usdin, B. Tommie, **725**

Vadeboncoeur, Betty, **567**
Van Orden, Phyllis, **254**
Van Pulis, Noelle, **455**
Varma, D.K., **441**
Vasi, John, **52**
Veit, Fritz, **113**
Vent, Marilyn S., **716-717**
Verdin, Jo Ann, **806**
Von Schon, Catherine V., **450**

Wahba, Susanne Patterson, **103, 794**
Walker, Guy, **102**
Walker, Jerry L., **83**
Walsh, Sandra, **270**
Walz, Carolyn F., **742**
Wanninger, Patricia Dwyer, **772**
Warden, Carolyn L., **424**
Warner, Edward S., **205, 645**
Wasylycia-Coe, Mary Ann, **557**
Waters, Richard, **70**
Watson, Jerry J., **220-221**
Watson, Paula de Simone, **256**
Way, James B., **138**
Weech, Terry L., **268, 365**
Weiss, Dana, **499**
Wellisch, Hans Hanan, **356, 641**
Wells, Dorothy P., **17**
Wells, Mary Baier, **515**
Wender, Ruth W., **409, 429, 716-717**
Werner, David J., **89**
Werner, Gloria, **724**
Werner, O. James, **389**
West, Richard T., **728**
Westerberg, Judy, **98**
Whalen, Lucille, **289**
Wheeler, Edd E., **253**
Whitbeck, George W., **285, 318**
White, Carol, **639**
White, Herbert S., **7, 16, 264, 463, 491**
White, Howard D., **781**

Whitlatch, Jo Bell, **10, 519**
Whitney, Stephen, **237**
Whittaker, Martha, **639**
Wiberley, Stephen E., Jr., **269**
Wiener, Paul B., **315**
Wiggins, Marvin E., **214**
Wilkinson, John, **544**
Wilkinson, John P., **154**
Williams, Edwin E., **118**
Williams, Jim, **776**
Williams, Martha E., **325, 347**
Williams, Robert V., **568**
Williams, Sally F., **526, 777**
Williamson, Nancy J., **304**
Wilson, Carolyn F., **800**
Wilson, Concepcion, **225**
Wilson, Constant D., **716-717**
Wilson, Joan W., **710, 735**
Wilson, R.G., **541**
Windsor, Donald A., **689, 707**
Wiseman, John, **545**
Wittig, Glenn R., **458**
Witucke, Virginia, **218, 779**
Wolfe, Charles B., **358**
Wolper, James, **122**
Wolters, Peter H., **536**
Wong, William Skeh, **785**
Wood, D.N., **306**
Wood, Floris W., **790**
Wood, M. Sandra, **705**
Woods, Joan B., **677-678**
Woods, Julia A., **33**
Woods, Lawrence, **503**
Woodsworth, Anne, **634**
Woolard, Wilma Lee, **226**
Wozny, Lucy Anne, **222**
Wright, Geraldine Murphy, **454**
Wright, James, **200**
Wright, John, **41**

Yagello, Virginia E., **128**
Yerkey, A. Neil, **290, 434**
Yokel, Robert A., **422**
Yu, Priscilla C., **37**

Zamora, Gloria J., **372, 438, 496**
Zelkind, Irving, **206**
Zubatsky, David S., **785**

ABOUT THE AUTHORS

DAVID F. KOHL is currently Undergraduate Librarian and Assistant Director for Undergraduate Libraries and Instructional Services at the University of Illinois-Urbana, with the rank of Associate Professor. Dr. Kohl did his graduate work at the University of Chicago. He has taught library administration at the University of Illinois Graduate School of Library and Information Science and has published numerous articles and monographs on library management and automation. His wide range of service in library management includes active participation in the ARL/OMS Library Consultant Program, the Washington State University's Managing for Productivity Program, and the Assessment Center Program for Potential Managers, sponsored jointly by the University of Washington Graduate Library School and the Washington State Library.

HUGH C. ATKINSON has been the University Librarian at the University of Illinois at Urbana-Champaign since September 1976. He was previously the Director of Libraries at the Ohio State University. Mr. Atkinson currently serves on the Board of the Association of Research Libraries and on the Board of Trustees for the Online Computer Library Center. He is a member of the OCLC User's Council, the American Library Association, and the Illinois Library Association. In addition to presenting many papers for national library conferences, Atkinson has authored several articles that appeared in recent issues of *Library Journal* concerning library technology and the library of the future. Also to his credit is a chapter, "Automation in Austerity," in *Austerity Management in Academic Libraries* (Scarecrow Press, 1984).